Macmillan Professional Masters

Contract Law

Macmillan Professional Masters

Law titles   *Law Series Editor* Marise Cremona

Contract Law

Ewan McKendrick
MA, BCL, LLB
Fellow of St Anne's College, Oxford and
Linnells Lecturer in Law in the University of Oxford

Law series editor: Marise Cremona
Senior Fellow, Centre for Commercial Law Studies
Queen Mary and Westfield College, University of London

Second Edition

MACMILLAN

First edition 1990
Reprinted six times
Second edition 1994

Published by
MACMILLAN PRESS LTD
Houndmills, Basingstoke, Hampshire RG21 2XS
and London
Companies and representatives
throughout the world

ISBN 0–333–62077–1

10   9   8   7   6   5   4   3   2
03   02   01   00   99   98   97   96   95

Printed in Malaysia

Contents

Part III   POLICING THE CONTRACT

12   A duty to disclose material facts?   193

13   Misrepresentation   202

Preface

My aim in writing the second edition of this book has not changed from the stated aim of the first edition: namely, to provide a clear and straightforward account of the basic rules of English contract law. I have also sought to introduce the reader to some of the debates about the nature, the scope and the functions of the law of contract and to discuss some of the wider controversies which surround certain basic doctrines of English contract law, such as consideration and privity. In discussing these issues I have attempted to build a bridge between this introductory work and some of the more advanced and detailed writings on the law of contract by making frequent reference throughout the book to both the periodical literature and the standard textbooks on the law of contract (full citations are contained in the bibliography located at the end of the book). My hope is that these references will encourage the reader to pursue the issues raised in this book in greater detail in the writings to which I have made reference.

Although contract law is generally thought of as a relatively stable area of law, a number of significant developments have occurred since the writing of the first edition. Some sixty new cases have been added to the text and a significant part of the text has been rewritten. The chapter on consideration has been largely recast in the light of the decisions of the Court of Appeal in *Williams* v. *Roffey Bros* and *Re Selectmove* and the work of the Law Commission in the area of privity of contract has necessitated a number of changes to the privity chapter. Perhaps the most significant development has been the adoption of the EC Directive on Unfair Terms in Consumer Contracts. The influence of Europe is likely to increase, and the development of a European Contract Law may be an idea whose time has come. One thing is certain: future editions of this book will have to take greater account of European and international developments.

Finally, I must acknowledge the debts which I have incurred in writing this edition. I would like to thank John Winckler at Macmillan but for whose enthusiasm this edition would never have seen the light of day. I must also acknowledge the assistance which I have derived from colleagues and students who have helped to clarify my thoughts and offered a number of constructive criticisms and suggestions. But my greatest debt is to my wife, Rose, and our children, Jenny, Sarah, Rachel and Katie. This edition of the book has come at the end of a long line of publishing commitments and it has involved yet further time spent away from the family home. I am grateful to them for their encouragement and support.

The book is dedicated to the memory of my grandparents.

I have endeavoured to state the law on the basis of the materials available to me at the end of April 1994.

EWAN McKENDRICK

Table of Cases

xxvi   *Table of Cases*

Table of Statutes

Canada

New Zealand

Europe

1 Introduction

1.1 Introduction

'If the "law of contract" were not already entrenched in the traditions of legal education, would anyone organise a course around it, let alone produce books expounding it?' (Wightman, 1989)

The fact that a lawyer can ask such a question would, no doubt, confound laymen. Yet it is true that the scope, the basis, the function and even the very existence of the law of contract are the subject of debate and controversy among academic lawyers.

But such questioning seems absurd. After all, we enter into contracts as a regular part of life and generally we experience no difficulty in so doing. A simple case is the purchase of a morning newspaper or the purchase of a bus ticket when travelling to work. What doubt can there possibly be about the existence of such contracts or their basis? But, behind the apparent simplicity of these transactions, there lurks a fierce controversy. In an introductory work of this nature we cannot give full consideration to these great issues of debate. The function of this chapter is simply to identify some of these issues so that the reader can bear them in mind when reading the ensuing chapters and to enable the reader to explore them further in the readings to which I shall make reference.

1.2 The Scope of the Law of Contract

A good starting point is the scope of the law of contract. Contracts come in different shapes and sizes. Some involve large sums of money, others trivial sums. Some are of long duration, while others are of short duration. The content of contracts varies enormously and may include contracts of sale, hire purchase, employment, and marriage. Nevertheless, we shall not be concerned with all such contracts in this book. Contracts of employment, marriage contracts, hire purchase contracts, consumer credit contracts, contracts for the sale of goods, contracts for the sale of land, mortgages and leasehold agreements all lie largely outside the scope of this book. Such contracts have all been the subject of distinct regulation and are dealt with in books on employment law, family law, consumer law, commercial law, land law and landlord and tenant law respectively. At this stage you might be forgiven if you asked the question: if this book is not about these contracts, what is it about and what is its value?

The answer to the first part of such a question is that this book is concerned with what are called the 'general principles' of the law of

contract and these general principles are usually derived from the
common law (or judge-made law). Treatises on the general principles of
the law of contract are of respectable antiquity in England and can be
traced back to Pollock (1875) and Anson (1879). This tradition has been
maintained today in works such as Treitel (1991), Anson (1984) and
Cheshire, Fifoot and Furmston (1991). One might have expected that
these treatises would have gradually disappeared in the light of the
publication of books on the contract of employment, the contract of hire
purchase etc., which subject the rules relating to such contracts to close
examination. Yet, textbooks on the 'general principles' of the law of
contract have survived and might even be said to have flourished.

The existence of such general principles has, however, been challenged
by Professor Atiyah (1986b) who maintains that these 'general' principles

> 'remain general only by default, only because they are being superseded
> by detailed *ad hoc* rules lacking any principle, or by new principles of
> narrow scope and application'.

Atiyah argues that 'there is no such thing as a typical contract at all'. He
maintains (1986a) that it is 'incorrect today to think of contract law as
having one central core with clusters of differences around the edges'. He
identifies the classical model of contract as being a discrete, two-party,
commercial, executory exchange but notes that contracts can be found
which depart from each feature of this classical model. Thus, some
contracts are not discrete but continuing (landlord and tenant relationships), some are not two-party but multiparty (the contract of
membership in a club), some are not commercial but domestic
(marriage), some are not executory (unperformed) but executed (fully
performed) and finally some do not depend upon exchange, as in the case
of an enforceable unilateral gratuitous promise. Atiyah concludes by
asserting that we must 'extricate ourselves from the tendency to see
contract as a monolithic phenomenon'.

Atiyah uses this argument in support of a wider proposition that
contract law is 'increasingly merging with tort law into a general law of
obligations'. But one does not need to agree with Atiyah's wider
proposition to accept the point that the resemblance between different
types of contracts may be very remote indeed. A contract of employment
is, in many respects, radically different from a contract to purchase a
chocolate bar. The considerations applicable to a contract between
commercial parties of equal bargaining power may be very different from
those applicable to a contract between a consumer and a multinational
supplier (see Chapter 17).

This fragmentation of the legal regulation of contracts has reached a
critical stage in the development of English contract law. The crucial
question which remains to be answered is: do we have a law of contract or
a law of contracts? My own view is that we are moving slowly in the
direction of a law of contracts as the 'general principles' decline in
importance.

Given this fragmentation, what is the value of another book on the general principles of contract law? The principal value is that much of the regulatory legislation concerning contracts has been built upon the foundation of the common law principles. So it remains important to have an understanding of the general principles before progressing to study the detailed rules which have been applied to particular contracts. The general principles of formation, privity, content, misrepresentation, mistake, illegality, capacity, duress and discharge apply to all contracts, subject to statutory qualification. These principles therefore remain 'general', but only 'by default'.

1.3 The Basis of the Law of Contract

The basis of the law of contract is also a matter of considerable controversy. Atiyah has written (1986e) that 'modern contract law probably works well enough in the great mass of circumstances but its theory is in a mess'. There are many competing theories which seek to explain the basis of the law of contract.

The classical theory is the will theory. Closely associated with *laissez-faire* philosophy, this theory attributes contractual obligations to the will of the parties. The law of contract is perceived as a set of power-conferring rules which enable individuals to enter into agreements of their own choice on their own terms. Freedom of contract and sanctity of contract are the dominant ideologies. Parties should be as free as possible to make agreements on their own terms without the interference of the courts or Parliament and their agreements should be respected, upheld and enforced by the courts. But today the will theory has been largely discredited. It is not possible to attribute many of the doctrines of contract law to the will of the parties. Doctrines such as those of consideration, illegality, frustration and duress cannot be ascribed to the will of the parties, nor can statutes such as the Unfair Contract Terms Act 1977.

The will theory has, however, been revived and subjected to elegant refinement by Professor Fried (1981). Fried maintains that the law of contract is based upon the 'promise-principle', by which 'persons may impose on themselves obligations where none existed before'. The source of the contractual obligation is the promise itself. But, at the same time, Fried concedes that doctrines such as mistake and frustration (Chapter 14) cannot be explained on the basis of his promise-principle. Other non-promissory principles must be invoked, such as the 'consideration of fairness ' or 'the encouragement of due care'.

But Fried's theory remains closely linked to *laissez-faire* ideology. He maintains that contract law respects individual autonomy and that the will theory is 'a fair implication of liberal individualism'. He rejects the proposition that the law of contract is an appropriate vehicle for engaging in the redistribution of wealth. But his theory is open to attack on two principal grounds.

The first is that it is difficult to explain many modern contractual doctrines in terms of liberal individualism or *laissez-faire* philosophy. The growth of standard form contracts and the aggregation of capital within fewer hands has enabled powerful contracting parties to impose contractual terms upon consumers and other weaker parties. The response of the courts and Parliament has been to place greater limits upon the exercise of contractual power. Legislation has been introduced to regulate employment contracts and consumer credit contracts in an effort to provide a measure of protection for employees and consumers. Such legislation cannot be explained in terms of *laissez-faire* ideology, nor can the expansion of the doctrines of duress and undue influence, or the extensive regulation of exclusion clauses which has been introduced by Parliament (see Chapter 11). Conceptions of fairness seem to underpin many of the rules of contract law (see Chapter 17). Such departures from the principles of liberal individualism have led some commentators to argue that altruism should be recognised as the basis of contract law (Kennedy, 1976), while others have argued that the law of contract should have as an aim the redistribution of wealth (Kronman, 1980). We shall return to this issue in Chapter 17.

A second attack on the promise-principle has been launched on the ground that, in many cases, the courts do not uphold the promise-principle because they do not actually order the promisor to carry out his promise. The promisee must generally content himself with an action for damages. But, as we shall see (in Chapter 20), the expectations engendered by a promise are not fully protected in a damages action. One of the principal reasons for this is the existence of the doctrine of mitigation (see 20.10). Suppose I enter into a contract to sell you 10 apples for £2. I then refuse to perform my side of the bargain. I am in breach of contract. But you must mitigate your loss. So you buy 10 apples for £2 at a nearby market. If you sue me for damages, what is your loss? You have not suffered any and you cannot enforce my promise. So how can it be said that my promise is binding if you cannot enforce it? Your expectation of profit may be protected but, where that profit can be obtained elsewhere at no loss to you, then you have no contractual claim against me. Your expectations have been fulfilled, albeit from another source.

Although you cannot enforce my promise, it is very important to note that in our example you suffered no loss and I gained no benefit. Let us vary the example slightly. Suppose that you had paid me in advance. The additional ingredients here are that you have acted to your detriment in reliance upon my promise and I have gained a benefit. Greater justification now appears for judicial intervention on your behalf. Can it therefore be argued that the source of my obligation to you is not my promise, but your detrimental reliance upon my promise or your conferment of a benefit upon me in reliance upon my promise. Atiyah has written (1986b) that 'wherever benefits are obtained, wherever acts of reasonable reliance take place, obligations may arise, both morally and in law'. This argument is one of enormous significance. It is used by Atiyah

(1979) in an effort to establish a law of obligations based upon the 'three basic pillars of the law of obligations, the idea of recompense for benefit, of protection of reasonable reliance, and of the voluntary creation and extinction of rights and liabilities'. The adoption of such an approach would lead to the creation of a law of obligations and, in consequence, contract law would cease to have a distinct identity based upon the promise-principle or the will theory (see further 1.4). This is why this school of thought has been called 'the death of contract' school (see Gilmore, 1974). We shall return to these arguments at various points in this book, especially in Chapters 20 and 21.

My own view is that Fried correctly identifies a strong current of individualism which runs through the law of contract. A promise does engender an expectation in the promisee and, unless a good reason to the contrary appears, the courts will call upon a defaulting promisor to fulfil the expectation so created. But the critics of Fried are also correct in their argument that the commitment to individual autonomy is tempered in its application by considerations of fairness, consumerism and altruism. These conflicting ideologies run through the entire law of contract (for a fuller examination of these ideologies under the titles of 'Market-Individualism' and 'Consumer-Welfarism' see Adams and Brownsword, 1987). The law of contract is not based upon one ideology; both ideologies are present in the case-law and the legislation. Indeed, the tension between the two is a feature of the law of contract. Sometimes 'market-individualism' prevails over 'consumer-welfarism', at other times 'consumer-welfarism' triumphs over 'market-individualism'. At various points in this book we shall have occasion to note these conflicting ideologies and the tensions which they produce within the law.

1.4 Contract, Tort and Restitution

A further difficulty lies in locating the law of contract within the spectrum of the law of civil obligations. Burrows (1983) has helpfully pointed out that the law of obligations largely rests upon three cardinal principles. The first principle is that expectations engendered by a binding promise should be fulfilled. Upon this principle is founded the law of contract. The second principle is that compensation must be granted for the wrongful infliction of harm. This principle is reflected in the law of tort. A tort is a civil wrong, such as negligence or defamation. Let us take an example to illustrate the operation of the law of tort. You drive your car negligently and knock me down. You have committed the tort of negligence. Harm has wrongfully been inflicted upon me and you must compensate me. The aim of the award of compensation is not to fulfil my expectations. It is to restore me to the position which I was in before the accident occurred; to restore the 'status quo' or to protect my 'reliance interest'.

The third principle is that unjust enrichments must be reversed. This principle is implemented by the law of restitution. There are three stages to a restitutionary claim. First, the defendant must be enriched by the receipt of a benefit; secondly, that enrichment must be at the expense of the plaintiff and, finally, it must be unjust for the defendant to retain the benefit without recompensing the plaintiff. The latter stage does not depend upon the unfettered discretion of the judge; there are principles to guide a court in deciding whether, in a particular case, it is unjust that the defendant retain the benefit without recompensing the plaintiff (see Goff and Jones, 1993 and Birks, 1985). The classic restitutionary claim arises where I pay you money under a mistake of fact. I have no contractual claim against you because there is no contract between us. Nor have you committed a tort. But I do have a restitutionary claim against you. You are enriched by the receipt of the money, that enrichment is at my expense, and the ground on which I assert that it is unjust that you retain the money is that the money was paid under a mistake of fact.

Contract, tort and restitution therefore divide up most of the law based upon these three principles and they provide a satisfactory division for the exposition of the law of obligations. This analysis separates contract from tort and restitution on the ground that contractual obligations are voluntarily assumed, whereas obligations created by the law of tort and the law of restitution are *imposed* upon the parties by the operation of rules of law. Occasionally, however, these three principles overlap, especially in the context of remedies (Chapter 20). Overlaps will also be discussed in the context of misrepresentation (Chapter 12) and privity (Chapter 7).

Finally, it must be noted that these divisions are not accepted by Professor Atiyah. His recognition of reliance-based and benefit-based liabilities cuts right across the three divisions. The writings of Atiyah deserve careful consideration, but they do not, as yet, represent the current state of English law. Although we shall make frequent reference to the writings of Atiyah, we shall not adopt his analysis of the law of obligations. Instead, it will be argued that the foundation of the law of contract lies in the mutual promises of the parties and, being founded upon such voluntary agreement, the law of contract can, in the vast majority of cases, be separated from the law of tort and the law of restitution.

1.5   Contract and Empirical Work

Very little empirical work has been done on the relationship between the rules that make up the law of contract and the practices of the community which the rules seek to serve. The limited work that has been done (see Beale and Dugdale, 1975 and Lewis, 1982) suggests that the law of contract may be relied upon in at least two ways. The first is at the planning stage. The rules which we shall discuss in this book may be very important when drawing up the contract and in planning for the future.

For example, care must be taken when drafting an exclusion clause to ensure, as far as possible, that it is not invalidated by the courts (see Chapter 11). Secondly, the law of contract may be used by the parties when their relationship has broken down. Here the rules of contract law have a less significant role to play than at the planning stage. The rules of contract law are often but one factor to be taken into account in the resolution of contractual disputes. Parties may value their good relationship and refuse to soil it by resort to the law. Litigation is also time-consuming and extremely expensive and so the parties will frequently resort to cheaper and more informal methods of dispute resolution. In the remainder of this book, we shall discuss the rules that make up the law of contract but it must not be forgotten that in the 'real world' the rules may be no more than chips to be used in the bargaining process on the breakdown of a contractual relationship.

1.6 A European Contract Law?

The subject-matter of this book is the English law of contract and so the focus is upon the rules that make up the English law of contract. But it should not be forgotten that we live in a world which is becoming more interdependent and where markets are no longer local or even national but are, increasingly, international. The creation of world markets may, in turn, encourage the development of an international contract and commercial law. There are two dimensions here. The first relates to our membership of the European Community; the second is the wider move towards the creation of a truly international contract law.

The first issue relates to the impact which membership of the European Community is likely to have on our contract law. As yet, membership has had little direct impact, but this is unlikely to remain the case. An example of the potential impact of membership of the European Community is provided by the recent EC Directive on Unfair Terms in Consumer Contracts (93/13/EEC), which will give to the courts greater powers to strike down unfair terms in consumer contracts which have not been individually negotiated. The purpose of this Directive, as stated in Article 1, is 'to approximate the laws, regulations and administrative provisions of the Member States relating to unfair terms in consumer contracts'. At the time of writing, it appears that the Directive will be implemented into UK law by regulations made under s.2(2) of the European Communities Act 1972. The Directive will be discussed in more detail in Chapter 17 but the issue which concerns us at this point is the potential which EC law has to intrude into domestic contract law. Some clue as to the likely reach of EC law can be found in Article 100A of the Treaty of Rome, which gives the Council of the European Community the power to adopt measures which have as their 'object the establishment and functioning of the internal market'. This Article formed the legal basis for the Unfair Terms Directive, as can be seen from its preamble where it is stated:

> 'whereas in order to facilitate the establishment of a single market and to safeguard the citizen in his role as consumer when buying goods and services by contracts which are governed by the laws of other Member States than his own, it is essential to remove unfair terms from those contracts'.

It can be argued that differences between the substantive laws of Member States do act as a restriction on intra-community trade because contracting parties are generally unsure of the legal rules which prevail in the different Member States and are therefore more hesitant about contracting with persons in other Member States. For example, an English supplier selling goods to an Italian customer will generally want to ensure that the contract is governed by English law because he is ignorant of the legal position in Italy. Conversely, the Italian customer will wish to ensure that the contract is governed by Italian law for the reason that he does not know the law in England. This gives rise to what lawyers call a 'conflict of laws'. If the law were to be the same in each Member State, these problems would not arise and a further barrier to intra-community trade would be removed. Thus far the Commission has not sought to use Article 100A of the Treaty of Rome in such an expansive manner but the potential is there and, as Dean has noted (1993), the Unfair Terms Directive 'could create a precedent for intervention in other areas of the law of contract'.

There is, however, a second development which is worthy of note, namely the establishment in 1980 of the Commission on European Contract Law (a non-governmental body of lawyers drawn from the Member States), which was set up with the purpose of drafting a statement of general Principles of Contract Law for all the EC countries. Professor Lando, the chairman of the Commission, has recently stated (1992) that there is 'no doubt that Europe needs a unification of the general principles of contract law and that a Uniform European Code of Obligations will enhance trade and other relationships in the Community'. Thus far the Commission's labours have not been particularly fruitful and it has only produced part of the statement of principles but there are hopes that a draft will be complete by the end of 1994. Yet, despite these initial difficulties, there are powerful voices which support the creation of a European Contract Law. For example, in 1989 the European Parliament passed a resolution on the preparation of a European Code of Private Law, the preamble to which stated: 'unification can be carried out in branches of private law which are highly important for the development of a Single Market, such as contract law'.

The creation and development of the Single Market within the European Community is likely to fuel demands for a single European Contract Law. Yet the difficulties which lie ahead should not be underestimated because it involves the bringing together of civilian and common law traditions. An example of the difficulties involved in bringing such traditions together is provided by the experience of the English and the Scottish Law Commissions. In the mid-1960s both Commissions commenced work on the codification of the law of contract but the project was suspended in 1973 after the withdrawal of the Scottish Law Commission. One ground which was cited by the Scottish Law Commission to justify its withdrawal was that it was becoming 'increasingly concerned at the areas of disagreement that still existed on fundamental issues'. The points of divergence were, indeed, substantial (England has a doctrine of consideration, whereas Scotland does not; Scotland has a doctrine of third party enforceable rights, while England presently does not). These differences are multiplied when it comes to reaching agreement at a European level. Not only are there differences of substance but there are differences of methodology: the civilians are more comfortable with statements of general principle, whereas common lawyers prefer to reason from the particular to the general and shy away from broad statements of principle.

While these difficulties are undoubtedly great, it is important to note that the aim of the Commission on European Contract Law is not to impose mandatory uniform rules on all Member States: rather it is to encourage harmonisation through the production of non-binding principles of law. This is very much a long-term goal. But as Europe grows closer together through stronger trade and political links, so the climate may be created in which an agreed and effective statement of general principles of contract law will become possible.

1.7 An International Contract Law?

A broader vision of the future is concerned with the internationalisation of contract law. There are, essentially, two different ways of proceeding. The first is the production of non-binding statements of principle or model contracts: the second is the attempt to impose mandatory uniform rules on the international community.

A notable example in the former category is provided by the International Institute for the Unification of Private Law (Unidroit) which has recently published, for the purposes of consultation, a document entitled Principles for International Commercial Contracts. These principles are contained in approximately 120 articles, each article being accompanied by a brief commentary setting out the reasons for its adoption and its likely practical application. These Articles are not intended to be imposed upon the commercial community in the form of mandatory rules. They are non-binding principles which, it is hoped, will be adopted by contracting parties across the world, by arbitrators, and by national legislatures seeking to update their law relating to international commercial contracts. The Unidroit principles should be seen alongside international standard form contracts, such as INCOTERMS (a set of standard trade terms sponsored by the International Chamber of Commerce) and the FIDIC (Federation Internationale des Igenieurs-Conseils) Conditions of Contract for Works of Civil Engineers, which have achieved widespread acceptance in international trade and international construction contracts respectively. There can be little to object to in such developments because they seek to bring about harmonisation through persuasion rather than imposition. Their alleged weakness is, however, the fact that they are not mandatory. They can therefore be ignored or amended by contracting parties and so are a rather uncertain method of seeking to achieve uniformity.

In an effort to ensure a greater degree of uniformity, it has been argued that there is greater scope for mandatory rules of law. But the attempt to impose uniform terms on the commercial community has given rise to considerable controversy. The most notable example of an international convention in this category is provided by the United Nations Convention on Contracts for the International Sale of Goods, commonly known as the Vienna Convention. Unlike earlier conventions, the Vienna Convention does not enable states to ratify the Convention on terms that it is only to be applicable if the parties choose to incorporate it into their contract. It provides that, once it has been ratified by a state, the Convention is applicable to all contracts which fall within its scope (broadly speaking, it covers contracts for the international sale of goods) unless the contracting parties choose to contract out of the Convention or of parts thereof. The Convention has been in force since 1988 and, although the United Kingdom has not yet ratified it, it has been ratified by a number of major trading nations, such as USA, France, Germany and China. Supporters of such Conventions argue that they promote the development of international trade by ensuring common standards in different nations. Contracting parties can then have greater confidence when dealing with a party from a different nation and such uniformity should result in lower costs because there will be no need to spend time arguing about which law should govern the transaction, nor will there be any necessity to spend time and money seeking to discover the relevant rules which prevail in another jurisdiction.

But such Conventions have also been the subject of considerable criticism. It is argued that they do not achieve uniformity because national courts are likely to adopt divergent approaches to their interpretation (some courts adopting a literal approach, others a purposive approach). In this way, the aim of achieving uniformity will be undermined. The Vienna Convention took many years to negotiate and, even now, 14 years after agreement was reached, it has not been adopted by all the major trading nations of the world. Furthermore, it is not at all clear how the Convention will be amended. The commercial world is constantly on the move and the law must adapt to the changing needs of the market if it is to facilitate trade. An international code which is difficult to amend is unlikely to meet the demands of traders. It is also argued that such

Conventions tend to lack clarity because they are drafted in the form of multi-cultural compromises in an effort to secure agreement and so lack the certainty which the commercial community requires. Lord Justice Hobhouse, writing extra-judicially, summed up these arguments when he wrote (1990) that 'international commerce is best served not by imposing deficient legal schemes upon it but by encouraging the development of the best schemes in a climate of free competition and choice... What should no longer be tolerated is the unthinking acceptance of a goal of uniformity and its doctrinaire imposition on the commercial community'.

While these arguments have a great deal of force, it should be noted that they do not deny the value of internationally agreed standards. But it is suggested that they do show that we should proceed by way of persuasion rather than imposition. Attempts to draft international standard form contracts and non-binding statements of the general principles of contract law should be encouraged as they are most likely to produce uniform standards which will meet the needs of contracting parties and, in so doing, lower the cost of concluding international contracts.

Part I

The Formation and Scope of a Contract

2 Agreement: Clearing the Ground

To say that contract is based upon the agreement of the parties may be a trite statement but it is also a statement which begs a number of questions. Two of these questions will be dealt with in this chapter. The first is: who decides whether or not the parties have indeed reached agreement? Is it the parties or is it the courts? The second question is: how is it decided that the parties have actually reached agreement?

2.1 Who Decides that an Agreement has been Reached?

When discussing the standard which is adopted in deciding whether or not a contract has been concluded a useful starting point, which is quoted in most of the reference works on the law of contract, is the judgment of Blackburn J in *Smith* v. *Hughes* (1871) LR 6 QB 597. He said:

'If, whatever a man's real intention may be, he so conducts himself that a reasonable man would believe that he was assenting to the terms proposed by the other party, and that other party upon that belief enters into the contract with him, the man thus conducting himself would be equally bound as if he had intended to agree to the other party's terms'.

This establishes the important point that the test for the existence and the scope of an agreement is objective rather than subjective. A subjective test attempts to ascertain the actual intention of the contracting parties, whereas an objective test examines what the parties said and did and not what they actually intended to say or do (see further 2.3). The commercial justification for the adoption of an objective test is that great uncertainty would be caused if a person who appeared to have agreed to certain terms could escape liability by claiming that he had no 'real' intention to agree to them.

Some confusion has, however, been caused by the judgment of Lord Diplock in *The Hannah Blumenthal* [1983] 1 AC 834. Lord Diplock stated that:

'to create a contract by exchange of promises between two parties where the promise of each party constitutes the consideration for the promise of the other, what is necessary is that the intention of each *as it has been communicated to and understood by the other* (even though that which has been communicated does not represent the actual state of mind of the communicator) should coincide'.

In *The Leonidas D* [1985] 1 WLR 925 Robert Goff LJ interpreted Lord Diplock as saying that the 'actual intentions of both parties should in fact coincide', which he took to be a reference to a subjective test. It is, however, highly unlikely that Lord Diplock intended to overturn established principles of contract law in such a way (see Atiyah, 1986f) and, in so far as he intended to state that the test was a subjective one, it is likely that, as was the case with Robert Goff LJ in *The Leonidas D*, his dicta will not be followed.

A good example of the application of the objective test is provided by *Centrovincial Estates plc* v. *Merchant Investors Assurance Company Ltd* [1983] Com LR 158. The plaintiffs let premises to the defendants at a yearly rent of £68 320, subject to review from December 25, 1982. The parties were obliged by their contract to endeavour to reach agreement before December 25 1982 on the then current market rental value of the property and to certify the amount of the current market rental value. In June 1982 the plaintiffs wrote to the defendants inviting them to agree that the current market rental value should be £65 000. The defendants accepted. When the plaintiffs received the defendants' written acceptance they immediately contacted the defendants to inform them that they had meant to propose £126 000 and not £65 000. The defendants refused to agree to this new figure and insisted that a contract had been concluded at a rental value of £65 000. So the plaintiffs sought a declaration that no legally binding agreement had been entered into between the parties. The Court of Appeal refused to grant such a declaration, holding that the parties had entered into a contract at a rental value of £65 000. Slade LJ said that:

> 'it is contrary to the well-established principles of contract law to suggest that the offeror under a bilateral contract can withdraw an unambiguous offer, after it has been accepted in the manner contemplated by the offer, merely because he has made a mistake which the offeree neither knew nor could reasonably have known when he accepted it'.

An alternative argument which was relied upon by the plaintiffs in *Centrovincial* was that the objective test of intention was founded upon the principle of estoppel. Estoppel is based upon the proposition that a representor will be prevented from going back on his representation when the representation was intended to be acted upon and is acted upon to his detriment by the representee (see further 5.25–5.27). The plaintiffs argued that the defendants had not relied upon the plaintiffs' offer to their detriment because the proposed rent of £65 000 was lower than the original rent of £68 320. This argument was rejected by the court on the ground that 'the mutual promises alone will suffice to conclude the contract'.

Professor Atiyah (1986f) has attacked the decision in *Centrovincial* on the ground that he can see no reason why an offeree should be entitled 'to create legal rights for himself by the bare act of acceptance when he has in no way relied upon the offer before being informed it was made as a result of a mistake and did not in reality reflect the intention of the offeror'. He has further argued that the decision of the House of Lords in *The Hannah Blumenthal* (above) lends support to his argument that *Centrovincial* was wrongly decided.

The *Hannah Blumenthal* concerned an agreement between two parties to settle a dispute by reference to arbitration. There was then a delay of some six years, during which time nothing happened in relation to the arbitration. When the buyers attempted to fix a date for the arbitration the sellers sought an order that the buyers were not entitled to proceed with the arbitration because of the delay which had occurred. One of the grounds relied upon by the sellers was that the parties had, by their silence and inactivity, agreed to abandon the reference to arbitration; the offer being made by the buyers and the acceptance by the sellers (see further 3.11). Lord Brandon held that there were two ways in which the parties could agree to abandon a contract to arbitrate. The first was where they actually agreed to do so. The second was where one party created a situation in which he was estopped from asserting that he had abandoned the contract. In the latter context it was held that the sellers must have 'significantly altered [their] position in reliance' upon their belief that the contract had been abandoned. Lord Diplock also placed emphasis upon the need for detrimental reliance, saying that this was 'an example of a general principle of English law that injurious reliance on what another person did may be a source of legal rights against him'. However it must be remembered that *Hannah Blumenthal* is a rather unusual case in that it was alleged that the parties had entered into a contract to abandon an arbitration by mere inactivity on both sides. In the absence of express communication between the buyers and the sellers, the only way of showing that the sellers had accepted the buyers' offer to abandon the arbitration was to show that they had acted in reliance on the fact that the contract had been abandoned. The function of reliance was therefore to provide *evidence* of the fact that the sellers had accepted the buyers' offer to abandon the agreement to arbitrate; it is not the case that the House of Lords was laying down a rule that such reliance was a prerequisite to the formation of any contract. Thus interpreted, *Hannah Blumenthal* does not cast doubt upon the correctness of *Centrovincial* because in *Centrovincial* the defendants' acceptance was evidenced by the fact that they wrote and accepted the plaintiffs' offer. In such a case, the acceptance concludes the contract without the need for any further act in reliance upon the offer.

2.2 A Residual Role for a Subjective Approach

It should not, however, be assumed that the subjective intentions of the parties are irrelevant to the law of contract. In many cases the subjective intentions of the parties will coincide with the interpretation put upon their intentions by the objective test and to that extent their subjective intentions are protected. Further, as was made clear by Slade LJ in *Centrovincial*, there are two situations in which the objective test is displaced by a subjective test.

The first arises where the offeree knows that the offeror is suffering from a mistake as to the terms of the offer; then the usual objective test is replaced by a subjective test. The operation of this rule can be seen in the case of *Hartog* v. *Colin and Shields* [1939] 3 All ER 566. The defendants entered into a contract to sell 3000 Argentinian hare skins to the plaintiffs. However by mistake they offered them for sale at 10¼d per pound instead of 10¼d per piece. When they discovered their mistake, the defendants refused to deliver the skins. The plaintiffs brought an action in respect of the defendants' non-delivery of the skins. It was held that they were not entitled to succeed because the negotiations had proceeded upon the basis that the skins were to be sold at a price per piece and that, as there were three pieces to the pound, the plaintiffs could not reasonably have thought that the defendants' offer matched their true intention. The plaintiffs were thereby prevented from snatching a bargain which they knew was not intended by the defendants.

The second situation in which the subjective intentions of the parties are relevant is where the offeree is at fault in failing to note that the offeror has made a mistake. Such was the case in *Scriven Bros* v. *Hindley* [1913] 3 KB 564. An auctioneer acting for the plaintiffs put up for sale lots of hemp and tow. The auction catalogue was misleading because it implied that the lots were the same when, in fact, the second lot only contained tow. Tow was considerably cheaper than hemp. The defendants bid for the lot thinking that it was hemp when in fact it was tow. The auctioneer did not realise that the defendants had misunderstood what was being auctioned; he merely thought that they had overvalued the tow. When the defendants discovered their mistake they refused to pay the price and so the plaintiffs sued them for the price. It was held that no contract for the sale of the tow had been concluded when the tow was knocked down to the defendants because the auctioneer intended to sell tow and the defendants intended to purchase hemp and the defendants' mistake had been induced by the carelessness of the plaintiffs in preparing the auction catalogue. The importance of the misleading nature of the auction catalogue can be seen in the fact that, had it not been misleading, a contract would have been concluded on the plaintiffs' terms because, in the usual case, an auctioneer is entitled to assume that a bidder knows what he is bidding for. Thus in the ordinary case a contract would have been concluded for the sale of tow.

A further situation in which it has been argued (see Spencer, 1974) that the subjective intentions of the parties are relevant arises where the parties are subjectively agreed but that subjective agreement is at variance with the result achieved by applying the objective test. Spencer gives the admittedly rather far-fetched example of two immigrants who have little command of the English language and who enter into a contract under which one is to sell to the other a 'bull'. Both parties intend to use the word 'bull' but they both think that the word 'bull' means cow. The application of the objective test, Spencer argues, leads to the conclusion that a contract has been concluded for the sale of a bull. But, as Spencer points out, this is absurd as the seller does not have a bull to sell and the buyer does not want one. He argues that while 'it may be acceptable for the law occasionally to force upon *one* of the parties an agreement he did not want . . . surely there is something wrong with a theory which forces upon *both* of the parties an agreement which neither of them wants'. Thus Spencer concludes that the subjective intentions of the parties must prevail. But if both parties in fact wished to contract to sell a cow and a cow was delivered and accepted then the law of contract would not force upon the parties an agreement which neither of them wanted because, in such a case, the objective approach would lead to the conclusion that a contract had been made for the sale of a cow. The actions of the parties, in delivering and accepting delivery of the cow, would displace the inference which had been raised by the words which they had used. There is thus no question of forcing upon the parties an agreement which neither of them wants and no need to invoke any reference to the subjective understandings of the parties.

It is important to understand that the subjective understandings of the parties will not generally prevail over their intention, objectively ascertained. As Lord Normand stated in *Mathieson Gee (Ayrshire) Ltd* v. *Quigley* 1952 SC (HL) 38, 'when the parties to a litigation put forward what they say is a concluded contract and ask the Court to construe it, it is competent for the Court to find that there was in fact no contract and nothing to be construed'. Conversely, it has been stated that 'if the parties' correspondence and conduct shows [objectively that they intend to make a contract] it will not, or may not, matter that neither privately intended to make a contact' (*The Amazonia* [1990] 1 Lloyd's Rep 238, 243). The existence or non-existence of a contract is ultimately a question for the court which will be decided by the application of the objective test and it is only in exceptional situations that resort will be had to a subjective test. We have noted only two such exceptional situations and it may be argued, as a basis for the development of the law, that they illustrate a wider proposition that the objective test must be applied by the court unless there is something unconscionable in the conduct of the party seeking to uphold the application of the objective approach, in which case the court may have regard to the subjective intentions of the parties.

2.3 The Objective Test

So the general rule is that the intention of the parties is to be assessed objectively. Thus far it has been assumed that there is only one objective test which can be applied by the courts but, in a recent article (Howarth, 1984), it has been argued that there are, in fact, three different interpretations of the objective test which can be applied by the courts.

The first is the standard of detached objectivity. This approach takes as its standpoint the perspective of the detached observer or the 'fly on the wall'. In other words, it asks what interpretation would a person watching the behaviour of the contracting parties place upon their words and actions. The second possible interpretation suggested by Howarth is to interpret the words as they were reasonably understood by the promisee (called 'promisee objectivity' by Howarth). This is the standard which finds the greatest support in the case law (see *Smith* v. *Hughes* (above)). The third and final interpretation is the standard of the reasonable person in the shoes of the person making the offer (called 'promisor objectivity' by Howarth). The approach which is preferred by Howarth is 'detached objectivity' but there is little judicial support for such a test (Vorster, 1987).

However the distinction which Howarth draws between 'promisor' and 'promisee' objectivity has been criticised on the ground that it is misleading because, in a bilateral contract, each party is both a promisor and a promisee (Vorster, 1987, especially pp. 276–8). Thus, for example, in *Scriven Bros* v. *Hindley* (above) the defendant purchaser was a promisor in relation to his promise to pay for the lot and a promisee concerning the auctioneer's promise to sell him the tow. On the other hand, the auctioneer was a promisor in relation to the promise to sell the lot and a promisee concerning the defendant's promise to purchase the lot. It is true that the nomenclature which Howarth employs is rather misleading but it should not blind us to his essential point, which is that there are two parties to a contract and that a court could elect to apply the perspective of one or other contracting party. One could meet the criticism by restyling the classification as 'plaintiff' and 'defendant' objectivity to underline the point that one is simply looking at the contract from the position of one or other contracting party.

Although it is true that, in our terminology, 'defendant' objectivity has the greatest support in the case law this may be a product of the way in which the cases have come before the courts rather than distinct judicial preference. The case of *Scriven Bros* v. *Hindley* (above) provides a good example of this point. In that case the court considered whether the plaintiffs were entitled to recover the price of the lot which they alleged that the defendants had contracted to buy. The emphasis of the court was upon the defendants' understanding of the offer made by the auctioneer. This was because the defence to the claim was based on the defendants' understanding of the offer and therefore the court was forced to examine that understanding. It is crucial to note that the defendants simply denied liability; they did not take the further step of asking the court to enforce their version of the 'contract'. This had the consequence that the court did not consider whether the defendants would have been able to sue the plaintiffs for breach of a contract to sell hemp. Had the defendants counterclaimed for breach of their version of the 'contract', the roles would have been reversed and the court would have been compelled to consider the plaintiffs' understanding of the bid made by the defendants.

The infrequency of such counterclaims by defendants means that 'defendant' objectivity is most commonly considered by the courts, but it does not follow that the courts are averse to applying 'plaintiff' objectivity; it is simply the case that they are not often asked by defendants to apply such a standard.

2.4 Has Agreement been Reached?

An instructive example of the approach which the courts adopt in deciding whether or not the parties have reached agreement is provided by the case of *Butler* v. *Ex-Cell-O Corporation (England) Ltd* [1979] 1 WLR 401. The sellers, Butler, offered to sell a machine tool to the buyers, the offer being made on Butler's standard terms of business, which included, *inter alia*, a price variation clause. The buyers sent an order for the machine tool which, in turn, was on their own standard terms of business, which made no provision for a price variation clause and stated that the price of the machine tool was to be fixed. The buyers' order form contained a tear-off acknowledgement slip, which stated that 'we [the sellers] accept your order on the terms and conditions stated thereon'. The sellers signed and returned this slip to the buyers, together with a letter stating that they were carrying out the order on the terms of their original offer. After constructing the machine tool, but before delivering it, the sellers sought to invoke the price variation clause contained in their original offer and claimed the additional sum of £2892. The buyers refused to pay this increase in price, claiming that they were not contractually bound to do so. The sellers accordingly sued the buyers for £2892 in damages. The Court of Appeal held that they were not entitled to recover the sum claimed because a contract had been concluded on the buyers' terms which did not include the price variation clause. Although the Court of Appeal was unanimous in holding that a contract had been concluded on the buyers' terms, the court was divided in its reasoning.

The reasoning of the majority, Lawton and Bridge LJJ, proceeded by applying the traditional 'mirror image' rule of contractual formation. According to this rule, the court must be able to find in the documents which passed between the parties a clear and unequivocal offer which is matched or 'mirrored' by an equally clear and unequivocal acceptance. A purported acceptance which does not accept all the terms of the original offer is not in fact a true acceptance at all but is a counter-offer which 'kills off' the original offer and amounts to a new offer which can in turn be accepted by the other party. Applying this, they held that the buyers' order could not be construed as an acceptance of the sellers' offer because it did not mirror exactly the terms of the sellers' offer and therefore amounted to a counter-offer. They held that this counter-offer was accepted by the sellers when they signed the tear-off acknowledgement on the buyers' order form. The letter accompanying the acknowledgement slip was held not to be an attempt to reintroduce the terms of the sellers' original offer and so was not a counter-offer, but was simply a means of identifying the order for the machine tool.

This traditional approach has a number of advantages. The first is that it provides some degree of certainty because legal advisers at least know the principles which the courts will apply in deciding whether or not a contract has been concluded. There is no separation between the formation of the contract and the ascertainment of the terms of the contract because the offer and acceptance must mirror each other exactly before a contract is concluded. Thus it gives the parties a clear standard against which to measure their conduct and sends out a message that a failure to reach agreement on all points may lead a court to hold that a contract has not been concluded. The second advantage of this approach is that it provides a standard which can be applied to every type of contract.

However the traditional approach has also been subjected to considerable criticism. One such criticism is that it is excessively rigid. It produces an 'all or nothing' result, in the sense that it is either the terms of the buyer or the terms of the seller which govern the relationship of the parties; the court cannot pick and choose between the respective sets of terms and conditions or seek to find an acceptable compromise. This is unfortunate in cases involving the 'battle of the forms' (as cases such as *Butler* are commonly called) where both parties may reasonably believe that their terms are the ones which govern their relationship and where a compromise may produce the fairest result on the facts of the case. The traditional approach has also been criticised in its application to battle of the forms cases on the ground that it encourages businessmen to continue to exchange their standard terms of business in the hope of getting the 'last shot' in and it places the party in receipt of the last communication in a very difficult position. If he refuses to accept the goods, it is likely that it will be held that no contract has come into existence, but if he accepts the goods it is possible that he will be held to have accepted them on the sellers' terms.

The strains on the traditional approach have led some judges to reject it in favour of a new approach. In *Butler* Lord Denning, who was in the minority, rejected the traditional mirror image approach to contractual formation, holding it to be 'out-of-date' (see too his judgment in the case of *Gibson* v. *Manchester City Council* [1978] 1 WLR 520, 523 when he said that 'to my mind it is a mistake to think that all contracts can be analysed into the form of offer and acceptance'). He held that the

'better way is to look at all the documents passing between the parties and glean from them, or from the conduct of the parties, whether they have reached agreement on all material points, even though there may be differences between the forms and conditions printed on the back of them'.

He also held that, even where the terms used by the parties were mutually contradictory, it was possible for a court to 'scrap' the terms and replace them by a 'reasonable implication'. Applying this reasoning, he held that the signing of the tear-off acknowledgement by the sellers was the 'decisive document', which made it clear that the contract was concluded on the buyers' terms.

This approach clearly conflicts with the mirror image approach to contractual formation because it adopts a two-stage approach. At the first stage, it must be decided whether a contract has been concluded and, at the second stage, it must be decided what are the terms of the contract. At the latter stage the court has considerable discretion in filling the gaps. The approach adopted by Lord Denning seeks to construct a more flexible framework for the law of contract which can accommodate inconsistent terms and an apparent lack of consensus within the law of contract.

This approach has in turn been criticised on the ground that it produces uncertainty because it gives too little guidance to the courts, or to legal advisers, in determining whether or not an agreement has been reached. Certainty is a particularly important commodity in the law of contract because businessmen will often want to know the standard which the law applies so that they can plan their affairs accordingly.

Despite the attempt by Lord Denning to introduce this new general approach to the issue of agreement, English law remains wedded to the traditional approach. This was confirmed by Lord Diplock in *Gibson* v. *Manchester City Council* [1979] 1 WLR 294, 297 when he said that, although there may be certain 'exceptional' cases which do not 'fit easily into the normal analysis of a contract as being constituted by offer and acceptance', these cases were very much the exception and they have not displaced the traditional rule. It would be a mistake, however, to think that the traditional rule is always rigidly applied by the judiciary. In *The Eurymedon* [1975] AC 154, 167 Lord Wilberforce stated that 'English law, having committed itself to a rather technical and schematic doctrine of contract, in application takes a practical approach, often at the cost of forcing the facts to fit uneasily into the marked slots of offer, acceptance and consideration'. We shall see, when discussing issues such as the application of the rules of offer and acceptance to transactions in the supermarket (see 3.2), that the courts do have some discretion in identifying the offer and the acceptance and so have some flexibility in applying the rules in a particular factual context.

In the next chapter we shall give consideration to the schematic approach to agreement by examining in greater detail the constituent elements of offer and acceptance. Then, in Chapter 4, we shall give further consideration to the application of the objective test.

Summary

1 The test for the existence of an agreement is objective rather than subjective. The justification for this is the need to promote certainty.

2   The objective test is, however, displaced by a subjective test where the offeree knows that the offeror is suffering from a mistake as to the terms of his offer and where the offeree is at fault in failing to note that the offeror has made a mistake.

3   There are three potential forms of the objective test: detached objectivity, plaintiff (or promisor) objectivity and defendant (or promisee) objectivity. The latter form has the greatest support in the case law but this may be a product of the way in which the cases have come before the courts rather than distinct judicial preference.

4   The courts apply the 'mirror image' rule in deciding whether or not a contract has been concluded. The acceptance must mirror the offer exactly. The general approach to contract formation advocated by Lord Denning has been rejected.

Exercises

1   Do you think that *Centrovincial Estates plc* v. *Merchant Investors Assurance Company* was correctly decided?

2   Andrew, an old man aged 80, agreed to sell his house to David for £6800. Andrew in fact meant to sell it for £68 000. David is now seeking to enforce the agreement. Advise Andrew.

3   Compare and contrast the reasoning of the majority and the minority in *Butler* v. *Ex-Cell-O Corporation*. Which approach do you prefer and why?

3 Offer and Acceptance

We noted in Chapter 2 that the courts adopt the 'mirror image' rule of contractual formation; that is to say they must find a clear and unequivocal offer which is matched by an equally clear and unequivocal acceptance. In this chapter we shall give more detailed consideration to the constituent elements of an offer and an acceptance. However, three points should be noted at the outset of our discussion.

The first point is that most of the cases which we shall discuss in this chapter are cases which came to court because one party was alleging that the other had broken the contract between them. This can be seen in *Butler* v. *Ex-Cell-O Corporation* [1979] 1 WLR 401 (see 2.4), where the discussion of the rules of offer and acceptance was crucial because the court had to find the existence of a contract and ascertain its terms before it could decide whether or not the buyers were in breach of contract. Thus the context of most of these cases is an allegation of *breach* of contract.

The second point which should be borne in mind relates to the way in which the courts use the requirements of offer and acceptance in deciding cases. Professor Atiyah has argued (1989) that the courts could either 'reason forwards' or they could 'reason backwards'. By 'reasoning forwards' Professor Atiyah means that the courts reason from the legal concepts of offer and acceptance towards the solution to the dispute. This is the traditional approach which has been adopted by the courts; they 'find' the existence of an offer and an acceptance and only then do they reason towards their conclusion. On the other hand the courts could 'reason backwards'; that is to say they could reason from the appropriate solution back to the legal concepts of offer and acceptance. On such a model the court can decide which solution it wishes to adopt and then fit the negotiations within the offer and acceptance framework to *justify* the decision which they have already reached. The distinction which Professor Atiyah is seeking to draw is a difficult one to grasp in the abstract but it is one to which we shall return when discussing some of the cases.

The third point is that, on a number of occasions, we shall note that great difficulty is experienced in accommodating many every day transactions within the offer and acceptance framework. This point will lead us to conclude by discussing the utility of the offer and acceptance model. With these preliminary points in mind let us examine the detailed rules of law relating to offer and acceptance.

3.1 Offer and Invitation to Treat

An offer is a statement by one party of a willingness to enter into a contract on stated terms, provided that these terms are, in turn, accepted by the party or parties to whom the offer is addressed. There is generally no requirement that the offer be made in any particular form; it may be made orally, in writing or by conduct.

Care must be taken, however, in distinguishing between an offer and an invitation to treat. An invitation to treat is simply an expression of willingness to enter into negotiations which, it is hoped, will lead to the conclusion of a contract at a later date. The distinction between the two is said to be primarily one of intention; that is, did the maker of the statement intend to be bound by an acceptance of his terms without further negotiation or did he only intend his statement to be part of the continuing negotiating process? Although the dichotomy is easy to state at the level of theory, it is not so easy to apply at the level of practice, as can be seen from the case of *Gibson* v. *Manchester City Council* [1978] 1 WLR 520 (CA) and [1979] 1 WLR 294 (HL).

In 1970 the defendant council prepared a brochure explaining how a council tenant could purchase his council house and sent a copy to those tenants who had previously expressed an interest in purchasing their council house. Mr Gibson completed the form contained in the brochure and sent it to the council, together with a request that he be told the purchase price of the house. The treasurer of the council wrote to inform him that the 'council may be prepared to sell the house' to him at a stated price and that if he wished to make a 'formal application' to purchase the house he should complete a further form. Mr Gibson completed the form, but he left the purchase price blank because he wished to know whether the council would repair the path to his house or whether he could deduct the cost from the purchase price. The council replied that the price had been fixed according to the condition of the property and so allowance had been made in the price for the condition of the path. Mr Gibson accepted this and asked the council to continue with his application. The council took the house off the list of houses for which they were responsible for maintenance and Mr Gibson carried out maintenance to the house. At this point the Labour Party gained control of the council after the local elections and promptly discontinued the policy of selling off council houses, unless a legally binding contract had already been concluded. The council refused to sell the house to Mr Gibson because they claimed that no contract had been concluded for the sale of the house.

The trial judge and the Court of Appeal held that a contract had been concluded between the parties. Lord Denning, in a broad and sweeping judgment, held that a contract had been concluded because there was agreement between the parties on all material points, even though the precise formalities had not been gone through. The House of Lords took a different view and held that no contract had been concluded. It was held that the letter written by the treasurer, which stated that the council *may* be prepared to sell, was not an offer as it did not finally commit the council to selling the house. It was simply an expression of their willingness to enter into negotiations for the sale of the house and was not an offer which was capable of being accepted. This was further evidenced by the fact that Mr Gibson was invited to make a 'formal application' to purchase the house and not to signify his agreement to the stated terms.

The difficulty in a case such as *Gibson* arises from the fact that it is not easy to ascertain when the preliminary negotiations end and a definite offer is made. The court must examine carefully the correspondence which has passed between the parties and seek to identify from the language used and from the actions of the parties whether, in its opinion, either party intended to make an offer which was capable of acceptance. *Gibson* shows that judges can and do differ in the results which they reach in this interpretative exercise and that each decision must ultimately rest on its own facts (contrast the decision of the Court of Appeal in *Storer* v. *Manchester City Council* [1974] 1 WLR 1403, where the court held that a contract had been concluded where the negotiations had advanced beyond the stage reached in *Gibson* but had not resulted in an exchange of contracts).

In a case such as *Gibson* the court is clearly engaged in trying to ascertain the intention of the parties from the documents which have passed between them (although it should be noted that, even in *Gibson*, the case was seen as a test case for 350 other similarly placed prospective purchasers and these purchasers would be presumed to have the same intention as Mr Gibson). There is, however, another group of cases, which concern certain stereotyped transactions, such as advertisements and shop-window displays, where the courts are less concerned with the intention of the parties and are more concerned to establish clear rules of law to govern the particular transaction. Professor Treitel has stated (1991) that 'it may be possible to displace these rules by evidence of contrary intention, but in the absence of such evidence [these rules of law] will determine the distinction between offer and invitation to treat, and they will do so without reference to the intention (actual or even objectively ascertained) of the maker of the statement'. These situations are discussed in sections 3.2-3.6.

3.2 Display of Goods for Sale

As a matter of principle, there are at least three different approaches which could be adopted to the display of goods for sale in a shop or supermarket. The first is to hold that the display of goods is an offer which is accepted when the goods are picked up by the prospective purchaser and put into his shopping basket. However, such a conclusion would have the undesirable consequence that a purchaser would be bound as soon as he picked up the goods and he could not change his mind and return them to the shelves without being in breach of contract. The second approach is to hold that the display of goods is an offer which is accepted when the purchaser takes the goods to the cash desk. This solution avoids the weakness of the first approach but it has been argued that it too is undesirable. Three criticisms have been levelled against this solution. The first is that it has been argued that a shop is a place for bargaining and not for compulsory sales and that to hold that the display of goods is an offer will take away the shopkeeper's freedom to bargain (Winfield, 1939). This argument can be countered by pointing out that, apart from second hand shops, bargaining is not a reality in the shops of today. Goods are displayed on a 'take it or leave it' basis. If the customer is not prepared to comply with the stated terms he can go elsewhere. Secondly it has been argued that this conclusion is undesirable because it takes away the freedom of the shopkeeper to decide whether or not to deal with a particular customer. It would compel the shopkeeper to trade with his worst enemy. However it is submitted that, in an era when shopping in vast superstores has become commonplace, such an argument can no longer be regarded as conclusive. Thirdly it has been argued that to treat a display of goods as an offer might result in the vendor being bound to a series of contracts which he would be unable to fulfil (see *Partridge* v. *Crittenden* [1968] 1 WLR 1204, discussed at 3.3). This objection can be countered by holding that the shopkeeper's offer is subject to the limitation that it is only capable of acceptance 'while stocks last'.

The third possible conclusion is that the display of goods constitutes an invitation to treat and that the offer is made by the customer when he presents the goods at the cash desk, where the offer may be accepted by the shopkeeper. This conclusion preserves the freedom of the shopkeeper to decide whether or not to deal with a particular customer but it can fail to protect the interests of the customer. For example, a customer who takes the goods to the cash desk may be told that the goods are in fact on sale at a higher price than the display price and there would be no way that the customer could compel the shopkeeper to sell the goods at the display price. It is true that the seller may be subject to criminal sanctions under the Trade Descriptions Act 1968 where he gives a misleading indication as to the price at which the goods or services are available for sale, but that does not assist the purchaser with his civil action. He is still left without a civil remedy.

In this simple everyday situation the rules of offer and acceptance simply do not demand that a particular conclusion be reached. Nor can the intention of the parties provide a useful guideline because, in truth, the parties often have no discernible intention one way or the other. The general rule which the courts have, in fact, adopted is that the display of goods in a shop window is an invitation to treat rather than an offer (*Fisher* v. *Bell* [1961] 1 QB 394). The application of this rule can be seen in the case of *Pharmaceutical Society of GB* v. *Boots Cash Chemists* [1953] 1 QB 401 (see Montrose, 1954). The defendants organised their shop on a self service basis. They were charged with a breach of the Pharmacy and Poisons Act 1933, which required that a sale of drugs take place under the supervision of a registered pharmacist. There was no pharmacist present close to the shelves, but a pharmacist supervised the transaction at the cash desk and was authorised to prevent a customer from purchasing any drug if he thought fit. It was held that the sale took place at the cash desk and not when the goods were taken from the shelves; the display of the goods was simply an invitation to treat and therefore there had been no breach of the Act.

However a rigid application of the rule established in *Boots* could lead to injustice in certain cases. An instructive example of a factual situation in which the application of the *Boots* test may lead to injustice is provided by the American case of *Lefkowitz* v. *Great Minneapolis Surplus Stores* 86 NW 2d 689 (1957). On two occasions the defendants placed an advertisement in a newspaper. The first advertisement stated 'Saturday 9 am sharp; 3 Brand new fur coats, worth to $100; First come first served, $1 each', and the second stated 'Saturday 9 am ... 1 Black Lapin Stole ... worth $139.50 ... $1.00; First Come, First Served'. On each of the Saturdays following publication of the advertisement the plaintiff was the first person in the store at 9am, but on both occasions the defendants refused to sell the goods to him. On the first occasion the reason given was a 'house rule' that the offer was intended for women only and on the second occasion he was informed that he knew the 'house rules'. The plaintiff brought a claim for damages for breach of contract. His claim in relation to the first advertisement was dismissed on the ground that the value of the fur coats was too speculative and uncertain to found a claim. But his claim for damages succeeded in relation to the second advertisement and he was awarded damages of $138.50. The Supreme Court of Minnesota held that the advertisement was an offer and not an invitation to treat and that the defendants were not entitled to confine their offer to women only because no such restriction was explicit in the offer itself. But would an English court conclude that these advertisements constituted an offer? Some authority can be adduced for treating a display of goods as an offer; in *Chapleton* v. *Barry UDC* [1940] 1 KB 532, it was held that the display of deck chairs for hire on a beach was an offer which was accepted by a customer taking a chair from the stack (see too *Carlill* v. *Carbolic Smoke Ball Co* [1893] 1 QB 256, discussed at 3.3). But if a court were to rely on the authority of *Chapleton* would it not be because the court thought that it was unfair to leave the plaintiff without a remedy? Would this not be an example of what Professor Atiyah calls 'reasoning backwards'; that the court feels that the plaintiff ought to have a remedy and it justifies that conclusion by treating the advertisement as an offer rather than an invitation to treat?

3.3 Advertisements

The general rule is that a newspaper advertisement is an invitation to treat rather than an offer. In *Partridge* v. *Crittenden* [1968] 1 WLR 1204, the appellant advertised Bramblefinch cocks and hens for sale at a stated price. He was charged with the offence of 'offering for sale' wild live birds contrary to the Protection of Birds Act 1954. It was held that the advertisement was an invitation to treat and not an offer and so the appellant was acquitted. Lord Parker CJ stated that there was 'business sense' in treating such advertisements as invitations to treat because if they were treated as offers the advertiser might find himself contractually obliged to sell more goods than he in fact owned. However, as we have seen, this argument is not conclusive because it could be implied that the offer is only capable of acceptance 'while stocks last'.

Nevertheless there are certain cases where an advertisement may be interpreted as an offer rather than an invitation to treat. The classic example is the case of *Carlill* v. *Carbolic Smoke Ball Co* (above). The defendants, who were the manufacturers of the carbolic smoke ball, issued an advertisement in which they offered to pay £100 to any person who caught influenza after having used one of their smoke balls in the specified manner, and they deposited £1000 in the bank to show their good faith. The plaintiff caught influenza after using the smoke ball in the specified manner. She sued for the £100. It was held that the advertisement was not an invitation to treat but was an offer to the whole world and that a contract was made with those persons who performed the condition 'on the faith of the advertisement'. The plaintiff was therefore entitled to recover £100.

3.4 Auction Sales

The general rule is that an auctioneer, by inviting bids to be made, makes an invitation to treat. The offer is made by the bidder which, in turn, is accepted when the auctioneer strikes the table with his hammer (*British Car Auctions Ltd* v. *Wright* [1972] 1 WLR 1519). The advertisement of an auction sale is generally only an invitation to treat (*Harris* v. *Nickerson* (1873) LR 8 QB 286), but it is unclear what is the effect of the addition of the words 'without reserve', that is that the auction is to take place without a reserve price. In *Warlow* v. *Harrison* (1859) 1 E & E 309, Martin B stated *obiter* that in such a case the auctioneer makes an offer that the sale will be without reserve and that that offer is accepted by the highest bidder at the auction. It should be noted that the offer is made by the *auctioneer* and not the owner of the goods, so that there is no concluded contract of sale (unless, perhaps, the auctioneer is the agent of the vendor). Such an analysis is not without its problems (see the debate between Slade, 1952, 1953, and Gower, 1952). The contract is presumably made with the highest bidder, but how can it be shown who is the highest bidder if the auctioneer does not bring down his hammer?

An alternative analysis put forward by Professor Gower (1952) is to the effect that the advertisement of the auction as being without reserve constitutes an offer to the whole world by the auctioneer that the sale will be without reserve and that offer is accepted by anyone who, in reliance upon the advertisement, attends and bids at the auction. The consequence of this analysis is that a contract is made with all those who attend the auction and bid in reliance upon the advertisement and that a withdrawal of the goods after bidding has begun constitutes a breach of contract with every such person at the auction. However Professor Gower argues that the only person who suffers damage as a result of the breach is the person who is the highest bidder and that breach is therefore the only one worth suing on.

But this analysis also has its problems. The problem of identifying the highest bidder remains because, until the hammer is brought down, there is always the possibility of a last minute bid being made. It also has the consequence that liability can be avoided by refusing to hold the auction at all because acceptance only takes place by attending *and bidding* at the auction. Despite these difficulties, it must be conceded that the intimation that an auction is to be held without reserve raises an expectation in those attending the auction that the goods will be sold to the highest bidder and that *Warlow* provides protection for these expectations and prevents an auctioneer ignoring a condition of the sale which he himself has set. *Warlow* may be another example of the courts reasoning backwards in that they decide that in such a case the bidder ought to have a remedy and they then accommodate that conclusion within the offer and acceptance framework, even though the fit is somewhat uneasy.

3.5 Tenders

Where a person invites tenders for a particular project the general rule is that the invitation to tender is simply an invitation to treat. The offer is made by the person who submits the tender and the acceptance is made when the person inviting the tenders accepts one of them. However in an appropriate case a court may hold that the invitation to tender was, in fact, an offer. Two cases are relevant here.

The first is *Harvela Investments Ltd* v. *Royal Trust Co of Canada* [1986] AC 207. The first defendants decided to sell their shares by sealed competitive tender. They invited the two parties most likely to be interested in the shares each to submit a single sealed offer for their shares and stated that they would accept the highest 'offer' received by them which complied with the terms of their invitation. The plaintiffs tendered a fixed bid of $2 175 000. The second defendant tendered a 'referential' bid of '$2 100 000 or . . . $101 000 in excess of any other offer . . . whichever is the higher'. The first defendants accepted the second defendant's bid, treating it as a bid of $2 276 000. But the House of Lords held that the first defendants were bound to accept the plaintiffs' bid. It was held that the invitation to tender was an offer of a unilateral contract to sell the shares to the highest bidder, despite the fact that the invitation asked the plaintiffs and the second defendant to submit an 'offer'. The bid submitted by the second defendant was held to be invalid because the object of the vendors' invitation was to ascertain the highest amount which each party was prepared to pay and this purpose would be frustrated by a referential bid.

The second case is *Blackpool and Fylde Aero Club Ltd* v. *Blackpool Borough Council* [1990] 1 WLR 1195 and it provides us with a very good example of the flexibility which the courts have in applying the rules relating to offer and acceptance. In 1983 the defendant local authority invited tenders for a concession to operate pleasure flights from Blackpool airport. The form of tender stated that 'the council do not bind themselves to accept all or any part of the tender. No tender which is received after the last date and time specified shall be admitted for consideration'. Tenders had to be received by the Town Clerk 'not later than 12 o'clock noon on Thursday 17th March 1983'. The plaintiffs posted their bid in the Town Hall letter box at about 11am on 17 March. A notice on the letter box stated that it was emptied each day at 12 o'clock noon. Unfortunately, on this particular day, the letter box was not emptied at 12 o'clock and so the plaintiffs' bid remained in the letter box until the morning of 18 March. The plaintiffs' bid was not considered by the Council because they considered it to be a late submission and the concession was awarded to another party. The plaintiffs brought an action for damages for, *inter alia*, breach of contract. The obvious difficulty which they faced was that they did not appear to be in a contractual relationship with the defendants because an invitation to tender is only an invitation to treat. The plaintiffs had therefore simply submitted an offer which the defendants had not accepted. But the Court of Appeal took a different approach. They held that the defendants were contractually obliged to consider the plaintiffs' tender and, for breach of that obligation, they were liable in damages. The court appeared to adopt a two-contract analysis. A contract was concluded with the party whose tender was accepted but the invitation to tender also constituted a unilateral offer to 'consider' any conforming tender which was submitted and that offer was accepted by any party who submitted such a tender. It is suggested that there are two problems with this approach.

The first lies in ascertaining the circumstances in which a court will see fit to imply an offer to consider all tenders submitted. The council did not expressly accept an obligation to consider conforming tenders yet the court saw fit to imply such a duty. Indeed, the court had to imply both a contract and its terms because the parties were not otherwise in a contractual relationship. The Court of Appeal relied upon a number of factors, none of which appear to be conclusive. The first was that the invitation to tender was directed to a small number of interested parties; the second was that, it was claimed, the duty to consider was consistent with the intention of the parties; finally, the court stated that the tender procedure was 'clear, orderly and familiar' and, the greater the precision, the easier it is for a court to spell out an offer which is capable of acceptance. But were there other factors of importance? Was there any significance in the fact that the defendants were a local authority (and so owed a fiduciary duty to rate-payers to act with reasonable prudence in their financial affairs) or in the fact that the plaintiffs were the existing holders of the concession and so may be said to have had a legitimate expectation of being considered? The answer to these questions remains unclear, although parties issuing an invitation to tender would be well advised to state expressly that they accepted no obligation to consider any tender submitted.

The second difficulty lies in determining the scope of this 'duty to consider'. Bingham LJ stated that the duty would have been breached had the defendants 'opened and thereupon accepted the first tender received, even though the deadline had not expired and other invitees had not yet responded' or if they 'had considered and accepted a tender admittedly received well after the deadline'. Could the defendants have rejected all the tenders? It would appear so. Stocker LJ stated that the obligation to consider 'would not preclude or inhibit the council from deciding not to accept any tender or to award the concession, provided the decison was bona fide and honest, to any tenderer'. So the obligation to consider tenders submitted does not preclude a local authority from removing a contractor from the tendering process when it discovers that there is a conflict of interest between a senior council employee and one of the tenderers (see *Fairclough Building Ltd* v. *Borough Council of Port Talbot* (1993) 62 Build. LR 82).

Finally, this two-contract analysis may have implications for those who submit tenders, as can be seen from the Canadian case of *The Queen in Right of Ontario* v. *Ron Engineering & Construction Eastern Ltd* (1981) 119 DLR (3d) 267. The defendants invited tenders on the basis that tenders had to be accompanied by a deposit which was to be forfeited if the tender was withdrawn or if the tenderer otherwise refused to proceed. The plaintiffs discovered, shortly after the tenders were opened, that they had made a mistake in the submission of their tender and they refused to proceed with the execution of the contract documents. They sued to recover their deposit of $150 000. It was held that they were not entitled to recover because the invitation to tender followed by the submission of a tender created a contract, the terms of which were that the plaintiffs were not entitled to recover their deposit if they refused to proceed with the contract. There is, as yet, no English case on this point but it is suggested that, in the light of the *Blackpool* case, an English court might reach the same conclusion.

3.6 Timetables and Vending Machines

It is remarkable how difficult it is to distinguish between an offer and an invitation to treat in many everyday transactions. A simple example is boarding a bus. One could say that the bus timetable and the running of the bus are an offer by the bus company which is accepted by boarding the bus (although it should be noted that most timetables contain express disclaimers of any obligation to provide the services contained in the timetable). Such was the view of Lord Greene in *Wilkie* v. *London Transport Board* [1947] 1 All ER 258, when he stated that the offer was made by the bus company and that it was accepted when a passenger 'puts himself either on the platform or inside the bus'. Alternatively, it could be said that the acceptance takes place when the passenger asks for a ticket and pays the fare. A further possibility is to say that the bus timetable is an invitation to treat, the offer is made by the passenger in boarding the bus and the acceptance takes place when the bus conductor accepts the money and issues a ticket. Finally it could be said that the bus conductor makes the offer when he issues the ticket and this offer is accepted by paying the fare and retaining the ticket.

In many ways the issue may seem to be an academic one, devoid of any practical consequence. But this is not the case. It has serious consequences if there is an exclusion clause contained on the back of the ticket (see further Chapter 11). If the first analysis is adopted then the exclusion clause is not part of the contract because the contract is concluded before the ticket is handed over. On the other hand if the final alternative is adopted then the exclusion clause is part of the contract because it is contained in the offer made by the conductor. A court might adopt the first of these alternatives in our exclusion clause example in order to protect the passenger but, would it also apply it where the same passenger boards the bus by mistake and wishes to get off the bus before it moves from the stop without paying for his fare? As Professor Treitel has stated (1991), the cases 'yield no single rule' and all that can be said is that 'the exact time of contracting depends in each case on the wording of the relevant document and on the circumstances in which it was issued'.

Other everyday examples could be provided which defy simple classification. What is the status of a menu outside a restaurant? What about a vending machine selling tea and coffee? The former is probably an invitation to treat but, in *Thornton* v. *Shoe Lane Parking Ltd* [1971] 2 QB 163, Lord Denning stated that an automatic machine which issued tickets outside a car park made a standing offer which was accepted by a motorist driving so far into the car park that the machine issued him with a ticket.

3.7 Acceptance

An acceptance is an unqualified expression of assent to the terms proposed by the offeror. There is no rule that acceptance must be made by words; it can be made by conduct, as was the case in *Carlill* v. *Carbolic Smoke Ball Co* (see above).

A purported acceptance which does not accept all the terms and conditions proposed by the offeror but which in fact introduces new terms is not an acceptance but a counter-offer, which is then treated as a new offer which is capable of acceptance or rejection. The effect of a counter-offer is to 'kill off' the original offer so that it cannot subsequently be accepted by the offeree. This rule can be seen in operation in the case of

Hyde v. *Wrench* (1840) 3 Beav 334. The defendant offered to sell some land to the plaintiff for £1000 and the plaintiff replied by offering to purchase the land for £950. The defendant refused to sell for £950. So the plaintiff subsequently wrote to the defendant agreeing to pay the £1000 but the defendant still refused to sell. It was held that there was no contract between the parties. The plaintiff's offer of £950 was a counter-offer which killed off the defendant's original offer so as to render it incapable of subsequent acceptance. It is this rule that acceptance must be unqualified which has given rise to difficulties in the battle of the forms cases, such as *Butler* v. *Ex-Cell-O Corp* (see above 2.4).

3.8 Communication of the Acceptance

The general rule is that an acceptance must be communicated to the offeror. The acceptance is generally only validly communicated when it is actually brought to the attention of the offeror. The operation of this rule was illustrated by Denning LJ in *Entores* v. *Miles Far East Corp* [1955] 2 QB 327. He said that if an oral acceptance is drowned out by an overflying aircraft, such that the offeror cannot hear the acceptance, then there is no contract unless the acceptor repeats his acceptance once the aircraft has passed over. Similarly, where two people make a contract by telephone and the line goes 'dead' so that the acceptance is incomplete then the acceptor must telephone the offeror to make sure that he has heard the acceptance. Where, however, the acceptance is made clearly and audibly, but the offeror does not hear what is said a contract is nevertheless concluded unless the offeror makes clear to the acceptor that he has not heard what was said. In the case of instantaneous communication, such as telephone and telex, the acceptance takes place at the moment the acceptance is received by the offeror and at the place at which the offeror happens to be (see *Brinkibon Ltd* v. *Stahag Stahl* [1983] 2 AC 34).

3.9 Acceptance in Ignorance of the Offer

An offer is effective when it is communicated to the offeree. This requirement generally does not give rise to problems, but difficulty does arise in the following type of case. X offers £100 for the safe return of his missing dog. Y returns the dog but is unaware of X's offer. Is Y entitled to the money? A good argument can be made out to the effect that Y should be entitled to the money. X has got what he wanted and there seems no reason in justice why he should not be required to pay what he has publicly promised to pay. At the same time Y has performed a socially useful act in returning the dog and he should be rewarded for so doing. On the other hand, in the case of a bilateral contract which imposes mutual obligations upon the parties, the effect of such a rule would be to subject the 'accepting' party to obligations of which he was unaware. For example, if X offered to sell the dog for £50 to the first person who returned it to him, Y, who returns the dog, unaware of the offer, should not thereby be held to have accepted an offer to purchase the dog for £50. In the light of these considerations it has been argued that the best approach to adopt is to hold that knowledge of the offer is not necessary in the reward type of case but that knowledge should be required in the case of bilateral contracts (Hudson, 1968).

However the rule which has been adopted in England is that a person who, in ignorance of the offer, performs the act or acts requested by the offeror is not entitled to sue as on a contract. The case of *Gibbons* v. *Proctor* (1891) 64 LT 594, which was thought to stand for the contrary proposition, appears on closer examination of the facts to be a case where the person claiming the reward knew of the offer at the time when the information was given to the police (Treitel, 1991). It is here that we see the importance of the schematic approach to agreement because it is not sufficient that the parties were, at some moment in time, in agreement; there must be a definite offer which is mirrored by a definite acceptance. For the same reason cross-offers which are identical do not create a contract unless or until they are accepted (*Tinn* v. *Hoffman & Co* (1873) 29 LT 271). These cases reinforce the point made in Chapter 2 that contract law adopts an objective rather than a subjective approach to agreement and therefore the fact that the parties are subjectively agreed is not conclusive evidence that a contract exists (contrast the view of Spencer discussed at 2.2).

Once it is shown that the offer has been communicated to the other party, a person who knows of the offer may do the act required for acceptance with some motive other than that of accepting the offer (*Williams* v. *Carwardine* (1833) 4 B & Ad 621). But the offer must have been present to his mind when he did the act which constituted the acceptance. Thus in *R* v. *Clarke* (1927) 40 CLR 227, where the party claiming the reward had forgotten about the offer of a reward at the time he gave the information, it was held that he was not entitled to the reward.

3.10   Prescribed Method of Acceptance

Where the offeror prescribes a specific method of acceptance, the general rule is that the offeror is not bound unless the terms of his offer are complied with. However the offeror who wishes to state that he will be bound *only* if the offer is accepted in a particular way must use clear words to achieve this purpose. Where the offeror has not used sufficiently clear words a court will hold the offeror bound by an acceptance which is made in a form which is no less advantageous to him than the form which he prescribed. This can be seen in the case of *Manchester Diocesan Council for Education* v. *Commercial and General Investments Ltd* [1969] 3 All ER 1593. The plaintiff decided to sell some property by tender and inserted a clause in the form of tender stating that the person whose bid was accepted would be informed by means of a letter sent to the address given in the tender. The defendant completed the form of tender and sent it to the plaintiff. The plaintiff decided to accept the defendant's tender and sent a letter of acceptance to the defendant's surveyor but not to the address on the tender. It was held that communication to the address in the tender was not the sole permitted means of communication of acceptance and that therefore a valid contract had been concluded. The defendant was not disadvantaged in any way by notification being given to its surveyor and, in any case, the stipulation had been inserted by the plaintiff, not the defendant, and so it was open to the plaintiff to waive strict compliance with the term provided that the defendant was not adversely affected thereby.

3.11 Acceptance by Silence

The general rule is that acceptance of an offer will not be implied from mere silence on the part of the offeree and that an offeror cannot impose a contractual obligation upon the offeree by stating that, unless the latter expressly rejects the offer, he will be held to have accepted it. The rationale behind this rule is that it is thought to be unfair to put an offeree to time and expense to avoid the imposition of unwanted contractual arrangements. The principal English authority on this point is *Felthouse* v. *Bindley* (1862) 11 CB (NS) 869. The plaintiff and his nephew entered into negotiations for the sale of the nephew's horse. The plaintiff stated that if he heard nothing further from his nephew then he considered that the horse was his at a price of £30 15s. The nephew did not respond to this offer but he decided to accept it and told the defendant auctioneer not to sell the horse because it had already been sold. Nevertheless, the auctioneer mistakenly sold the horse and so the plaintiff sued the auctioneer. The auctioneer argued that the plaintiff had no title to sue because his offer to buy the horse had not been accepted by his nephew and this argument was upheld by the court on the ground that the nephew's silence did not amount to an acceptance of the offer. The application of the general rule to the facts of *Felthouse* has been the subject of criticism on the ground that the uncle had waived the need for communication of the acceptance and the nephew had manifested his acceptance by informing the auctioneer that the horse had been sold (see Miller, 1972).

But the rule itself has not emerged unscathed from the line of cases represented by *The Hannah Blumenthal* (see 2.1), where the House of Lords held that a contract to abandon a reference to arbitration could be concluded by the silence of both parties. As Bingham J noted in *Cie Francaise d'Importation et de Distribution SA* v. *Deutsche Continental Handelsgesellschaft* [1985] 2 Lloyd's Rep 592, 599, this line of authority does 'some violence ... to familiar rules of contract such as the requirement that acceptance of an offer should be communicated to the offeror unless the requirement of communication is expressly or impliedly waived'. But no case actually sought to overrule or to question explicitly the correctness of *Felthouse* v. *Bindley* and the reasoning in these cases was distorted by the fact that neither arbitrators nor courts had, at common law, the power to dismiss an arbitration for want of prosecution and so the courts were asked to employ any common law doctrine which appeared even remotely suitable to enable them to reach a commercially just solution, namely that the agreement to arbitrate had been abandoned. Now that Parliament has intervened in the form of s.102 of the Courts and Legal Services Act 1990 and given to arbitrators the power to dismiss a claim for want of prosecution, the courts no longer need to engage in such subterfuge, nor to distort the rules relating to offer and acceptance (see *The Amazonia* [1990] 1 Lloyd's Rep 238, 243).

Instead it is submitted that these arbitration cases remind us that the rule that silence does not amount to an acceptance is not an absolute one and that it does admit of exceptions. For example, a course of dealing between the parties may give rise to the inference that silence amounts to acceptance. It is also unclear whether the general rule will apply where the offeree assumes that his silence has been effective to conclude a contract and then acts in reliance upon that belief. It is suggested that, in such a case, the general rule should give way and a court should hold that a contract has been concluded between the parties (see Miller, 1972). As we have noted, the purpose behind the general rule is to protect the offeree and therefore it should not apply where its application would cause hardship to the offeree. However where the offeree only mentally assents to the offer but does not act in reliance upon it, it is suggested that the general rule should apply because, otherwise the offeree would be able to speculate against the offeror, by stating that he had accepted the offer when the contract was a good one for him and by stating that he had not accepted it when the contract turned out to be a bad one. Therefore it is submitted that some positive action is required on the part of the offeree to provide evidence that he has in fact accepted the offer.

3.12   Exceptions to the Rule Requiring Communication of Acceptance

The rule that acceptance must be communicated to the offeror is not an absolute one. For example, the terms of the offer may demonstrate that the offeror does not insist that the acceptance be communicated to him (*Carlill* v. *Carbolic Smoke Ball Co* see above 3.3). The offeror may be prevented by his conduct from arguing that the acceptance was communicated to him (*Entores* v. *Miles Far East Corporation*, see above 3.8). But the major and most controversial exception relates to acceptances sent through the post.

As a matter of theory any one of a number of possible solutions could be used to ascertain when an acceptance sent by post takes effect. It could be when the letter is posted, when it reaches the address of the offeror, when it is read by the offeror or when, in the ordinary course of the post, it would reach the offeror. The general rule which English law has adopted can be traced back to *Adams* v. *Lindsell* (1818) 1 B & Ald 681, which is now understood to stand for the proposition that acceptance takes place when the letter of acceptance is posted by the offeree.

However the justifications put forward in support of this rule are, to say the least, rather tenuous (see Gardner, 1992). The first justification is that the Post Office is the agent of the offeror and so receipt of the letter by the agent is equivalent to receipt by the offeror. This justification is open to the criticism that it cannot be said in any meaningful sense that the Post Office is the agent of the offeror because the Post Office has no power to contract on behalf of the offeror. The second justification is that the offeror has chosen to start negotiations through the post and so the risk of delay or loss in the post should be imposed upon him. However it is not necessarily the offeror who has started the negotiations through the post. It could be the case that the offeree initiated negotiations through the post by asking the offeror for the terms on which he was prepared to do business. Nevertheless, it must be conceded that this justification has some element of validity because, in *Henthorn* v. *Fraser* [1892] 2 Ch 27, it was held that the postal rule only applies where it is reasonable to use the post. However it is reasonable to use the post where the parties live at a distance from each other; it is not necessary for the offeror to have commenced the negotiations by post. So it is not entirely true to say that the offeror has accepted the risk of delay in the post. A more promising justification is that the offeree should not be prejudiced once he has dispatched his acceptance and he should be able to rely on the efficacy of his acceptance. This argument is a strong one but it could be met by providing that, once the acceptance has been posted, the offeror can no longer revoke his offer; it does not demand that the acceptance be treated as taking effect when it is dispatched. In fact, it may be that the explanation for the initial adoption of the rule lies in the public perception of the postal service in the middle of the nineteenth century (Gardner, 1992). The uniform penny post was introduced in 1837. At around the same time postage began to be pre-paid rather than paid for on receipt and the cutting of letter boxes in doors meant that a letter need no longer be handed to the addressee individually. These factors, Gardner argues, meant that the public perception of the time was that a letter, once posted, would reach its destination 'without further subvention from outside the system' and that this led to the 'notional equation of the posting of a letter with its delivery'. In the modern world this perception seems ridiculous: with the advent of truly instantaneous means of communication, the idea that posting is equivalent to delivery is not credible. This theory may help explain why it was that the judiciary in the late nineteenth century (in cases such as *Henthorn* v. *Fraser* (above) and *Byrne* v. *Van Tienhoven* (1880) 5 CPD 344, see 3.14) began to confine the postal rule within narrow limits. As quicker methods of communication, such as the telephone, were developed, so the equation of posting with delivery began to look increasingly anomalous. Indeed, on this basis it can be said that the postal rule is now 'something of a museum piece', continuing to exist in a world which bears no relationship to the world in which the rule was introduced and therefore serving a purpose which is entirely different from the one intended by those who initially adopted and developed the rule.

Not only are the justifications for the general rule weak, but the operation of the rule can give rise to manifest injustice. Take the following example. X makes an offer to Y and states that it will be open for acceptance until 5 pm on Friday. Applying the general rule Y may validly 'accept' that offer by posting his acceptance at 4.45 on Friday afternoon, even though it will not reach X until Monday or Tuesday of the following week. It is true that X could avoid such hardship by stating in his offer that the acceptance must *reach* him by 5pm on Friday (see below) but the fact that the parties can contract out of the general rule is no justification for the general rule itself.

In addition to creating injustice, the general rule gives rise to practical difficulties. Two such difficulties will be dealt with here. The first arises where the letter of acceptance is lost in the post. A logical application of the general rule leads to the result that a contract has been concluded because the acceptance takes effect when it is posted and not when it reaches the offeror. This was held to be the case in England in *Household Fire Insurance* v. *Grant* (1879) 4 Ex D 217. But in Scotland this view was rejected by Lord Shand in *Mason* v. *Benhar Coal Co* (1882) 9 R 883. He stated that, in his opinion, no contract came into existence when the acceptance was posted but never reached the offeror. It is suggested that the latter rule is the preferable one because it is the offeree who has sent the acceptance and so he is in the best position to know when his acceptance is likely to reach the offeror and to take steps to check that it does so reach the offeror. Nevertheless English law is presently committed to the view that a contract is concluded on the posting of the letter of acceptance even where it gets lost in the post, although Professor Treitel has argued (1991) that, where the reason for the loss of the letter is that it has been incorrectly addressed by the offeree, then the acceptance should not take place on posting because, while the offeror may take the risk of delay or loss in the post, he does not take the further risk of carelessness by the offeree.

The second practical difficulty arises where the offeree posts his acceptance and then sends a rejection by a quicker method so that the rejection reaches the offeror before the acceptance. Once again a logical application of the general rule leads to the result that the contract was concluded when the letter of acceptance was posted and so the subsequent communication is not a revocation of the offer but a breach of contract, which may be accepted or rejected by the offeror. But it can be argued that it would be absurd to hold that a contract has been concluded when both parties have relied on the fact that there was no contract (although in such a case it could be argued that both parties have entered into a second contract under which they agreed to abandon their rights and obligations under the first contract). On the other hand it can be argued that to hold that the contract was not concluded when the letter of acceptance was posted allows the offeree to speculate at the offeror's expense by sending a rejection by a faster means where the contract turns out to be a bad one for him. It is unclear which of these approaches will be adopted in English law (for contrasting views see the Scottish case *Countess of Dunmore* v. *Alexander* (1830) 9 S 190 and the South African case *A to Z Bazaars (Pty) Ltd* v. *Minister of Agriculture* 1974 (4) SA 392).

Given these practical difficulties to which the general rule gives rise it is no surprise to find that the postal rule is subject to some limitations. In the first place, as we have seen, it must have been reasonable for the offeree to use the post (see *Henthorn* v. *Fraser* (above)). Secondly, the offeror can avoid the operation of the rule by stating that the acceptance will only be effective when it actually reaches him. Thirdly, it is interesting to note that the rule has not been adopted in many other cases where the parties are not dealing face to face. Thus in *Entores* v. *Miles Far East Corp* (above) it was held that the postal rule did not apply to telexes and that it was confined to non-instantaneous forms of communication. Therefore a distinction has been drawn between instantaneous and non-instantaneous forms of communication; only the latter being caught by the postal rule. This distinction is likely to pose difficulties in its application to new forms of technology but it is suggested that, in the case of communication via computers, communication is virtually instantaneous and therefore is unlikely to be governed by the postal rule. The widest exception to the general rule was recognised in *Holwell Securities Ltd* v. *Hughes* [1974] 1 WLR 155, where it was suggested that the postal rule ought not to apply 'where it would lead to manifest inconvenience and absurdity'.

The width of the latter exception illustrates the weakness of the arguments which have been put forward to support the general rule but, rather than recognise that it is the general rule which is the source of the problem, the English courts have chosen to widen the scope of the exceptions to the general rule. It is submitted that the better approach would be to abolish the general rule and replace it with the normal rule that acceptance takes place when the acceptance is received by the offeror, subject to the qualification that the offeror cannot revoke the offer once the acceptance has been posted.

3.13 Acceptance in Unilateral Contracts

A unilateral contract is a contract whereby one party promises to pay to the other a sum of money or to do some other act if that other party will do or refrain from doing something without making a promise to that effect. Classic examples are the reward cases or *Carlill* v. *Carbolic Smoke Ball Co* (see 3.3). The effect of classifying a contract as unilateral rather than bilateral is that acceptance can be made by fully performing the requested act; there is no need to give advance notification of acceptance. The principal difficulty lies in determining when the offer can be withdrawn, which, in turn, depends upon when the offer has been 'accepted'. For example X offers Y £10 000 if Y will walk from London to Newcastle. Does Y accept the offer when he expresses an intention to accept the offer, when he reaches York, or only when he gets to Newcastle? The general rule which English law has adopted was described by Goff LJ in *Daulia Ltd* v. *Four Millbank Nominees Ltd* [1978] Ch 231, in the following terms:

> 'Whilst I think the true view of a unilateral contract must in general be that the offeror is entitled to require full performance of the condition which he has imposed and short of that he is not bound, that must be subject to one important qualification, which stems from the fact that there must be an implied obligation on the part of the offeror not to prevent the condition becoming satisfied, which obligation it seems to me must arise as soon as the offeree starts to perform'.

The willingness of the courts to imply an obligation not to 'prevent the condition becoming satisfied' can be seen by contrasting the following two cases. The first is *Errington* v. *Errington* [1952] 1 KB 290. A father bought a house for £750 and took out a mortgage for £500. His son and daughter-in-law moved into the house and the father stated that if they paid off the mortgage the house was theirs. The couple moved into the house and began to pay off the mortgage, without promising to continue with the payments. The father died and the father's personal representatives sought to revoke the arrangement. The Court of Appeal held that they could not do so because the 'father's promise was a unilateral contract', which could not be revoked once the couple had embarked upon performance provided that they did not leave performance 'incomplete and unperformed'.

On the other hand, a different result was reached in the case of *Luxor (Eastbourne) Ltd* v. *Cooper* [1941] AC 108. The plaintiff agreed with the defendants that if he introduced a purchaser who would buy the defendants' two cinemas for at least £185 000 each, he would be paid a commission. The plaintiff succeeded in introducing to the defendants a purchaser who was ready and willing to complete the purchase, but the defendants refused to proceed with the sale. It was held that the plaintiff was not entitled to the commission because it was only payable on completion of the sale. The House of Lords refused to imply a term that the defendants would do nothing to prevent the plaintiff from earning his commission because it was contrary to the common understanding of the parties which was that the plaintiff took 'the risk in the hope of a substantial remuneration for a comparatively small exertion'.

3.14   Termination of the Offer

There are five principal methods by which an offer may be terminated. The first is that the offer may be withdrawn. An offer can be withdrawn by the offeror at any time before it has been accepted. However to withdraw an offer the notice of withdrawal must actually be brought to the attention of the offeree. There is no requirement that the offeror himself must be the one to bring the withdrawal to the attention of the offeree. Thus in *Dickinson* v. *Dodds* (1876) 2 Ch D 463, the defendant offered to sell a house to the plaintiff for £800, the offer to be left open until Friday. On Thursday the defendant sold the house to a third party and the plaintiff was informed of this by another third party. Nevertheless the plaintiff sent the defendant his letter of acceptance on the Friday. It was held that no contract had been concluded between the parties because the offer had been withdrawn before it was accepted.

The rule that the withdrawal must be brought to the attention of the offeree has odd effects in relation to offers sent throught the post. This can be seen in the case of *Byrne* v. *Van Tienhoven* (1880) 5 CPD 344. The defendants sent the plaintiffs an offer on 1 October. This offer was received by the plaintiffs on 11 October and they sent off an immediate acceptance. However, in the meantime, the defendants had sent, on 8 October, a letter revoking their offer, which reached the plaintiffs on 20 October. It was held that a contract was concluded between the parties on 11 October. To be effective the withdrawal must be drawn to the attention of the other party and, for this purpose, the postal rule does not apply, so that the revocation only takes effect when it actually reaches the other party. So the purported withdrawal could not take effect until 20 October but, by that time, a contract had already been concluded and the withdrawal was therefore too late. This case is a good example of the objective approach which the courts adopt to the issue of agreement because at no time were the parties actually subjectively agreed; by the time the plaintiffs accepted the offer on 11 October, the defendants had already dispatched their 'withdrawal' of the offer.

Although it is clear that the revocation must be brought to the attention of the offeree it is not entirely clear when the revocation is treated as being brought to his attention. It could be when the letter reaches his business or it could be when he actually reads it. There is no clear English authority on this point, although in *The Brimnes* [1975] QB 929, the Court of Appeal held that, in the case of a revocation sent by telex during ordinary business hours, the revocation was effective when it was received on the telex machine. There was no requirement that it actually be read by any particular person within the organisation.

Secondly, an offer can be terminated by a rejection by the offeree. We have already seen how a rejection or a counter-offer has the effect of 'killing off' the original offer (*Hyde* v. *Wrench* (see 3.7)). Thirdly, an offer may be terminated by lapse of time. An offer which is expressly stated to last only for a specific period of time cannot be accepted after that date. An offer which specifies no time limit is deemed to last for a reasonable period of time.

Fourthly, an offer which is stated to come to an end if a certain event occurs cannot be accepted after that event has actually taken place.

Finally, an offer may be terminated by the death of the offeror, although the law is not entirely clear on this point. On one view it could be said that death always terminates an offer because the parties cannot enter into an agreement once one of the parties is dead. However it seems to be the case that an offeree cannot accept an offer once he knows that the offeror has died but that his acceptance may be valid if it is made in ignorance of the fact that the offeror has died, provided that the contract is not one for the performance of personal services. There is no authority on the position where it is the offeree who dies. The generally accepted view is that on the offeree's death the offer comes to an end by operation of law.

3.15   The Limits of Offer and Acceptance

We have noted at various points in this chapter how difficult it is to fit many everyday transactions within the offer and acceptance framework. Simple examples which give rise to difficulty are boarding a bus, buying goods in a supermarket and making a contract through the post. The battle of the forms poses difficulties for the businessman. These difficulties have led some commentators to doubt the utility of the offer and acceptance model. It is true that there are difficulties with the offer and acceptance model but these problems are often experienced because of the tension between the court's wish to give effect to the intention of the parties, their desire to achieve a just result on the facts of the case and the need to establish a clear rule which can be applied to all such cases in the future.

Some commentators argue that there is too much uncertainty within the present law. Certainty is an extremely important commodity in the law of contract. A greater degree of certainty could be provided by adopting legislative formulae to prescribe solutions for difficult and uncertain areas, such as the battle of the forms. An example of this approach is Article 19 of the United Nations Convention on Contracts for the International Sale of Goods (more commonly known as the Vienna Convention) which provides that:

(1)   A reply to an offer which purports to be an acceptance but contains additions, limitations or other modifications is a rejection of the offer and constitutes a counter-offer.

(2)   However, a reply to an offer which purports to be an acceptance but contains additional or different terms which do not materially alter the terms of the offer constitutes an acceptance, unless the offeror, without undue delay, objects orally to the discrepancy or dispatches a notice to that effect. If he does not so object, the terms of the contract are the terms of the offer with the modifications contained in the acceptance.

(3)   Additional or different terms relating, among other things, to the price, payment, quality and quantity of the goods, place of delivery, extent of one party's liability to the other or the settlement of diputes are considered to alter the terms of the offer materially'.

This type of approach seeks to achieve a solution which is practical, without being excessively rigid, and which is easy to apply. Yet Article 19 in turn has been criticised for being uncertain (see Vergne, 1985). For example, is any alteration proposed by the offeree an 'addition, limitation or other modification' or does some form of *de minimis* rule apply? Secondly, although the definition of materiality in paragraph (3) is helpful, it is clearly not exhaustive, but it is unclear how much further it goes. It is important to note that none of the many legislative solutions proposed for battle of the forms cases have escaped criticism (see McKendrick, 1988). The variety of battle of the forms cases is such that no single formula can provide an acceptable solution to all possible cases. Absolute certainty of this type is unattainable because of the infinite variety of intentions held by contracting parties. It is submitted that English law is unlikely to be improved by the adoption of such formulations, which will still give rise to uncertainty and yet impose an unacceptable level of rigidity.

Other commentators argue that the present rules can give rise to injustice in certain cases. This could be ameliorated by the adoption of Lord Denning's general approach in *Butler* v. *Ex-Cell-O Corporation* but, as we have noted (see 2.4), the general approach has its own problems because it gives rise to so much uncertainty.

It is submitted that the present law strikes a reasonable balance between the need for certainty and the desire to achieve a just result which is consistent with the intention of the parties. The offer and acceptance model has a core of well-established rules which are understood by lawyers and which are capable of being understood by the business community. At the same time the model is applied with some degree of flexibility by the courts so that a conclusion can be reached which is consistent with the intention of the parties. The present state of the law cannot be said to be entirely satisfactory but it is better than a system which imposes an unacceptable level of rigidity or a system which imposes an unacceptable level of uncertainty.

Summary

1 An offer is a statement by one party of a willingness to enter into a contract on stated terms, provided that these terms are, in turn, accepted by the party to whom the offer is addressed.
2 An offer must be distinguished from an invitation to treat. A display of goods in a shop and advertisements are, subject to cases such as *Carlill* v. *Carbolic Smoke Ball Co.* regarded as invitations to treat. An auctioneer, by inviting bids to be made, makes an invitation to treat (except, perhaps, where the auction is to take place without a reserve price) and an invitation to parties to submit a tender is generally an invitation to treat.
3 An acceptance is an unqualified expression of assent to the terms proposed by the offeror. An acceptance must generally be communicated to the offeror.
4 A purported acceptance which does not mirror the terms of the offer is not an acceptance but a counter-offer which kills off the original offer.

5   An offer cannot be accepted by someone who is ignorant of the existence of the offer or by someone who does not have the offer in his mind when he does the act which he alleges constitutes the acceptance.

6   Where the offeror prescribes a specific method of acceptance, the general rule is that the offeror is not bound unless the terms of his offer are complied with.

7   The general rule is that acceptance of an offer will not be implied from mere silence on the part of the offeree.

8   A letter of acceptance takes effect whenever it is posted, provided that it was reasonable for the offeree to have used the post. This rule applies even where the letter gets lost in the post and never reaches the offeror. It is unclear what is the legal position where the offeree posts his acceptance and then sends a rejection by a quicker method so that the rejection reaches the offeror before the acceptance.

9   In the case of a unilateral contract the offeror is only bound by full performance of the requested act but, in certain cases, the court will imply an obligation on the part of the offeror not to prevent completion of performance, which obligation arises as soon as the offeree starts to perform.

10 An offer may be terminated by revocation, rejection by the offeree, lapse of time, the occurrence of a stipulated event and, possibly the death of one or other of the parties. In the case of revocation the general rule is that the revocation must actually be brought to the attention of the offeree.

Exercises

1   Distinguish between an offer and an invitation to treat. Give examples to illustrate the distinction.

2   Do you think that *Lefkowitz* v. *Great Minneapolis Surplus Stores* would be followed in this country? Give reasons for your answer.

3   In offer and acceptance cases do the courts 'reason forwards' or 'reason backwards'?

4   What is the 'postal rule'? Do you think it is a good rule?

5   Do you think Article 19 of the United Nations Convention on Contracts for the International Sale of Goods is an improvement upon the principles established in *Butler* v. *Ex-Cell-O Corp*?

6   Billy wishes to know whether or not he can refuse to carry out the following arrangements without finding himself in breach of contract. Advise him.

   (a) Billy offered to sell his car to Jimmy for £5000 and stated that he would assume that Jimmy had accepted his offer unless he informed Billy to the contrary. Jimmy has not been in contact with Billy but he has contacted his bank manager and agreed a loan to purchase the car.

   (b) Billy offered to sell a consignment of bricks to Jimmy subject to his terms and conditions which stated that Jimmy would be responsible for collecting the bricks. Jimmy accepted the offer, subject to his terms and conditions which stated that Billy would be responsible for delivery of the bricks. Billy still possesses the bricks.

   (c) Billy offered to sell his golf clubs to Jimmy. Jimmy immediately replied by letter accepting Billy's offer but, due to his carelessness in wrongly addressing the letter, the acceptance never reached Billy.

4 Certainty and Agreement Mistakes

In Chapter 2 we noted that the test for the existence of an agreement is objective rather than subjective. In this chapter we shall consider the application of the objective test in two areas, namely certainty and mistake.

4.1 Certainty

In order to create a binding contract, the parties must express their agreement in a form which is sufficiently certain for the courts to enforce. The traditional reason for this is that it is for the parties, and not the courts, to make the contract. The function of the court is limited to the interpretation of the contract which the parties have made and it does not extend to making contracts on their behalf (Fridman, 1962). This sentiment was classically expressed by Viscount Maugham in *Scammell and Nephew Ltd* v. *Ouston* [1941] AC 251 when he said that

> 'in order to constitute a valid contract the parties must so express themselves that their meaning can be determined with a reasonable degree of certainty. It is plain that unless this can be done . . . consensus ad idem would be a matter of mere conjecture'.

The traditional stance has to be tempered, however, in its application to commercial contracts where businessmen wish to avoid rigid agreements which give them no room to manoeuvre in a fluctuating economy. It is not uncommon for building and civil engineering contracts to contain terms which permit the contractor to vary the work which he is required to do, or which make provision for a variation of the time for performance or for the price to be recalculated in the light of events occurring during the agreement. A good example of such flexibility is provided by clause 51 of the current version of the Institute of Civil Engineers Conditions of Contract which provides:

'(1) The Engineer:

(a) shall order any variation to any part of the Works that may in his opinion be necessary for the completion of the Works and

(b) may order any variation that for any other reason shall in his opinion be desirable for the completion and/or improved functioning of the Works.

Such variations may include additions omissions substitutions alterations changes in quality form character kind position dimension level or line and changes in any specified sequence method or timing of construction required by the Contract and may be ordered during the Defects Correction Period'.

Such a clause is an essential ingredient of any long-term construction contract because it obliges the contractor to carry out such additional work and it also entitles the contractor to be paid for that work under the terms of the contract. The desire to provide the parties with a degree of flexibility is not the only factor which impels the courts towards the conclusion that agreements are enforceable. The courts are also reluctant to find that no contract has been concluded where the parties have acted on the assumption that a contract has been entered into (*Percy Trentham Ltd* v. *Archital Luxfer* [1993] 1 Lloyd's Rep 25, 27).

Thus this area of law is characterised by a tension between the traditional refusal of the courts to make a contract for the parties and the desire of the courts to put into effect what they believe to be the intention of the parties. The dominant judicial philosophy may be said to be one which leans in favour of upholding an agreement and treating it as a valid contract. Thus in *Hillas* v. *Arcos* (1932) 147 LT 503, Lord Wright said:

> 'Business men often record the most important agreements in crude and summary fashion . . . It is . . . the duty of the court to construe such documents fairly and broadly, without being too astute or subtle in finding defects'.

However there are limits to the benevolence of the courts. Lord Wright himself recognised that such a liberal approach did not mean that 'the court is to make a contract for the parties'. In comparing these two statements of Lord Wright we can see that he is making a contrast between 'construing' (or interpreting) a contract and 'making' a contract; the former being legitimate, the latter being illegitimate. Some academic commentators have accepted the existence of such a distinction (Fridman, 1962) but others have subjected it to heavy criticism (Samek, 1970 and Ellinghaus, 1971). In application the distinction is by no means obvious. This is so for two reasons. The first is that the test for the existence of an agreement is objective and, as we have seen in cases such as *Gibson* v. *Manchester City Council* [1979] 1 WLR 294 (see 3.1), the courts can and do differ in the application of this test. Secondly, as is clear from the judgment of Viscount Maugham in *Scammell* v. *Ouston* (quoted above), the courts do not insist upon absolute certainty: 'a reasonable degree of certainty' will suffice. There is no hard and fast line between what is certain and what is uncertain. What is sufficiently certain to one judge may be uncertain to another. Thus the distinction between 'construing' a contract and 'making' a contract is one of degree and not one of kind.

A consequence of this is that the approach which the courts have adopted has not been wholly consistent, with some judges being more willing than others to find the existence of a contract. This inconsistency was present in the cases at the time of the formulation of the rules in *Hillas*

v. *Arcos* (above) and it has continued to the present day. This can be demonstrated by reference to the following two pairs of contrasting decisions.

The first pair consists of *May and Butcher* v. *R* [1934] 2 KB 17 and *Hillas* v. *Arcos*. In *May and Butcher* the parties entered into a written agreement under which the British government was to sell tentage to the plaintiff and the agreement provided that the price and date of payment 'shall be agreed upon from time to time'. It was held that, the parties not having reached agreement on these matters, no contract had been concluded because, according to Lord Buckmaster, 'an agreement between two parties to enter into an agreement in which some critical part of the contract matter is left undetermined is no contract at all'. On the other hand a different approach was adopted in the case of *Hillas* v. *Arcos* (above). In 1930 the parties entered into a contract under which the plaintiffs bought from the defendants 22 000 standards of 'softwood goods of fair specification'. The 1930 contract also contained a provision which stated that the plaintiffs had an option 'of entering into a contract with sellers for the purchase of 100 000 standards for delivery during 1931'. When the plaintiffs sought to exercise this option the defendants argued that the clause was too uncertain to be enforced. This argument was rejected by the House of Lords, who held that the words could be given a reasonable meaning and that therefore the option was binding. Lord Tomlin said that, before the conclusion that no contract has been completed is reached 'it is necessary to exclude as impossible all reasonable meanings which would give certainty to the words'. But it should be noted that in *Hillas* there was a prior contract between the parties which assisted the court in giving a meaning to the option clause.

The second pair of decisions demonstrates that the inconsistency is still present in the cases today. The two cases are *Queensland Electricity Generating Board* v. *New Hope Collieries Pty Ltd* [1989] 1 Lloyd's Rep 205 and *Walford* v. *Miles* [1992] 2 AC 128. In the former case the parties entered into a contract under which New Hope Collieries agreed to supply the Board with coal for a period of 15 years. It is very difficult to draft a supply contract which is to last for such a long period of time. Some idea of the difficulties involved can be obtained by imagining a contract draftsman in 1994 seeking to assess the impact of possible events up to the year 2009 on the obligations contained in the contract. How can a contract draftsman possibly see into the future with any degree of accuracy? These difficulties are particularly acute when it comes to finding an acceptable formula for the price of the product over the lifetime of the contract. The contract in *Queensland Electricity* made provision, for the first five year period of the contract, for a scale of base prices and the contract also contained elaborate 'escalation' or 'price variation' clauses for adjusting the base prices to reflect changes in New Hope's costs. Although provision was made for the general terms of the contract to continue beyond the initial five-year period, clause 2.5 of the agreement stated that '[t]he base price and provisions for variations in prices for changes in costs for purchases after 31 December 1982 shall be agreed by the parties thereto in accordance with clause 8' (which set out the broad criteria to be applied in setting the new pricing structure). The agreement also contained a comprehensive arbitration clause. One of the issues which arose before the Privy Council was whether or not the contract was enforceable after the first five years. It was argued that the contract was too uncertain because no price had been agreed for the supply of coal. The Privy Council rejected this argument in robust terms. Sir Robin Cooke stated:

'in cases where the parties have agreed on an arbitration or valuation clause in wide enough terms, the Courts accord full weight to their manifest intention to create continuing legal relations. Arguments invoking alleged uncertainty, or alleged inadequacy in the machinery available to the Courts for making contractual rights effective, exert minimal attraction . . . their Lordships have no doubt that here, by the agreement, the parties undertook implied primary obligations to make reasonable endeavours to agree on the terms of supply beyond the initial five-year period and, failing agreement and upon proper notice, to do everything reasonably necessary to procure the appointment of an arbitrator. Further, it is implicit in a commercial agreement of this kind that the terms of the new price structure are to be fair and reasonable as between the parties. . .'

This liberal approach should, however, be contrasted with the more restrictive approach adopted by the House of Lords in *Walford* v. *Miles* (above). The defendants were the owners of a company and they entered into negotiations with the plaintiffs for the sale of the company to the plaintiffs. On 17 March 1987 the parties entered into an agreement under which the plaintiffs promised to provide a comfort letter from their bank which confirmed that they had the financial resources to pay the price which was being asked for the company. In return the defendants agreed to deal exclusively with the plaintiffs and to terminate any negotiations then current between the defendants and any other prospective purchasers of the company. The plaintiffs complied with their side of the agreement but the defendants subsequently decided not to deal with the plaintiffs and they agreed to sell the company to a third party on 30 March 1987. The plaintiffs sought to recover damages in respect of the breach of the agreement of 17 March, while the defendants argued that the agreement was unenforceable on the ground that it was too uncertain.

The agreement of 17 March was both a 'lock-out' agreement (in that it sought to prevent the defendants from continuing negotiations with third parties) and a 'lock-in' agreement (in that it purported to oblige the defendants to negotiate exclusively with the plaintiffs). Both aspects were held by the House of Lords to be unenforceable. The lock-out agreement could not be enforced because it was not limited to a specified period of time and the argument that a term should be implied that it was to last a reasonable period of time was decisively rejected. That argument had found favour with Bingham LJ in the Court of Appeal who stated that a reasonable time 'would end once the parties acting in good faith had found themselves unable to come to mutually acceptable terms'. But the House of Lords dismissed the argument on the ground that it 'would indirectly impose upon [the defendants] a duty to bargain in good faith'. The lock-in aspect of the agreement was also held to be unenforceable on the ground that an agreement to negotiate is not an enforceable contract because it is too uncertain to have any binding force (in this respect following the decision of the Court of Appeal in *Courtney and Fairbairn Ltd* v. *Tolaini Brothers (Hotels) Ltd* [1975] 1 WLR 297). The plaintiffs sought to meet this argument by asserting that, in order to give 'business efficacy' to the agreement of 17 March, it was necessary to imply a term that the defendants were obliged to continue the negotiations in good faith, with the result that they were only entitled to terminate the negotiations if they had a 'proper reason', subjectively assessed, for doing so. Lord Ackner rejected this argument. He doubted whether a court could properly be expected to decide whether a contracting party subjectively had a good reason for terminating negotiations. He further stated that a 'concept of a duty to carry on negotiations in good faith is inherently repugnant to the adversarial position of the parties involved in negotiations' and that 'each party is entitled to pursue his (or her) own interest, so long as he avoids making misrepresentations'. Thus, he held, either party was entitled to withdraw from the negotiations at any time and for any reason and the plaintiffs' claim was therefore held to be without foundation.

It is suggested that the decision in *Walford* is a regrettable one for three reasons. The first is that the refusal to countenance the existence of an undertaking to negotiate in good faith sits rather uneasily with the willingness of the Privy Council in *Queensland Electricity* to imply an obligation to use reasonable endeavours to agree on the terms of supply of coal after five years. The difference between an obligation to use 'reasonable endeavours' to reach agreement and an obligation to negotiate in 'good faith' is not at all clear and it is particularly unfortunate that the decision in *Queensland Electricity* was not cited to the court in *Walford*. The second is that the decision makes it difficult to draft an enforceable 'lock-out' or 'lock-in' agreement, despite the commercial purposes which are served by such agreements in enabling contracting parties to buy time to put together a bid with no competition from a third party or to purchase a period of time in which to negotiate exclusively with another party in an effort to persuade him to conclude a contract. It is possible to draft an enforceable lock-out agreement provided that the duration of the agreement is confined to a limited period of time, such as 14 days (see *Pitt* v. *PHH Asset Management Ltd* [1993] 4 All ER 961). But it is extremely difficult, if not impossible, to draft an enforceable lock-in agreement because of the refusal of the House of Lords to recognise an obligation to negotiate in good faith for the period in which the parties are prohibited from conducting negotiations with third parties. Finally, the rejection of a role for an obligation to negotiate in good faith may render a number of clauses in long-term contracts unenforceable in English courts (see further 14.9).

So it can be seen from these cases that the approach adopted by the courts does seem to differ. The court in *Hillas* and *Queensland Electricity Generating Board* was more willing than the court in *May and Butcher* and *Walford* v. *Miles* to uphold the agreement entered into by the parties. It is the more liberal approach in *Hillas* and *Queensland* which has been followed with the greatest regularity in the cases (see, for example, *Foley* v. *Classique Coaches* [1934] 2 KB 1). Judges generally do not want to 'incur the reproach of being the destroyer of bargains' (per Lord Tomlin in *Hillas* v. *Arcos*) and therefore they tend to gravitate towards upholding and enforcing agreements. Nevertheless, it must be borne in mind that the distinction between 'construing' a contract and 'making' a contract is one of degree and that judges will continue to differ in their approach, with some preferring to adopt a more restrictive approach, as in *May and Butcher* v. *R* and *Walford* v. *Miles*.

4.2 Vagueness

The uncertainty may arise from one of a number of different sources. In the first place, the terms of the agreement may be too vague for the courts to enforce. Such was the case in *Scammell and Nephew Ltd* v. *Ouston* (above), where the parties entered into an agreement to buy goods on 'hire purchase'. It was held that this agreement was too vague to be enforced because there were many different types of hire purchase agreements in use, these agreements varied widely in their content and it was not clear what type of hire purchase agreement was envisaged.

However, as we have noted, the courts are reluctant to find that an agreement is so vague that it cannot be enforced. There are a number of devices available to a court which does not wish to find that an agreement is too vague to be enforced. The court may be able to ascertain the meaning of the phrase by reference to the custom of the trade in which the parties are contracting (*Shamrock SS Co* v. *Storey and Co* (1899) 81 LT 413), or it may be able to enforce the agreement by severing a clause which is meaningless (*Nicolene Ltd* v. *Simmonds* [1953] 1 QB 543) or, finally, the court may be able to interpret the vague phrase in the light of what is reasonable (*Hillas* v. *Arcos* (above)).

4.3 Incompleteness

Alternatively, the agreement may be incomplete because the parties have failed to reach agreement upon a particular issue. It is at this point that cases such as *May and Butcher* and *Hillas* become relevant. Once again, however, a number of devices are available to a court which wishes to avoid the conclusion that the agreement is incomplete and therefore cannot be enforced. The first is to invoke section 8(2) of the Sale of Goods Act 1979 which provides that where the price of goods in a contract of sale is not 'determined' by the contract (on which see section 8(1) of the Act) 'the buyer must pay a reasonable price' (see also section 15(1) of the Supply of Goods and Services Act 1982). This section only comes into play where the contract is silent as to the price; where, as in *May and Butcher*, provision is made for calculating the price but the provision is not implemented then the section is inapplicable. Secondly, where, as in *Hillas* v. *Arcos*, the parties have agreed criteria by which an incomplete matter can be resolved it is much easier for the court to uphold the agreement.

Thirdly, the contract itself may provide for machinery to resolve the dispute between the parties. It is possible for that machinery to be provided by one of the contracting parties. Thus in *May and Butcher* v. *R.* Viscount Dunedin stated that 'with regard to price it is a perfectly good contract to say that the price is to be settled by the buyer' and this rule has been applied to consumer credit contracts where the lender is given the power unilaterally and in its absolute discretion to vary the rate of interest subject to notice to the debtor (see *Lombard Tricity Finance Ltd* v. *Paton* [1989] 1 All ER 918). Difficulties do, however, emerge where the machinery has, for some reason, failed to come into effect. It was once thought that such a failure was fatal to the existence of an enforceable contract because the court would not substitute its own, different machinery for that agreed by the parties. This view was, however, rejected by the House of Lords in *Sudbrook Estates Ltd* v. *Eggleton* [1983] 1 AC 444. A lease gave to tenants (the lessees) an option to purchase the premises at a price to be agreed upon by two valuers, one to be nominated by the lessors and the other by the lessees and, in default of agreement, by an umpire to be appointed by the valuers. When the lessees sought to exercise the option the lessors refused to appoint a valuer and claimed that the option clause was void for uncertainty. It was held by the House of Lords that the crucial question in each case was whether the machinery agreed upon by the parties was an essential factor in determining the price to be paid or whether it was simply a means of ensuring that a fair price was paid. It was only where the machinery was essential and had not been implemented that the agreement would be held to be incomplete and not binding. An example of machinery which may be held to be essential is the appointment of a particular valuer because of his special skill or his special knowledge. On the facts, it was held, Lord Russell dissenting, that the reference to the valuers was an indication that the price was to be a reasonable and fair one and that the machinery for appointing the valuers was subsidiary to the main purpose of ascertaining a fair and reasonable price. Therefore, given that the machinery was not essential, the House of Lords was able to substitute its own machinery for ascertaining the price to be paid and an inquiry was ordered into what was the fair value of the premises.

4.4   A General Rule?

The general impression which is left by a study of the English case law on uncertainty is that the courts have adopted a rather piecemeal approach, which has resulted in a degree of inconsistency in the case law. The courts have not laid down a general rule which could provide a unifying basis for the law in this area. Such a general rule has been adopted in America in section 2–204 of the Uniform Commercial Code which states that 'even though one or more terms are left open a contract for sale does not fail for indefiniteness if the parties have intended to make a contract and there is a reasonably certain basis for giving an appropriate remedy'. It is a matter for consideration whether such a general rule would constitute an improvement upon the present state of English law. It would provide a basis for a coherent development of the law, but it would also bring its own problems of interpretation. For example, how would the courts decide whether the parties had an intention to contract and what meaning would be given to the phrase a 'reasonably certain basis for giving an appropriate remedy'? Although these problems of interpretation would remain, it is suggested that the adoption of such a rule would improve the present state of the law.

4.5   A Restitutionary Approach?

It should not be assumed, however, that the law of contract, and the law of contract alone, can resolve all the problems raised by agreements which appear to lack certainty. A role may be found for the law of restitution, as can be seen from the case of *British Steel Corp* v. *Cleveland Bridge and Engineering Co Ltd* [1984] 1 All ER 504. The parties entered into negotiations for the manufacture by the plaintiffs of steel nodes for the defendants. The defendants sent the plaintiffs a letter of intent which stated their intention to place an order for the steel nodes and proposed that the contract be on the defendants' standard terms. The plaintiffs refused to contract on these terms. Detailed negotiations then took place over the specifications of the steel nodes, but no agreement was reached on matters such as progress payments and liability for loss arising from late delivery and no formal contract was ever concluded. After the final node had been delivered the defendants refused to pay for them. The plaintiffs brought an action against the defendants, who counterclaimed for damages for late delivery or delivery of the nodes out of sequence. Robert Goff J discussed three possible analyses of the plaintiffs' claim.

The first was to hold that an executory contract had come into existence after the letter of intent had been sent. But he rejected this solution on the ground that, since the parties were still negotiating and had not reached agreement, it was impossible to say what were the material terms of the contract. The second solution was to hold that there was a unilateral contract or a standing offer made by the defendants which, if acted upon before it was lawfully withdrawn, would result in a contract. But, because of the disagreement between the parties, Robert Goff J held that it could not be assumed from the fact that the plaintiffs had commenced the work that a contract had thereby been created on the terms of the defendants' standing offer. The third solution, and the one which Robert Goff J adopted, was to allow the plaintiffs to recover in a restitutionary action for the reasonable value of the work which they had done. He held that, because the defendants had requested the plaintiffs to deliver the nodes, they had received a benefit at the expense of the plaintiffs and that it was unjust that they retain that benefit without recompensing the plaintiffs for the reasonable value of the nodes. The conclusion which was reached in the case was not altogether satisfactory because, no contract having been concluded, the defendants' counterclaim for damages for breach of contract was held to be without foundation. But, if the defendants had argued that the plaintiffs' *restitutionary* claim should have been reduced on the ground that the defects in the final product had reduced the value of the benefit which they had received as a result of the work done by the plaintiffs, their argument might have been successful (see *Crown House Engineering Ltd* v. *Amec Projects Ltd* (1990) 47 Build LR 32 and, more generally, Ball, 1983 and McKendrick, 1988). So, instead of liberalising the rules relating to certainty (or possibly in addition to such liberalisation), an alternative approach would be to hold that no contract was concluded and look to the emerging law of restitution for a solution.

4.6 Mistake Negativing Consent

This is an extremely difficult area of law. It is important to distinguish at the outset between two different types of mistake. The first is called common mistake and arises where both parties enter into the contract sharing the same mistake which nullifies their contract (see further 14.2–14.7). In this type of case the parties do initially reach agreement but that agreement may subsequently be set aside on the ground of the parties' shared mistake. The second type of mistake, and the type with which we shall be concerned here, may be called an 'offer and acceptance' mistake because it negatives consent and prevents a contract coming into existence on the ground that one party is labouring under a mistake or the parties are at cross-purposes. Professor Goodhart has written (1941) that 'there is no branch of the law of contract which is more uncertain and difficult than that which is concerned with the effect of mistake on the formation of a contract'.

Despite this uncertainty, it is at least clear that the mere fact that one party to the contract is mistaken in his 'innermost mind' is not sufficient, of itself, automatically to render a contract void. This is because, as we have seen, the courts have adopted an objective rather than a subjective test of agreement (see 2.1). The objective test of agreement considerably reduces the scope of the doctrine of mistake and this restriction is traditionally justified on the ground that it promotes certainty in commercial transactions. Despite these restrictions, mistake can operate to negative consent in the following cases.

The first case arises where the terms of the offer and acceptance suffer from such latent ambiguity that it is impossible reasonably to impute any agreement between the parties. The classic, if confusing, case in this category is *Raffles* v. *Wichelhaus* (1864) 2 H & C 906. The defendants agreed to buy from the plaintiffs a cargo of cotton to arrive 'ex Peerless from Bombay'. There were, unknown to the parties, two ships called 'Peerless' and both sailed from Bombay. The defendants meant the Peerless which sailed in October, whereas the plaintiffs meant the Peerless which sailed in December. When the cotton eventually arrived, the defendants refused to accept delivery because they argued that the plaintiffs were obliged to deliver the cotton on the Peerless which sailed in October, not the Peerless which sailed in December. The plaintiffs therefore sued for the price of the cotton. Judgment was given for the defendants but, as no reasoned judgment was given in the case, it is not clear whether judgment was given for the defendants because there was no contract or because there was a contract to deliver the cotton on the October Peerless, which the plaintiffs had breached. Despite the obscurity of the case *Raffles* has generally been understood by contract lawyers to stand for the proposition that latent ambiguity in the terms of an offer and acceptance can operate to negative consent in an appropriate case.

The second case is where one contracting party is under a mistake as to the terms of the contract, and that mistake is known to the other contracting party. Here the normal rule of objective interpretation is replaced by a subjective test (see *Hartog* v. *Colin and Shields* [1939] 3 All ER 566, discussed at 2.2). In *Smith* v. *Hughes* (1871) LR 6 QB 597 a buyer purchased from a seller a quantity of oats in the belief that they were old oats when, in fact, they were new oats and therefore unsuitable for the buyer's proposed use. When he discovered his mistake the buyer refused to accept the oats and the seller sued for the price. The jury found in favour of the buyer but the Court of Queen's Bench ordered a new trial because of a misdirection given to the jury by the trial judge. The Court of Queen's Bench held that a distinction must be drawn between two different types of case. The first is where the buyer correctly understands that the seller's offer is an offer to sell oats but the buyer mistakenly believes these oats to be old oats, and this mistake is known to the seller. In such a case the seller is not under an obligation to inform the buyer that he has made an mistake. The responsibility lies with the buyer to ensure that the oats are as he believed them to be; he cannot escape from what is a bad bargain for him by arguing that it is the responsibility of the seller to inform him of his error (see further Brownsword, 1987). In the second class of case the seller knows that the buyer is mistaken, but this time the buyer is mistaken as to the *terms* of the seller's *offer*. The buyer mistakenly believes that the seller's offer is an offer to sell old oats and the seller knows that the buyer has thus misunderstood his offer. In such a case there is an offer and acceptance mistake and the seller is under an obligation to inform the buyer of the true nature of his offer.

The third case is where there is a mistake as to the identity of the other contracting party. The identity of the person with whom one is contracting or proposing to contract is often immaterial. However, a mistake is sufficiently material to negative consent if one party is mistaken as to the *identity* of the other contracting party. Where the mistake is simply one as to the *attributes* of the other contracting party the mistake is not sufficiently fundamental to render the contract void. The distinction between identity and attributes can best be understood by contrasting the following two cases.

In *Cundy* v. *Lindsay* (1878) 3 App Cas 459, a dishonest person called Blenkarn, who gave his address as 37, Wood Street, Cheapside, ordered handkerchiefs from the plaintiffs. Blenkarn signed his name to make it look like Blenkiron & Co, a respectable firm who carried on business at 123 Wood Street and who were known by reputation to the plaintiffs. The plaintiffs duly sent the handkerchiefs to 'Blenkiron & Co, 37 Wood St' where Blenkarn received them. He did not pay for the goods, but rather sold them to the defendants. When they discovered their mistake, the plaintiffs sought to recover the goods from the defendants. The question whether the contract between the plaintiffs and Blenkarn was void for mistake was crucial to the defendants' rights. A contract which is void is set aside for all purposes. So, if the contract was void, Blenkarn could not have obtained title to the goods and was therefore incapable of giving title to the defendants. But a contract which is voidable remains a good contract until it is set aside by the innocent party. Therefore, if the contract was merely voidable on the ground of fraud then, provided Blenkarn sold the goods to the defendants before the contract between the plaintiffs and Blenkarn was set aside by the plaintiffs, the defendants would have obtained good title. However it was held that the contract was void because the plaintiffs did not intend to deal with Blenkarn but with Blenkiron and Co, a firm which they knew; thus they had made a mistake as to identity.

On the other hand a different result was reached in the case of *King's Norton Metal Co* v. *Edridge Merrett & Co Ltd* (1897) 14 TLR 98. The plaintiffs sent goods on credit to Hallam and Co, which purported to be a large firm in Sheffield, but was in fact an impecunious rogue called Wallis. Wallis failed to pay for the goods and sold them to the defendants. The plaintiffs, when they discovered their mistake, sought to recover the goods from the defendants. But it was held that the plaintiffs had not made a mistake as to the identity of Wallis. They intended to contract with the writer of the letters; they had simply made a mistake as to one of his attributes, namely his creditworthiness, and so the defendants got good title to the goods. The distinction between the two cases is that the mistake in *Cundy* was a mistake as to identity because the plaintiffs intended to deal with an identifiable third party (Blenkiron & Co, a company which they knew), whereas in *Kings Norton* the plaintiffs had not heard of Hallam and Co and simply intended to contract with the writer of the letters.

This distinction between a mistake as to identity and a mistake as to attributes has led to acute difficulties where the contracting parties meet face to face. The difficulties begin with the case of *Phillips* v. *Brooks* [1919] 2 KB 243. A man called North entered the plaintiff's shop and asked to see some pearls and rings. He selected a ring and produced a cheque book to pay for it, saying that he was Sir George Bullough (a wealthy man known to the plaintiff) and gave Sir George's address. The plaintiff checked the address in a directory and let North take the ring away for a cheque, which was later dishonoured. North pledged the ring to the defendant, from whom the plaintiff sought to recover it or its value. It was held that he could not do so because the contract between the plaintiff and North was not void; no mistake as to identity having been made. The plaintiff intended to contract, and did contract, with the person in his shop. The defendants therefore had good title to the ring.

However, a different approach was adopted in the case of *Lake* v. *Simmonds* [1927] AC 487. The plaintiff, a jeweller, was insured against loss of his stock by theft, with the exception of jewellery entrusted to a customer. A woman called Ellison, who pretended to be the wife of a wealthy customer, Mr Van der Borgh, took 2 pearl necklaces 'on approval' for her supposed husband and never returned them. The plaintiff sought to recover for his loss under the insurance policy. The House of Lords held that the plaintiff was entitled to recover as he had not entrusted the jewellery to Ellison because he did not in fact consent to her obtaining possession of the jewellery. There was a fundamental mistake both about the identity of the rogue, in that the plaintiff would never have entrusted the jewellery simply to the postman or to a messenger, and about the identity of the person to whom the jewellery was to be delivered, because Mr Van der Borgh was a well-known and wealthy customer (see *Citibank NA* v. *Brown Shipley & Co Ltd* [1991] 2 All ER 690, 700). Such a conclusion appears to be inconsistent with *Phillips* but Lord Haldane sought to reconcile the instant case with *Phillips* on the ground that in *Phillips* the sale was concluded before any mention was made of Sir George Bullough, so the mistake did not induce the contract. However it is not clear that this finding is consistent with the facts as found by the trial judge in *Phillips*.

The issue was reconsidered by the Court of Appeal in *Ingram* v. *Little* [1961] 1 QB 31. The plaintiffs, who were two sisters, were visited by a rogue who called himself Hutchinson and who wished to buy their car. He produced a cheque to pay for it, but one of the plaintiffs said that they would not accept a cheque. The rogue then said that he was a certain P. G. M. Hutchinson of Stanstead House, Caterham. Neither of the plaintiffs had heard of this person, but one of them went to the Post Office, checked in the telephone directory and confirmed that there was such a person. Believing the rogue to be P. G. M. Hutchinson they allowed him to take the car on handing over the cheque, which later proved to be worthless. The rogue then sold the car to the defendants. When the plaintiffs discovered their mistake they sought recovery of the car from the defendants. The Court of Appeal held that the contract between the plaintiffs and the rogue was void because of a mistake as to identity. They held that there was a prima facie presumption that a party contracts with the person in front of him, but held that the presumption was displaced on the facts of the case. The decisive factor appears to be that the plaintiffs refused to accept the rogue's offer to enter into a contract on terms that he paid by cheque until they had checked his identity in the telephone directory, which showed that his identity was crucial to the creation of a contract. It should be noted, however, that it was not the fact that they consulted a directory which was decisive because the shopkeeper in *Phillips* v. *Brooks* also consulted a directory. The vital factor appears to be the *purpose* behind consulting the directory. If, as in *Ingram*, it is relevant to the decision to enter into the contract, the identity is crucial but if, as in *Phillips*, it is relevant only to the method of payment then the mistake is as to attributes, namely creditworthiness.

The final case on this point is the decision of the Court of Appeal in *Lewis* v. *Avery* [1972] 1 QB 198. A rogue, calling himself the actor Richard Greene, offered to buy the plaintiff's car. He signed a cheque, but the plaintiff did not want him to take the car away until the cheque had been cleared. In order to persuade the plaintiff to allow him to take the car away immediately, the rogue produced an admission pass to Pinewood Studios, bearing the name Richard A Greene, his address, his photograph and an official stamp. The plaintiff then let the rogue take the car in return for a cheque, which proved to be worthless. The rogue then sold the car to the defendant, from whom the plaintiff sought recovery when he discovered his mistake. In giving judgment for the defendant the Court of Appeal held that there was nothing to displace the prima facie presumption that the plaintiff intended to deal with the party in front of him and they confined *Ingram* to its 'special facts'. The 'special facts' would appear to be that in *Ingram* no contract was concluded until the plaintiffs had ascertained the rogue's identity, thus the mistake was as to identity. On the other hand, in *Lewis* a contract had been concluded and the identity of the rogue was only crucial to the method of payment; thus the mistake was one as to his attributes, namely his creditworthiness.

It can be seen from this brief discussion of the leading cases that the distinction between a mistake as to identity and a mistake as to attributes is a very fine one. The fineness of the distinction was recognised by Devlin LJ in an important dissenting judgment in *Ingram*. He suggested that the more appropriate solution was to divide the loss between the parties in such proportion as is just in all the circumstances. Such a solution would avoid the apparent harshness of cases such as *Ingram* and *Lewis* where the plaintiff either gets everything or he gets nothing and there are few distinguishing facts between the cases. However it is unlikely that such a reform will be introduced in the foreseeable future either by the courts or by Parliament. This is because the common law has traditionally set its face against such loss splitting devices, preferring to use an all or nothing solution, and Parliament is unlikely to intervene because such a proposal was rejected as long ago as 1966 by the Law Reform Committee on the ground that a power of apportionment would give rise to too much uncertainty and would create excessive complexity in an effort to do justice between all the parties to the dispute.

There is a temptation to conclude that each case 'rests on its own facts' (per Waller J in *Citibank NA* v. *Brown Shipley & Co Ltd* [1991] 2 All ER 690, 700) and to leave it at that. But the law cannot be left in such an unprincipled state. It is suggested that the courts in future are, in fact, likely to follow *Lewis* in preference to *Ingram*. This is so for three reasons. The first is the effect of the presumption that a contracting party intends to contract with the person in front of him and that presumption will only be displaced upon 'special facts'. The second is that the courts have sought to protect third party rights and such a policy would be frustrated by holding that the contract was void on the ground of mistake. The third and final reason is the strength of the objective approach which, as we have seen in this chapter, is applied by the courts in determining whether or not a contract has been concluded.

Summary

1 An agreement must be expressed with sufficient certainty before it will be enforced by the courts.
2 The principal causes of uncertainty are vagueness and incompleteness.
3 There are, however, a number of devices available to a court which wishes to avoid the conclusion that an agreement is too uncertain to be enforced.
4 It should not be forgotten that a remedy may be found in the law of restitution where it is held that the agreement is too uncertain to constitute a contract.
5 A mistake may negative consent and prevent a contract coming into existence where one party is labouring under a mistake or the parties are at cross purposes.
6 Mistake does, however, operate within very narrow confines. Mistake has been held to negative consent where the terms of the offer and acceptance suffer from such latent ambiguity that it is impossible reasonably to impute any agreement between the parties, where one party was under a mistake as to the terms of the contract and that mistake was known to the other party and where there was a mistake as to the identity (not attributes) of the other contracting party.
7 Where the parties are dealing face to face there is a prima facie presumption that a party contracts with the person in front of him but, as in *Ingram* v. *Little*, that presumption can be displaced by 'special facts'.

Exercises

1 Compare and contrast the decisions of the House of Lords in *May and Butcher* v. *R* and *Hillas* v. *Arcos*.

2 List the devices which are available to a court which wishes to avoid the conclusion that an agreement is too uncertain to be enforced.

3 Would any advantage be obtained by introducing into English law a provision equivalent to section 2–204 of the American Uniform Commercial Code?

4 Distinguish between common mistake and unilateral mistake. Give some examples of the distinction.

5 What is the difference between a contract which has been held to be void and one which has been held to be voidable?

6 Compare and contrast the decisions of the Court of Appeal in *Ingram* v. *Little* and *Lewis* v. *Avery*.

5 Consideration and Form

It is clear that no legal system treats all agreements as enforceable contracts. In every legal system there exist rules which identify the types of agreement that are to be treated as enforceable contracts. The function of these rules is to give what we shall call the 'badge of enforceability' to certain agreements. In English law that function is performed principally by the doctrine of consideration and, to a lesser extent, by a doctrine of formalities. Of course, it could be argued that the rules relating to duress, misrepresentation and illegality play a role in identifying those agreements which are to be treated as enforceable contracts (see Atiyah, 1986c) and, to some extent, this is true. But English law has, historically, viewed the requirements of consideration and form as being separate and distinct from doctrines such as duress and this is the approach which we shall adopt in this chapter.

5.1 Requirements of Form

A legal system may grant the 'badge of enforceability' only to those agreements which are entered into in a certain form. Historically, English law has placed considerable reliance upon requirements of form. The Statute of Frauds 1677 required that certain classes of contracts be evidenced in writing, but most of its provisions were repealed in 1954. Requirements of form are therefore no longer a significant feature of English contract law, except in a residual category of contracts. For example, a lease for more than three years must be by deed (Law of Property Act 1925 ss. 52, 54(2)) and a unilateral gratuitous promise is only enforceable if it is made by deed. Compliance with this requirement is relatively straightforward; a document bearing the word 'deed' or some other indication that it is intended to take effect as a deed must be signed by the individual maker of the deed, that signature must be attested by one witness if the deed is signed by the maker (there must be two witnesses if the deed is signed at his direction) and it must be delivered, that is to say, there must be some conduct on the part of the person executing the deed to show that he intends to be bound by it (Law of Property (Miscellaneous Provisions) Act 1989, s.1(2), (3)). The requirement that the deed be under seal was abolished by section 1 of the Law Reform (Miscellaneous Provisions) Act 1989.

Bills of exchange (Bills of Exchange Act 1882 s.3(1)) and bills of sale (Bills of Sale Act 1878 (Amendment) Act 1882) must be in writing, while contracts for the sale or other disposition of an interest in land (Law of Property (Miscellaneous Provisions) Act 1989, s.2) must be made in writing. Contracts of guarantee (Statute of Frauds Act 1677 s.4) must be *evidenced* in writing. However it is vital to note that, apart from the case of gratuitous promises made by deed, such formal requirements do not replace consideration; they are an additional requirement.

Professor Atiyah has argued that 'insistence on form is a characteristic of primitive and less well-developed legal systems' (1989, p. 172). Yet many major legal systems in the world continue to place heavy reliance upon formal requirements. Many provinces in Canada (see Fridman, 1986) and states in Australia (see Greig and Davis, 1987) are still governed by the Statute of Frauds, either in its original or a modified form. Scotland, which does not have a doctrine of consideration, places great emphasis upon formal requirements. In Scotland many contracts can be constituted in any form and be proved by any form. But certain contracts (*obligationes literis*), of which the principal example is contracts relating to heritage (land and buildings), must be entered into or constituted in writing. Other contracts, such as a contract of loan of a sum of money in excess of £8.33, innominate and unusual contracts and gratuitous obligations, can be created informally but must be proved by the writ or oath of the party alleged to be bound (see McBryde, 1987).

What are the functions of such formal requirements? Professor Fuller (1941) has identified three functions. The first is the evidentiary function; in cases of dispute a formal requirement, such as writing, provides evidence of the existence and content of the contract. For this reason businessmen frequently reduce their contracts to writing, even though it is not mandatory to do so. Secondly, formalities have a cautionary function, 'by acting as a check against inconsiderate action'. A requirement that a contract be made by deed impresses upon the parties the importance of the agreement into which they are about to enter. This cautionary function has recently been recognised by Parliament in sections 60 and 61 of the Consumer Credit Act 1974, which provide that a regulated consumer credit agreement is not 'properly executed' unless it complies with certain formal requirements which are designed to ensure, as far as possible, that the consumer is fully informed of the nature and consequences of the agreement before entering into it. Such formal, statutory paternalistic requirements may become an increasingly common feature of English contract law. The third function of formalities is the channelling function, that is to say, formalities provide a simple and external test of enforceability.

On the other hand, requirements of form are attended by considerable disadvantages. In the first place formalities tend to be cumbersome and time-consuming. It would be ridiculous and impractical to insist that every contract be reduced to writing, so that every time I bought by morning newspaper I had to sign a written contract. This leads to a second difficulty which is that, given that it is impractical to apply formal requirements to all contracts, which contracts should be governed by requirements of form? For example, in England contracts of guarantee must be evidenced in writing, but no such requirement applies to contracts of indemnity. Yet the two contracts are very similar and the cases have 'raised many hair-splitting distinctions of exactly that kind which bring the law into hatred, ridicule and contempt by the public' (*Yeoman Credit Ltd* v. *Latter* [1961] 1 WLR 828, 835). Section 2 of the Law Reform (Miscellaneous Provisions) Act 1989 (above) threatens to be equally productive in litigation terms as the courts have already experienced some difficulty in deciding which terms have to be made in writing (see *Spiro* v. *Glencrown Properties Ltd* [1991] Ch 537, *Record* v. *Bell* [1991] 1 WLR 853; *Tootal Clothing Ltd* v. *Guinea Properties Ltd* (1992) 64 P & CR 452; and *Pitt* v. *PHH Asset Management Ltd* [1993] 4 All ER 961). The Scots have also encountered the same problem. Scotland has the anachronistic rule that contracts of loan of over £8.33 must be proved by the writ or oath of the party alleged to be bound. It is extremely difficult, if not impossible, to identify any rational theory which explains why certain contracts are subjected to requirements of form while others are not. It is equally difficult to explain why some contracts must actually be in writing, while others need only be evidenced in writing. Other difficult questions arise. What type of writing is required? Must the contract be signed? What constitutes a signature? These issues have all been the subject of extensive litigation under the Statute of Frauds 1677 (see Treitel, 1991 pp. 165–9) and are an inevitable concomitant of a system based upon requirements of form.

A final difficulty created by requirements of form arises where an 'innocent' party has acted to his detriment upon a 'contract' which did not comply with the relevant formalities. A good illustration of the difficulties which can arise is provided by cases concerning the (now repealed) s.40(1) of the Law of Property Act 1925. In *Wakeham* v. *Mackenzie* [1968] 1 WLR 1175 the deceased orally promised the plaintiff that he would leave his house to her if she moved into his house and looked after him until his death. She complied with his request but he failed to leave the house to her on his death. Could the plaintiff enforce the oral contract despite the fact that it did not comply with the formal requirements of s.40(1) of the Law of Property Act 1925 (which, it must be remembered, re-enacted part of s.4 of the Statute of Frauds 1677)? At common law the answer was 'no' because the defect in form rendered the contract unenforceable (but not void). But it was held that the contract was enforceable in equity under the doctrine of part performance. The doctrine of part performance was developed by equity in response to the hardships created by a strict application of the Statute of Frauds. The doctrine came into play where the acts of the plaintiff were referable to the alleged contract, it was a fraud for the defendant to rely on the Statute, the contract was specifically enforceable and there was proper evidence of the agreement. All these requirements were satisfied on the facts of *Wakeham*. It was not easy to reconcile the existence of the doctrine of part performance with the Statute of Frauds; in truth, it was incompatible with the Statute but it mitigated the hardships which would otherwise have been caused by its rigorous application. Although s.40(1) of the 1925 Act has now been repealed by s.2(8) of the Law of Property (Miscellaneous Provisions) Act 1989, similar problems are likely to arise under the 1989 Act. As we have noted, s.2(1) requires that a contract for the sale or other disposition of an interest in land be 'made in writing'. It follows from this that, where there is no writing, there is no contract and so nothing for part performance to bite on to. So what will be the position of the party who relies to his detriment on there being an enforceable contract for the sale of land when there is, in fact, no contract because it was not 'made in writing'? The answer is that he will be in a rather precarious position. However s.2(5) expressly states that 'nothing in this section affects the creation or operation of resulting, implied or constructive trusts' and so it may be that the constructive trust and proprietary estoppel will be called upon to play a role similar to that played by the doctrine of part performance in relation to s.40(1) of the 1925 Act.

There is no doubt that there are genuine difficulties experienced by legal systems which place heavy reliance upon requirements of form. But, as we have seen, formalities do perform useful evidentiary and cautionary functions. Although it is highly unlikely that Parliament will ever re-enact the Statute of Frauds, Parliament can usefully continue its practice of imposing requirements of form where it is satisfied that such requirements will 'provide a check against inconsiderate action' (as in the case of ss.60 and 61 of the Consumer Credit Act 1974 (above)). When it does so it can also devise a solution which will protect those who are in need of protection, while ensuring that the formalities do not become a trap for the unwary (see s.127 of the Consumer Credit Act 1974 which, as against the debtor, places severe restrictions upon the enforceability of regulated consumer credit agreements which are not 'properly executed' but otherwise gives the court considerable discretion to reach an appropriate solution).

5.2 Consideration Defined

Having largely rejected formal requirements, English law has developed a doctrine of consideration to play the principal role in selecting those agreements to be given the 'badge of enforceability'. However the basis of the doctrine of consideration has been a battleground for leading contract scholars in recent years. The orthodox interpretation of consideration is that it is based upon the idea of 'reciprocity'; that a promisee should not be able to enforce a promise unless he has given or promised to give something in exchange for the promise or unless the promisor has obtained (or been promised) something in return. The classic definition was expressed in *Currie* v. *Misa* (1875) LR 10 Ex 153 in the following terms:

'a valuable consideration, in the sense of the law, may consist either in some right, interest, profit or benefit accruing to the one party, or some forbearance, detriment, loss or responsibility given, suffered or undertaken by the other'.

However, this orthodox interpretation has been subjected to a powerful challenge by Professor Atiyah (1986c). Atiyah argues that there is no coherent doctrine of consideration based upon reciprocity. He states that

'the truth is that the courts have never set out to create a doctrine of consideration. They have been concerned with the much more practical problem of deciding in the course of litigation whether a particular promise in a particular case should be enforced. . . When the courts found a sufficient reason for enforcing a promise they enforced it; and when they found that for one reason or another it was undesirable to enforce a promise, they did not enforce it. It seems highly probable that when the courts first used the word "consideration" they meant no more than there was a "reason" for the enforcement of a promise. If the consideration was "good", this meant that the court found sufficient reason for enforcing the promise.'

Professor Treitel has, in turn, launched a vigorous counter-attack on Atiyah's thesis. Treitel argues (1991) that English law does, in fact, recognise the existence of a 'complex and multifarious body of rules known as the "doctrine of consideration"'. He rejects the argument that consideration means a reason for the enforcement of a promise and maintains (1976) that such a proposition is a 'negation of the existence of any applicable rules of law' because it does not tell us the circumstances in which the courts will find the existence of such a 'good reason'.

Yet even Treitel has to admit (1976) that in some cases the courts have 'invented' consideration, that is to say the courts 'have treated some act or forbearance as consideration quite irrespective of the question whether *the parties* have so regarded it'. This concession is necessary if the cases are to be reconciled with the traditional theory. Atiyah argues (1986c) that 'Professor Treitel has himself invented the concept of an invented consideration because he finds it the only way in which he is able to reconcile many decisions with what he takes to be the "true" or "real" doctrine'. Although Atiyah challenges the orthodox interpretation of consideration, he does recognise that the presence of 'benefit or detriment is normally a good reason for enforcing a promise'. But, he argues, '[it] does not in the least follow that the presence of benefit or detriment is always a sufficient reason for enforcing a promise; nor does it follow that there may not be other very good reasons for enforcing a promise'.

The difference between the two schools of thought is that Treitel adheres to the benefit/detriment analysis (suitably expanded to encompass cases of 'invented consideration') while Atiyah maintains that there are other 'good reasons' for the enforcement of a promise. In the remaining sections of this chapter we shall consider whether the cases can be accommodated within a 'benefit/detriment' analysis or whether there are, as Atiyah argues, other reasons which support the enforcement of promises.

5.3 The Many Functions of Consideration

As the law of contract has developed, so it would appear that the functions of the doctrine of consideration have gradually changed. Professor Simpson has argued (1975) that at an early stage in its development consideration played a multi-functional role within the law of contract. He states that 'the old action for breach of promise catered for what we would call bilateral contracts - that is transactions involving both sides doing things - in terms of the doctrine of consideration and the concept of a condition'. He then recounts how during the nineteenth century the doctrines of offer and acceptance and intention to create legal relations were 'superimposed upon the sixteenth century requirement of consideration and made to perform some of the same functions' and concludes (at p. 263) that 'all this seems to me to have produced rather too many doctrines chasing a limited number of problems. To put my point differently there is something to be said for throwing out old doctrine when importing new'. The refusal of English law to 'throw out' the doctrine of consideration has given rise to considerable problems in the twentieth century as the courts have sought, largely without success, to ascertain the relationship between consideration and other emerging doctrines of the law of contract. This has proved to be a particularly pressing problem in relation to the rise of the doctrine of duress and the willingness of the courts and some academics to re-analyse some of the old consideration cases in terms of duress rather than consideration (see 5.13 and 17.2). This has led some of the judiciary to advocate a more 'flexible' approach to the doctrine of consideration. A good example of this process can be found in the judgment of Russell LJ in *Williams* v. *Roffey Bros & Nicholls (Contractors) Ltd* [1991] 1 QB 1, 18 when he stated that:

'in the late twentieth century I do not believe that the rigid approach to the concept of consideration to be found in [the early nineteenth century case of] *Stilk* v. *Myrick* is either necessary or desirable. Consideration there must still be but, in my judgment, the courts nowadays should be more ready to find its existence so as to reflect the intention of the parties to the contract where the bargaining powers are not unequal and where the finding of consideration reflect the true intention of the parties.'

But this 'watering-down' of consideration makes it very difficult to ascertain the purpose behind the modern doctrine of consideration, or to locate its function within the law of contract. The approach of Russell LJ appears to be that its function should be to 'reflect the intention of the parties to the contract', which suggests that it should, perhaps, become an aspect of the doctrine of intention to create legal relations. This is a controversial suggestion and not one which reflects the traditional understanding of the relationship between consideration and intention to create legal relations (see 5.29) but it does reflect the uncertainty which currently surrounds the role and functions of consideration within modern contract law.

5.4   Consideration and Motive

Before we enter into a discussion of the substance of the doctrine of consideration, one further preliminary point must be made. That point relates to the distinction between consideration and motive. In *Thomas* v. *Thomas* (1842) 2 QB 851 a testator, shortly before he died, expressed the desire that his widow should have the house for the rest of her life. After his death, his executors promised to carry out the testator's desire provided that the widow paid £1 per annum towards the ground rent and kept the house in repair. Now, although the testator's desire was the motive for the transaction, that desire was not the consideration; rather, the consideration was the widow's promise to pay £1 and to keep the house in good repair. It was only the latter which was of value in the eyes of the law.

5.5   The Scope of the Doctrine

The rules which make up the doctrine of consideration may be divided into three categories. The first is that consideration must be sufficient but it need not be adequate (5.6–5.16), the second is that past consideration is not good consideration (5.18) and the third is that consideration must move from the promisee (5.19). Once we have ascertained the scope of the doctrine of consideration, we shall consider the extent to which the law of contract protects those who rely to their detriment upon promises which are not supported by consideration (5.20–5.30).

5.6   Consideration Must Be Sufficient But It Need Not Be Adequate

The first rule of the doctrine of consideration is that consideration must be sufficient but it need not be adequate. That is to say, the courts will not enforce a promise unless something of value is given in return for the promise. This is what is meant by saying that consideration must be 'sufficient'. On the other hand, the courts do not, in general, ask whether adequate value has been given in return for the promise or whether the agreement is harsh or one-sided (although here a significant role is played by the doctrines of duress and undue influence, on which see generally Chapter 17). This is what is meant by saying that consideration need not be 'adequate'. So if a house worth £160 000 is sold for £1 that is sufficient consideration, even though it is manifestly inadequate. In the following sections (5.7–5.17) we shall discuss in greater detail the scope of the rule that consideration must be sufficient but that it need not be adequate.

5.7 Trivial Acts

The maxim that consideration must be sufficient but need not be adequate has resulted in very trivial acts being held to constitute consideration. The classic illustration is *Chappell & Co* v. *Nestle* [1960] AC 87. Nestle offered for sale gramophone records in return for 1/6d and 3 wrappers from their chocolate bars. The House of Lords held that the wrappers themselves, although of very trivial economic value, were nevertheless part of the consideration. This was so even though Nestle threw away the wrappers. As Lord Somervell said:

'a contracting party can stipulate for what consideration he chooses. A peppercorn does not cease to be good consideration if it is established that the promisee does not like pepper and will throw away the corn.'

Atiyah has argued (1986c) that this case does not fit within the 'benefit/detriment' analysis because it would be 'ridiculous to assert that the sending or the receipt of the wrappers necessarily involved an actual detriment to the sender or a benefit to the defendants'. He argues that the receipt of the wrappers was not a benefit but was the motive which inspired the promise and that therefore this was a case in which a court would have enforced a promise despite the lack of benefit to the promisee. Treitel has replied (1976) by asserting that Atiyah has failed to take account of the principle that the courts will not investigate the adequacy of the consideration and that, once it is realised that consideration need only be of *some* value, 'there is no doctrinal difficulty in holding that a piece of paper or some act or forbearance of very small value can constitute consideration'.

The crucial question which must now be asked is: what does the law of contract recognise as 'value'? Professor Treitel has stated (1991) that consideration must have 'some economic value', even though that value cannot be 'precisely quantified'. But, as we shall see, the courts have not adopted a consistent approach to the identification of 'value' or 'benefit'. In some cases (such as *Foakes* v. *Beer*, below 5.15), they have ignored a factual benefit obtained by the promisor and held that no consideration was provided because, as a matter of *law*, the promisor was not benefited.

In other cases (such as *Cook* v. *Wright,* below 5.9), the courts have found the existence of consideration despite the apparent lack of either benefit to the promisor or detriment to the promisee. Some cases have adopted an extremely subjective interpretation of benefit (see, for example, *Bainbridge* v. *Firmstone* (1838) 8 A & E 743), but in other cases the courts have adopted an objective interpretation (see, for example, *White* v. *Bluett,* below 5.8). The emphasis in the important recent decision of the Court of Appeal in *Williams* v. *Roffey Bros & Nicholls (Contractors) Ltd* [1991] 1 QB 1 (see further, 5.11–5.14) was on the need to identify a 'practical benefit' to the promisor rather than 'a benefit in the eyes of the law' but this approach has not been carried through into all aspects of the doctrine of consideration (see *Re Selectmove* (1994) *The Times* January 13, discussed further at 5.15). One of the most difficult tasks in analysing the doctrine of consideration is to stabilise the concept of value or benefit (see further 5.17).

5.8   Intangible Returns

It is clear that 'natural affection of itself is not a sufficient consideration' (*Bret* v. *JS* (1600) Cro Eliz 756). In *White* v. *Bluett* (1853) 23 LJ Ex 36, a son's promise not to bore his father with complaints about the father's distribution of his property among his children was held not to be good consideration for the father's promise not to sue the son on a debt owed by the son to the father. Pollock CB said that the son had not provided any consideration as he had 'no right to complain' to his father (because it was for the father to decide how he wanted to distribute his property) and so, in giving up his habit of complaining, he had not provided any consideration. But the decision is open to attack on two possible grounds.

The first is that it ignored the 'practical benefit' which the father obtained in being freed from the complaints of his son. The emphasis on practical benefit in recent cases such as *Williams* v. *Roffey Bros* (above) suggests that this aspect of *White* may be open to criticism. That this is so can be demonstrated by reference to the recent case of *Pitt* v. *PHH Asset Management Ltd* [1993] 4 All ER 961. The defendants, acting as undisclosed agents of mortgagees, put a cottage on the market for £205 000. Both the plaintiff and a Miss Buckle were interested in purchasing the property and made competing bids. The plaintiff made a bid of £200 000 which the defendants accepted 'subject to contract'. The next day Miss Buckle increased her offer to £210 000 and the acceptance of the plaintiff's offer was withdrawn. Discussions then took place between the plaintiff and the defendants' agent. The plaintiff threatened to seek an injunction to halt the sale to Miss Buckle and also said that he would inform her of his loss of interest in the property so that she would be free to lower her offer in the absence of a rival bidder. The outcome of these negotiations was that it was agreed that the property should be sold to the plaintiff for £200 000 and that the vendors would not consider any further offers for the property provided that the plaintiff agreed to exchange contracts within two weeks of receipt of the contract. But in breach of the agreement the cottage was sold to Miss Buckle for £210 000. The plaintiff sued the defendants for damages for breach of contract. One of the defences which was invoked by the defendants was that the plaintiff did not provide any consideration for the promise not to consider other offers because he had only promised to be ready, willing and able to proceed to exchange of contracts, which he was already obliged to do. But the Court of Appeal held that the plaintiff had supplied consideration for the promise. In the first place, the plaintiff agreed not to apply for an injunction to restrain the sale to Miss Buckle. Peter Gibson LJ said that he could not see how the plaintiff could have succeeded with this claim but he held that the defendants were nevertheless freed from the 'nuisance value' of having to defend such a claim. Secondly, consideration was provided by the plaintiff agreeing not to carry out his threat to make trouble with Miss Buckle; once again, the removal of that 'nuisance' provided 'some consideration'. Finally, the promise of the plaintiff to proceed to exchange within two weeks was also held to amount to consideration. The court therefore held that 'these three items constituted valuable consideration sufficient to support the. . .agreement' and upheld the plaintiff's claim. The difficulty with the case is not so much in the result (as the third item seems clearly to constitute consideration) but the emphasis which the court placed upon the benefit which the defendants obtained by being free of 'nuisance claims'. This does not sit very easily with the refusal of the court to find consideration on the facts of *White* (although it must be said that, where the 'nuisance' consists of a threat of litigation (as in the case of the injunction), the courts have been particularly willing to find the existence of consideration, see further 5.9).

The second ground on which *White* is open to attack is that the son did act to his detriment in refraining from making complaints. He was doing nothing wrong in complaining to his father, so in that sense he did have a 'right' to complain, and in giving up that right he provided consideration. This aspect of *White* should be contrasted with the American case of *Hamer* v. *Sidway* (1891) 27 NE 256. An uncle promised to pay his nephew $5000 if the nephew refrained from 'drinking liquor, using tobacco, swearing and playing cards or billiards for money' until he (the nephew) was 21. This promise was held to be enforceable because the nephew had a legal right to engage in such activities, and in giving up his rights he had provided consideration for the promise. Professor Atiyah has argued (1986c) that *Hamer* is a case which does not fit within the 'benefit/detriment' analysis because there was no benefit to the uncle (apart from the fact that he wanted his nephew to abstain from such practices, but that is a matter of motive, not benefit), nor was there a detriment to the nephew (on the ground that giving up smoking is a benefit rather than a detriment). Rather, Atiyah argues, this is a case in which the nephew was induced to act on the promise and the court thought it just to enforce the promise. But the court did not perceive matters in this way. It was of the opinion that the nephew had incurred a detriment because he had 'restricted his lawful freedom of action within certain prescribed limits upon the faith of the uncle's agreement' (see, too, Treitel, 1976).

Hamer is not at all easy to reconcile with *White*. It might be said that it is not necessary to reconcile them because *Hamer* is an American case and so not binding on an English court. While this is true, it is often assumed that *Hamer* does represent English law (see, for example, Beale, Bishop and Furmston, 1990, p. 90). It may be that the cases can be reconciled on the ground that the promise of the son in *White* was too uncertain to constitute consideration for the father's promise (Anson, 1984, p. 90) or on the ground that the activities of the son in *White* were thought to be less socially valuable (bordering on duress?) and therefore less deserving of protection than the conduct of the nephew in *Hamer*. Even if *Hamer* does represent English law, it must be noted that there is a limit to the principle which it establishes, namely that, if the nephew had never intended to drink, smoke, swear or gamble because, for example, he had a religious objection to engaging in such practices, then he could not have enforced his uncle's promise. This is because 'it is not consideration to refrain from a course of conduct which it was never intended to pursue' (*Arrale* v. *Costain Civil Engineering Ltd* [1976] 1 Lloyd's Rep 98, 106).

5.9   Compromise and Forbearance to Sue

A promise not to enforce a valid claim is good consideration for a promise given in return, as is a promise not to enforce a claim which is doubtful in law. On the other hand, it is clear that a promise not to enforce a claim which is known to be invalid is not good consideration for a promise given in return (*Wade* v. *Simeon* (1846) 2 CB 548). The difficulty lies in the case where the claim is clearly bad in law but is believed by the promisee to be good. In *Cook* v. *Wright* (1861) 1 B & S 559 the plaintiffs honestly believed that the defendant was under a statutory obligation to reimburse them in respect of certain expenditure which they had incurred in work on a street adjoining the house in which the defendant was residing. The defendant denied that he was under such an obligation, but he eventually promised to pay a reduced sum after he was threatened with litigation if he did not pay. When the defendant discovered that he was not in fact under a statutory obligation to pay, he refused to honour his promise. He maintained that his promise was not supported by consideration because the plaintiffs had given nothing in return for it. But the court held that the promise was supported by consideration and that he was liable to pay the sum promised. Nevertheless, it is difficult to find the consideration supplied by the plaintiffs. They had given up an invalid claim and in so doing they had suffered no detriment and the defendant was not benefited in any way by their promise to accept the reduced sum in full satisfaction of their invalid claim. It could be argued that the plaintiffs' honest belief in the validity of their claim provided the consideration. But consideration must actually be of value in the eyes of the law and not merely something believed to be of value by the parties. Alternatively, it could be argued that the defendant benefited because he escaped the vexation which is inherent in litigation. Such a rationale proves too much because it would apply equally where the claim was known to be bad and yet we know from *Wade* v. *Simeon* (above) that a promise not to enforce a claim which is known to be bad is not good consideration for a promise given in return (unless it is possible to confine *Wade* v. *Simeon* on public policy grounds, namely that proceedings should not be instituted where the claim is known to be a bad one). *Cook* is therefore a case which is very difficult to accommodate within the 'benefit/detriment' analysis (although it should be noted that Treitel (1976) includes the case within his category of 'invented' consideration).

5.10 Performance of a Duty Imposed by Law

The question whether performance of a duty (or a promise to perform a duty) which one is already under an obligation to perform can constitute consideration for a promise given in return is currently a very controversial one in English contract law. The orthodox position is clear: performance of an existing duty imposed by law and performance of a contractual duty owed to the promisor do not constitute consideration, while performance of a duty imposed by a contract with a third party does constitute consideration. But today the position is not so clear. The source of the problem is the decision of the Court of Appeal in *Williams* v. *Roffey Bros & Nicholls (Contractors) Ltd* [1991] 1 QB 1, in which it was held that performance of an existing contractual duty owed to the promisor could constitute good consideration. Having reached this conclusion, the question which now arises is whether this approach can also be applied to performance of a duty imposed by law.

Prior to *Williams* v. *Roffey Bros*, the law was relatively clear: performance of (or a promise to perform) a duty imposed by law was not good consideration for a promise given in return (*Collins* v. *Godefroy* (1831) 1 B & Ad 950). The rule was generally supported on the ground that it prevented public officials extorting money in return for the performance of their existing legal duties. But in other cases the rule could give rise to hardship because it ignored real benefits obtained by the promisor or real detriments incurred by the promisee. So it is no surprise to learn that the rule has come under some scrutiny.

The leading case is *Ward* v. *Byham* [1956] 1 WLR 496. The father of an illegitimate child promised to pay the mother of the child £1 per week provided that the child was well looked after and happy. The mother was under a legal duty to look after the child. The mother sued the father when he stopped making the payments. The father argued that the mother had not provided any consideration for his promise because, by looking after the child, she was simply carrying out her existing legal duty. Denning LJ rejected this argument and launched a direct assault on the general rule. He held that the mother provided consideration by performing her legal duty to support the child. He stated that the father was benefited by the mother's promise to look after the child, just as he would have been benefited if a neighbour had promised to look after the child for reward. Lord Denning returned to this theme in *Williams* v. *Williams* [1957] 1 WLR 148 when he said:

> 'a promise to perform an existing duty is, I think, sufficient consideration to support a promise, so long as there is nothing in the transaction which is contrary to the public interest'.

Although this statement of principle has much to commend it, the majority of the Court of Appeal in *Ward* did not agree with it. Rather, they affirmed that performance of an existing legal duty does not constitute consideration, but they found consideration in the fact that the mother had promised to do more than her legal duty by promising to keep the child 'happy'. There is no doubt that a promise to do more than one is legally obliged to do is good consideration (*Glasbrook Ltd* v. *Glamorgan CC* [1925] AC 270). But there must be some doubt about the application of this rule to the facts of *Ward* because it could only be said that the mother did more than she was legally obliged to do by promising to keep the child 'happy'. Yet, we have already noted that natural affection of itself is not a sufficient consideration (*Bret* v. *JS*, discussed at 5.8). Whatever doubts we may harbour about the validity of this approach, it should be noted that its focus is upon detriment to the mother in that it is argued that she did *more* than she was legally obliged to do. An alternative analysis of the case is to look at in terms of benefit to the father. Thus in *Williams* v. *Roffey Bros* (above) Glidewell LJ (at p. 13) interpreted *Ward* as a case in which the father obtained a '*practical benefit*' as a result of the mother's promise that the child would be well looked after and happy (although contrast the view of Purchas LJ at p. 20). Whatever might be said about this emphasis on practical benefit as a matter of principle (see 5.12) it is clear that it is not the approach which the majority actually adopted on the facts of *Ward*. So, as a matter of authority, the rule that performance of a duty imposed by law does not constitute consideration remains intact, at least for now. But it may not be able to withstand the onslaught on the existing duty rule commenced by the Court of Appeal in *Williams* v. *Roffey Bros* (see 5.11).

5.11   Performance of a Contractual Duty Owed to the Promisor

Until recently the rule which English law adopted was that performance of an existing contractual duty owed to a promisor was no consideration for a fresh promise given by that promisor. The rule was not a popular one:

indeed, it was once stated that it has done the 'most to give consideration a bad name' (Patterson, 1958). The origin of the rule can be traced back to the old case of *Stilk* v. *Myrick* (1809) 2 Camp 317 and 6 Esp 129. Stilk was a seaman who agreed with the defendants to sail to the Baltic and back at a rate of pay of £5 per month. Originally, there were eleven men in the crew, but two men deserted during the voyage. The master was unable to find replacements for the deserters and so he agreed with the remainder of the crew that he would share the wages of the two deserters between them if they would work the ship back to London. The crew members agreed. When they returned to London, Stilk demanded his share of the money but the master refused to pay. Stilk sued for the money. He was unsuccessful in his claim. The case was reported twice and, unfortunately, the two reports differ as to the reason for the failure of Stilk's claim.

In the Espinasse report Stilk was unsuccessful on grounds of policy; the policy ground being that a successful claim would open up the prospect of sailors on the high seas making unreasonable and extortionate demands upon their masters as the price for performing their contractual duty to bring the ship back to the home port. In Campbell's report Stilk's claim failed, not on grounds of policy, but because he had provided no consideration for the master's promise as he had only done what he was already contractually obliged to do.

The difference between these two reports is crucial. If the former report is correct, it is possible to confine the rule to cases where there is a possibility of duress being exercised. Where such fear is absent, there is no objection to the enforcement of the promise. However, Espinasse is not highly regarded as a law reporter and it was the second, wider rule derived from Campbell's report which was accepted into English law (see *North Ocean Shipping Co* v. *Hyundai Construction Co* [1979] QB 705).

But the existing duty rule laid down in Campbell's report of *Stilk* has always been controversial. Thus Professor Atiyah has argued that cases such as *Stilk* and *Ward* v. *Byham* (above, 5.10) cannot be accommodated within the 'benefit/detriment' analysis because, as a matter of fact, there was a benefit to the promisor and a detriment to the promisee but nevertheless there was held to be no consideration. In *Stilk* there is little doubt that, as a matter of fact, the master of the ship was benefited by Stilk's promise to work the ship back home, yet the court concluded that no consideration had been provided. The defenders of the orthodox interpretation of consideration attempt to meet this argument by asserting that it is *legal* benefit or *legal* detriment which is important and not factual benefit or factual detriment. But, as Corbin has pointed out (1963), this does not explain *why* the courts have resorted to the concepts of legal benefit and detriment.

Given these criticisms of *Stilk* it is perhaps surprising that it stood unchallenged for as long as it did. There are two possible reasons for this. The first is that the one case which appeared to be flatly inconsistent with *Stilk* remained buried in the Law Reports, rarely being cited in the books or in the courts. That case is *Raggow* v. *Scougall & Co* (1915) 31 TLR 564.

The plaintiff was employed by the defendants for a period of two years at a certain salary. During the period of the contract war broke out and the defendants' business was detrimentally affected. Rather than close the business the parties entered into a new agreement under which the plaintiff agreed to accept a lower salary until the end of the war, when the original agreement would be revived. The plaintiff accepted the reduced salary for a period of time but then brought an action claiming his salary at the old rate, arguing that the defendants had provided no consideration for his promise to accept a lower salary. Darling J held that the agreement was supported by consideration and that the action therefore failed. He held that the parties had in fact torn up the old agreement and made a new one by mutual consent and stated that he was glad to be able to arrive at this conclusion because the plaintiff was seeking to do a 'very dishonest thing'. The case has been rarely cited since and it has never been used as the basis for an attack on the decision in *Stilk* itself.

The second factor which contributed to the fact that *Stilk* survived serious judicial assault is the two exceptions which exist to the original rule. The first arises where the promisee has done, or has promised to do, more than he was obliged to do under his contract. In *Hanson* v. *Royden* (1867) LR 3 CP 47, the plaintiff was promoted from able seaman to second mate and it was held that, in carrying out the job of second mate, he had done more than he was obliged to do under his contract and so had provided consideration for the promise of extra pay. The second situation arises where, before the new promise was made, circumstances had arisen which entitled the promisee to refuse to carry out his obligations under his contract. In *Hartley* v. *Ponsonby* (1857) 7 E & B 872, seventeen of a crew of thirty-six deserted and only four or five of the remaining crew were able seamen. The desertion of such a large proportion of the crew rendered it unsafe to continue the voyage and would have entitled the remaining seamen to abandon the voyage. The seamen agreed to continue the voyage on being promised extra pay on its completion. The master refused to fulfil his promise on their return to the home port but it was held that the seamen were entitled to enforce the master's promise because, in agreeing to continue with the voyage when they were not obliged by the terms of their contract to do so, they had provided consideration.

However, a more wide-ranging attack on *Stilk* was launched by the Court of Appeal in what is now the seminal case of *Williams* v. *Roffey Bros & Nicholls (Contractors) Ltd* [1991] 1 QB 1. The defendant contractors entered into a contract to refurbish a block of flats. They subcontracted the carpentry work to the plaintiff for a price of £20 000. The plaintiff ran into financial difficulties after having completed part of the work. The cause of his difficulties was partly attributable to the fact that he had underpriced the job and partly because of his own inability to supervise his workforce. It was in the interest of the defendants to ensure that the plaintiff completed the work on time because if, as a result of delay or non-performance by the plaintiff, the defendants were late in completing the work they would incur liability to their employers under the terms of a 'penalty' clause contained in the main contract. So the defendants called a meeting with the plaintiff in order to discuss the situation. At that meeting it was agreed that the defendants would pay to the plaintiffs an extra £10 300 at the rate of £575 per flat on completion to ensure that the work was completed on time. The plaintiff subsequently finished eight more flats but the defendants paid him only a further £1500. The plaintiff then ceased work on the flats and brought a claim against the defendants for the £10,300 promised. One of the grounds on which the defendants denied the existence of a liability to pay was that the plaintiff had provided no consideration for the promise of extra payment: he had simply promised to perform his existing contractual duties and that, according to *Stilk* v. *Myrick*, did not constitute good consideration. The Court of Appeal rejected the defendants' argument and held that the plaintiff had provided consideration and that he was entitled to bring an action for damages (although it should be noted that the plaintiff was not awarded full expectation damages).

The Court of Appeal adopted a very pragmatic approach to the issue. They held that the defendants had obtained a *practical benefit* as a result of the plaintiff's promise to complete the work on time and that practical benefit was, for this purpose at least, sufficient to constitute consideration. The proposition for which *Williams* stands as authority was summed up by Glidewell LJ in the following words:

'(i) if A has entered into a contract with B to do work for, or to supply goods or services to, B in return for payment by B and (ii) at some stage before A has completely performed his obligations under the contract B has reason to doubt whether A will, or will be able to, complete his side of the bargain and (iii) B thereupon promises A an additional payment in return for A's promise to perform his contractual obligations on time and (iv) as a result of giving his promise B obtains in practice a benefit, or obviates a disbenefit, and (v) B's promise is not given as a result of economic duress or fraud on the part of A, then (vi) the benefit to B is capable of being consideration for B's promise, so that the promise will be legally binding'.

Two immediate problems arise. The first is: what exactly was the practical benefit which the defendants obtained? The second is: how can this conclusion be reconciled with *Stilk* v. *Myrick*? These issues must be examined with some care.

5.12 Practical Benefit

There was no one practical benefit which the defendants were held to have obtained as a result of the plaintiff's promise. The court relied upon a number of factors in identifying the practical benefit obtained. The first was that the plaintiff continued with the work and did not breach his sub-contract. The second was that the defendants were spared the 'trouble and expense of engaging other people to complete the carpentry work'. The third was that they avoided incurring a penalty under the main contract for delay in completion of the work. The fourth factor was that a 'rather haphazard method of payment' was replaced by a 'more formalised scheme involving the payment of a specified sum on the completion of each flat'. Finally, by directing the plaintiff to complete one flat at a time, the defendants 'were able to direct their other trades to do the work in the completed flats which otherwise would have been held up until the plaintiff had completed his work'.

The first three factors are controversial. The first adopts a Holmesian conception of contract law so that 'the duty to keep a contract at common law means a prediction that you must pay damages if you do not keep it - and nothing else'. Thus Purchas LJ stated (at p. 23) that, although in 'normal circumstances the suggestion that a contracting party can rely on his own breach to establish consideration is distinctly unattractive' on the facts of the case the plaintiff had given up his right to 'cut his losses' by deliberately breaching the contract with the defendants. To adopt such an approach is to refuse to recognise that the defendants under the original contract had bought not simply the right to damages in the event of non-performance, but the right to performance itself. The same approach can be adopted in relation to the second factor. The benefit of not having to look for alternative carpenters was a benefit which the defendants paid for under the original contract and were entitled to receive. The third factor is scarcely more convincing. If the defendants had been compelled to pay out under the penalty clause because of the plaintiff's failure to complete on time they would have been entitled to recover that sum from the plaintiff by way of damages (although there was, admittedly, a risk that the plaintiff would not have been in a financial position to pay damages). The fourth and fifth factors do appear to be capable of constituting consideration (even on orthodox grounds) if the plaintiff did actually accept a new obligation to complete the flats one by one. Unfortunately, it is not clear from the judgments whether any new obligation was assumed because elsewhere in the judgments it is stated that the plaintiff simply performed his existing contractual duties. So the fourth and fifth factors are at best equivocal and it is not at all easy to pinpoint exactly what the practical benefit was on the facts. Are the factors cumulative or not? Does a promise to complete the work in itself confer a practical benefit or must one show 'something more', such as the avoidance of liability under a penalty clause?

Williams has been applauded as a pragmatic decision, giving effect to the 'realities' of the situation. Modifications of contracts, it is argued, are in the public interest; both parties should be encouraged to bargain their way out of an unanticipated difficulty and this can best be done by giving effect to the variations which the parties have agreed. But this is to tell only half of the story. Modifications are not necessarily in the public interest. There is a competing interest in holding parties to their original bargain. When I employ a sub-contractor to do work for me for £20 000, I do not mean £20 000 plus whatever else he can extract from me by conduct short of duress. The deal is £20 000; not a penny more, not a penny less. In jumping on the practical benefit bandwagon, the Court of Appeal has not only failed to identify practical benefit with sufficient precision, it has also failed to place sufficient weight on the need to hold contracting parties to the terms of their original bargain.

5.13   Consideration and Duress

Even if the practical benefit hurdle can be overcome, we are left with our second problem. How can *Williams* be reconciled with *Stilk* v. *Myrick*? The Court of Appeal in *Williams* were adamant that *Stilk* had not been overruled: rather, it had been 'refined' and 'limited'. Yet the two cases are very similar. If the defendants in *Williams* received a practical benefit, can the same not be said of the master of the ship in *Stilk*? He was practically benefited by the promise of Stilk to work the ship back home, yet that benefit was held not to constitute consideration. The Court of Appeal attempted to resolve this problem by explaining *Stilk* as a duress case. This could have been done relatively easily. After all, Espinasse's report was explicitly based upon considerations of public policy and there were other cases in which public policy had been relied upon by the courts (see, for example, *Harris* v. *Watson* (1791) Peake 102). But this relatively straightforward approach was not for the Court of Appeal. The court chose to cite Campbell's report but in substance they followed Espinasse. Thus Purchas LJ stated (at p. 21) that *Stilk* was a case arising out of 'the extraordinary conditions existing at the turn of the 18th century under which seamen had to serve their contracts of employment on the high seas. There were strong public policy grounds at that time to protect the master and owners of a ship from being held to ransom by disaffected crews'. But where is the evidence for this on the facts of *Stilk*? As Gilmore (1974) has pointed out, the contract in *Stilk* was concluded on shore, not the high seas. We have no evidence that Stilk applied any pressure upon the master. The only real evidence of duress can be found in the Espinasse report but the Court of Appeal chose not to rely upon that evidence.

But even if *Stilk* is now a duress case, what does this tell us about the case? Here we encounter the problem which we noted above (5.3) of working out the relationship between consideration and duress. In *The Alev* [1989] 1 Lloyd's Rep 138, 147, Hobhouse J said that 'now that there is a properly developed doctrine of the avoidance of contracts on the grounds of economic duress, there is no warrant for the Court to fail to recognise the existence of some consideration even though it may be insignificant and even though there may be no mutual bargain in any realistic use of that phrase'. This approach advocates a more liberal approach to consideration, maintaining that the courts should be readier to find consideration now that they know that they can always set aside the contract on the ground of duress. On this analysis, there was consideration on the facts of *Stilk* (because the master was practically benefited by Stilk's promise to work the ship back home). So a contract was initially concluded but that contract was then set aside on the ground of duress exerted by Stilk which prevented him from enforcing the contract.

Some commentators have gone even further than advocating a more liberal approach to the identification of consideration and argued that there are 'good reasons why the doctrine of economic duress ought to *displace*, and not be in addition to, the doctrine of consideration in "extortion situations", provided, of course, that it can be rationalized' (Phang, 1990). This is difficult to understand. Duress cannot 'displace' consideration because they perform different functions. Consideration is relevant to the question whether or not a contract has been concluded. But duress is a vitiating factor; that is to say, it is a ground upon which an otherwise valid and subsisting contract can be set aside. The two issues cannot be collapsed into one.

So it is suggested that, after *Williams* v. *Roffey Bros*, *Stilk* should be interpreted as a case in which there was consideration but that the contract was set aside on the ground of duress. This view does not yet command universal support. For example, in *Anangel Atlas Compania Naviera SA* v. *Ishikawajima-Harima Heavy Industries Co Ltd (No. 2)* [1990] 2 Lloyd's Rep 526, 544–545 Hirst J, after expressing his approval of the emphasis upon practical benefit on the facts of *Williams* v. *Roffey*, stated that *Stilk* still applied where there is 'a wholly gratuitous promise'. This is difficult to follow. Why was Stilk's promise wholly gratuitous, when the promise of the plaintiff in *Williams* was not? As has already been stated, there is very little to distinguish between the two cases. This failure to provide a coherent, fresh analysis of *Stilk* in the light of *Williams* v. *Roffey* further underlines the confusion which currently exists in this area of the law.

5.14   Alternative Analyses

We have now discussed the principal difficulties with, and analyses of, *Williams* v. *Roffey* and *Stilk* v. *Myrick*. There are, however, two other theories which are worthy of brief mention. The first was adopted by the Supreme Court of New Hampshire in *Watkin & Son Inc* v. *Carrig* (1941) 21 A 2d 591. The parties entered into a written contract under which the plaintiff agreed to excavate a cellar for the defendant for a fixed price. Shortly after commencing the work the plaintiff discovered the presence of solid rock in the area which he had agreed to excavate. Discussions took place between the parties and the defendant agreed to pay a price which was approximately nine times the amount of the original contract price. The plaintiff did the work and then sued to recover the promised sum. The defendant argued that there was no consideration to support the promise to pay the additional sum. The argument was rejected. The trial judge found that the written contract between the parties had been superseded by a new agreement which was enforceable. In giving up their rights to sue each other under the original written contract, the parties provided consideration for their agreement to abandon that contract. The second contract was then supported by consideration. Applying this type of reasoning to *Stilk* we can say that, if Stilk had been able to show that the original contract had been abandoned by the mutual agreement of the parties, then that abandonment would have been supported by consideration and the agreement to pay the higher rate would then have been enforceable. But this is a very difficult test to apply in practice because how do the courts decide whether there is a variation of one contract or a replacement of one contract by another? Yet the answer to this question is vital because if it is a variation there is no consideration to support it, while if a second contract has been concluded then it is, in fact, supported by consideration and so is enforceable. Purchas LJ in *Williams* stated (at p. 20) that he was unable to accept 'the attractive invitation' to follow *Watkins and it is suggested that he was right to do so because of the difficulties which arise in putting it into practice.*

The final analysis which can be offered of *Williams* is that it is moving English law in the direction of the conclusion that consideration should only be a requirement for the formation of a contract and that it should not be required for the modification of a contract. This point is not a new one. Sir Frederick Pollock stated in 1950 that 'the doctrine of consideration has been extended, with not very happy results, beyond its proper scope, which is to govern the formation of contracts, and has been made to regulate the discharge of contracts'. The distinction between formation and modification has been recognised in America where s.2–209(1) of the Uniform Commercial Code dispenses with the requirement of consideration in the case of agreements to modify an existing contract. To some extent this view is based on the idea that variations of contracts are in the public interest (see Halson, 1990 and 1991) and therefore it is open to the criticism that it does not place sufficient weight on the need to hold parties to the terms of their original bargain. If that bargain is subsequently altered by a fresh bargain then there is obviously no objection to the enforcement of the fresh bargain. But if that bargain is purportedly changed by what is no more than a gift, then there is a lot to be said for the argument that such a gift should be treated like any other gift and only enforced if it is in the form of a deed.

5.15 Part Payment of a Debt

A close relation of the old rule that performance of an existing contractual duty owed to the promisor does not constitute consideration is the rule that a promise to accept part payment of a debt in discharge of the entire debt is not supported by consideration. The debtor is already contractually obliged to repay the entire debt and so provides no consideration for the creditor's promise to accept part payment (unless, for example, the debtor agrees to repay the debt at an earlier date, in which case he does provide consideration). This rule can be traced back to *Pinnel's case* (1602) 5 Co Rep 117a and was upheld by the House of Lords in *Foakes* v. *Beer* (1884) 9 App Cas 605 (although it should be noted that the rule is the subject of numerous common law limitations, see Treitel, 1991, pp. 116–20, and for the equitable evasions of this rule, see 5.25).

In *Foakes* a creditor promised to abandon her claim to interest on the debt but it was held that her promise to forbear was unsupported by consideration. Although such an agreement is not supported by consideration, in many cases a creditor will, as a matter of fact, be benefited by receipt of part payment because, in the words of Corbin (1963), 'a bird in the hand is worth much more than a bird in the bush'. So how can this refusal to recognise the efficacy of a practical benefit in *Foakes* be reconciled with *Williams* v. *Roffey*? Curiously, *Foakes* was not cited to the court in *Williams* v. *Roffey* and, given that *Foakes* is a decision of the House of Lords, to the extent that the two cases cannot be reconciled it is *Williams* which should give way. It is interesting to note that in *Foakes* Lord Blackburn registered his disagreement with the rule in *Pinnel's case* on the basis of his

'conviction that all men of business, whether merchants or tradesmen, do every day recognise and act on the ground that prompt payment of part of their demand may be more beneficial to them than it would be to insist on their rights and enforce payment of the whole. Even where the debtor is perfectly solvent, and sure to pay at last, this is often so. Where the credit of the debtor is doubtful it must be more so.'

This is the same emphasis on practical benefit which was adopted by the Court of Appeal in *Williams*, yet it did not win the day in the House of Lords in *Foakes*. The majority of their Lordships decided that such a practical benefit did not constitute good consideration in law.

This creates acute difficulties in distinguishing between *Foakes* v. *Beer* and *Williams* v. *Roffey Bros*. It has been argued that a promise to release part of a debt is different from a promise to pay more for the performance of an existing contractual obligation. But it is hard to see the difference: in both cases less than full performance is accepted as full performance. The fact that in one it is by receiving less and in the other it is by paying more should not be allowed to detract from that essential point.

The relationship between *Foakes* v. *Beer* and *Williams* v. *Roffey* was recently considered by the Court of Appeal in *Re Selectmove Ltd* (1994) *The Times* January 13. Peter Gibson LJ refused to extend *Williams* v. *Roffey* to the *Foakes* v. *Beer* situation on the ground that 'it would in effect leave the principle in *Foakes* v. *Beer* without any application. When a creditor and a debtor who are at arm's length reach agreement on the payment of the debt by instalments to accommodate the debtor, the creditor will no doubt always see a practical benefit to himself in so doing'. He continued: '*Foakes* v. *Beer* was not even referred to in the *Williams* case, and it is in my judgment impossible, consistently with the doctrine of precedent, for this Court to extend the principle of the *Williams* case to any circumstances governed by the principle of *Foakes* v. *Beer*. If that extension is to be made, it must be by the House of Lords or, perhaps even more appropriately, by Parliament after consideration by the Law Commission'. This approach does not deny the inconsistency between the two rules: it simply leaves it to the House of Lords or Parliament to sort out the mess. A choice must be made between the two cases: we cannot have practical benefit operating in one case and legal benefit in the other case with no rational explanation for the continued existence of such inconsistent rules.

5.16 Performance of a Duty Imposed by Contract with a Third Party

Despite the difficulty which English law has experienced in recognising that performance of an existing contractual duty owed to a promisor is good consideration, performance of a contractual duty owed to a third party has been clearly recognised as good consideration for a long period of time. In *Shadwell* v. *Shadwell* (1860) 9 CB (NS) 159, the plaintiff, who was engaged to Ellen Nicholl, received a letter from his uncle, in which the uncle promised to pay the plaintiff £150 per year after he was married. The plaintiff sued to enforce the promise and it was held that he could do so because he had provided consideration for his uncle's promise by marrying Ellen (the nephew was at the time contractually bound to marry her). The proposition that performance of a contractual duty owed to a third party can constitute consideration has recently been affirmed by the House of Lords in *The Eurymedon* [1975] AC 154 (see 7.6 for a full discussion of this case).

In *Jones* v. *Waite* (1839) 5 Bing NC 341 it was held that a promise to perform (as opposed to actual performance of) a contractual duty owed to a third party did not constitute consideration. But in *Scotson* v. *Pegg* (1861) 6 H & N 295 and *Pao On* v. *Lau Yiu Long* [1980] AC 614 it was held that such a promise could constitute consideration and the latter view is the one which is accepted by most scholars. It has always been difficult to explain why performance of an existing contractual duty owed to a third party can constitute consideration when the law has had such difficulty in recognising that performance of an existing contractual duty owed to a promisor does constitute consideration (although it should be noted that both *Shadwell* v. *Shadwell* and *Scotson* v. *Pegg* are treated by Treitel (1976) as examples of 'invented' consideration). It is here that the duress analysis may provide us with the key (and note, in this context, that the Court of Appeal in *Williams* derived some assistance from one of the three party cases, namely *Pao On* (above)). In the three party cases such as *Shadwell* v. *Shadwell*, there is not even a hint of duress. Indeed, it is difficult to see how the nephew in *Shadwell* could ever use the situation to apply pressure on the uncle. The fear of duress being absent, the courts saw no objection to the enforcement of a promise to pay in return for the performance of a duty imposed by contract with a third party (although it must be conceded that is is not easy to explain *Shadwell* even on the practical benefit test: in what sense did the uncle receive a practical benefit as a result of the marriage of his nephew to Ellen Nicholl?).

5.17   Conceptions of Value

It can readily be seen from the cases which we have discussed that the courts adopt an inconsistent approach to the identification of a benefit or detriment. In *Foakes* v. *Beer* the court ignored an obvious factual benefit to the creditor. Yet in *Cook* v. *Wright, Shadwell* v. *Shadwell* and *Scotson* v. *Pegg* the court found the existence of consideration upon the flimsiest of evidence. It will not do to say, as does Professor Treitel, that in some cases the courts have 'invented' consideration because that does not tell us why they have invented consideration, nor does it tell us when they are likely to invent it again in the future. Nevertheless, it must be conceded that the courts do tend to employ the language of 'benefit' and 'detriment'. But their use of 'benefit' and 'detriment' is inconsistent, which suggests that, on occasions, the courts do, as Atiyah argues, enforce a promise because there was a 'good reason' so to do. The most recent emphasis in *Williams* v. *Roffey Bros* (above) is upon 'practical benefit' but we have seen that it is not at all easy to identify what the court actually means by this phrase and we have also seen that the Court of Appeal in *Re Selectmove* felt unable to extend that approach to the *Foakes* v. *Beer* situation. The inconsistency therefore remains unresolved and the conclusion which must be reached is that the English courts have built a theory of consideration upon the foundations of benefit and detriment without subjecting to stringent analysis the coherency of their conceptions of benefit and detriment (see further Atiyah, 1986c).

5.18   Past Consideration

If I promise to reward you for acts which you have already performed prior to my promise, the general rule is that you cannot enforce my promise because the consideration which you have provided is past. By 'past consideration' lawyers mean that your consideration was already completed before I made my promise, so that you have not given anything new in return for my promise. The rule that past consideration is not good consideration is closely linked to the bargain theory of consideration. The fatal objection is that there is no reciprocity; the promisee does not give anything in return for the promise of the promisor. Thus it would appear that the past consideration rule is unaffected by the recent upheavals caused by *Williams* v. *Roffey Bros* (above) because the point in the past consideration cases hinges, not on the distinction between legal benefit and practical benefit, but on the need to show that the promise was made as part of the bargain. The focus is upon the identification of a bargain, not upon the type of benefit received.

It follows from this that, as a general rule, if two parties have already made a binding contract and one of them subsequently promises to confer an additional benefit on the other party to the contract, that promise is not binding because the promisee's consideration, which is his entry into the original contract, is past. In *Roscorla* v. *Thomas* (1842) 3 QB 234, the defendant agreed to sell a horse to the plaintiff. Shortly afterwards the defendant added a promise that he would give a warranty as to the soundness of the horse. It was held that the defendant's promise was unenforceable because the only consideration which the plaintiff had provided was his entry into the original contract of sale and that consideration was past. The courts do, however, have some degree of latitude in applying this rule and do not always take a strictly chronological view of the sequence of events. If the court is satisfied that the new promise and the act of the promisee which is alleged to be the past consideration are, in fact, part of the same overall transaction, the exact order in which the events occurred will not be decisive (*Thornton* v. *Jenkyns* (1840) 1 Man & G 166). In identifying whether consideration is actually past or not, the courts look, not to the wording of the contract, but to the actual sequence of events. Thus, in *Re McArdle* [1951] Ch 669, a promise made 'in consideration of your carrying out' certain work was held to be unenforceable as the consideration for it was past. Although the wording of the contract suggested that the work was to be done at some future time it had, as a matter of fact, been done prior to the making of the contract and was therefore past.

The rule as to past consideration is a harsh one. In *Eastwood* v. *Kenyon* (1840) 11 A & E 438, the guardian of a young girl raised a loan to educate the girl and to improve her marriage prospects. After her marriage, her husband promised to pay off the loan. It was held that the guardian was unable to enforce this promise because the consideration which he had provided, which was bringing up and financing the girl, was past. The court conceded that the husband might have been under a moral obligation to pay, but that moral obligation could not be converted into a legal obligation because of the absence of consideration.

The harshness of the past consideration rule has been mitigated to some extent by the doctrine of implied assumpsit. Where the act of the promisee was performed at the request of the promisor and, subsequent to the performance of the act by the promisee, the promisor promises to pay for it, then such a promise may be enforceable. An early example is *Lampleigh* v. *Brathwait* (1615) Hob 105. The defendant, who was under sentence of death, requested the plaintiff to ride to Newark to obtain a pardon from King James I. The plaintiff did so. The defendant then promised to pay the plaintiff £1000. It was held that the plaintiff could enforce the contract. But the doctrine of implied assumpsit operates within narrow confines. The Privy Council in *Pau On* v. *Lau Yiu Long* [1980] AC 614 held that three conditions must be satisfied by a promisee who wishes to invoke the doctrine. The first is that he must have performed the original act at the *request* of the promisor. The second is that it must have been clearly understood or implied between the parties when the act was originally requested that the promisee would be rewarded for doing the act. The third is that the eventual promise of payment after the act was completed must be one which, had it been made prior to or at the time of the act, would have been enforceable.

Parliament has also intervened to mitigate the hardships caused by the past consideration rule by providing that an antecedent debt or liability is good consideration for a bill of exchange (Bills of Exchange Act 1882 s.27(1)(b)) and by providing that a written acknowledgement of a debt by a debtor shall be deemed to have accrued on and not before the date of acknowledgement (Limitation Act 1980 s.27(5)).

5.19   Consideration Must Move from the Promisee

A person to whom a promise is made can only enforce the promise if he himself provides consideration for the promise. If the consideration is provided by a third party, the promisee cannot enforce the promise (*Tweddle* v. *Atkinson* (1861) 1 B & S 393, discussed further at 7.1).

5.20 Reliance Upon Non-bargain Promises

A plaintiff who is able to establish the existence of consideration can, absent any other vitiating factors, bring an action on the contract to enforce the defendant's promise. But what of the plaintiff who relies to his detriment upon a promise of the defendant which is not supported by consideration? Can he enforce that promise or recover compensation for the extent to which he has detrimentally relied upon it? Once again the debate between Treitel and Atiyah assumes enormous significance. If Treitel is correct, and consideration is built upon reciprocity, then such a promise cannot be enforced because of the lack of consideration (although more limited effect may be given to the promise). But, if Atiyah is correct and consideration means a reason for the enforcement of a promise, then such a promise may be enforceable where the court can find a 'good reason' for its enforcement.

A factual situation which will provide a useful background to our discussion of these issues is provided by the American case of *Ricketts* v. *Scothorn* 57 Neb 51 (1898). Scothorn was at work when her grandfather gave her a promissory note under which he promised to pay her $2000 at 6 per cent per annum. On giving her the promissory note he told her that none of his other grandchildren worked and now 'you don't have to'. Scothorn gave up work in reliance upon his promise but, when her grandfather died, his executors refused to honour his promise. Could she enforce the promise? Her claim does appear to be a just one because she acted to her detriment in reliance upon the promise. But how do we reconcile such a claim with the doctrine of consideration which, as we have seen, requires that something of value be given in return for the promise? Two possible arguments suggest themselves. The first is that Scothorn did, in fact, provide consideration by giving up her work. The second is to challenge the rule that a promise is unenforceable if it is unsupported by consideration.

It may seem rather odd to canvass the first argument when purporting to discuss reliance upon promises which are unsupported by consideration. But plaintiffs do, as a matter of practice, attempt to bring themselves within the fold of the doctrine of consideration before embarking upon the more hazardous task of seeking to persuade a court to enforce a promise which is unsupported by consideration. The issues are also related because, the wider the scope of the doctrine of consideration, the less need there is to find a substitute for consideration. So it is here that the liberal approach to consideration in *Williams* v. *Roffey Bros* (above, 5.11) becomes important because it minimises the need for plaintiffs to have resort to estoppel and hence diminishes the practical significance of the limitations from which estoppel presently suffers (such as the fact that it cannot be used to create a cause of action, see 5.22). In *Williams* itself Russell LJ stated (at p. 17) that he 'would have welcomed the development of argument. . .on the basis that there was . . . an estoppel and that the defendants, in the circumstances prevailing, were precluded from raising the defence that their undertaking to pay the extra £10 300 was not binding'. But it is not at all clear that the estoppel argument would have succeeded on the facts of *Williams* (see 5.22) and, for present purposes, that point is irrelevant. The point which is being made here is that there was no need for the plaintiff to resort to estoppel because he won on the consideration point. Why should a plaintiff make life difficult for himself by pleading estoppel (and possibly recovering less by way of compensation, see 5.28) when he can take the easy route and invoke the doctrine of consideration? It is sometimes argued that estoppel should be developed to play a much wider role, similar to that played by estoppel in America in s.90 of the Restatement (Second) Contracts. But it is important to note that in America consideration operates within relatively narrow confines and so the need for a more developed doctrine of estoppel is apparent. *Williams* v. *Roffey Bros* has chosen to develop English law in a different direction by expanding the doctrine of consideration and hence diminishing the practical need for a more elaborate doctrine of estoppel. On the other hand, should the more restrictive approach to consideration adopted in *Foakes* v. *Beer* (5.15) prevail, then the need for a broader doctrine of estoppel will become apparent (and note in this context the extent to which estoppel has already operated to limit the scope of the rule in *Foakes* v. *Beer*, see 5.25). The relationship between the scope of consideration and the role of estoppel is therefore a close one.

5.21   The Role of Consideration

We have already seen that consideration is a rather elastic doctrine and that the courts have scope to 'invent' consideration. Could a court not find or invent consideration in a case such as *Ricketts*? The difficulty is that the grandfather did not request Scothorn to give up her work and so there does not appear to be any bargain under which she promised to give up work in return for the promised sum of money. But could we not imply such a bargain? After all, the grandfather must have known that Scothorn would be likely to give up work as a result of his promise. Should a court not imply that, where it is foreseeable to a promisor that a promisee will act to her detriment in reliance upon his promise, the reliance of the promisee is at the request of the promisor and so constitutes consideration?

Such an approach was, however, rejected by the English Court of Appeal in *Combe* v. *Combe* [1951] 2 KB 215. A husband promised to pay his wife £100 per annum on their separation. The husband did not make any of the payments and six years later the wife brought an action to recover the arrears. She argued that she had supplied consideration for her husband's promise because she had refrained from applying to court for a permanent maintenance order. But the Court of Appeal held that there was no request, express or implied, by the husband that the wife should refrain from applying to the court for maintenance. Therefore no consideration was provided for the husband's promise and it was unenforceable.

But there were facts in *Combe* upon which the court could have implied a request by the husband that the wife forbear from applying for maintenance (see Goodhart, 1951 and 1953, but contrast the alternative explanation of the case put forward by Denning, 1952, p. 2). Indeed, cases can be found in which a court has been prepared to make such an implication. For example, in *Alliance Bank* v. *Broom* (1864) 2 Dr & Sm 289, the defendant owed £22 000 to the plaintiff bank. The bank demanded some security for the loan and this was promised by the defendant. The defendant failed to honour his promise and, when the bank sought to enforce it, he argued that his promise was not supported by consideration and was therefore unenforceable. The court held that the promise was enforceable because, as a result of the defendant's promise, the plaintiffs had refrained from suing him to recover the debt and the defendant had therefore received 'the benefit of some degree of forbearance' (contrast *Miles* v. *New Zealand Alford Estate Co* (1886) 32

Ch D 267). Although the defendant had not expressly requested the plaintiffs to forbear, the court felt able to imply such a request. But why did the court imply a request on the facts of *Allied Bank* but not in *Combe*? The answer to that question is unclear. It could be argued that the bank in *Allied Bank* was much more likely to institute proceedings than was the wife in *Combe* and therefore it was easier for the court to imply such a request. Alternatively, it could be argued that the reason for the court's refusal to imply a request on the facts of *Combe* was that the 'justice of the case [did] not require that it should be' implied because the wife had an income in excess of that of her husband and she had delayed for six years in bringing her action (see Atiyah, 1986c). Whatever the precise ground of distinction between the two cases, it is clear that the courts do have considerable discretion in implying such a request. The readier they are to find a request, the wider will be the scope of the doctrine of consideration and hence the need to find a substitute for consideration will be radically diminished.

5.22 Estoppel

Where, as in *Ricketts* and *Combe*, the court is unable to find the existence of consideration, can the promise be enforced despite the absence of consideration? The orthodox answer is that such a promise will not be enforced. But limited effects may be given to the promise under the doctrine of estoppel. The essential ingredients of estoppel were defined by Lord Birkenhead in *Maclaine* v. *Gatty* [1921] 1 AC 376, 386, in the following terms:

'where A has by his words or conduct justified B in believing that a certain state of facts exists, and B has acted upon such belief to his prejudice, A is not permitted to affirm against B that a different state of facts existed at the same time'.

But the picture is in fact more complicated than this quotation from the judgment of Lord Birkenhead would suggest. In the first place Lord Birkenhead was referring to estoppel by representation but, under the umbrella of 'estoppel', there are, in fact, many distinct doctrines; estoppel by representation, promissory estoppel, proprietary estoppel, estoppel by convention and related doctrines such as waiver and variation. It is not easy to identify the relationship between these different types of estoppel. The second difficulty lies in ascertaining whether there is a single unifying principle which unites these different estoppels (see Jackson, 1982). The final difficulty lies in discerning the relationship between estoppel and the doctrine of consideration.

The latter point needs some amplification before we embark upon an analysis of the leading cases. If the courts were to hold that a promise was enforceable simply because a promisee had acted upon it to his detriment, then a great hole would arguably be blown in the doctrine of consideration (see 5.28). But, as Denning LJ stated in *Combe* v. *Combe* (above), 'the doctrine of consideration is too firmly fixed to be overthrown by a side-wind'. So estoppel must be reconciled with consideration. The reconciliation achieved by the courts is a rather uneasy one and is summed up in the well-worn maxim that estoppel can be used as a 'shield but not as a sword'. This means that estoppel cannot be used to create a new cause of action. The estoppel must relate to the existing legal rights of the promisor; that is to say, there must be a pre-existing legal relationship between the parties under which the promisor promises to give up some of his rights under that relationship. The effect of the estoppel is to prevent the promisor going back on his promise where the promisee has acted upon it to his detriment. But, where there is no pre-existing legal relationship between the parties, as in *Combe* v. *Combe*, then the promisee cannot invoke estoppel because such an estoppel would create a completely new cause of action. To permit an estoppel to create a new cause of action would, on traditional analysis, undermine the doctrine of consideration. But how can this analysis be applied to a case such as *Stilk* v. *Myrick* (5.11)? *Stilk* is more difficult than *Combe* because in *Stilk* there was a pre-existing contractual relationship between the parties. So, had estoppel been invoked, would it have been used to create the cause of action? It is suggested that it would and so an argument based upon estoppel would have been rejected on the facts of *Stilk*. The original contract did not give Stilk the right of action which he was asserting. He could only establish the right to the extra pay by relying upon the separate promise of the master to share the wages. The promise of the master to accept a more onerous obligation was not supported by consideration and so could not be enforced simply by proof that Stilk had relied upon it to his detriment (see also *Williams* v. *Roffey Bros* [1991] 1 QB 1, 13, cf. pp. 17–18).

In the remaining sections of this chapter we shall consider the orthodox cases in which estoppel is used as a 'shield'. We shall then discuss some cases in which it has been sought to use estoppel as a 'sword' and conclude by analysing the relationship between these cases and the doctrine of consideration.

5.23   Estoppel by Representation

Estoppel clearly acts as a shield in the case of estoppel by representation. The basic principle is that a person who makes a representation of existing fact which induces the other party to act to his detriment in reliance on the representation will not be permitted subsequently to act inconsistently with that representation. It is a rule of evidence which *permanently* prevents a representor from averring or proving facts which are contrary to his own representation (see *Avon County Council* v. *Howlett* [1983] 1 WLR 603, 622, per Slade LJ). There are two particular features of this estoppel. First, the representation must be one of fact. This limitation was initially established at common law, but was extended to its equitable counterpart in the controversial decision of the House of Lords in *Jorden* v. *Money* (1854) 5 HL Cas 185. Therefore the doctrine does not apply to representations of law or intention. Although the courts have shown some inclination to construe a representation of fact from what appears to be a statement of intention (see Thompson, 1983), a promise is clearly beyond the scope of the doctrine. The second feature of this type of estoppel is that it operates as a defence; it does not create a cause of action. In *Avon County Council* v. *Howlett* (above) the defendant was overpaid by his employers, the plaintiffs. They sought to recover the money as paid under a mistake of fact. The defendant argued that the plaintiffs were estopped from pursuing their claim because they had made a representation of fact to him that he was entitled to the money and he had spent the money in reliance upon their representation. The Court of Appeal upheld the defendant's argument. The effect of the estoppel was to act as a 'shield' and to defeat a claim which would otherwise have succeeded.

5.24 Waiver and Variation

The role of estoppel as a shield can also be seen in cases where contracting parties agree to modify or abandon an existing contract. A preliminary point must be made here, which is that consideration applies to the discharge or variation of a contract as well as to its formation (although, as we have noted (5.14), the extension of consideration to the discharge or variation of a contract is a controversial one and, after the decision of the Court of Appeal in *Williams* v. *Roffey Bros* (above), it is arguable that consideration should no longer be applied to the modification of a contract). Where the discharge or variation is capable of benefiting either contracting party then the variation or discharge is supported by consideration and is enforceable (*WJ Alan & Co Ltd* v. *El Nasr Export and Import Co* [1972] 2 QB 189). But where the variation or discharge can confer a benefit upon only one contracting party then the agreement is not supported by consideration. The classic example is the creditor who agrees to accept part payment of a debt in discharge of the entire debt (5.15). In such a case the variation can only operate to the benefit of the debtor and so is unsupported by consideration.

A variation which is unsupported by consideration has no contractual effect. But effect may be given to a promise to forego rights under the doctrine of waiver. A variety of meanings have been attributed to the word waiver (see *The Kanchenjunga* [1990] 1 Lloyd's Rep 391, 397–399 and Dugdale and Yates, 1976) and the present scope of the doctrine is a matter of some uncertainty. It is essential that a distinction be drawn between 'waiver by election' and 'waiver by estoppel' (see further 19.8). Waiver by election arises where a contracting party has to choose between the exercise of two inconsistent rights (such as the right to affirm the contract or the right to terminate performance for breach, see 19.8) and has nothing to do with our present inquiry. Waiver by estoppel, on the other hand, is of relevance in this context but it seems to be virtually indistinguishable from equitable estoppel and appears to have been subsumed within the larger doctrine of equitable or promissory estoppel (see, for example, *Prosper Homes* v. *Hambro's Bank Executor & Trustee Co* (1979) 39 P & CR 395, 401). So we shall consider the elements of waiver within our discussion of promissory estoppel. Here it is sufficient to give one example of the operation of the doctrine of waiver.

In *Hickman* v. *Haynes* (1875) LR 10 CP 598, the parties entered into a contract for the sale of goods. The buyer subsequently requested the seller to delay the delivery of the goods. The seller agreed and tendered delivery on the later date, but the buyer refused to accept delivery. The seller brought an action for damages against the buyer, who argued that the seller could not succeed because he was in breach of contract in failing to deliver on time. The court held that the buyer had waived his right to demand delivery on time and that he could not subsequently reassert it without the giving of reasonable notice (see on the giving of reasonable notice *Charles Rickard Ltd* v. *Oppenhaim* [1950] 1 KB 616). It should be noted that, in contrast to *Avon County Council* v. *Howlett* (above), the estoppel in *Hickman* was invoked by the *plaintiff* and the effect of the waiver was to enable a claim to succeed which otherwise would have failed.

5.25   Promissory Estoppel

As we have already noted, there is a very close relationship between the doctrines of waiver and promissory (or equitable) estoppel. The leading case on promissory estoppel is *Hughes* v. *Metropolitan Railway Co* (1877) 2 App Cas 439. A landlord gave six months' notice to a tenant, requiring him to carry out certain repairs. The tenant responded by inquiring whether the landlord wished to purchase his interest in the premises for £3000. The landlord entered into negotations for the purchase of the lease but, when these negotiations broke down, he sought to forfeit the lease because the tenant had not carried out the repairs within six months of his original notice. The House of Lords held that the tenant was entitled to equitable relief against forfeiture of the lease on the ground that the running of the six month period was suspended during the negotiations to purchase the lease and did not recommence until the negotiations broke down.

Hughes lay in obscurity for many years until it was resurrected by Denning J in the famous case of *Central London Property Ltd* v. *High Trees House Ltd* [1947] KB 130. In 1937 the plaintiffs let a block of flats in London to the defendants on a 99 year lease at an annual rent of £2500. In 1940 the defendants discovered that, as a result of the outbreak of war and the evacuation of people from London, they were unable to let many of the flats. So the plaintiffs agreed to reduce the rent to £1250. This promise to accept a reduced rent was unsupported by consideration. At the end of the war in 1945 the property market had returned to normal and the flats were fully let. The plaintiffs demanded that the defendants resume payment of the entire rent from 1945, but the defendants refused to pay. Denning J held that the plaintiffs were entitled to demand the entire rent from the date of their notice in 1945. The interest of this case lies in the new life which it breathed into promissory estoppel which, for present purposes, may be defined as follows:

> 'where, by words or conduct, a person makes an unambiguous representation as to his future conduct, intending the representation to be relied on and to affect the legal relations between the parties, and the representee alters his position in reliance on it, the representor will be unable to act inconsistently with the representation if by so doing the representee would be prejudiced'.

This definition of promissory estoppel can be divided into five elements.

The first is that there must be a promise or a representation as to future conduct which is intended to affect the legal relations between the parties and which indicates that the promisor will not insist on his strict legal rights against the promisee. The promise or representation must be clear and unequivocal so that the promisor does not lose his rights simply because he has failed throughout to insist upon strict performance of the contract by the promisee. Although this requirement originated in estoppel by representation, it has since been extended to cases of promissory estoppel and waiver.

The second element is that the promise or representation must have been relied upon by the promisee. There are dicta which suggest that the the promisee must have acted to his 'detriment' in reliance upon the promise but the better view is that it is sufficient to show that the promisee committed himself to a course of action which he would not otherwise have adopted. The third requirement is that it must be 'inequitable' for the promisor to go back upon his promise. This will usually be satisfied by demonstrating that the promisee has acted in reliance upon the promise (although see *The Post Chaser* [1981] 2 Lloyd's Rep 693, where the promisee acted in reliance upon the promise but could not show that it was 'inequitable' for the promisor to go back upon his promise).

The fourth element is that the effect of promissory estoppel is generally suspensory; it does not extinguish the promisor's rights. In *Hughes* v. *Metropolitan Railway Co* (above) the landlord's right to enforce the repairing covenant was not extinguished. It was suspended and could be resurrected by his giving reasonable notice. But in *High Trees* the estoppel had permanent effects because Denning J stated that the lessors would not have been entitled to demand the rent waived between 1940 and 1945. Such a proposition is difficult to reconcile with *Foakes* v. *Beer* (see 5.15) and has been criticised (see Treitel, 1991). But the better view is that, in cases of post-breach representations or where it is not possible or practicable to return the parties to their original position, then promissory estoppel may have permanent effects (see Dugdale and Yates, 1976 and Thompson, 1983).

The final point is that promissory estoppel cannot act as a cause of action; it acts as a shield but not as a sword (see *Combe* v. *Combe* (above)).

5.26 Estoppel by Convention

So far we have been dealing with cases in which estoppel acted as a shield and did not create a new cause of action. But the effect of estoppel by convention may be to create a cause of action. The leading authority is *Amalgamated Investment and Property Co* v. *Texas Commerce International Bank Ltd* [1982] QB 84, where estoppel by convention was defined in the following terms:

> 'when the parties have acted in their transaction upon the agreed assumption that a given state of facts is to be accepted between them as true, then as regards that transaction each will be estopped against the other from questioning the truth of the statement of facts so assumed'.

In the *Texas Bank* case the common assumption of the parties was that they had entered into a contract of guarantee under which the plaintiffs had promised to guarantee loans made by a subsidiary of the defendants to a subsidiary of the plaintiffs. In fact, the wording of the guarantee covered loans made by the defendants, but not loans made by the defendants' subsidiary. When the plaintiffs went into liquidation the defendants applied money which they owed to the plaintiffs in discharge of the plaintiffs' alleged liability under the guarantee. The plaintiffs sought a declaration that the defendants were not entitled to apply the money in such a way because the guarantee was not effective to cover the loans made by the subsidiary. But the court held that the parties had entered into the guarantee under the shared assumption that the guarantee did cover such loans and the effect of the estoppel was to prevent the plaintiffs from denying the efficacy of the guarantee. So the defendants used the estoppel as a shield to the plaintiffs' claim for a declaration. But could they have sued on the guarantee to recover the sums which they alleged were due? The majority (Brandon LJ and Lord Denning) held that they could have done so, but Brandon LJ held that, in such a case, it would be the contract and not the estoppel which created the cause of action. This point is difficult to understand. The contract of guarantee was not enforceable. Only the estoppel could validate the contract and thereby render the guarantee enforceable. Thus stated, is it not the estoppel which creates the cause of action?

5.27 Proprietary Estoppel

Whatever doubts we may harbour about the ability of estoppel by convention to create a cause of action, there can be no doubt that proprietary estoppel can be used to found a cause of action. Cases of proprietary estoppel can be divided into two broad categories. The first group of cases relate to the situation in which a landowner 'stands by' while another person improves his land in the mistaken belief that he is the owner of the land. In the second group of cases the promisee relies to his detriment upon the landowner's promise that he has or will be given an interest in the land (for a useful summary of the ingredients of proprietary estoppel see the judgment of Nourse LJ in *Brinnand* v. *Ewens* (1987) 19 HLR 415).

The operation of proprietary estoppel can be illustrated by reference to the case of *Pascoe* v. *Turner* [1979] 1 WLR 431. The plaintiff and the defendant lived together for a number of years. The plaintiff left the defendant and went to live with another woman, but he told the defendant that the house and everything in it was hers. In reliance upon this assurance, the defendant spent some £230 in repairs upon the house. The plaintiff subsequently decided that he wanted the house and he sued for possession. The defendant counterclaimed for a declaration that the house and everything in it was hers and her counterclaim succeeded in the Court of Appeal. Although she had not provided any consideration for the plaintiff's promise, the defendant had acted to her detriment in reliance upon his promise. This created an equity in her favour and that equity could only be satisfied by an order that the plaintiff convey to her the fee simple in the house. The effect of the estoppel in *Pascoe* was clearly to create a new cause of action. There was no pre-existing legal relationship between the parties and yet the promise of the plaintiff was enforced, despite the absence of consideration.

According to orthodox analysis, proprietary estoppel may be triggered by detrimental reliance by a promisee upon a promise, express or implied, that he will acquire rights in or over the promisor's land (*Dillwyn* v. *Llewelyn* (1862) D, F & G 517, *Inwards* v. *Baker* [1965] 2 QB 29). It should not, however, be thought that the courts will in all cases order the promisor to convey the fee simple to the promisee. More limited forms of relief may be granted (see *Inwards* v. *Baker* (above)). The remedy granted depends upon all the circumstances of the case and it is difficult to discern any principled basis upon which the courts decide what is the most appropriate remedy (but see the useful analysis by Moriarty, 1984).

Thus far, proprietary estoppel has been confined to cases in which a promisee has been induced to believe that he will acquire an interest in the promisor's land, although Megaw LJ recognised in *Western Fish Products* v. *Penwith DC* [1981] 2 All ER 204, 218 that it may extend to the case where the promisee is induced to believe that he will acquire an interest in other forms of property. There is, as yet, no clear authority which suggests that proprietary estoppel extends beyond such cases (but see *Pacol Ltd* v. *Trade Lines Ltd* [1982] 1 Lloyd's Rep 456).

However there are some dicta which suggest a more expansive role for proprietary estoppel. In *Crabb* v. *Arun DC* [1976] Ch 179 Scarman LJ said he did not find the distinction between 'promissory and proprietary estoppel' helpful and in *Amalgamated Investment and Property Co Ltd* v. *Texas Commerce International Bank Ltd* (above) Robert Goff J called proprietary estoppel an 'amalgam of doubtful utility'. Oliver J identified a much broader base for proprietary estoppel in *Taylor Fashions Ltd* v. *Liverpool Victoria Trustees Co Ltd* [1982] QB 133. The focus of his inquiry was upon

> 'whether, in particular individual circumstances, it would be unconscionable for a party to be permitted to deny that which, knowingly or unknowingly, he has allowed or encouraged another to assume to his detriment rather than to inquiring whether the circumstances can be fitted within the confines of some preconceived formula serving as a universal yardstick for every form of unconscionable behaviour'.

This type of approach has been labelled 'unhelpful' by Treitel (1991, p. 136) on the ground that it provides 'no basis on which a legal doctrine capable of yielding predictable results can be developed'. On the other hand, the present restriction upon the scope of proprietary estoppel cannot be justified. Why is it that detrimental reliance upon a promise to create an interest in property can create a cause of action, but that detrimental reliance upon any other promise cannot create a cause of action? No answer has been provided to this question. The only possible objection is that such a wide-ranging jurisdiction of the type advocated by Oliver J would be irreconcilable with the doctrine of consideration. And that is the issue which we must now consider.

5.28   The Relationship between Estoppel and Consideration

The relationship between estoppel and consideration has recently been exhaustively analysed by the High Court of Australia in *Walton Stores (Interstate) Ltd* v. *Maher* (1988) 164 CLR 387. The parties were involved in the negotiation of a major leasing and construction project. The plaintiff was the owner of land which he hoped to lease to the defendants. It was also intended that the plaintiff would demolish the existing building on the site and erect a new building to the defendants' specifications. The negotiations reached an advanced stage and solicitors were instructed to prepare the formal documents. The plaintiff signed the requisite documents and they were forwarded to the defendants' solicitors for execution and exchange. He was informed by his solicitors that the contracts had been sent to the defendants and he believed that they would shortly exchange and complete. Because of this belief and because the project was one of extreme urgency, the plaintiff began to demolish the building on his land. Meanwhile, the defendants were beginning to have second thoughts about the deal and they instructed their solicitors to 'go slow', even though they knew that the plaintiff had commenced work on the site. After the plaintiff had completed a substantial amount of the work, the defendants informed him that they had decided to withdraw from the project. The plaintiff sought a declaration that a binding agreement existed between the parties and consequential relief. His difficulty was that no exchange had ever taken place. However he argued that the defendants were estopped from withdrawing from their implied promise to complete the contract.

The defendants argued that the plaintiff could not use estoppel to create a cause of action. There was no pre-existing legal relationship between the parties and therefore nothing to which an estoppel could apply. The defendants' argument was rejected by the High Court who, by a majority, held that promissory estoppel could, in an appropriate case, create a cause of action; it could act as a sword as well as a shield. They held that such a proposition was not irreconcilable with the doctrine of consideration because the function of the estoppel was not 'to make a promise binding' or to make good the expectations engendered by a promise, but to 'avoid the detriment' which the promisee would suffer as a result of the unconscionable conduct of the promisor in departing from the terms of his promise (the differences between a contract and an equity created by an estoppel are fully set out in the judgment of Brennan J). A simple example will illustrate the distinction. Let us suppose that someone promises to pay me £500 and I act on that promise to my detriment by spending £300 which I would not otherwise have spent. Enforcement of the promise would give me £500 (and hence protect my expectation interest), whereas 'avoiding a detriment' would give me only £300 (thus protecting my reliance interest). The former is the province of the law of contract and hence demands consideration, the latter is the province of estoppel and so does not require consideration. So to protect my reliance interest does not necessarily undermine the doctrine of consideration. The High Court also rejected the argument that it was necessary to establish a pre-existing legal relationship between the parties before estoppel could be invoked. As *Walton Stores* amply demonstrates, the action of the promisor in going back upon his promise can be as unconscionable where there is no pre-existing legal relationship between the parties as when there is such a relationship.

The difficulty which remains lies in ascertaining when it is unconscionable for a promisor to go back upon his promise where there is no pre-existing legal relationship between the parties. As was pointed out by Mason CJ and Wilson J, a failure to fulfil a promise does not of itself amount to unconscionable conduct. It therefore follows that mere reliance upon a promise will not suffice to bring promissory estoppel into play; something more must be established. That 'something more' they held could be

'found, if at all, in the creation or encouragement by the party estopped in the other party of an assumption that a contract will come into existence or a promise will be performed and that the other party relied on that assumption to his detriment to the knowledge of the first party'.

These factors were all present on the facts of *Walton Stores*. It may be that there are other factors which will be found to be relevant but these can be worked out over time. The judgments of the majority are of immense importance in their demonstration that such an approach does not undermine consideration and in their establishment of a principled foundation for the resolution of future disputes. This first, crucial step having been taken by the High Court of Australia, all that remains is for a bold House of Lords to sweep aside *Combe* v. *Combe* and follow in its footsteps.

5.29   Conclusion: The Future of Consideration

After the decision of the Court of Appeal in *Williams* v. *Roffey Bros* (above, 5.11), the future of consideration in English contract law is somewhat uncertain. The Court of Appeal did not attempt expressly to throw out the doctrine; its stated aim was to 'limit' and 'refine' the rule in *Stilk* v. *Myrick* by placing emphasis upon the need to identify practical benefit rather than legal benefit. But the inference which one draws from the tenor of the judgments is that the court, particularly Russell LJ, saw the doctrine as a technicality which, on occasions, could operate to prevent the court from giving effect to the intention of the parties. Far from being an essential ingredient of a contract, the court appeared to regard consideration as a vitiating factor; that is to say, they perceived it as a doctrine which operated to set aside what was an otherwise valid and subsisting contract. More than that, they regarded it as a 'technical vitiating factor'; in other words, it was a vitiating factor which could not distinguish between modifications which were in the public interest and those which were not. That task, they thought, could be better achieved through the invocation of the doctrine of duress. The centrality of consideration to the creation of a contract was therefore thrown into doubt by the court.

   If the courts choose to develop this argument it could lead to the abolition of consideration as a doctrine. This approach has been adopted in Article 3.1 of the Draft Unidroit Statement of Principles for International Commercial Contracts, which states that 'a contract is concluded, modified or terminated by the mere agreement of the parties, without any further requirement'. The note to the Article states that consideration is of 'minimal practical importance' and that its elimination 'can only bring about greater certainty and reduce litigation'. While this may be true in the context of international commercial contracts, the task of limiting the scope of the law of contract must be entrusted to some set of rules. That task has traditionally been performed by consideration which has insisted that there must be a bargain between the parties; that is to say, both parties must contribute something to the transaction. Admittedly, the task of identifying the existence of a bargain has not always been easy, but is English law really ready to abandon the requirement of a bargain in favour of the more nebulous requirement of 'mere agreement'?

A more limited argument is that the vital question in future cases should be: did the parties have an 'intention to contract'? The role of consideration would then be confined to answering this particular question. If the parties had an intention to contract, there would be consideration; if not, there would be none. This appears to be the approach of Russell LJ in *Williams* when he said that 'the courts nowadays should be more ready to find [the existence of consideration] so as to reflect the intention of the parties'. This would take consideration into close proximity with the doctrine of intention to create legal relations (see Chapter 6). While this test may be relatively easy to operate in the commercial context, it is not at all obvious that the question whether the parties had an intention to contract will be any easier to answer than the question whether or not there was consideration (in the bargain sense) to support the agreement. It is the responsibility of those who advocate the abolition of the doctrine of consideration to formulate a precise set of alternative rules to mark out the limits of the law of contract.

Summary

1 English contract law does not generally insist upon requirements of form.
2 The classical definition of consideration is that a promisee should not be able to enforce a promise unless he has given or promised to give something in exchange for the promise or unless the promisor has obtained (or been promised) something in return.
3 Consideration must be sufficient but it need not be adequate and it must be something which the law regards as being of value. Natural love and affection does not constitute value for this purpose.
4 It is not clear when performance of an existing duty can constitute consideration. The orthodox view is that performance of a contractual duty owed to a third party does constitute consideration but that performance of an existing legal duty and performance of an existing contractual duty owed to the promisor does not constitute good consideration. The reason for the doubt relates to the scope of the decision of the Court of Appeal in *Williams* v. *Roffey Bros* which suggests that performance of an existing (contractual) duty can constitute consideration where it results in a 'practical benefit' to the promisor.
5 Part payment of a debt does not constitute good consideration for the discharge of the entire debt, although it must be said that it is not easy to reconcile *Foakes* v. *Beer* with *Williams* v. *Roffey Bros.*
6 Past consideration is not good consideration. The harshness of this rule is mitigated by the doctrine of implied assumpsit.
7 Consideration must move from the promisee.
8 Where the act of the promisee can be shown to be at the request, express or implied, of the promisor then the act of the promisee will constitute good consideration.
9 Estoppel can act as a shield but not as a sword. There must be a pre-existing legal relationship between the parties under which the promisor promises to

give up some of his rights under that relationship. The effect of the estoppel is to prevent the promisor going back on his promise where the promisee has acted in reliance upon it.

10 The maxim that estoppel acts as a shield but not as a sword operates in the case of estoppel by representation, waiver and promissory estoppel, but not in the case of proprietary estoppel (the position is unclear in relation to estoppel by convention).

11 It is a matter for debate whether the English courts should follow the High Court of Australia and conclude that, in an appropriate case, promissory estoppel can create a cause of action.

Exercises

1 What is meant by the maxim 'consideration must be sufficient but it need not be adequate'? Give examples to illustrate your answer.

2 Can performance of an existing duty ever constitute consideration? Should it ever constitute consideration?

3 What is a 'practical benefit'?

4 Can *Williams* v. *Roffey Bros* be reconciled with *Foakes* v. *Beer*?

5 What is past consideration? Do you think that the decision of the court in *Eastwood* v. *Kenyon* is (a) correct as a matter of principle and (b) fair?

6 What is implied assumpsit?

7 What is estoppel'? How many different types of estoppel are there and what is the relationship between them?

8 Describe the fact situation in the following two cases and explain their legal significance:

(a) *Combe* v. *Combe* [1951] 2 KB 215

(b) *Central London Property Trust Ltd* v. *High Trees House Ltd* [1947] KB 130.

9 What is meant by the phrase 'estoppel can act as a shield but not as a sword'? Can estoppel ever act as a sword?

6 Intention to Create Legal Relations

6.1 Introduction

The fact that the parties have reached agreement does not necessarily mean that they have concluded a legally enforceable contract, even where the agreement is supported by consideration. The following fact situation will demonstrate the point. I promise to pay my wife £50 if she will type the manuscript of this chapter of the book. My wife agrees. Does this agreement create a legally enforceable contract? On the face of it there appears to be no reason why it should not. We have reached agreement and the agreement is supported by consideration. But it is likely that an English court would conclude that we had not entered into a legally binding contract because we lacked an 'intention to create legal relations', which has been held to be an essential element in any contract. Before examining the relevant case law, we must stop and contemplate the juristic basis of this doctrine of intention to create legal relations.

It could be said that the doctrine is based on the intention of the parties, objectively interpreted; that is to say, my wife and I did not intend that our agreement would have legal consequences. But my wife certainly expected to receive the £50 if she typed the manuscript, although it is unlikely that either of us intended that she would have to go to court to get her money. However to say that we did not intend that she would have to go to court to get her money is not the same thing as saying that, if the case did come to court, that we thought her action would fail.

Alternatively, it could be said that the doctrine is based upon public policy; that is to say that, as a matter of policy, the law of contract ought not to intervene in domestic situations because the courts would then be swamped by trifling domestic disputes. Thus the Scottish Law Commission has stated (1977) that 'it is, in general, right that courts should not enforce entirely social engagements, such as arrangements to play squash or to come to dinner, even though the parties themselves may intend to be legally bound thereby'. In such a case it is for the court to decide, as a matter of policy, whether the agreement is 'entirely social' and hence not legally enforceable.

6.2 Balfour v. Balfour

The approach which has been adopted in the English courts is best illustrated by reference to the case of *Balfour* v. *Balfour* [1919] 2 KB 571.

A wife sought to enforce a promise by her husband to pay her £30 per month while he worked abroad. The action failed because the wife had not provided any consideration for the promise of her husband and because it was held that the parties did not intend their agreement to 'be attended by legal consequences'. Atkin LJ said that 'agreements such as these are outside the realm of contracts altogether. The common law does not regulate the form of agreements between spouses. . . . The consideration that really obtains for them is that natural love and affection which counts for so little in these cold Courts'.

But how did Atkin LJ know that the parties did not intend to create legal relations? Did he inquire into the intention of the parties or did he lay down this rule as a matter of policy? It appears from his judgment that he was more concerned with policy than with ascertaining the intention of the parties because he said that

'it would be of the worst possible example to hold that agreements such as this resulted in legal obligations which could be enforced in the Courts. . . The small Courts of this country would have to be multiplied one hundredfold if these arrangements were held to result in legal obligations.'

It was the need to prevent what was, in the opinion of the court, unnecessary litigation and the desire of the court to keep the law out of the marriage relationship ('each house is a domain into which the King's writ does not seek to run') which were the predominant factors behind the finding that there was no intention to create legal relations.

However it does not necessarily follow from the fact that the judgment of Atkin LJ is based primarily upon considerations of policy that the intention of the parties is thereby completely irrelevant. The rule laid down in *Balfour* has been interpreted subsequently as a *presumption* that parties to a domestic agreement do not intend to create legal relations. Cases concerning intention to create legal relations are thus commonly divided into two categories; the first, concerning domestic and social agreements, where the presumption is that the parties did not intend to create legal relations and the second, concerning commercial agreements, where the presumption is that the parties did intend to create legal relations. Both presumptions may be rebutted by evidence of contrary intention. But the fact that the initial presumption may be rebutted by evidence of contrary intention does not mean that the presumption itself is based upon the intention of the parties. Rather, as the judgment of Atkin LJ in *Balfour* makes clear, the initial presumption is a matter of policy. The policy which underpins these presumptions is one of 'keeping contract in its place; to keep it in the commercial sphere and out of domestic cases, except where the judges think it has a useful role to play' (Hedley, 1985).

6.3 Rebutting the Presumption

Although we have noted that evidence of intention is relevant to the rebuttal of the presumption, even here the role of intention is, at best, marginal. This is so for two reasons. The first is that in the case of many domestic and social agreements the parties have no discernible intention one way or the other. The second reason is that it is a very difficult task to rebut a presumption because of the strength of the initial presumption. In domestic agreements 'clear' evidence is required of an intention to create legal relations, whereas in commercial cases the presumption of legal relations is a 'heavy one' which is not discharged easily (*Edwards* v. *Skyways* [1964] 1 WLR 349). The marginal role of intention will be demonstrated by examining the scope of the two presumptions and then the factors which have been held to be relevant to the rebuttal of these presumptions.

6.4 Domestic and Social Agreements

As we have seen, an agreement between a husband and a wife is presumed not to be legally enforceable (*Balfour* v. *Balfour* (above)). Similarly, agreements between parents and children are presumed not to be legally binding. In *Jones* v. *Padavatton* [1969] 1 WLR 328, a mother persuaded her daughter, who was a secretary in Washington DC, to give up her work and read for the English Bar by promising to pay her $200 maintenance per month. After the daughter had begun to read for the Bar, the agreement was varied. The mother bought a house in London so that the daughter could live there rent free and the rent from letting out the other rooms to tenants would provide the daughter with her maintenance. Eventually, after the daughter had had more than one unsuccessful attempt at passing the Bar examinations, the mother and daughter fell out. The mother came to England and sought to gain possession of the house. The daughter relied upon their agreement as a defence to her mother's action. The Court of Appeal held that the agreement was not intended to be legally binding and that the mother was entitled to possession (see too *Hardwick* v. *Johnson* [1978] 1 WLR 683).

Social arrangements are also presumed not to give rise to legal relations. In *Lens* v. *Devonshire Social Club The Times* 4 December 1914, it was held that the winner of a competition held by a golf club could not sue for his prize because no-one involved in the competition intended that legal consequences should flow from entry into the competition.

The presumption may, of course, be rebutted by evidence of contrary intention, but a mere subjective intention to create legal relations will not suffice. There must be some objective evidence of a contrary intent. Although a complete list cannot be drawn up of the factors to which the court will have regard in considering whether or not the presumption has been rebutted, in practice the following three factors are among the most important.

The first is the context in which the agreement is made. If an agreement is entered into by family members in what the courts perceive to be a 'business context' the court will be readier to infer that the presumption has been rebutted. In *Snelling* v. *John G Snelling Ltd* [1973] 1 QB 87, it was held that legal relations were created when three brothers, who were directors of a family company, entered into an agreement relating to the running of the company. Similarly where a husband and a wife are about to separate or have separated the presumption does not operate because in such a case the parties 'bargain keenly' and do not rely on 'honourable understandings' (*Merritt* v. *Merritt* [1970] 1 WLR 1121, 1123 per Lord Denning).

Secondly, the court will have regard to any reliance which has been placed upon the agreement. Where one party has acted to his detriment on the faith of the agreement a court may be more willing to conclude that the agreement was intended to have legal consequences. Such was the case in *Parker* v. *Clark* [1960] 1 WLR 286. The defendants, who were an elderly couple, suggested that the plaintiffs, who were their friends, come to live with them. The plaintiffs were agreeable to the proposal but pointed out that, if they were to live with the defendants, they would have to sell their own house. The defendants replied stating that the problem could be resolved by the defendants leaving to the plaintiffs a share of their house in their will. The plaintiffs accepted this offer, sold their house, lent the balance of the money to their daughter to enable her to purchase a flat and moved in with the defendants. However the parties soon began to disagree over certain matters and the result was that the defendants asked the plaintiffs to leave. The plaintiffs left the house to avoid being evicted and brought an action against the defendants for breach of contract. The defendants argued that there was no contract between them because of a lack of intention to create legal relations. It was held that the parties had intended to create legal relations. Devlin J stated that

> 'I cannot believe . . . that the defendant really thought that the law would leave him at liberty, if he so chose, to tell the [plaintiffs] when they arrived that he had changed his mind, that they could take their furniture away, and that he was indifferent whether they found anywhere else to live or not.'

Similarly, there is some authority for the proposition that an agreement between workmates under which one is to provide the other with a lift to work in return for a contribution towards the petrol does not create legal relations with regard to journeys to be undertaken in the future (see Upjohn LJ in *Coward* v. *Motor Insurers' Bureau* [1963] 2 QB 259, 271) but that it does create legal relations with regard to journeys which have already been undertaken (see Lord Cross in *Albert* v. *Motor Insurers'*

Bureau [1972] AC 301, 340). In these cases the determining factor appears to be the fact that the parties have acted in reliance upon the agreement. The courts are reluctant to allow the parties to go back on their agreement once it has been acted upon.

Finally, the court will consider the certainty of the agreement which has been entered into by the parties. In *Vaughan* v. *Vaughan* [1953] 1 QB 762, it was held that a promise by a husband to allow his deserted wife to stay in the matrimonial home did not have contractual force because its vagueness evidenced that it was neither intended to have, nor was understood as having, contractual force. The husband did not state how long she could live there, nor did he indicate the terms on which she could stay. Similarly, the uncertainty of the agreement in *Jones* v. *Padavatton* (above) was a factor which persuaded the court to hold that there was no intention to create legal relations, despite the fact that the daughter had detrimentally relied upon the agreement. The daughter had been in London for six years and this was held to be long enough to complete her Bar exams. The mother's promise of support could not be treated as lasting indefinitely.

6.5 Commercial Agreements

The presumption is that parties to commercial agreements do intend to create legal relations and the presumption is a heavy one. The operation of the presumption can be seen in the case of *Esso Petroleum Ltd* v. *Commissioners of Customs and Excise* [1976] 1 WLR 1. Esso supplied garages with World Cup Coins in 1970, instructing the garages to give away one coin with every four gallons of petrol sold. It was sought to subject these coins to a purchase tax on the ground that they had been sold. On the facts it was held that the coins were not supplied under a contract of sale. But the House of Lords divided on the issue of whether or not there was an intention to create legal relations. The majority, Lord Simon, Lord Wilberforce and Lord Fraser, held that there was an intention to create legal relations. They placed heavy reliance on the onus of proof in commercial transactions and on the fact that Esso envisaged a bargain of some description between the garage owner and the customer. But the minority, Lord Russell and Viscount Dilhorne, relying upon the language of the advertising posters which said that the posters were 'going free' and the minimal value of the coins, held that there was no intention to create legal relations (see too *J Evans & Son (Portsmouth) Ltd* v. *Andrea Merzario Ltd* [1976] 1 WLR 1078).

The presumption may be rebutted by an express term of the contract which states that the parties do not intend to create legal relations. The parties must, however, make their intention clear. Thus agreements for the sale of land are usually made 'subject to contract' and, on that ground, do not create legal relations. At common law a collective agreement entered into between trade unions and an employer was held not to give rise to legal relations (*Ford Motor Co Ltd* v. *AEF* [1969] 1 WLR 339). This common law rule has been reinforced by a statutory presumption to the effect that a collective agreement is conclusively presumed not to have been intended by the parties to be a legally enforceable contract unless it is in writing and expressly provides to the contrary (see s.179, Trade Union and Labour Relations (Consolidation) Act 1992).

The most interesting example in this category is, however, what is known as an honour clause. In *Rose and Frank Co* v. *J R Crompton and Bros Ltd* [1925] AC 445, an agreement stated 'this arrangement is not entered into as a formal or legal agreement, and shall not be subject to legal jurisdiction in the Law Courts but is only a definite expression and record of the purpose and intention of the parties concerned to which they each honourably pledge themselves'. The court held that this agreement was not a legally binding contract because it was not intended that it would have such an effect. The courts interpret such clauses restrictively and clear words must be used to create such an honour clause (see *Home Insurance Co* v. *Administratia Asiguraliror* [1983] 2 Lloyd's Rep 674, 677).

Summary

1   An intention to create legal relations is an essential element in any contract.
2   In cases of domestic and social agreements the presumption is that the parties did not intend to create legal relations. The presumption may be rebutted by 'clear' evidence to the contrary.
3   Factors which may persuade a court to hold that the presumption has been rebutted include the context in which the agreement was made (that is, was it a business context?) and any reliance which has been placed upon the agreement.
4   In cases involving commercial agreements the presumption is that the parties did intend to create legal relations. This presumption is also a 'heavy' one.
5   Clear evidence is required to rebut the presumption. The presumption has been rebutted in cases of agreements to sell land 'subject to contract', collective agreements and 'honour clauses'.

Exercises

1   Is the doctrine of intention to create legal relations based on considerations of policy or does the court genuinely seek to discover the intention of the parties?
2   Reagan Ltd are considering inserting an 'honour clause' in their contract with their major supplier, Jones Ltd. Advise them as to the advantages and disadvantages of such a course of action.
3   John offers £50 to any one who will remove rubbish from his garden. The following people comply with the terms of his offer:

   (a) his wife, Beatrice;
   (b) his ex-wife, Brenda;
   (c) his mistress, Belinda;
   (d) his son, Billy;

(e) his nephew, Brian, whom he had never seen before;
(f) his god-child, Bernard; and
(g) his next-door neighbour, Benedict.

Advise John whether or not, in these circumstances, any legally enforceable contracts have been concluded.

7 Privity

7.1 Introduction

The doctrine of privity of contract consists of two distinct general rules. The first is that a third party cannot be subjected to a burden by a contract to which he is not a party. The second is that a person who is not a party to a contract cannot claim the benefit of it, even though the contract was entered into with the object of benefiting that third party. The former rule is not at all controversial: it would be wholly unreasonable for a legal system to enable two parties to subject a third party to a contractual obligation of which he was completely unaware. The second rule is, however, extremely controversial and is presently under review by the Law Commission (1991). It is this aspect of privity which will form the principal subject-matter of this chapter and any discussion of the reform of privity is confined exclusively to this limb of the doctrine.

English law has not, however, always adopted the rule that a third party cannot take the benefit of a contract to which he is not a party. Some old authorities can be found in the books in which a third party has been held to be entitled to sue upon a contract (see *Dutton* v. *Poole* (1677) 2 Lev 211 and, more generally, Flannigan, 1987). But the doctrine as we know it today was established in two principal cases. The first is *Tweddle* v. *Atkinson* (1861) 1 B & S 393. In this case John Tweddle and William Guy entered into an agreement under which each promised to pay a sum of money to William Tweddle on the occasion of William Tweddle's marriage to William Guy's daughter. The agreement between them further stated that 'it is hereby further agreed . . . that the said William Tweddle has full power to sue the said parties in any Court of law or equity for the aforesaid sums hereby promised and specified'. However, William Guy failed to pay the promised sum and, on his death, William Tweddle sued the executor of William Guy for the promised amount. It was held that he could not maintain such a cause of action. Now there was one obvious reason why he could not sue; he had provided no consideration for William Guy's promise. The consideration had been provided by John Tweddle. Indeed, Wightman, Crompton and Blackburn JJ all appeared to base their judgments on the rule that a stranger to the consideration cannot enforce the promise. There is therefore no need to explain the result in *Tweddle* on the basis of an independent doctrine of privity.

The second leading case is *Dunlop Pneumatic Tyre Company Ltd* v. *Selfridge* [1915] AC 847. In this case the plaintiffs attempted to operate a price fixing ring. For this purpose they extracted a promise from dealers called Dew & Co that they in turn would obtain a written undertaking from any third party to whom they sold Dunlop products that the third party would not sell at a price below Dunlop's list price. The defendants, Selfridge, bought Dunlop products from Dew and gave the required undertaking to Dew but nevertheless sold Dunlop products at less than the list price. In these circumstances Dunlop brought an action for an injunction and damages against Selfridge. The action failed. The majority held that the action failed because Dunlop had provided no consideration for the promise of Selfridge; the consideration had been provided by Dew. But Viscount Haldane, in a judgment which has since assumed considerable significance, held that, independently of the need for consideration, it was a fundamental principle of English law that 'only a person who is a party to a contract can sue on it' and that, because Dunlop were not a party to the contract between Dew and Selfridge, they could not sue on it.

Tweddle and *Dunlop* both demonstrate that there is a very close relationship between the doctrines of privity and consideration. Indeed, on one view, there is no difference between the doctrine of privity and the rule that consideration must move from the promisee (see Furmston, 1960). Privity then becomes swallowed up in the larger rule that consideration must move from the promisee. *Tweddle* and *Dunlop* are both consistent with this view because the majority view in each case was that the plaintiff could not sue because he had not provided consideration for the defendant's promise. Despite the strength of this argument, the more widely accepted view, and the one subsequently adopted by the House of Lords in the cases of *Scruttons Ltd* v. *Midland Silicones Ltd* [1962] AC 446, and *Beswick* v. *Beswick* [1968] AC 58, is that expressed by Viscount Haldane in *Dunlop*, namely that the doctrine of privity is separate and distinct from the rule that consideration must move from the promisee. The following example is often used to illustrate the point. X makes a promise to Y and Z to pay £100 to Z in exchange for consideration provided by Y. In such a case Z is privy to the contract but cannot maintain an action against X unless he has provided consideration for X's promise. In such a case privity and consideration consititute two hurdles for Z to surmount and not one (see *Kepong Prospecting Ltd* v. *Schmidt* [1968] AC 810).

However, even those who maintain that privity and the rule that consideration must move from the promisee are two separate rules, nevertheless concede that there is a very strong relationship between privity and consideration and that it is very difficult to reform one without the other. Yet the Law Commission in a recent Consultation Paper (1991) has argued that it is possible to separate out the two doctrines and to reform the privity rule without also reforming consideration. The Law Commission maintain that the two doctrines raise 'two separate issues of policy'. The first relates to who can enforce the contract and the second concerns the types of promises that can be enforced. The first issue is the concern of the doctrine of privity, while the second is the province of consideration. Thus they conclude that 'we believe that the third party rule, i.e., that third parties cannot enforce contracts made for their benefit, can be reformed without prejudicing the rule that consideration must move from the promisee'. This is a controversial proposition and it is not at all clear what is meant when it is said that the rule that consideration must move from the promisee is not 'prejudiced' by any such reform. Given that the Law Commission concede that both *Tweddle* and *Dunlop* were decided 'on the consideration point', does this mean that they would be decided the same way even under the Law Commission's proposals? If so, what is the point of embarking upon reform of the doctrine of privity if plaintiffs are then to be met by the argument that they still cannot sue because they have not provided any consideration? The view of the Law Commission appears to be that consideration today does not play the multi-functional role which it played in the nineteenth century (see 5.3) so the fact that *Tweddle* was decided 'on the consideration point' does not mean that it would be so decided today. But this view is not one which is universally shared. This is an issue to which we shall return after we have considered the development and the current state of the doctrine of privity in English law.

7.2   The Development of Privity and the Challenge of Lord Denning

Although *Dunlop* appeared to root privity firmly into English law, a serious attempt was subsequently made by Lord Denning to uproot it. His clearest attack was launched in the case of *Smith and Snipes Hall Farm Ltd* v. *River Douglas Catchment Board* [1949] 2 KB 500, when he said that a promise deliberately made was enforceable

> 'not only at the suit of the party who gave the consideration, but also at the suit of one who was not a party to the contract, provided that it was made for his benefit and that he has a sufficient interest to entitle him to enforce it, subject always, of course, to any defences which may be open to him on the merits'.

This judgment is one of enormous significance. It recognises that the doctrine of privity is, in many cases, commercially inconvenient and that it also produces results which are fundamentally unjust. The result in *Dunlop* may be said to be fundamentally unjust because, in the words of Lord Dunedin, it made it possible

> 'for a person to snap his fingers at a bargain deliberately made, a bargain not in itself unfair, and which the person seeking to enforce it has a legitimate interest to enforce'.

Yet, it is important to insert a word of warning here. The source of the injustice which Lord Dunedin identified in *Dunlop* was not the doctrine of privity but the doctrine of consideration: he said that the case was 'apt to nip any budding affection which one might have had for the doctrine of consideration'. This underlines, once again, the difficulty of reforming privity without also reforming the rule that consideration must move from the promisee. The same criticisms can be levelled against both rules.

Despite recognising the inconvenience to which the doctrine of privity gives rise and its potential for unfairness, the House of Lords chose to reject the views of Lord Denning and re-establish the doctrine of privity in the case of *Scruttons Ltd* v. *Midland Silicones Ltd* (above). Lord Reid stated that

> 'although I may regret it, I find it impossible to deny the existence of the general rule that a stranger to a contract cannot in a question with either of the contracting parties take advantage of provisions of the contract, even where it is clear from the contract that some provision in it was intended to benefit him'.

Despite this decision Lord Denning continued his attack upon the doctrine of privity. He launched a further assault in the Court of Appeal in the case of *Beswick* v. *Beswick* [1966] 3 WLR 396, but once again his views were overruled by the House of Lords ([1968] AC 58). *Beswick* concerned a contract under which Peter Beswick sold his coal round and the goodwill of his business to his nephew John Beswick in return for a promise to pay £6 10/- a week to Peter Beswick for the rest of his life and thereafter £5 a week to Peter Beswick's widow for the rest of her life. The nephew ceased making payments to the widow shortly after Peter Beswick's death. The widow brought an action to compel the nephew to continue making the payments and the House of Lords held that she was entitled to such an order. The crucial point to note is that the widow *failed* in the action which she brought in her own name: she was not privy to the contract between Peter Beswick and John Beswick and so could not bring a claim on it. She only succeeded in her capacity as administratrix of her husband's estate (when a person dies the administrator or administratrix of the estate, broadly speaking, acquires the rights of the deceased). So, in the final analysis, no exception was created to the doctrine of privity because it was as if Peter Beswick himself was suing and, of course, he was privy to the original agreement.

While all the judgments delivered in the House of Lords in *Beswick* affirmed the existence of the doctrine of privity, the doctrine did not escape judicial criticism. Lord Reid referred to the report of the Law Revision Committee (Cmnd. 5449) which had reported in 1937 and which had recommended that English law adopt the rule that 'where a contract by its express terms purports to confer a benefit directly on a third party it shall be enforceable by the third party in his own name'. After noting that the Committee's recommendation had not been implemented, he continued:

> 'if one had to contemplate a further long period of Parliamentary procrastination, this House might find it necessary to deal with this matter'.

Some 12 years later, after still further Parliamentary procrastination, Lord Scarman expressed similar sentiments in the case of *Woodar Investment Development Ltd* v. *Wimpey Construction U.K. Ltd* [1980] 1 WLR 227, when he said:

'I hope the House will reconsider *Tweddle* v. *Atkinson* and the other cases which stand guard over this unjust [privity] rule.'

Parliament is still procrastinating but it is suggested that it is highly unlikely that the judges will pick up the gauntlet thrown down by Lord Reid and Lord Scarman. Far from using Parliamentary procrastination as a justification for judicial abolition or reform of the doctrine of privity, such procrastination is likely to be used as a justification for the preservation of the status quo. It would be a bold court which abolished a doctrine which has been accepted as part of English law since 1861. In fact, one of the most striking features of the development of the doctrine of privity is that, while the judges in cases such as *Midland Silicones* and *Woodar* have expressed regret at the present state of the law, they have, Lord Denning apart, been remarkably orthodox in their interpretation and application of the doctrine. Indeed, the decision of the House of Lords in *Midland Silicones* constituted a much criticised extension of the doctrine of privity (see 7.6) and in *Woodar* the House of Lords rejected a device which would have enabled the courts to avoid some of the unfair consequences produced by the application of the privity doctrine (see 7.4). Other such evasive devices have been similarly rejected by the courts (see 7.9). Although occasional instances can be found in which the courts have been prepared to evade privity (see the judgments of Dunn LJ in *Northern Regional Health Authority* v. *Derek Crouch Construction Co Ltd* [1984] 2 All ER 175 and May LJ in *Norwich City Council* v. *Harvey* [1989] 1 All ER 1180), these remain isolated examples and there is little prospect of radical judicial reform of the doctrine of privity on the horizon (contrast the Australian case of *Trident General Insurance Co Ltd* v. *McNiece Bros Pty Ltd* (1988) 165 CLR 107, noted by Reynolds, 1989). The most that can be expected from the courts is a gradual widening of the exceptions to the general rule (see 7.7).

So if reform is to be introduced it is more likely to come from Parliament. As we have noted, reform of the privity rule is under consideration by the Law Commission. A Consultation Paper was issued in 1991 and a report may be forthcoming in 1995. But even if the Commission recommend reform or abolition of the doctrine of privity and produce a draft Bill to give effect to their recommendations, space still has to be found on the Parliamentary timetable to implement such reform. The Law Commission does not have a particularly impressive track record in terms of securing the implementation of their recommendations and, unless Parliament is persuaded that the commercial inconvenience of the doctrine of privity is such that England is losing substantial trade as a result of its continued existence, it is suggested that it is unlikely to rush to implement any proposals brought forward. Notwithstanding these reservations, it remains the case that, if reform is to be brought about, it is more likely to be achieved by Parliament than the courts.

7.3 The Scope of the Doctrine of Privity

Thus far we have been discussing cases in which a third party has sought to enforce a contract to which he was not a party. Before discussing the various exceptions to this rule, it is necessary to consider three other issues relating to the scope of the doctrine of privity. The first relates to the contractual remedies which are available to the promisee against the promisor and whether such remedies can be of any benefit to the third party (7.4), the second is the extent to which a contract between two parties can impose obligations upon a third party (7.5) and the third is the question whether a third party can rely upon an exclusion clause contained in a contract between the plaintiff and another party as a *defence* to the plaintiff's action against him in tort (7.6). Once we have considered these three issues we will discuss the situations in which English law does in fact recognise the existence of enforceable third party rights.

7.4 Action by the Contracting Party

If A and B enter into a contract under which, in return for some act to be performed by B, A agrees to pay £50 to C, a failure by A to pay the £50 to C will constitute a breach of contract between A and B. Although the doctrine of privity precludes C from bringing an action against A, it does not prevent B from suing A. In such a case what remedies does B have against A and can these remedies be of any use to C? There are at least four actions which B could bring against A.

The first possibility is to bring an action for damages for breach of contract. The difficulty here is that B does not appear to have suffered any loss as a result of A's breach and so his damages are likely to be nominal (although if the £50 was to be paid to discharge a debt owed by B to C then B might be entitled to more than nominal damages; see Windeyer J in *Coulls* v. *Bagot's Executor* (1967) 119 CLR 460, 501–2). But even if B could recover substantial damages this would be of no avail to C because the damages recovered by B would be held on his own behalf and not on behalf of C. So B would not be under any obligation to give any portion of the damages recovered to C (although in the case of a debt owed by B to C, B would remain liable to repay the debt).

Secondly, B could seek to recover damages on behalf of C. Some authority for such a proposition was provided by Lord Denning in the case of *Jackson* v. *Horizon Holidays* [1975] 1 WLR 1468. In this case the plaintiff entered into a contract with the defendants under which the defendants promised to provide the plaintiff and his family with a holiday of a certain standard. The holiday did not comply with the promised standard and the defendants admitted that they were in breach of contract. The plaintiff was awarded damages of £1,100, which included £500 for 'mental distress'. The defendants appealed, alleging that the damages awarded were excessive. The appeal was dismissed but the ratio of the decision is unclear. James LJ dismissed the appeal, apparently on the ground that £500 was the correct figure to compensate the plaintiff for the loss which he had suffered (presumably his loss had been increased as a result of his witnessing the distress and disappointment suffered by the other members of his family). Orr LJ simply concurred. However Lord Denning took a more radical approach. He held that £500 was excessive if it was regarded solely as compensation for the plaintiff's own loss. But he nevertheless upheld the award on the ground that the plaintiff could recover, not only in respect of his own loss, but also in respect of the losses suffered by the rest of his family; the latter compensation being held by the plaintiff on trust for the rest of his family. Lord Denning instanced other examples where such a principle would operate: a vicar making a contract for a coach trip for the church choir, a host making a contract with a restaurant for dinner for himself and his friends. In all such cases Lord Denning thought that the contracting party could, in the event of breach, recover damages on behalf of himself and the other members of the group.

However, the view of Lord Denning was disapproved by the House of Lords in *Woodar Investment Development Ltd* v. *Wimpey Construction U.K. Ltd* [1980] 1 WLR 227. Purchasers of land agreed to pay £850 000 to the vendors and £150 000 to a third party on completion of the contract. One question which arose was whether, if the purchasers were in breach of contract, the vendors could recover damages in respect of the £150 000 payable to the third party. In considering this issue, the House of Lords took the opportunity to disapprove of the judgment of Lord Denning in *Jackson*. They did not disapprove of the result of the case; that was justified on the ground that the damages awarded did in fact represent the loss which the plaintiff himself had suffered. But they established in clear terms that English law does not allow a plaintiff to recover damages on behalf of a third party (although see the criticisms levelled against *Woodar* by Dillon J in *Forster* v. *Silvermere Golf and Equestrian Centre Ltd* (1981) 125 SJ 397 where he stated that the rule which it established was 'a blot on our law and thoroughly unjust'). It is, however, important to note that Lord Wilberforce did not shut the door completely on Lord Denning's proposition; he left the door slightly ajar by saying that *Jackson* could possibly be supported as

'an example of a type of contract, examples of which are persons contracting for family holidays, ordering meals in restaurants for a party, hiring a taxi for a group, calling for special treatment'.

This 'special treatment' would be that the contracting party could recover damages on behalf of the group. However, no appellate court has yet applied this 'special treatment'. So, these special cases apart, it is clear that a promisee cannot recover damages on behalf of a third party and so, in our example, B would not be able to recover damages on behalf of C.

Thirdly, B could seek an order of specific performance against A (that is an order of the court that the promisor carry out his promise). This was of course what happened in *Beswick* v. *Beswick* (above). Such a remedy would be of supreme significance to C because it would ensure that he obtained the £50 promised to him by A. However it must be noted that specific performance is a discretionary remedy which, as a general rule, is only available where damages are inadequate and, while it was available on the facts of *Beswick*, it should not be assumed that it is widely available (see further 21.9). B would therefore have to show that damages were not an adequate remedy and that none of the traditional bars to specific performance were applicable before such an order could be made. It should also be noted that there does not appear to be any procedure by which C could compel B to sue A, so that B could refuse to sue A and thereby leave C without a remedy. If the promise which B sought to enforce was a negative one then B could, in an appropriate case, be entitled to an injunction to restrain the threatened breach of contract by A (see further 21.10).

Finally, if the promise made by A to B had been a promise not to sue C and A nevertheless, in breach of contract with B, had commenced an action against C, B could ask the court, in its discretion, to stay the proceedings against C (*Snelling* v. *John G Snelling* [1973] QB 87, but contrast *Gore* v. *Van Der Lann* [1967] 2 QB 31).

7.5 Interference with Contractual Rights

As we noted at the beginning of this chapter, the general rule is that a third party cannot be subjected to a burden by a contract to which he is not a party. However a contract between two parties may nevertheless impose certain obligations upon a third party. The first such obligation is that a third party must not seek to persuade one contracting party to break his contract with the other. Thus, it is a tort for a third party, without lawful justification, to interfere intentionally or recklessly with a contract between A and B, either by persuading A to break his contract with B or by preventing A from performing his contract with B by the use of some direct or indirect unlawful means. The case of *Lumley* v. *Gye* (1853) 2 El & Bl 216, provides a useful illustration of the operation of this tort. The plaintiff was a theatre owner who entered into a contract with a famous opera singer, Miss Wagner, under which she was to sing only at his theatre for a period of time. The defendant, who was the owner of a rival theatre, procured Miss Wagner to break her contract with the plaintiff by promising to pay her more than she was receiving from the plaintiff. When Miss Wagner, in breach of contract, refused to continue to perform at the plaintiff's theatre, the plaintiff brought an action against the defendant alleging that the defendant had induced Miss Wagner to break her contract with him and that this had caused him loss. It was held that the defendant had indeed committed a tort and the plaintiff was therefore entitled to claim damages from the defendant to compensate him for his loss.

It has also been argued that a third party who acquires property in the knowledge that that property is affected by a contract between two other parties is bound by the terms of that contract and may be restrained from acting inconsistently with the terms of the contract. This indeed occurred in the case of *Tulk* v. *Moxhay* (1848) 2 Ph 774. The plaintiff sold land subject to a restrictive covenant that the land must not be built upon but must be preserved in its existing condition. After a number of conveyances the land was eventually conveyed to the defendant, who had notice of the covenant but nevertheless sought to build on the land. It was held that the plaintiff was entitled to an injunction to restrain the proposed building. The defendant was therefore bound by an agreement to which he was not a party simply because he had notice of the covenant. The question which arises is whether this principle applies only within the rather rarefied atmosphere of land law and restrictive covenants or whether it is of general application. The answer is that it is a matter of land law and, even within the confines of land law, the scope of the principle has been narrowed; for example the plaintiff must now show that he has retained ownership of other land in the immediate vicinity which is capable of being benefited by the covenant.

However the prospect of extending the scope of *Tulk* v. *Moxhay* beyond the province of restrictive covenants was held out by the Privy Council in *Lord Strathcona Steamship Co* v. *Dominion Coal Co Ltd* [1926] AC 108. The owner of a ship chartered her to the plaintiffs for a number of summer seasons. The owner sold the ship during the winter season. After a series of sales the ship was bought by the defendants who, although aware of the charterparty at the date of purchase, nevertheless refused to deliver the ship to the plaintiffs for the summer season. The Privy Council held that the defendants were bound by the terms of the charterparty and granted the plaintiffs an injunction to restrain the defendants from using the ship in any way inconsistent with the terms of the charterparty.

The result of the case does not seem to be entirely unfair. A person who buys property subject to the rights of third parties will generally pay a lower price for the property and, if he could then take advantage of the rules of privity to disregard those rights, he would thereby free the property and be able to sell it at a considerable profit. Nevertheless, it is difficult to reconcile *Strathcona* with the rule that a contract of hire only creates personal and not proprietary rights and that therefore the purchaser should be free to ignore the contract of hire. *Strathcona* is therefore an extremely controversial case (see Gardner, 1982 and

Tettenborn, 1982) and, indeed, in the case of *Port Line Ltd* v. *Ben Line Steamers Ltd* [1958] 2 QB 146, Diplock J said that he thought the case was wrongly decided and refused to follow it (contrast *Swiss Bank Corporation* v. *Lloyds Bank Ltd* [1979] Ch 548 where Browne-Wilkinson J followed *Strathcona* on the ground that it was the equitable counterpart of the tort of knowing interference with contractual rights). The present standing of *Strathcona* is therefore unclear. In *Law Debenture Trust Corporation* v. *Ural Caspian Oil Corporation Ltd* [1993] 1 WLR 138, 144, Hoffmann J accepted that *Strathcona* was still good law but stated that the real difficulty was that 'neither the *Strathcona* case nor the *Swiss Bank* case make it entirely clear when the principle applies and when it does not'. Only two things are clear. The first is that *Strathcona* 'does not provide a panacea for outflanking the doctrine of privity of contract' (*Law Debenture Trust Corporation* v. *Ural Caspian Oil Corporation Ltd* (above)). The second is that it can only apply where the purchaser has actual knowledge of the contract at the time of the purchase and the only remedy available is an injunction restraining the purchaser from acting inconsistently with the contract. The plaintiff cannot obtain a specific performance order requiring the purchaser to carry out the terms of the contract (*Port Line Ltd* v. *Ben Line Steamers Ltd* (above); *Law Debenture Trust Corporation* v. *Ural Caspian Oil Corporation Ltd* (above)).

7.6 Exclusion Clauses and Third Parties

In some cases defendants have sought to rely on an exclusion clause contained in a contract between the plaintiff and another party as a defence to the plaintiff's action in tort. In such cases, in the absence of an implied contract between the plaintiff and the defendant, defendants have sought to invoke the doctrine of 'vicarious immunity', that is to say they have argued that, as employees or agents of a contracting party (the contracting party being the party with whom the plaintiff has contracted), they are entitled to the benefit of any exclusion clause negotiated by that contracting party. Some authority for the existence of such a doctrine can be found in the case of *Elder Dempster* v. *Paterson, Zochonis and Co* [1924] AC 522 (for the different interpretations of this confusing case see Treitel, 1991, pp. 552–3).

But this authority was decisively rejected by the House of Lords in *Scruttons Ltd* v. *Midland Silicones Ltd* (above). The plaintiffs, who were the owners of a drum of chemicals, entered into a contract with a firm of carriers for the transportation of the drum. Under the contract the carriers limited their liability to the plaintiffs to $500. Stevedores, who were employed by the carriers to discharge the drum, negligently dropped it and the plaintiffs brought an action in tort against them in respect of the resulting damage. The stevedores sought to rely on the limitation clause contained in the contract between the plaintiffs and the carriers but it was held that they could not do so because they were not privy to that contract. The House of Lords held that English law knew of no doctrine of vicarious immunity and that, in any case, the limitation clause only referred to the carriers and so was incapable of providing protection for the stevedores. This conclusion gave rise to considerable commercial inconvenience because it made it extremely difficult for an employer to give his employees and agents the benefit of an exclusion clause negotiated by the employer, even where the exclusion clause was a valid and legitimate method of allocating the risks under the contract between the employer and the plaintiff.

So it is not surprising that attempts have been made to mitigate the rigours of *Midland Silicones*. Furmston has argued (1960) that, in an appropriate case, the exclusion clause in the contract between the plaintiff and the carrier should enable the defendant to invoke the defence of *volenti non fit injuria* where it can be shown from the exclusion clause that the plaintiff willingly accepted the risk of injury as a result of the negligence of the third party. Alternatively, it could be argued that the effect of the exclusion clause is, in an appropriate case, to demonstrate that the plaintiff has assented to the risk of damage by the third party and that the effect of the exclusion clause is therefore to negative or limit the duty of care which would otherwise be owed by the third party to the plaintiff (see Lord Roskill in *Junior Books Ltd* v. *Veitchi Ltd* [1983] 1 AC 520, 546 and see also *Norwich City Council* v. *Harvey* [1989] 1 All ER 1180). These possibilities have not really been developed in the courts. Rather the courts have sought to find the existence of a contract between the plaintiff and the third party, under which the third party can enjoy the same immunity as that given to his principal under the contract.

The origins of this approach can be found in the judgment of Lord Reid in *Midland Silicones*. Lord Reid thought that stevedores might be able to claim the protection of an exclusion clause

> 'if (first) the bill of lading makes it clear that the stevedore is intended to be protected by the provisions in it which limit liability, (secondly) the bill of lading makes it clear that the carrier, in addition to contracting for these provisions on his own behalf, is also contracting as agent for the stevedore that these provisions should apply to the stevedore, (thirdly) the carrier has authority from the stevedore to do that, or perhaps later ratification by the stevedore would suffice, and (fourthly) that any difficulties about consideration moving from the stevedore were overcome'.

Lord Reid therefore envisaged that, at the moment the carrier signed the contract, two contracts would come into existence; the first between the owner and the carrier and the second between the owner and the stevedore. But, at that moment in time, it is extremely difficult to find any consideration supplied by the stevedore; indeed, at the moment of signing the contract, it might not be known which firm of stevedores is to unload the goods. Lord Reid's solution was therefore not entirely satisfactory.

The issue was reconsidered by the Privy Council in *New Zealand Shipping Co Ltd* v. *A.M. Satterthwaite & Co Ltd* (*The Eurymedon*) [1975] AC 154, in which the stevedores were held to be entitled to the benefit of the exclusion clause contained in the contract between the consignors and the carriers. The fact situation was similar to *Midland Silicones* except that the bill of lading was much more complex and clearly sought to give the stevedores the benefit of the exclusion clause. The first three of Lord Reid's four conditions were satisfied. The bill of lading expressly extended the benefit of the exclusion clause to any servants, agents and independent contractors employed by the carriers. The carriers had also contracted as the agents of the stevedores and they were authorised by the stevedores so to act. The principal problem lay in locating the consideration provided by the stevedores for the consignor's offer of immunity and in accommodating the solution within the offer and acceptance framework. The solution adopted by the Privy Council proceeded in the following stages. First, they held that when the consignors signed the bill of lading they made a unilateral offer to all the world that anyone who unloaded their goods at the port of discharge would be entitled to the benefit of the exclusion clause. Secondly, they held that this offer was accepted by the stevedores unloading the goods at the port of discharge and at that moment a binding contract came into existence. The consideration supplied by the stevedores was the performance of their contractual duty owed to the carriers and, as we noted at 5.16, performance of a contractual duty owed to a third party is good consideration for a promise given by the plaintiff.

Although this analysis is an improvement upon the solution advocated by Lord Reid in *Midland Silicones*, it gives rise to three further problems. The first problem is that a court may decide that the main contract cannot be interpreted as an offer of immunity to the sub-contractor and, equally, the sub-contractor may find it difficult to persuade the court that the main contractor was acting as his agent when he entered into the main contract (*Southern Water Authority* v. *Carey* [1985] 2 All ER 1077). The second difficulty is that, as we have already noted (3.9), an 'acceptance' is not generally valid if it was made in ignorance of the existence of the offer. In most of these cases, when the stevedores unloaded the goods, they did so in pursuance of a contract with the carriers and were unlikely to be aware of the owner's offer. Does this mean that the stevedores cannot claim the benefit of the exclusion clause? The Privy Council in *The New York Star* [1981] 1 WLR 138, brushed aside such technicalities and deprecated the use of such 'fine distinctions' in an effort to diminish the applicability of the principles established in *The Eurymedon*. So it would appear that there is no requirement that the stevedores must be aware of the offer at the time of their acceptance (see too *Celthene Pty Ltd* v. *WKJ Hauliers Pty Ltd* [1981] 1 NSWLR 606).

The third problem is that the *Eurymedon* solution cannot be invoked by the stevedore who damages the goods before he starts to unload them because the acceptance of the owner's offer only takes place when the stevedore begins to unload the goods (see *Raymond Burke Motors Ltd* v. *Mersey Docks & Harbour Co* [1986] 1 Lloyd's Rep 155). Despite this last difficulty, the approach adopted by the majority in *The Eurymedon* displays a welcome, if rather isolated, willingness to evade the undesirable consequences of the doctrine of privity, even although it is at the cost of a rather cavalier approach to the rules of offer, acceptance and consideration (contrast the approach adopted by the majority of the Supreme Court of Canada in the seminal case of *London Drugs Ltd* v. *Kuenhe & Nagel International Ltd* (1992) 97 DLR (4th) 261, where the court chose not to adopt a *Eurymedon* type analysis but instead held that employees were entitled to take the benefit of a contractual limitation clause contained in a contract between their employer and the plaintiffs if (i) the limitation of liability clause either expressly or impliedly extended its benefit to the employees seeking to rely on it and, (ii) the employees were acting in the course of their employment and had been performing the very services provided for in the contract at the time at which the loss was suffered).

7.7   Evading the Rule

As we noted above (7.2), the courts are unlikely to abolish the doctrine of privity. Until such time as Parliament chooses to enact any recommendations for reform which the Law Commission may make, the most likely development is for the courts to widen the scope of the exceptional situations in which a third party can sue to enforce a contract. The importance of these exceptions should not be underestimated; they are examples of cases in which English law does recognise the existence of enforceable third party rights.

It should be noted that there is some disagreement as to what exactly constitutes an exception to the rule. For example, in the case of collateral contracts (7.8) and agency (7.9) the plaintiff or principal is regarded as being privy to the contract and so it could be argued that they are not true exceptions to the rule. But they are treated as exceptions here because in effect, if not in theory, they undermine the privity rule. With this point in mind let us give further consideration to these exceptions.

7.8   Collateral Contracts

One useful device which may be available to a court which wishes to evade the clutches of the doctrine of privity is to find the existence of a collateral contract between the promisor and the third party. A good illustration of the utility of the collateral contract device is the case of *Shanklin Pier Ltd*

v. *Detel Products Ltd* [1951] 2 KB 854. Contractors employed by the plaintiffs to paint the plaintiffs' pier were instructed by the plaintiffs to use paint manufactured by the defendants. The contract to purchase the paint was actually made between the contractors and the defendants but a representation was made by the defendants to the plaintiffs that the paint would last for seven years. The paint only lasted three months. It was held that the plaintiffs were entitled to bring an action for breach of contract against the defendants on the ground that there was a collateral contract between them to the effect that the paint would last for seven years, the consideration for which was the instruction given by the plaintiffs to their contractors to order the paint from the defendants.

The collateral contract device has also been usefully employed in cases of hire-purchase. In many cases consumers are unaware of the exact legal technicalities of a hire-purchase agreement. These technicalities are that the dealer will sell the goods to the finance house who in turn will lease the goods to the consumer on hire-purchase terms. Thus the contracts are between the dealer and the finance house and between the finance house and the consumer; there is no contract between the dealer and the consumer. But in *Andrews* v. *Hopkinson* [1957] 1 QB 229, it was held that the dealers' false warranty as to the roadworthiness of a car gave rise to a collateral contract between the dealer and the consumer, thereby enabling the consumer to bring an action against the dealer for breach of contract.

The limitation of the collateral contract device, however, is that the court must be able to find evidence upon which to imply such a contract and that consideration must be found to support the collateral contract. The latter requirement can give rise to some difficulty, as is illustrated by the case of *Charnock* v. *Liverpool Corporation* [1968] 1 WLR 1498. The plaintiff's car was damaged in an accident and he left his car to be repaired by the defendant garage, the defendants having promised to do the repairs reasonably quickly. The car was repaired under a contract between the plaintiff's insurance company and the defendants. But it was held that the plaintiff could nevertheless bring an action in respect of the defendants' failure to carry out the repair reasonably quickly. It was held that there was consideration to support the collateral contract because, although there was no detriment to the plaintiff, the defendants were benefited by virtue of the opportunity given to them to enter into a contract with the insurance company for the repair of the car (note that Treitel, 1976, treats this as a case of 'invented' consideration and Atiyah, 1986c, p. 223 argues that this is a case of 'fictitious consideration' because the 'real' consideration was supplied by the insurers and not by the plaintiff).

7.9 Agency

It would cause great commercial hardship if a businessman who appointed an agent to enter into a contract on his behalf was prevented by the doctrine of privity from suing upon that contract himself. So the doctrine of agency exists to give the businessman such a right of action. An agency relationship arises where one party, the agent, is authorised by another, the principal, to negotiate and to enter into contracts on behalf of the principal. Once an agency relationship is created the agent is thereby authorised to commit the principal to contractual relationships with third parties. Agency is now a specialised area of law and we will not deal with it in this book, except to give a very brief account of the relationship between agency and privity (for fuller consideration of the doctrine of agency see Treitel, 1991, ch. 17).

When the agent discloses to the third party that he is acting as an agent of a principal and he concludes the contract within the scope of his authority, the general rule is that the contract is made between the principal and the third party and the agent cannot sue or be sued on the contract. Such a transaction is not generally regarded as an exception to the doctrine of privity because the function of the agent is to negotiate the contract on behalf of his principal and once he has done that he 'drops out of the picture', leaving his principal as the true party to the contract.

However there are certain aspects of the law of agency which appear to flout the doctrine of privity. One such aspect is the rule that a principal may, in certain limited circumstances, sue upon the contract even though the agent has not disclosed to the third party that he is acting as an agent for the principal (see Treitel, 1991, pp. 631–4). In these situations the third party can find himself in a contractual relationship with a person of whose existence he was blissfully unaware at the time that he entered into the contract. The ability of a principal to ratify the unauthorised act of his agent is also said to be an exception to the doctrine of privity (see Treitel, 1991, pp. 626–30).

Privity also appears to be flouted by the controversial case of *Watteau* v. *Fenwick* [1893] 1 QB 346. In this case the agent, who was the manager of a public house, was prohibited by his principal (the owner of the public house) from purchasing cigars on credit for the purpose of the business. Despite this prohibition, the agent purchased cigars in his own name on credit from the plaintiffs, who were unaware of the existence of the principal and therefore unaware of the prohibition placed upon the agent. It was held that the principal was nevertheless bound by the contract and was liable to the plaintiffs. The rationale of the case appears to be that the principal, by employing the agent as his manager, was regarded as having given the agent the authority which was usually given to managers of a public house, which included the authority to purchase cigars. Further, the agreement between the principal and agent, under which the agent's authority was restricted, was not binding on a third party who was unaware of that restriction. So the principal was bound. But *Watteau* demonstrates that agency and privity are strange bedfellows. It is highly anomalous that the existence of an agency relationship should enable a plaintiff to sue a defendant who expressly disavows any intention to benefit the plaintiff third party, whereas privity, in cases such as *Tweddle*

v. *Atkinson* (see 7.1), prevents a plaintiff third party from suing a defendant who has expressly declared an intention to benefit the plaintiff.

7.10 The Trust Concept

We have already noted that if A and B enter into a contract under which, in return for some act to be performed by B, A agrees to pay £50 to C, a failure by A to pay the £50 to C will constitute a breach of contract between A and B. There is no doubt that, in such a case, B has a right to sue A for breach of contract. A further question which may be asked is: in what capacity does B hold his contractual right to sue A for breach of contract? The answer to this question would appear to be an obvious one, namely that he holds it in his own capacity and for his own benefit. An alternative answer, however, is that he holds his contractual right to sue A on trust for the benefit of C. A trust is an equitable obligation to hold property on behalf of another. In this case the subject matter of the trust is the right of B to sue A for breach of contract and that right of action can be held by B on trust for C (it is often referred to by lawyers as a 'trust of the promise'). The property right created by the trust enables the beneficiary, C, to enforce the trust in his own name, although he was not a party to the agreement.

Such an analysis was adopted by the House of Lords in *Les Affréteurs Réunis* v. *Walford* [1919] AC 801. A term of a charterparty between a shipowner and a charterer stated that the shipowner would pay a commission to the broker who had negotiated the contract but was not party to the contract. It was held that the broker was a beneficiary of the trust, the subject matter of the trust being the contractual right of action created by the promise of the shipowner to pay the broker, and that, as the beneficiary, he could enforce the promise. On the facts of *Walford*, the finding of an intention to create a trust of the promise appears to be no more than a fiction designed to do justice on the facts of the case by enabling the broker to sue the shipowner. The device may have been inelegant and artificial, but it effectively evaded the doctrine of privity. Indeed, Corbin argued (1930) that this was a device by which privity might be discarded in its entirety when a third party could show that he was the intended beneficiary of a promise and greater use of the trust of a promise device was recently urged by Mason CJ and Wilson J in the High Court of Australia in *Trident General Insurance Co Ltd* v. *McNiece Bros Pty Ltd* (1988) 165 CLR 107.

However, since *Walford* was decided, the English courts have had a change of heart and this device is now practically defunct. The courts have undermined this device by insisting upon strict proof of an intention to create a trust of the promise (*Re Schebsman* [1944] Ch 83), instead of treating the requirement of intention as a fiction which simply enabled the court to invoke the doctrine. To establish the existence of a trust of the promise it must now be shown that the promisee intended the benefit of the contract to be enjoyed by the third party (*Vandepitte* v. *Preferred Accident Corp. of New York* [1933] AC 70) and the promise to benefit the third party must be intended to be irrevocable. By a rigorous insistence upon compliance with these requirements, the courts have rendered this device practically insignificant.

7.11   The Role of the Law of Tort

Instead of bringing a contractual action, a third party may elect to bring an action against the promisor in the tort of negligence. Three cases illustrate this process. The first is *Ross* v. *Caunters* [1980] Ch 297. The defendant, who was a solicitor, failed to inform a testator that attestation of a will by the spouse of a beneficiary would invalidate any gift to that beneficiary. The plaintiff, whose husband had signed the will, sued the defendant in negligence for the loss of her gift under the will. It was held that the plaintiff was entitled to recover from the defendant because the defendant had been negligent and there was a close relationship of proximity between the defendant and the plaintiff since the defendant could forsee that the plaintiff, as an individual, would suffer damage as a result of his negligence. Now the point to note here is that the plaintiff was not privy to the contract between the solicitor and the testator, nor had she provided any consideration, but the *effect* of granting a remedy in tort was to put the plaintiff in the position which she would have been in had the contract between the defendant and the testator been performed by the defendant with reasonable care. Rules of privity and consideration were circumvented by framing the action in tort (for criticism see Jaffey, 1985).

Notwithstanding these criticisms, *Ross* was recently followed by the Court of Appeal in our second case, *White* v. *Jones* [1993] 3 WLR 730 (an appeal is, at the time of writing, before the House of Lords). The facts were very similar to *Ross* except that in this case the solicitors' negligence took the form of an unreasonable delay in drawing up the will. The testator had previously fallen out with the plaintiffs (his daughters) and had cut them out of his will. He was later reconciled with them and so he instructed the defendants to prepare a new will which was to include bequests of £9000 to each of the plaintiffs. Unfortunately, the testator died before the new will could be executed. The plaintiffs successfully brought a claim in tort against the defendants and recovered £9000 each in damages on the ground that the defendants had been negligent in causing unnecessary delay in the drawing up of the will. The interesting point here relates to the role of contractual doctrines, such as privity, in the resolution of the case. The defendants argued that 'privity of contract would be undermined by the recognition of a duty owed by the solicitor to the beneficiary'. But Steyn LJ rejected the argument in a robust fashion stating that the argument was 'simply an echo of the long buried notion that because there is no liability in contract there can be none in tort'. Sir Donald Nicholls VC argued that a 'coherent system of law demands that there should be an effective remedy' against the defendants. He noted that the law of contract was unable to provide an effective remedy both because of the privity doctrine (which prevented the plaintiffs from bringing a claim) and because a claim by the testator's estate in contract was of no use to the plaintiffs (because any money so received would have been distributed under the will from which the plaintiffs had been cut out) and so he resorted to the tort of negligence for a remedy. He concluded that it was 'eminently fair, just and reasonable that the solicitor should be liable in damages' to the plaintiffs in tort because 'otherwise there is no sanction in respect of the solicitor's breach of his professional duty'. In this way the Court of Appeal gave its express approval to the use of the tort of negligence to fill in the gaps of the law of contract, in this case a gap caused by the privity rule.

The third and more infamous case is *Junior Books Ltd* v. *The Veitchi Co Ltd* [1983] 1 AC 520. The defendants were contractors who specialised in laying floors. The plaintiffs had entered into a contract with the main contractors for the construction of a factory but they nominated the defendants to lay the factory floor. So the main contractors sub-contracted the laying of the floor to the defendants. The plaintiffs argued that the floor had been laid defectively by the defendants and claimed damages from them, including the cost of replacing the factory floor. Thus they were seeking to be put in the position in which they would have been if the sub-contractors had laid the floor in accordance with their contract with the main contractors. Once again it should be noted that there was no contract between the defendants and the plaintiffs. The contracts were between the defendants and the main contractors and between the main contractors and the plaintiffs. Nevertheless, the House of Lords held that the plaintiffs were entitled to succeed in an action in tort against the defendants because of the extremely close relationship between the parties. The crucial elements in this relationship appear to be, firstly, the fact that the plaintiffs relied upon the skill of the defendants in laying the floor, as indicated by the fact that they nominated the defendants to do the work and, secondly, the fact that the defendants assumed an obligation towards the plaintiffs. It is not easy to see in what respects the defendants did assume an obligation towards the plaintiffs because the contractual relationships between the parties were structured in such a way that the defendants did *not* assume any direct responsibility towards the plaintiffs. In later cases courts have held that the assumption of a contractual responsibility by a sub-contractor to a main contractor makes it very difficult to establish that the sub-contractor has assumed an additional obligation in tort to the plaintiff (see *Simaan General Contracting Co* v. *Pilkington Glass Ltd (No 2)* [1988] QB 758).

In any event *Junior Books* is a highly anomalous case. The damaged floor was not the cause of personal injury, nor did it damage any other property of the plaintiffs. It was simply the case that the floor was less valuable than it would have been had the contracts been performed according to their terms. To allow the plaintiffs to recover in respect of such damage in a tort action conflicts with the general rule that, where the defect simply renders the product less valuable, the plaintiff's remedy, if any, lies in contract (see *D & F Estates Ltd* v. *Church Commissioners for England* [1989] AC 177).

The tort action therefore provides only a limited exception to the doctrine of privity. The most obvious limitation is that the promisor must have been negligent; it would not avail the plaintiff in *Tweddle* v. *Atkinson* where the defendant was not negligent but simply refused to carry out his promise. The second limitation is that there must be an extremely close relationship between the plaintiff and the defendant in order to justify the imposition of a duty of care upon the defendant.

7.12   Assignment

We have already seen that, if A and B enter into a contract under which, in return for some act to be performed by B, A agrees to pay £50 to C, C will be prevented by the doctrine of privity from suing to enforce the contract. However if B validly assigns to C his contractual rights against A then, provided the assignment has been validly made, C may sue A for the money. It is highly anomalous that English law allows for the assignment of rights which have already been created, but prevents A and B from conferring enforceable rights upon C from the very outset of their agreement.

Although at common law it was not possible to assign rights, rights can be assigned in equity or under s.136(1) of the Law of Property Act 1925 (for the detailed requirements of each method of assignment see Treitel, 1991, ch. 16). The principal disadvantage of assignment from the perspective of the assignee is that any defence which would have succeeded against the assignor will also succeed against the assignee; the assignee takes 'subject to equities'.

7.13   Negotiable Instruments

A negotiable instrument is a type of written promise under which the right to enforce that promise may be transferred either by delivery or by delivery and indorsement of the person to whom the debt was payable. The principal categories of negotiable instruments are bills of exchange, cheques and promissory notes. For example, a cheque is a written order by a person ('the drawer') to his bank ('the drawee') to pay on demand a stated sum of money to a named person. Now that person can transfer the cheque to another party and that third party can demand payment from the bank, even though he was not privy to any contract with the bank and has not himself furnished the bank with any consideration. The advantage of a negotiable instrument as compared with an assignment is that a bona fide holder for value who is without notice of any defect in the title of the transferor obtains a good title and is able to demand payment and therefore does not take 'subject to equities'.

7.14 Statutory Exceptions

There are a number of statutory exceptions to the doctrine of privity. These exceptions have no coherent rationale but are largely responses to the exigencies of the moment. The importance of these statutory exceptions should not be underestimated. One commentator has remarked that 'but for the statutory exceptions, the doctrine of privity would undoubtedly have been abolished long ago upon it having become widely appreciated that, for example, third parties had no right to the proceeds of life insurance policies taken out for their benefit' (Flannigan, 1987). Thus section 11 of the Married Women's Property Act 1882 states that where a man has insured his life for the benefit of his wife and children the policy shall create a trust in favour of the objects therein named. Third parties have been allowed, in certain circumstances, to sue on fire or marine insurance policies (Marine Insurance Act 1906 s.14(2)) and an injured third party may recover compensation from the insured's insurance company once he has obtained judgment against the insured (Road Traffic Act 1972 s.148(4)). Section 56 of the Law of Property Act 1925 provides that 'a person may take an immediate or other interest in land or other property, or the benefit of any condition, right of entry, covenant or agreement over or respecting land or other property, although he may not be named as a party to the conveyance or other instrument'. Finally, under section 2 of the Carriage of Goods by Sea Act 1992 a person who becomes the lawful holder of a bill of lading shall, by virtue of becoming the holder of the bill, have transferred to and vested in him all rights of suit under the contract of carriage as if he had been a party to that contract from the outset (similar principles apply to sea waybills and to ship's delivery orders).

7.15 The Need for Reform?

Although English law recognises the existence of a number of exceptions to the doctrine of privity, it cannot be claimed that the present state of the law is satisfactory. There are a number of deficiencies. The first is that the doctrine of privity fails to give effect to the expressed intentions of the parties (see, for example, *Tweddle* v. *Atkinson* (above, 7.1)). The second is that the numerous exceptions make the law unduly complex. Some of the evasive devices used are artificial, as in the case of the trust of the promise device and the collateral contract device. The contorted reasoning of the Privy Council in *The Eurymedon* demonstrates the unnecessary complexities which can arise in seeking to give effect to the intention of the contracting parties in extending the benefit of an exclusion clause to a third party. The third deficiency is that the doctrine is commercially inconvenient (see, for example, the difficulties which have arisen in the stevedore cases (7.6) and the fact that commercial transactions such as insurance and carriage of goods by sea have had to be put on a statutory footing). The final deficiency is that the application of the doctrine can sometimes lead to results which are fundamentally unjust (see *Tweddle* v. *Atkinson* (above)). The argument for reform has therefore been largely won. The difficulty which now arises relates to the scope and shape of any reform. Here consensus has not yet been achieved. The difficulties which will arise in relation to the reform of the doctrine of privity should not be underestimated.

The most comprehensive proposals for reform in this country have recently been put forward by the Law Commission in a Consultation Paper (1991, and see Beatson, 1992). The Law Commission's provisional recommendation is that a 'third party should be able to enforce a contract in which the parties intend that he should receive the benefit of the promised performance and also intend to create a legal obligation enforceable by him'. The first part of this test will be relatively easy to satisfy because in cases such as *Tweddle* v. *Atkinson* it is obvious that the third party (the son) is to receive the benefit of the promised performance (in that case the money). The difficulty will lie in satisfying the second test. Did the parties intend to give the third party a legally enforceable right or did they intend the arrangement to be binding only as between the two of them? Again this would not be much of a problem on the facts of *Tweddle* as there was an express statement in the agreement that the son was to have a right of action. But must there be such an express statement before the court will conclude that there was an intention to create a legal obligation enforceable by the third party? The cause of certainty would be enhanced if the right was so limited but such a restriction would cause practical problems in certain industries. For example, in the stevedore cases (7.6) it will probably not be clear at the time at which the contract of carriage is concluded who is to unload the goods at their destination, so express designation of the third party in the contract is impractical. So should the law allow express designation of a class or should the court have power to imply that it was the intention of the parties to create such a legal obligation? The Law Commission suggest that to require express designation of the third party would be too restrictive but have not yet formed a final view. How would the double intention test apply to the facts of *Junior Books* v. *Veitchi* (7.11)? Could the defendants argue that their contract with the main contractors was the limit of their obligations and that it could not be implied that they intended to create in the plaintiffs a legal obligation enforceable by them? And would the Law Commission's proposals apply to the facts of *White* v. *Jones* (7.11; see the discussion of this point at paras 5.41–5.43 of the Consultation Paper)?

Other practical problems will arise if reform is to be implemented. If the third party sues on the contract, will the defendant be able to rely on any defences which would have been available to him in an action brought by the other party to the contract? It can be argued that it is unfair to the third party that he should be bound by terms of which he was unaware, but it is equally unfair to the defendant to allow his defences to be outflanked by such third party action. The Law Commission provisionally recommend that 'the rights of the third party against the promisor should be subject to the promisor's defences, set-offs and counterclaims which would have been available to the promisor in an action by the promisee'.

Problems will also arise where the two parties to the original contract purport to vary or cancel their agreement. Can they do so without incurring liability to the third party? At what point in time does the third party acquire a right of action so that his consent must be obtained to any variation or cancellation of the contract? There are a number of possible answers. The parties could never have such a right, or they could have it until the third party is aware of the contract, until the third party adopts the contract, until he accepts or assents to the contract, or until he materially alters his position in reliance upon the contract. It is very difficult to decide which approach is the best one for all cases and the Law Commission has left the matter open for consultation. Difficulties will also arise in relation to double liability. If the third party has a cause of action as well as the original party to the contract, the party in breach could be made to pay twice for the same breach. Steps must be taken to reduce the possibility of double liability. And what about the existing exceptions relating to insurance, road traffic etc where English law presently recognises the existence of third party rights? The Law Commission provisionally recommend that 'in the interests of certainty, existing legislative exceptions to the third party rule should be preserved', although in the short run this will create a rather odd patchwork of third party rights. Finally, will it be possible to circumvent any limitation placed upon the scope of the third party right by an action in tort (see, for example, *Junior Books*, which was a Scottish case and Scots law recognises the existence of enforceable third party rights, yet the plaintiffs still had to have resort to the law of tort to secure a remedy)?

These are all difficult questions and they must be faced up to by any advocate of reform of the present privity rule. But there is one problem which is peculiar to the Law Commission's proposals, which is that they do not seek to reform consideration at the same time. When the Law Revision Committee put forward proposals for reform in 1937, they also included reform of consideration within their proposals. The Law Commission, on the other hand, expressly state that the rule that consideration must move from the promisee will not be 'prejudiced' by their proposed reform. The scope of the consideration rule will therefore become crucial to the success or otherwise of the proposed reform. How will it apply to cases such as *Tweddle* and *Dunlop* (see 7.1)? Who is the 'promisee' for the purposes of the rule that consideration must move from the promisee? The Law Commission would appear to be of the view that, once the parties to the contract have provided consideration, the third party may take advantage of the consideration which has been provided by these contracting parties. Such a solution could be consistent with an extended bargain view of consideration with the third party simply joining in the bargain which the other two parties have made. On the other hand, it is possible to interpret the requirement that consideration must move from the promisee as meaning that 'consideration must move from the party seeking to enforce the promise' (Treitel, 1991, p. 527). On this analysis of the rule, *Tweddle* and *Dunlop* would be wholly unaffected by the Law Commission's proposals, notwithstanding the fact that in *Tweddle* both fathers expressly declared that the plaintiff was to have a right of action on the agreement. On the other hand, it can be argued that, even if the second view of the consideration rule is accepted, the effect of the decision of the Court of Appeal in *Williams* v. *Roffey Bros & Nicholls (Contractors) Ltd* [1991] 1 QB 1 (see 5.11), is radically to reduce the practical problems caused by the doctrine of consideration so that the courts could find consideration in most of these cases. The relationship between the proposed new right of action and the doctrine of consideration should be addressed more clearly so that the new right of action is not emasculated at its birth in consideration difficulties (although it can be argued that, in practice, problems will not arise here because a court would not interpret legislation in such a way as to frustrate its purpose). The problems could be largely eliminated if it was expressly provided that the rule that consideration must move from the promisee was abolished.

In the light of all of these difficulties, it could be said that to reform the doctrine of privity is to cause more problems than it solves. The new third party right is too uncertain in scope and threatens to cut across existing contractual allocation of risks. This is particularly so in the case of the construction industry where collateral warranties are in constant use. Sub-contractors and other participants in the construction process will often be asked to give a warranty to the building owner (for example, as to the quality of his work, its fitness for purpose, the materials used etc.). This warranty is in addition to their obligations under the sub-contract with the main contractor. Many sections of the construction industry are content with the operation of these collateral warranties because they establish clear lines of liability and they do not want these arrangements to be upset by new third party rights of uncertain ambit which may interfere with their (careful) allocation of risk. While this argument has its merits, it is not ultimately convincing. The first objection is that collateral warranties are expensive and time-consuming because they have to be obtained from all the participants in the construction process. The second is that it does not apply to the *Tweddle* v. *Atkinson* type situation where both parties expressly state that the third party should have a right of action. Such a statement is presently unenforceable in English law and such a limited reform would not upset the operation of collateral warranties in the construction industry. The third point is that such reasoning is all very well for those who can afford to consult lawyers and pay for them to draft collateral warranties, but it does little to help the Mrs Beswicks of this world. Finally, it is unlikely that Parliament will accept reform which exempts the construction industry from its scope and so, even if reform will cause one or two problems in the construction industry, in the final analysis these problems do not outweigh the benefits which will be obtained by radical reform of the doctrine of privity.

Summary

1 The doctrine of privity consists of two distinct rules.
2 The first is that a third party cannot be subjected to a burden by a contract to which he is not a party.
3 The second is that a person who is not a party to a contract cannot claim the benefit of it, even though the contract was entered into with the object of benefiting that third party.
4 Although the two rules are generally thought to be distinct, there is a very close relationship between the doctrine of privity and the rule that consideration must move from the promisee.
5 Where, in breach of contract with a promisee, a promisor has failed to confer a benefit on a third party, the promisee may bring an action for breach of contract against the promisee. The promisee may be able to obtain damages, specific performance or a stay of proceedings but the general rule is that a promisee cannot recover damages on behalf of a third party.
6 A third party who seeks to procure a contracting party to break his contract without lawful justification commits a tort.
7 A third party cannot generally claim the protection of an exclusion clause contained in a contract between the plaintiff and another party as a defence to the plaintiff's action in tort. However, if the case falls within the scope of *The Eurymedon* then the third party may be able to enjoy such protection.
8 There are a number of exceptional cases in which English law does recognise the existence of enforceable third party rights.
9 In limited circumstances a court may be prepared to find the existence of a contract between the promisor and the third party which is collateral to the contract between the promisor and the promisee.
10 An agent may bring into existence a contract between his principal and a third party. An agency relationship arises where one party, the agent, is authorised by another, the principal, to negotiate and to enter into contracts on behalf of the principal.
11 Where an intention to create a trust can be shown to exist, a promisee may hold his right to sue the promisor on trust for the third party beneficiary, who can therefore sue to enforce the promise.
12 In limited circumstances a third party may be able to bring an action in the tort of negligence against a negligent promisor.
13 There are a large number of statutory exceptions to the doctrine of privity.
14 Provided that the relevant formalities are complied with a promisee may assign his right to sue the promisor to a third party.

Exercises

1 Explain the relationship between the doctrine of privity and the rule that consideration must move from the promisee.

2 John and Sarah go out for a meal at Freddy's restaurant. Sarah pays for the meal. John's meal is inedible. What remedies are available to Sarah? If Sarah refuses to sue, could John sue? (see *Lockett* v *AM Charles Ltd* [1938] 4 All ER 170)

3 In what circumstances can a defendant claim the protection of an exclusion clause contained in a contract to which he was not a party?

4 List the exceptional cases in which English law does recognise the existence of enforceable third party rights. Do these exceptions undermine the rule?

5 Do you think that English law should adopt the recommendations put forward by the Law Commission in their recent Consultation Paper? What difficulties are likely to arise in reforming privity and how should they be resolved?

Part II

The Content of a Contract

8 What is a Term?

Having considered what the law recognises as a valid, enforceable contract and who is bound by that contract, we shall now consider the contents of a contract. This section is divided into four chapters. In this chapter we shall consider what constitutes a term of the contract; in Chapter 9 we shall discuss the sources of contractual terms; in Chapter 10 we shall consider the classification of contractual terms; and in Chapter 11 we shall analyse a particular type of contractual term, the exclusion or limitation clause.

8.1 What is a Term?

A contract consists of a number of terms. However not everything that is said or written during the course of negotiations constitutes a term of the contract. An example will illustrate the point. Suppose that I agree to sell my word processor to my neighbour. During the course of negotiations he may ask me many things about it; its age, how often it has been used, whether it can do footnotes, the speed of the printer and so on. But the conclusion of the contract may consist simply of my statement 'I will sell you the word processor for £500' and his statement 'I accept'. It is, however, highly unlikely that these two statements would be held to constitute the entirety of the contract. It is equally unlikely that all my answers to my neighbour's questions would be regarded as terms of the contract. My answers could, in fact, be classified in one of three ways.

The first is that some answers could be treated as mere statements of opinion or 'mere puffs' and will have no legal effect (for example a statement that the printer 'goes like a bomb'; see further 13.3). The principal distinction however, is between the second and the third categories; that is, between a term and a mere representation (note that in some cases the distinction is drawn between 'warranties' and 'mere representations', but this terminology will not be used here because it leads to confusion when, in Chapter 10, we seek to distinguish between a condition and a warranty (both of which are terms of a contract)). The distinction between a term and a mere representation is important because, if a statement is held to be a term of the contract, a failure to comply with it will be a breach of contract, entitling the innocent party to a remedy for breach of contract. On the other hand, if the statement is held to be a mere representation, the innocent party cannot claim that there has been a breach of contract because the statement was not a term of the contract. His remedy, if any, is to seek to have the contract set aside or claim damages for misrepresentation (see further, Chapter 13).

Whether a statement is a contractual term or a mere representation depends, ultimately, on the intention with which the statement was made. In considering the intention with which a particular statement was made, the courts have, once again, adopted an objective approach to intention. The cases have established some principles (see 8.2-8.4) to guide the court in deciding whether a statement is a term or a mere representation. No one principle is decisive; in every case the court must assess the relative importance of each principle (see Lord Moulton in *Heilbut, Symons & Co* v. *Buckleton* [1913] AC 30, 50–51).

8.2   Verification

A statement is unlikely to be a term of the contract if the maker of the statement asks the other party to verify its truth. In *Ecay* v. *Godfrey* (1947) 80 L1 LR 286, a seller of a boat stated that the boat was sound but advised the buyer to have it surveyed. His statement was held to be a mere representation. On the other hand, in *Schawel* v. *Reade* [1913] 2 IR 64, the plaintiff, while examining a horse with a view to buying it for stud purposes, was told by the defendant: 'You need not look for anything; the horse is perfectly sound. If there was anything the matter with this horse I should tell you'. In reliance upon this statement the plaintiff bought the horse without examining it. It was subsequently discovered that the horse was totally unfit for stud purposes and it was held that the defendant's statement was a term of the contract (contrast *Hopkins* v. *Tanqueray* (1854) 15 CB 130).

8.3   Importance

A statement is likely to be a term of the contract where it is of such importance to the person to whom it is made that, had it not been made, he would not have entered into the contract. In *Couchman* v. *Hill* [1947] KB 554, a heifer was put up for sale at an auction but no warranty was given as to its condition. The plaintiff asked the defendant whether the heifer was in calf and stated that he was not interested in purchasing it if it was. He was told that it was not in calf. Approximately seven weeks after the purchase the heifer suffered a miscarriage and died. The plaintiff brought an action for breach of contract. The statement that the heifer was not in calf was held to be a term of the contract because of the importance attached to it by the plaintiff (contrast *Oscar Chess Ltd* v. *Williams* [1957] 1 WLR 370, discussed at 8.4).

8.4   Special Knowledge

If the maker of a statement has some special knowledge or skill compared to the other party, the statement may be held to be a contractual term. On the other hand if the parties' degrees of knowledge are equal or if the person to whom the statement is made has the greater knowledge, the statement may be held to be a mere representation. These propositions can be illustrated by reference to the following two cases.

The first is *Oscar Chess Ltd* v. *Williams* (above), in which the defendant sold a car to the plaintiffs for £290. The car was described as a 1948 Morris 10; in fact it was a 1939 model (which was worth only £175). The defendant had obtained the information that the car was a 1948 model in good faith from the car log book, but the log book was subsequently discovered to be a forgery. It was held that the defendant's statement as to the age of the car was not a term of the contract but a mere representation. The plaintiffs, who were car dealers, were in at least as good a position as the defendant to know the true age of the car. On the other hand, in *Dick Bentley Productions Ltd* v. *Harold Smith (Motors) Ltd* [1965] 1 WLR 623, the plaintiff asked the defendants, who were car dealers, to find him a 'well vetted' Bentley car. The defendants found a car which they sold to the plaintiff and which they stated had done only 20 000 miles since a replacement engine had been fitted. It had in fact done 100 000 miles. It was held that the defendants' statement as to the car mileage was a term of the contract; the defendants, being car dealers, were in a better position than the plaintiff to know whether their statement was true.

8.5 The Consequences of the Distinction Between a Term and a Mere Representation

Although the distinction between a term and a mere representation is important, it is not quite as fundamental as it used to be. At the beginning of this century it was important because damages were only available for misrepresentation in a very narrow range of circumstances. But now, both at common law and under the Misrepresentation Act 1967, damages are available for misrepresentation in a much wider range of circumstances (see 13.9). The distinction is now primarily relevant to the *amount* of damages recoverable rather than to whether damages are recoverable at all (although there do remain cases in which damages are not recoverable for misrepresentation, see 13.9). If the statement is held to be a term, breach will generally entitle the innocent party to recover damages which will have the effect of putting him in the position which he would have been in had the contract been performed (called his 'expectation interest'), whereas if it is a representation, damages will generally be assessed on the basis of the extent to which the representee has incurred loss through reliance on the misrepresentation (the 'reliance interest') (see further Chapter 20).

The distinction between a term and a representation is also relevant to the ability to set aside the contract. In the case of misrepresentation, the representee is always, in principle, entitled to set aside the contract (see 13.8), while in the case of a term the innocent party can only set aside the contract where the term which has been broken is a condition (see 10.3) or is an 'innominate term' and the consequences of the breach have been sufficiently serious (see 10.5). The meaning of 'set aside' also differs between the two contexts (see further 13.8). In the case where the contract is set aside on the ground of misrepresentation, the contract is set aside both retrospectively and prospectively so that the aim of setting the contract aside is to restore both parties to their pre-contractual position. But in the case where a contract is set aside for breach, it is set aside prospectively only and the setting aside does not have retrospective consequences (see 19.7).

8.6   Can a Representation be Incorporated into a Contract as a Term?

This may seem a strange question to ask given that we have spent a chapter arguing that the two are separate and distinct. The issue can be illustrated by reference to the case of *Pennsylvania Shipping Co* v. *Compagnie Nationale de Navigation* [1936] 2 All ER 1167. A tanker was chartered from the defendants by the plaintiffs. Prior to the conclusion of the contract, the defendants provided the plaintiffs with incorrect information about the heating of the ship. This information was subsequently incorporated into the contract. When the plaintiffs discovered the true position, they sought, *inter alia*, to have the contract set aside on the ground of misrepresentation. Branson J held that the representation became 'merged in the higher contractual right' and that there was therefore no need to set aside the contract on the ground of misrepresentation; the plaintiffs' claim was for breach of contract (contrast *Compagnie Francaise des Chemin de Fer Paris-Orleans* v. *Leeston Shipping Co* (1919) 1 Ll LR 235). However section 1(a) of the Misrepresentation Act 1967 now provides that a representee who has entered into a contract after a misrepresentation has been made to him may rescind the contract for misrepresentation, even though the misrepresentation is subsequently incorporated into the contract, provided that he would otherwise be entitled to rescind the contract. This may be of very great significance where the representee is unable to rescind the contract for breach because, for example, the term which has been broken is a warranty (see further 10.3). In such a case, provided the relevant conditions for rescission for misrepresentation are satisfied (on which see 13.8), he may nevertheless be entitled to rescind for misrepresentation.

Summary

1 A contract consists of a number of terms.
2 A term must be distinguished from a statement of opinion or 'mere puff' (which has no legal effect) and a mere representation (which generates a claim for misrepresentation).
3 The question whether a statement is a term or a mere representation depends upon the intention with which the statement was made. Factors to which the court will have regard in deciding this issue include whether the maker of the statement advised the other party to verify the truth of his statement, the importance of the statement and the respective states of knowledge of the parties.
4 In certain circumstances the term/representation dichotomy may be crucial to the recoverability of damages but it is more likely that it will be relevant to the amount of damages recoverable. Where a term of the contract has been broken damages will generally protect the promisee's expectation interest, but in the case of a misrepresentation damages will only protect the misrepresentee's reliance interest.
5 A representee who has entered into a contract after a misrepresentation has been made to him may rescind the contract for misrepresentation, even though the misrepresentation is subsequently incorporated into the contract, provided that he would otherwise be entitled to rescind for misrepresentation.

Exercises

1 Why do lawyers distinguish between a term and a mere representation?
2 Distinguish between a term and a mere representation. What are the consequences of this distinction?
3 John, a specialist race-horse trainer, wished to buy a horse from Fred, who was a farmer who had little knowledge of horses. John believed that the horse was a potential champion and, during the course of negotiations, he asked Fred if he could inspect the horse. Fred said there was really no need as his stable-boy had assured him that the horse would make a 'brilliant race horse'. In reliance on Fred's statement, John bought the horse. When the horse was delivered to John, he found it had a serious leg injury which made it useless as a race-horse. John wishes to know whether his remedy lies for breach of contract or for misrepresentation. Advise him.
4 What is the effect of s.1(a) of the Misrepresentation Act 1967?

9 The Sources of Contractual Terms

9.1 Introduction

There are two principal sources of contractual terms: express terms and implied terms. Express terms are the terms which are agreed specifically by the contracting parties and implied terms are those terms which are not specifically agreed by the contracting parties but which are implied into the contract by the courts or by Parliament. We shall deal with implied terms at 9.8. Here we shall focus our attention on express terms.

Express terms may be agreed orally or in writing. Where the contract is made orally the ascertainment of the contractual terms may involve difficult questions of fact, but the task of a judge is simply to decide exactly what was said by each of the parties. More particular difficulties arise in the case of written contracts. Three such difficulties will be dealt with here. The first and fundamental issue is whether the court can go beyond the written agreement in an attempt to discover the existence of additional terms to the contract (9.2). The second is whether a person is necessarily bound by the terms of a contract which he has signed (9.3). The third and final issue is whether written terms can be incorporated into a contract, either by notice (9.4) or by a course of dealing (9.5). Once we have discussed these issues we shall consider the approach which the courts adopt towards the interpretation of contracts (9.6).

9.2 The Parol Evidence Rule

Once the contracting parties have elected to enshrine their contract in a written document, the courts have held that, as a general rule, the parties cannot adduce extrinsic evidence to add to, vary or contradict the written document; the document is the sole repository of the terms of the contract (*Jacobs* v. *Batavia & General Plantations Trust Ltd* [1924] 1 Ch 287). This rule has been called the 'parol evidence rule'. The purpose behind this rule is said to be the promotion of certainty; that is to say, once the parties have gone to the trouble of drawing up a written document, one party should not be able to allege with impunity that there were, in fact, other terms which were, for some reason, not incorporated into the final written document.

If this rule were to be applied rigidly to all cases there is no doubt that it would produce considerable injustice. For example, the written document may have been procured by fraud and so one party would wish to lead extrinsic evidence to prove that fraud. So it is no surprise to find that the parol evidence rule is not an absolute rule, but is the subject of numerous exceptions. We will now consider the scope of these exceptions and then consider their implications for the status of the rule.

The first exception is that the rule does not apply where the written document was not intended to contain the whole of the agreement (*Allen* v. *Pink* (1838) 4 M & W 140). As Wedderburn has remarked (1959) this exception reduces the rule to 'no more than a self-evident tautology . . . when the writing is the whole contract, the parties are bound by it and parol evidence is excluded; when it is not, evidence of the other terms must be admitted'. The Law Commission in its report (No 154 Cmnd 9700 (1986)) agreed with this observation, adding that the parol evidence rule is 'no more than a circular statement'. On this view the parol evidence rule does not give rise to injustice because it will never prevent a party from leading evidence of terms which were intended to be part of the contract. On the other hand it must be remembered that the the courts will presume that a document which looks like the contract is the whole contract. However, this presumption is rebuttable and the presumption operates with less strength today than in former times and it is therefore highly unlikely that the parol evidence rule will preclude a party from leading evidence of terms which were intended to be part of the contract.

Parol evidence is also admissible to prove terms which must be implied into the agreement (*Gillespie Bros & Co* v. *Cheney, Eggar & Co* [1896] 2 QB 59); to prove a custom which must be implied into the contract (*Hutton* v. *Warren* (1836) 1 M & W 466); to show that the contract is invalid on the ground of misrepresentation, mistake, fraud or *non est factum* (on which see 9.3 and *Campbell Discount Co* v. *Gall* [1961] 1 QB 431); to show that the document should be rectified; to show that the contract has not yet come into operation or that it has ceased to operate (*Pym* v. *Campbell* (1856) 6 E & B 370) and to prove the existence of a collateral agreement (*Mann* v. *Nunn* (1874) 30 LT 526). The latter exception is of particular significance because in one case extrinsic evidence was actually used to *contradict* the terms of the written agreement. In *City and Westminster Properties (1934) Ltd* v. *Mudd* [1959] Ch 129, a lease entered into by the parties contained a covenant which stated that the tenant could use the premises for business purposes only. The tenant had been induced to sign the lease by an oral assurance given by the lessors' agent that the lessors would not raise any objection to the tenant continuing his practice of residing in the premises. In an action by the lessors to forfeit the lease on the ground that the tenant was using the premises for residential purposes, it was held that evidence of the assurance given by the lessors' agent was admissible to prove the existence of a collateral agreement, despite the fact that it contradicted the express terms of the written lease. This case has been subjected to some criticism and it does appear to be inconsistent with earlier cases such as *Angell* v. *Duke* (1875) 32 LT 320 and *Henderson* v. *Arthur* [1907] 1 KB 10. However, if the collateral agreement is truly a separate agreement, then there is no reason why it should not be contrary to the terms of the written agreement. That said, it must be conceded that the effect of the decision is largely to undermine the parol evidence rule.

The parol evidence rule has been subjected to considerable criticism. The exceptions are so wide that they subvert the purpose of the rule in promoting certainty. Indeed, the width of the exceptions is such that it must now be doubted whether there is a 'rule' in English law that parol evidence is not admissible to add to, vary or contradict the written document. In the light of these criticisms the Law Commission provisionally recommended in 1976 (Working Paper No 76) that the parol evidence rule be abolished but, in its more recent report (No 154 Cmnd 9700), it concluded that no legislative action need be taken for two reasons. The first was that the rule did not preclude the courts from having recourse to extrinsic evidence where such a course was consistent with the intention of the parties. The second reason was that any legislative change would be more likely to confuse than clarify the law. Therefore the 'rule' remains in existence but it must be remembered that it is a rule which, because of the width of the exceptions, is unlikely to have significant effects in practice.

9.3   Bound by Your Signature?

Despite the existence of numerous exceptions to the parol evidence rule, English law does attach some importance to the sanctity of written documents and this can be seen in the general rule that a person is bound by a document which he signs, whether he reads it or not. This proposition can be derived from the case of *L'Estrange* v. *F Graucob Ltd* [1934] 2 KB 394. The plaintiff bought an automatic slot machine from the defendants. She signed an order form which contained a clause which excluded liability for all express and implied warranties. When the plaintiff discovered that the machine did not work she brought an action against the defendants for breach of an implied warranty that the machine was fit for the purpose for which it was sold. Judgment was given for the defendants on the ground that they had excluded their liability by virtue of the exclusion clause which was incorporated into the contract by the plaintiff's signature, even though the exclusion clause was in 'regrettably small print' and had not been read by the plaintiff. Given the widespread use of contracts which rely heavily upon the use of small print, such a rule appears singularly unfortunate, especially in its application to consumers. In this respect a more realistic view was taken by the Ontario Court of Appeal in *Tilden Rent-a-Car Co* v. *Clendenning* (1978) 83 DLR (3d) 400. The court recognised that many standard form printed contracts are signed without being read or understood and they held that a signature could only be relied upon as evidence of genuine consent when it was reasonable for the party relying on the signed document to believe that the signer did assent to the onerous terms proposed. In the case of consumer contracts, English law may now reach the same conclusion, albeit by a different route, as a result of the EC Directive on Unfair Terms in

Consumer Contracts (see 1.6 and 17.7). Article 5 of the Directive states that 'in the case of contracts where all or certain terms offered to the consumer are in writing, these terms must always be drafted in plain, intelligible language'. Apart from the difficulties involved in ascertaining what this phrase actually means, it is not clear what sanctions are available in respect of any non-compliance. Although the Directive provides that an unfair term shall not be binding upon a consumer, it is not expressly declared that a provision which is not in 'plain, intelligible language' is itself unfair. It may be that the presence of language which is not 'plain' and 'intelligible' will only be a factor in deciding whether or not a term is unfair. It is also unclear what effect Article 5 will have on a case such as *L'Estrange* v. *Graucob*. It certainly appears that the language of the contract in *L'Estrange* was not plain and intelligible and so, had it been a consumer contract, it could now be argued that the exclusion clause was not binding upon the consumer because it was an unfair term (note also the role of the Unfair Contract Terms Act 1977 (see 11.9–11.15) which places significant controls upon exclusion clauses of the type found in *L'Estrange*). Aside from the possible impact of the EC Directive, the rule in *L'Estrange* does not apply where the signature has been procured by fraud, misrepresentation or the defence of *non est factum* is made out. Fraud and misrepresentation will be dealt with in Chapter 13. Here we shall discuss the defence of *non est factum*.

The defence of *non est factum* is a defence of respectable antiquity in English law. It was originally applied to the case where an illiterate person signed a deed which had been read to him incorrectly by another person. In such a case the illiterate person was not bound by the deed; to put it in technical terms, he could plead *non est factum*, which means 'this is not my deed'. The effect of *non est factum* is to render the deed void so that a third party cannot obtain good title under it (see further on the issue of third party rights the discussion at 4.6). As the doctrine has developed, it has had to grapple with the problem that it is seeking to reconcile two competing policies. These policies are, firstly, the injustice of holding a person to a bargain to which he has not brought a consenting mind and the second is the necessity of holding a person to a document which he has signed, especially where innocent third parties rely to their detriment upon the validity of the signature.

These two competing policies can be seen at work in the important decision of the House of Lords in *Saunders* v. *Anglia Building Society* (also referred to as *Gallie* v. *Lee*) [1971] AC 1004. A widow of 78 made a will in which she left her house to her nephew. However the nephew wished to raise money immediately on the security of the home. The widow was prepared to help her nephew to raise the money provided that she was permitted to live in her home for the rest of her life rent free. The difficulty for the nephew was that he did not want to raise the loan in his own name because he was afraid that his wife would get her hands on the money. So he arranged that a friend of his should raise the money on the security of the house. The nephew arranged for the preparation of a document assigning the house to the friend for £3000. The widow did not read the document because her glasses were broken, but she signed it after the friend told her that it was a deed of gift to the nephew. The friend raised money on a mortgage with the respondent building society but he made no payment either to the building society, the nephew or the widow. The building society sought to recover possession of the property from the widow, who invoked the defence of *non est factum*. Here we have the clash of the competing policies which we noted above. On the one hand there is the injustice of holding the widow to an agreement to which she had not brought a consenting mind, but on the other hand there is the need to protect the building society which had innocently relied to its detriment upon the widow's signature. The House of Lords gave greater weight to the second policy than the first and held that the defence of *non est factum* was not made out on the facts of the case. As Scott LJ stated in *Norwich and Peterborough Building Society* v. *Steed (No. 2)* [1993] QB 116, 125, the law almost invariably protects the innocent third party because 'the signer of the document has, by signing, enabled the fraud to be carried out, enabled the false documents to go into circulation'. It is the signer of the document who must therefore bear the consequences and to further that goal *non est factum* is kept within very narrow confines. Its scope can best be considered by asking ourselves three questions.

The first question is: to whom is the plea available? As originally conceived, the doctrine only applied to those who were unable to read. However in *Saunders* it was held that the doctrine was not confined to those who are blind or illiterate. It extends to those 'who are permanently or temporarily unable through no fault of their own to have without explanation any real understanding or purport of a particular document, whether that be from defective education, illness or innate incapacity'. Their Lordships did not say that the defence could never be available to a person of full capacity, but it would only be available to him in the most exceptional of cases and would not be available simply because he was too busy or too lazy to read the document.

The second question is: for what type of mistake is the defence available? Initially it was held that the defence was available if the mistake went to the heart of the transaction (*Foster* v. *MacKinnon* (1869) LR 4 CP 704). But in *Howatson* v. *Webb* [1907] 1 Ch 537 Warrington J drew a distinction between a mistake as to the 'character' of the document and a mistake as to its 'content', only the former being sufficient to support a plea of *non est factum*. However this distinction was rejected by the House of Lords in *Saunders* on the ground that it was 'arbitrary'. Instead it was held that the difference between the document as it was and as it was believed to be must be radical or substantial or fundamental. This test was not satisfied on the facts of *Saunders* because the widow wished to benefit her nephew by enabling him to raise money on the security of the house and the document which she signed was in fact intended to do this, although it was designed to do it by a different route, namely by assignment to the friend instead of by gift to the nephew.

The third and final question is: in what circumstances is a person precluded from relying on the defence? The principal circumstance in which the defence is not available arises where there is carelessness on the part of the person who signs the document. In *United Dominions Trust Ltd* v. *Western* [1976] QB 513, the defendant signed a loan agreement with the plaintiff company in connection with the purchase of a car and he left it to the garage owner to fill in the details, including the price. The garage owner increased the price of the car and the plaintiff company paid over the money to the garage owner in good faith. The court held that the onus was on the defendant to show that, in allowing the form to be filled in by the garage owner, he had acted carefully. It was held that he had wholly failed to discharge that onus and therefore could not invoke the defence of *non est factum* (see also *Norwich and Peterborough Building Society* v. *Steed (No. 2)* [1993] QB 116, 128).

It is clear that English law has given considerable weight to the idea that a person should be able to rely on the signature of a contracting party. Such protection would be undermined by a wide defence of *non est factum* because it would render agreements void and thus detrimentally affect third party rights. However it should not be assumed that, where the defence of *non est factum* fails, the person who signs the document will therefore be left without a remedy. He may have a remedy in misrepresentation, fraud or undue influence (see *Avon Finance Co* v. *Bridger* [1985] 2 All ER 281). But the important point to note is that misrepresentation, fraud and undue influence only render the contract voidable and so greater protection is thereby afforded to third party rights.

9.4 Incorporation of Written Terms

Contracting parties may agree to incorporate a set of written terms into their contract. Three hurdles must be overcome before such terms can be incorporated. The first is that notice of the terms must be given at or before the time of concluding the contract. It is therefore crucial to determine the *precise* moment at which the contract was concluded. In *Olley* v. *Marlborough Court Ltd* [1949] 1 KB 532, a notice in the bedroom of a hotel, which purported to exempt the hotel proprietors from any liability for articles lost or stolen from the hotel, was held not to be incorporated into a contract with a guest, whose furs were stolen from her bedroom, because the notice was not seen by the guest until after the contract had been concluded at the hotel reception desk.

Secondly, the terms must be contained or referred to in a document which was intended to have contractual effect. It is a question of fact whether or not a document was intended to have contractual effect and the issue must be decided by reference to current commercial or consumer practices. In *Chapleton* v. *Barry UDC* [1940] 1 KB 532, the plaintiff hired a deck chair from the defendants. On paying his money he was given a ticket, which, unknown to him, contained a number of conditions, including an exclusion clause. The plaintiff was injured when he sat in the deck chair and it gave way beneath him. He sued the defendants, who relied by way of defence on the exclusion clause contained in the ticket. It was held that they could not rely on the exclusion clause because it was contained in a mere receipt which was not intended to have contractual effect.

Thirdly, and finally, reasonable steps must be taken to bring the terms to the attention of the other party. In *Parker* v. *South Eastern Railway* (1877) 2 CPD 416, it was established that the test is whether the defendant took reasonable steps to bring the notice to the attention of the plaintiff, not whether the plaintiff actually read the notice. Thus, in *Thompson* v. *London, Midland and Scottish Railway Co Ltd* [1930] 1 KB 41, an exclusion clause contained in a railway time-table was held to be validly incorporated despite the fact that the plaintiff was illiterate and therefore unable to read the clause. The result may be different, however, where the party seeking to rely on the exclusion clause knows of the disability of the other party (*Richardson, Spence and Co Ltd* v. *Rowntree* [1894] AC 217).

What amounts to reasonable notice is a question which depends upon the facts and circumstances of the individual case. In *Thompson* the defendants were held to have taken reasonable steps to bring the exclusion clause to the attention of the plaintiff, even though it was contained on page 552 of the timetable and the timetable cost 1/5 of the price of the railway ticket. It is doubtful whether such a liberal view would be taken today (see, for example, *The Mikhail Lermontov* [1990] 1 Lloyd's Rep 579, 594). If the clause is not referred to on the front of the ticket (*Henderson* v. *Stevenson* (1875) LR 2 Sc & Div 470)) or if the reference to the clause is obliterated (*Sugar* v. *London, Midland and Scottish Railway Co* [1941] 1 All ER 172) the clause is less likely to be incorporated into the contract. Similarly, the more unusual or unreasonable the exclusion clause, the greater the degree of the notice required by the courts. In *J Spurling Ltd* v. *Bradshaw* [1956] 1 WLR 461, Denning LJ said that some clauses would need to be printed in red ink on the face of the document with a red hand pointing to it before the notice could be held to be sufficient.

All of the 'incorporation' cases which we have considered so far are concerned with attempts to incorporate exclusion clauses into a contract. They generally evince a restrictive approach to incorporation, particularly in cases such as *Spurling* v. *Bradshaw* (above) where Lord Denning enunciated his 'red hand rule'. It could be argued that such a restrictive approach is confined to exclusion clauses and, indeed, that, since the enactment of the Unfair Contract Terms Act 1977, which gives the courts considerable power to control exclusion clauses (see 11.9–11.15), there is little need for such a restrictive approach, even in the case of exclusion clauses. But a recent case shows that the restrictive approach is very much alive and, further, that it is not confined to exclusion clauses.

The recent case is *Interfoto Picture Library Ltd* v. *Stiletto Visual Programmes Ltd* [1989] QB 433 (see further Macdonald, 1988a). The defendants ordered photographic transparencies from the plaintiffs, not having dealt with them before. The plaintiffs duly sent them 47 transparencies, together with a delivery note which contained a number of conditions. Condition 2 stated that a holding fee of £5 per day was payable for every day the transparencies were kept in excess of fourteen days. The defendants put the transparencies to one side and forgot about them. They eventually returned them after approximately one month. The plaintiffs then sent the defendants an invoice for £3783.50, which the defendants refused to pay. In an action by the plaintiffs to recover the £3783.50, the Court of Appeal held that condition 2 was not incorporated into the contract because insufficient notice had been given to the defendants of its terms and that, in the absence of express provision in the contract, the plaintiffs were only entitled to a restitutionary award of £3.50 per transparency per week. It was held that a party who seeks to incorporate into a contract a term which is particularly onerous *or* unusual must prove that the term has been fairly and reasonably drawn to the attention of the other party. Bingham LJ argued that cases on sufficiency of notice are concerned with the question 'whether it would in all the circumstances be fair (or reasonable) to hold a party bound by any conditions . . . of an unusual and stringent nature'. The utility of this general principle must surely be debatable and its application to the present facts even more so. The defendants were businessmen and were surely capable of reading the conditions on the delivery note. If they did not do so, they must be deemed to have accepted the risk that the terms might prove to be unacceptable to them. The objection that the terms were particularly onerous could possibly have been dealt with by arguing that condition 2 was a penalty clause, a point suggested by Bingham LJ. The difficulty with this argument is that the penalty clause rule only applies to sums payable on a breach of contract (see 21.7) and the defendants might not have been in breach of contract in retaining the transparencies beyond 14 days (for example, the plaintiffs could have operated a two-tier price structure, with one fee being payable for the first 14 days and a different fee thereafter). But even if the penalty clause rule was inapplicable, any unfairness in the terms sought to be incorporated into a contract should be dealt with directly, through a general doctrine of unfairness or unconscionability or, in the consumer context, by the EC Directive on Unfair Terms in Consumer Contracts (see 17.6) and not by distorting the rules relating to the incorporation of terms into a contract. There is no need to apply different standards on the issue of incorporation according to the severity of the term sought to be incorporated; the same test should be applied to all terms, regardless of their severity.

9.5 Incorporation by a Course of Dealing

Terms may also be incorporated into a contract by a course of dealing. The courts have never defined course of dealing with any degree of precision, but some useful guidance was given by the House of Lords in

McCutcheon v. *David MacBrayne Ltd* [1964] 1 WLR 125. There it was held that the course of dealing must be both regular and consistent. What constitutes a 'regular' course of dealing depends upon the facts of the particular case. Thus, in *Henry Kendall Ltd* v. *William Lillico Ltd* [1969] 2 AC 31, the House of Lords held that 100 similar contracts over a period of three years constituted a course of dealing. But in *Hollier* v. *Rambler Motors (AMC) Ltd* [1972] 2 QB 71, three or four contracts over a period of five years was held not to be a course of dealing between a consumer and a garage. The position may, however, be different where the contracting parties are commercial parties of equal bargaining power. In *British Crane Hire Corporations Ltd* v. *Ipswich Plant Hire Ltd* [1975] QB 303, a clause was incorporated into the contract on the basis of two previous transactions and the custom of the trade. The court placed emphasis on the fact that the parties were of equal bargaining power, they were both in the trade and such conditions were habitually incorporated into these contracts.

The course of dealing must not only be regular, it must also be consistent. In *McCutcheon* v. *David MacBrayne Ltd* (above) a ferry belonging to the defendants sank and the plaintiff's car was lost. In the resulting action by the plaintiff, the defendants sought to rely on an exclusion clause contained in a risk note which, contrary to their usual practice, they had not asked the plaintiff's brother-in-law (who made the arrangement for the shipping of the plaintiff's car) to sign. The defendants argument failed in the House of Lords because it was held that there was no consistent course of dealing on the basis of which the exclusion clause could be incorporated into the contract. Lord Pearce said that there was no consistent course of dealing because the previous transactions had always been in writing (that is, by the signing of the risk note) and in the present case the transaction was entirely oral. But this is surely to take the requirement of consistency too far because the only reason for the defendants' reliance upon the course of dealing argument was that they had forgotten to ensure that the risk note was signed. If that forgetfulness, of itself, also had the effect of precluding them from relying upon the course of dealing argument, cases of incorporation by a course of dealing will be very rare (see further Macdonald, 1988b). It is suggested that the better view of the case is that the evidence failed to establish a consistent course of dealing because, although on some occasions the brother-in-law had been asked to sign the risk note, there were other occasions when he had not been asked to sign. On this basis there was clearly no consistent course of dealing.

From the regularity and consistency of the course of dealing will be inferred knowledge of the conditions. In *McCutcheon* Lord Devlin said that previous dealings were only relevant if they proved actual knowledge of the terms and assent to them, but this view was not shared by other judges in the case and appears to have been rejected by the House of Lords in *Henry Kendall Ltd* v. *William Lillico Ltd* (above). However, where it can be shown that one party knows that the other has forgotten to include his usual exclusion clause and seeks to take advantage of it, he will not be allowed to do so and the exclusion clause will be incorporated, even in the absence of a regular and consistent course of dealing.

9.6 Interpretation

Once the terms of the contract have been ascertained, they must be interpreted to ascertain their 'true' meaning. Many contractual disputes arise out of disagreements over the proper interpretation of a particular phrase in a contract and most of them hinge upon the precise wording and context of the contract. When it comes to the interpretation of contracts, precedents are of relatively limited value: 'a decision on a different clause in a different context is seldom of much help on a question of construction' (*Surrey Heath Borough Council* v. *Lovell Construction Ltd* (1990) 48 Build LR 113, 118). Nevertheless, there are some broad principles which emerge with some clarity from the case law.

The starting-point is that it is for the courts, not the parties, to decide what is the proper interpretation of the contract. The guiding principle which the courts apply is that, in interpreting (or, as lawyers usually say, 'construing') the contract, the court must seek to ascertain and give effect to the intention of the parties. However in many cases the process of imputing an intention to the parties is an extremely artificial one, which is sharply influenced by the court's view of the 'desirability' of the contract term which it is called upon to interpret. There is no better illustration of this than the approach which the courts have adopted to the interpretation of exclusion clauses, where rules of interpretation have been used with particular venom in order to place difficult obstacles in the way of those who seek to exclude their liability towards others (see further 11.5–11.7). That this is indeed the case was recognised by Lord Diplock when he said that 'the reports are full of cases in which what would appear to be very strained constructions have been placed upon exclusion clauses' (*Photo Production Ltd* v. *Securicor Transport Ltd* [1980] AC 827).

With this point in mind let us examine the way in which the courts seek to ascertain the intention of the parties. The general rule is that the intention of the parties must be ascertained from the document in which they have elected to enshrine their agreement (*Lovell & Christmas Ltd* v. *Wall* (1911) 104 LT 85). It is only in very limited circumstances that the courts can go outside the four corners of the document. Therefore the actual words used in the document are of crucial significance. In *Lovell & Christmas Ltd* v. *Wall* (above) Cozens-Hardy MR stated that 'it is the duty of the court . . . to construe the document according to the ordinary grammatical meaning of the words used therein'. But it should not be thought that English courts are 'left behind in some island of literal interpretation' (per Lord Wilberforce in *Prenn* v. *Simmonds* [1971] 1 WLR 1381). In the latter case Lord Wilberforce stated that 'the time has long passed when agreements . . . were isolated from the matrix of facts in which they were set and interpreted purely on internal linguistic considerations'. He said that the court 'must enquire beyond the language and see what the circumstances were with reference to which the words were used, and the object, appearing from those circumstances, which the person using them had in view'.

However the following types of evidence are not generally admissible. Evidence of pre-contractual negotiations is generally inadmissible because, during the negotiating process, the parties' positions are constantly changing and it is only the final document which actually records their agreement. Where there is an ambiguity in the final written document, evidence of pre-contractual negotiations may be admissible to show that the parties had attached a particular meaning to that phrase (*The Karen Oltman* [1976] 2 Lloyd's Rep 708). Evidence of conduct subsequent to the making of the contract is also inadmissible because, were it otherwise, the contract could mean one thing on the day on which it was signed but mean something completely different one month after it was signed by virtue of the conduct of the parties after the making of the contract (*Schuler AG* v. *Wickman Machine Tool Sales* [1974] AC 235). However evidence of conduct subsequent to the making of the contract may be relevant to a plea of estoppel (*James Miller & Partners Ltd* v. *Whitworth Street Estates (Manchester) Ltd* [1970] AC 583). Finally, evidence of the parties' subjective intentions is not admissible (*Prenn* v. *Simmonds* (above)). Although the ascertainment of the intention of the parties is the guiding principle which underpins the process of interpretation, the intention of the parties is to be ascertained from an *objective* assessment of the wording of the contract and of the surrounding circumstances.

One further principle which the courts apply when interpreting contracts should also be mentioned. It is the *contra proferentem* rule, according to which any ambiguity in a clause is interpreted against the party seeking to rely on it (the rule is discussed in greater detail in its application to exclusion clauses at 11.5). This rule gives to contracting parties an incentive to draft their contracts in clear and precise terms, because if they fail to do so, any doubt in a clause will be resolved against the party seeking to rely on it. The rule has also been reinforced by the EC Directive on Unfair Terms in Consumer Contracts which in Article 5 states that written terms offered to a consumer must be drafted in 'plain, intelligible language' and that 'where there is doubt about the meaning of a term, the interpretation most favourable to the consumer shall prevail' (although, as we have noted (9.2), some doubt surrounds the remedy, if any, which is available in the event of non-compliance with the requirements of Article 5).

9.7 Rectification

Once the contract has been interpreted, one of the parties may argue that the written agreement, as interpreted, fails to reflect the agreement which the parties actually reached. In such a case the court may be asked to rectify the document so that it accurately reflects the agreement which the parties did reach. Such was the case in *Lovell & Christmas Ltd* v. *Wall* (above) where the plaintiff asked the court to adopt a particular interpretation of the contract and, when that argument failed, sought to have the contractual document rectified. However it should be noted that there is a distinction between interpretation and rectification, although in many cases the line between the two is a fine one. Interpretation is the process of ascribing a meaning to a term which is uncertain. Rectification, on the other hand, is a process whereby a document, the meaning of which has already been ascertained, is rectified so that it gives effect to the intention of the parties. Nevertheless it must be conceded that there are cases in which the courts have corrected minor errors in the expression of a document by a process of construction rather than by rectification. Thus in *Nittan (UK) Ltd* v. *Solent Steel Fabrication Ltd* [1981] 1 All ER 633, the Court of Appeal read 'Sargrove Electronic Controls Ltd' as if it read 'Sargrove Automation' and thereby avoided the need to rectify the document. However this process of construction will only be used to correct very minor errors.

Rectification is a remedy which is concerned with defects not in the making, but in the recording, of a contract. This distinction can be illustrated by reference to the case of *Frederick E Rose (London) Ltd* v. *William H Pim Jnr & Co Ltd* [1953] 2 QB 450. The plaintiffs were asked to supply certain buyers of theirs with a quantity of 'Moroccan horsebeans known here as feveroles'. The plaintiffs did not know what feveroles were and so they asked the defendants, who replied that they were simply horsebeans. So the parties entered into a contract for the supply by the defendants to the plaintiffs of 'horsebeans'. At the time of making the contract both parties believed that 'horsebeans' were 'feveroles'. It later transpired that 'feveroles' were a more expensive variety of horsebean than the type which had been supplied to the plaintiffs under the contract. When the plaintiffs' buyers claimed damages from the plaintiffs on the ground that the horsebeans which had been supplied to them were not 'feveroles', the plaintiffs sought to have the contract with the defendants rectified by the insertion of the word 'feveroles'. The Court of Appeal refused to rectify the contract. This was not a case in which the document failed to record the intention of the parties. The document did reflect their prior agreement; it was simply the case that the parties were under a shared misapprehension that 'horsebeans' were 'feveroles'.

Rectification is an equitable discretionary remedy. As such, it is only available in the discretion of the court. Originally the courts were reluctant to exercise this discretion but gradually they have become more willing to do so. In deciding whether to rectify a document a court will have regard to the following considerations.

The first is that a court will only rectify a document where 'convincing proof' is provided that the document fails to record the intention of the parties (*Joscelyne* v. *Nissen* [1970] 2 QB 86). A high degree of proof is needed so that certainty is not undermined (*The Olympic Pride* [1980] 2 Lloyd's Rep 67, 73). The second is that the document must fail to record the intention of *both* parties. Unilateral mistake is insufficient of itself to base a claim to rectification (*Riverlate Properties* v. *Paul* [1975] Ch 133). But where one party mistakenly believes that the document correctly expresses the parties' common intention, and the other party is aware of that mistake, rectification may be available (*A Roberts and Co Ltd* v. *Leicestershire County Council* [1961] Ch 555). Thirdly, the document must have been preceded by a concluded contract or by a 'continuing common intention'. It is no longer the case that a prior contract is a prerequisite to rectification. In *Joscelyne* v. *Nissen* (above) a father and daughter agreed that the daughter would purchase the father's business and would, in return, pay all the expenses of the father's home, including the gas, electricity and coal bills. The formal contract signed by the parties made no mention of the fact that the daughter had agreed to pay these bills. There was no prior contract to which the court could have regard but it was held that there was sufficient evidence of a continuing common intention that the daughter pay the gas, electricity and coal bills to enable the court to rectify the agreement to give effect to their common intention. Finally, rectification will not be granted in favour of a plaintiff who has been guilty of excessive delay in seeking rectification, nor will it be granted against a bona fide purchaser for value without notice.

9.8   Implied Terms

In addition to the terms which the parties have expressly agreed a court may be prepared to hold that other terms must be implied into the contract. Such terms may be implied from one of three sources.

The first is statute. Parliament has, in numerous instances, seen fit to imply terms into contracts. It is clear that these statutorily implied terms are not based upon the intention of the parties but on rules of law or public policy. As an illustration of statutorily implied terms we shall give very brief consideration to sections 12–15 of the Sale of Goods Act 1979. Thus it is an implied condition of a contract for the sale of goods that the seller has the right to sell the goods (s.12(1)) and there is an implied warranty that the goods are free from charges or incumbrances in favour of third parties (s.12(2)). There is also an implied condition that goods sold by description shall correspond with the description (s.13(1)) and that goods sold by sample shall correspond with the sample (s.15). In the case of a seller who sells goods in the course of a business, there is an implied condition that the goods supplied under the contract are of merchantable quality, except in relation to defects drawn to the buyer's attention before the contract was concluded or, in the case where the buyer examines the goods, as regards defects which that examination ought to reveal (s.14(2)). Finally, where the seller sells goods in the course of a business and the buyer makes known to the seller any particular purpose for which the goods are being bought, there is an implied condition that the goods supplied under the contract are reasonably fit for that purpose (s.14(3)). The function of these implied terms is not to give effect to the intention of the parties but to provide some protection for the expectations of purchasers, particularly consumers. This element of 'consumer protection' is further evidenced by the fact that the Unfair Contract Terms Act 1977 places severe restrictions upon the ability of sellers to exclude the operation of these implied terms and, indeed, as against a consumer, they cannot be excluded (see further 11.11).

The second source of implied terms are terms implied by custom. A contract may be deemed to incorporate any relevant custom of the market, trade or locality in which the contract is made (*Hutton v. Warren* (1836) 1 M & W 466), unless the custom is inconsistent with the express terms of the contract or its nature (*Palgrave, Brown & Son Ltd v. SS Turid (Owners)* [1922] 1 AC 397). A custom will generally be implied into a contract where it can be shown that the custom was generally accepted by those doing business in the particular trade in the particular place and was such that an outsider making inquiries could not fail to discover it (*Kum v. Wah Tat Bank Ltd* [1971] 1 Lloyd's Rep 439). A custom which satisfies these requirements binds both parties, whether they knew of it or not.

The third source of implied terms are terms implied at common law. There are, broadly speaking, two types of terms which are implied at common law (the distinction was recognised by Lord Bridge in *Scally* v. *Southern Health and Social Services Board* [1992] 1 AC 294, 306–7). The first type are sometimes called terms 'implied in fact'. This nomenclature seeks to convey the idea that the term is being implied as a matter of fact to give effect to what the court perceives to be the unexpressed intention of the parties. The test which must be satisfied before such a term will be implied into a contract is a stringent one. The test which is frequently employed by the courts is the 'officious bystander' test, the origin of which lies in the following statement:

> 'Prima facie that which in any contract is left to be implied and need not be expressed is something so obvious that it goes without saying; so that, if while the parties were making their bargain an officious bystander were to suggest some express provision for it in the agreement, they would testily suppress him with a common "Oh, of course"' (MacKinnon LJ in *Shirlaw* v. *Southern Foundries Ltd* [1939] 2 KB 206).

To put it another way: the implication must be 'necessary to give the transaction such business efficacy as the parties must have intended' (*The Moorcock* (1889) 14 PD 64). These tests were summarised by Lord Simon in *BP Refinery (Westernport) Pty Ltd* v. *Shire of Hastings* (1978) ALJR 20, 26 in the following terms:

> 'for a term to be implied, the following conditions (which may overlap) must be satisfied: (1) it must be reasonable and equitable; (2) it must be

necessary to give business efficacy to the contract, so that no term will be implied if the contract is effective without it; (3) it must be so obvious that "it goes without saying"; (4) is must be capable of close expression; (5) it must not contradict any express term of the contract'.

Although the reasonableness of the term is a relevant factor in deciding whether or not to imply a term into the contract, it must be emphasised that the court does not have power to imply a term into a contract simply because it is reasonable to do so. Although Lord Denning has advocated such an approach (*Liverpool CC* v. *Irwin* [1976] QB 319) it has been rejected by the House of Lords, who insisted that the term must be a necessary one before it will be implied (*Liverpool CC* v. *Irwin* [1977] AC 239; see also *Hughes* v. *Greenwich London Borough Council* [1994] AC 170). The necessity test at least allows the court to base its reasoning on the intention of the parties and it avoids the court being seen overtly to be 'making' the contract for the parties (on which see 4.1).

So a high standard must be satisfied before such a term will be implied into a contract. Attempts to imply a term have therefore failed where one of the parties did not know of the term which it was alleged must be implied (*Spring* v. *NASDS* [1956] 1 WLR 585) and where it was not clear that both parties would in fact have agreed to the term (*Luxor (Eastbourne) Ltd* v. *Cooper* [1941] AC 108). The courts are also reluctant to imply a term where the parties have entered into a carefully drafted written contract containing detailed terms agreed between them: in such a case a court is likely to presume that the written contract constitutes a complete code and so refuse to imply any term into it (*Shell UK Ltd* v. *Lostock Garages Ltd* [1976] 1 WLR 1187). Further, as Lord Simon stated in *BP Refinery (Westernport) Pty Ltd* v. *Shire of Hastings* (above), a term will not be implied into a contract if it would be inconsistent with the express wording of the contract (see also *Duke of Westminster* v. *Guild* [1985] QB 688). However, where the meaning of the express term is in doubt and the court is called upon to interpret that term, an implied term may, by a process of interpretation, be invoked to cut down or limit the literal scope of the express term so that the express and the implied terms can thus coexist 'without conflict' (*Johnstone* v. *Bloomsbury Health Authority* [1992] QB 333, 350–1 per Browne-Wilkinson VC, although contrast the approach of Stuart-Smith LJ who suggests (pp. 343–5) that a term implied in law (see below) may prevail over an express inconsistent term of the contract).

Secondly terms, known as terms 'implied in law', may be implied into all contracts of a particular type. Thus terms are frequently implied into contracts of employment and into contracts between landlords and tenants, not on the basis of the relationship between the particular parties, but as a general incidence of the relationship of employer and employee or landlord and tenant. To take the employment relationship as our example, there is an implied term that an employee will serve his employer faithfully and that he will indemnify his employer for liabilities incurred as a result of his wrongful acts in the course of his employment (*Lister* v. *Romford Ice & Cold Storage Co Ltd* [1957] AC 555). Equally it has been held that there is an implied term to the effect that the employer must not 'without reasonable and proper cause conduct [himself] in a manner calculated or likely to destroy or seriously damage the relationship of confidence and trust between the parties' (*Courtaulds Northern Textiles Ltd* v. *Andrew* [1979] IRLR 84). In these cases and the many other cases in which the courts have implied terms into contracts of employment it seems clear that the implication is not based on the 'officious bystander' test, but on some less stringent test which reflects the court's perception of the nature of the relationship between an employer and an employee and whether such an implied term is suitable or 'reasonable' for incorporation in all such contracts (for an example in the context of a landlord and tenant relationship see *Liverpool CC* v. *Irwin* (above)). As Lord Bridge put it in *Scally* v. *Southern Health and Social Services Board* [1992] 1 AC 294, 306, there is 'a clear distinction between the search for an implied term necessary to give business efficacy to a particular contract and the search, *based on wider considerations*, for a term which the law will imply as a necessary incident of a definable category of contractual relationship' (emphasis added, but note the criticisms of Phang, 1993, pp. 243–50).

Summary

1 Once the contracting parties have elected to enshrine their contract in a written document, the courts have held that, as a general rule, the parties cannot adduce extrinsic evidence to add to, vary or contradict the written document.

2 This 'rule' is called the parol evidence rule but it is the subject of so many exceptions that it is unlikely to have significant effects in practice.

3 As a general rule a person is bound by a document which he signs, whether he reads it or not, except where his signature has been procured by fraud, misrepresentation or the defence of *non est factum* is made out.

4 *Non est factum* means this is not my deed. It is a defence which is available to those who are permanently or temporarily unable through no fault of their own to have without explanation any real understanding of a particular document. The difference between the document as it was and as it was believed to be must be radical or substantial or fundamental. A person who signs the document carelessly, without bothering to read it properly, cannot invoke the defence.

5 Contracting parties may agree to incorporate a set of written terms into their contract. In order to do so notice must be given at or before the time of contracting, be contained in a document which was intended to have contractual effect and reasonable steps must be taken to bring the terms to the attention of the other party.

6 Terms may also be incorporated into a contract by a course of dealing. The course of dealing must be both regular and consistent.

7 When interpreting a contract the court must seek to ascertain and give effect to the intention of the parties. The intention of the parties must generally be derived from the document in which they have expressed their agreement.

8 Evidence of pre-contractual negotiations, of conduct subsequent to the making of the contract and of the parties' subjective intentions is generally inadmissible.

9 Rectification is a remedy which is concerned with defects not in the making, but in the recording, of a contract. It is an equitable discretionary remedy.

10 A court will only rectify a document where 'convincing proof' is provided that the document fails to record the intention of the parties, where the document fails to record the intention of *both* parties (unless one party knows that the other is mistaken) and the document must have been preceded by a concluded contract or by a 'continuing common intention'.

11 Terms may be implied into a contract by statute, by custom or by the common law. In the case of 'terms implied in fact' a court cannot imply a term simply because it would be reasonable to do so; it must be necessary to imply such a term (in other words it must pass the 'officious bystander' test).

Exercises

1 What is the 'parol evidence rule'? List the principal exceptions to the rule.

2 What is *non est factum*? In what circumstances is the defence available to an adult of full capacity?

3 Is it correct to say that the cases on sufficiency of notice are concerned with the question 'whether it would in all the circumstances be fair (or reasonable) to hold a party bound by any conditions . . . of an unusual and stringent nature'?

4 When is a course of dealing 'regular and consistent'?

5 What types of evidence are inadmissible when a court seeks to interpret a written contract?

6 What is rectification? When is it available?

7 In what circumstances may a term be implied into a contract? Do courts ever imply terms into a contract on the basis that it was 'just and reasonable' so to do?

10 The Classification of Contractual Terms

10.1 The Classification of Terms

Not all contract terms are of equal significance; some are more important than others. For example, if I were to enter into a contract to buy a new car, the make of the car, its roadworthiness and the price would be much more important to me than its colour. This fact has long been reflected in contract law in the distinction which has traditionally been drawn between a condition and a warranty.

A condition is an essential term of the contract which goes to the root or the heart of the contract. Thus, in the example of my purchase of a new car, the terms as to the make of the car, its roadworthiness and the price would all be conditions. A warranty, on the other hand, is a lesser, subsidiary term of the contract, such as the term relating to the colour of the car (unless it was part of the description of the car, in which case it would be treated as a condition under s.13(1) of the Sale of Goods Act 1979; see 9.8). The distinction between a condition and a warranty is vital in the event of a breach of contract. A breach of a condition enables the party who is not in breach of contract ('the innocent party') *either* to terminate performance of the contract and obtain damages for any loss suffered as a result of the breach *or* to affirm the contract and recover damages for the breach. A breach of a warranty only enables the innocent party to claim damages, that is to say he cannot terminate performance of the contract and must therefore continue to perform his obligations under the contract. So if, in our example, I wished to terminate the contract to purchase the car and to return the car to the sellers it would be essential for me to show that the sellers had broken a condition of the contract because, if the sellers had only broken a warranty, I would be confined to a remedy in damages.

It may seem odd to discuss the classification of contractual terms at this stage in the book if the primary significance of the classification relates to breach of contract. However the justification for doing so lies in the fact that the distinction is an important one in contract law and we shall encounter it on a number of occasions before we reach the chapter on breach of contract (Chapter 19).

10.2 What is a 'Condition'?

Before embarking upon a more detailed discussion of the distinction between a condition and a warranty, it is necessary to deal with a preliminary point relating to the meaning of the word 'condition'. The word 'condition' can be used in a number of different senses and it is important to have a clear grasp of the meanings which contract lawyers ascribe to this word. In the first place it could mean some event upon which the existence of the contract hinges. Such conditions are commonly called contingent conditions. These conditions may be of two types; conditions precedent and conditions subsequent. A condition precedent provides that the contract shall not become binding until the occurrence of a specified event (*Pym* v. *Campbell* (1856) 6 E & B 370). For example, I enter into an agreement to buy a car but the agreement provides that it shall not become binding until the car passes a road test; if the car fails the road test no contract comes into existence. A condition subsequent provides that a previously binding contract shall come to an end on the occurrence of a stipulated event. So if I enter into a binding contract, supported by consideration, under which I promise to pay £50 a month to my daughter Jenny until she gets married, the occurrence of her marriage will determine the contract between us. In both cases the effect of the occurrence of the condition is to terminate the agreement without either party being in breach of contract because, in the case of the condition precedent, neither party promised that the condition would be fulfilled and, in the case of the condition subsequent, neither party promised that the condition would not occur.

However we are not concerned here with such contingent conditions; we are concerned with promissory conditions. A promissory condition is a term of a contract under which one party promises to do a particular thing and a failure on his part to perform the promised act constitutes a breach of contract.

10.3 Distinguishing Between a Condition and a Warranty

Having established that we are discussing promissory conditions, it is now necessary to explain how it is decided whether a term is a condition or a warranty. We shall approach this issue by examining the situations in which a term has been held to be a condition. A term may be held to be a condition in one of three ways: by statutory classification, by judicial classification or by the classification of the parties .

Firstly, a term may be classified as a condition by statute. We have already noted (see 9.8) that sections 12–15 of the Sale of Goods Act 1979 imply certain terms into contracts for the sale of goods. These sections also classify these implied terms; thus the implied terms as to merchantable quality, fitness for purpose and compliance with description and sample are declared to be conditions, whereas the implied term that the goods are free from charges and incumbrances in favour of third parties is stated to be a warranty.

Secondly, a term may be classified as a condition by the courts. There are two grounds, apart from the stipulation of the parties, on which courts may decide that a term is a condition. The first is where performance of the term goes to the root of the contract so that, by necessary implication, the parties must have intended that the term should be treated as a condition, breach of which would entitle the other party to treat himself as discharged (see *Couchman* v. *Hill* [1947] KB 544, discussed at 8.3)). Although the term must go to the root of the contract, it need not be the case that every breach of the term should deprive the innocent party of substantially the whole benefit which it was intended that he would obtain from the contract (*Bunge Corp* v. *Tradax Export SA* [1981] 1 WLR 711). When seeking to ascertain the significance of the term which has been broken the courts will have regard to the views and practices of the commercial community. As Kerr LJ recently stated, the court is, in the absence of any other 'more specific guide', making 'what is in effect a value judgment about the commercial significance of the term in question' (*State Trading Corporation of India Ltd* v. *M Golodetz Ltd* [1989] 2 Lloyd's Rep 277, 283). In particular, where a decision has been made by an experienced trade arbitrator or tribunal as to the status of a particular term and that decision is based upon the commercial significance of the term, the courts will be extremely reluctant to interfere with the finding of that arbitrator or tribunal (*State Trading Corporation of India Ltd* v. *M Golodetz Ltd* [1989] 2 Lloyd's Rep 277, 284 and *The Naxos* [1990] 1 WLR 1337, 1348).

The second ground on which a court may decide that a term is a condition is that binding authority requires the court to hold that the term is a condition. In some industries parties trade on standard terms and a decision that a particular standard term is a condition will affect not only that contract, but also all subsequent contracts of that type. Thus a stipulation in a voyage charterparty relating to the time at which the vessel is expected ready to load is generally treated as a condition (*The Mihalis Angelos* [1971] 1 QB 164). The governing factor here is the need for certainty. But certainty carries with it a price. That price is that, in some cases, a party has been held to be entitled to terminate for breach of a condition, even though the breach has caused him little or no hardship. The most infamous example is, perhaps, *Arcos Ltd* v. *E A Ronaasen & Son* [1933] AC 470. Timber, described in the contract as half an inch thick, was bought to be used in making cement barrels. The timber, as delivered, was 9/16 inch thick but this did not impair its utility for making cement barrels. Nevertheless the buyers were held to be entitled to reject the timber, even though their motive in doing was so clearly that the market price for timber had fallen. As Professor Brownsword has recently stated (1992), 'the objection to the decision in *Arcos* is not so much that the buyers were allowed to act unreasonably or inefficiently by rejecting goods which they could use, but that they were allowed to reject such goods in order to take advantage of a falling market. In short, the objection is that the buyers acted in bad faith'. The buyers can be said to have acted in bad faith because the reason which they gave for exercising the right to terminate (the thickness of the timber) was not the 'real reason' and further that the 'real reason' was not attributable to the consequences of the breach but to the fact that they had entered into what had turned out to be a bad bargain. The courts are not presently concerned to ascertain the 'real reason' for the decision to terminate: as long as the party asserting the right to terminate does actually possess it the courts will not inquire into the motives behind its assertion. Arguably, the courts are right to adopt this approach because of the cost and uncertainty which would be created by inquiries into the actual motives of the party seeking to exercise the right to terminate.

The third method of classification is the parties' own classification of the contractual term. Thus, if a contract states that a particular term is a condition, the term will generally be regarded as a condition; similarly where the contract expressly states that breach of the term will entitle the other party to terminate performance of the contract. This ability to classify a term as a condition gives an extremely powerful weapon to contracting parties, as can be seen from the case of *Lombard North Central plc* v. *Butterworth* [1987] QB 527. A contract for the hire of computers stated in clause 2 of the agreement that it was of the essence of the contract that the hirer should pay each instalment promptly. The hirer failed to pay certain instalments promptly, whereupon the owners retook possession of the computers and sued the hirer for damages. The Court of Appeal held that making punctual payment of the essence of the contract was sufficient to turn the failure to pay a single instalment into a repudiation of the contract, thus entitling the plaintiff owners to terminate the contract and recover, not only in respect of arrears as at the date of termination, but also the loss of future instalments (subject to a discount for accelerated receipt of the future rentals). The court held that there was no restriction upon the right of the parties to classify the relative importance of the terms of their contract. It has been objected that such a principle 'does not always lead to a desirable result' (Bojczuk, 1987) but Mustill LJ refused to subject such terms to the control of the penalty clause jurisdiction (see 21.5) on the ground that to do so would be 'to reverse the current of more than 100 years' doctrine, which permits the parties to treat as a condition something which would not otherwise be so'.

However the court must be satisfied that the parties intended to use the word condition in its technical sense. In *Schuler AG* v. *Wickman Machine Tool Sales Ltd* [1974] AC 235, clause 7(b) of a four year distributorship agreement stated that 'it shall be a condition of this agreement that [Wickman] shall send its representatives to visit [six named UK manufacturers] at least once in every week for the purpose of soliciting orders'. Wickman failed to make some visits to the named manufacturers. Schuler claimed that they were therefore entitled to terminate the agreement because Wickman had broken a 'condition' of the agreement. This argument was rejected by the House of Lords. Lord Reid held that the use of the word 'condition' was an 'indication', perhaps even a ' strong indication', that the parties intended the term to be a condition in the technical sense, but it was by no means 'conclusive' evidence. He held that the more unreasonable the consequences of treating a term as a condition in its technical sense, the less likely it was that the parties intended to use the word 'condition' in such a way. On the facts, the consequence that a 'failure to make even one visit' would entitle Schuler to terminate the contract 'however blameless Wickman might be' was so unreasonable that it compelled Lord Reid to interpret 'condition' in clause 7(b) in its non-technical sense.

Although contracting parties are free to create conditions by stipulating that performance of a particular obligation shall be of the essence of the contract, it is vital to note that *both parties* must agree to this classification before the term can enjoy the status of a condition. The position is entirely different where *one party* serves a notice on the other party purporting to make performance of a particular obligation 'of the essence of the contract'. Let us suppose that one party fails to comply with the terms of a warranty, thus giving rise only to a claim for damages. Can the innocent party give the party in breach notice requiring him to perform the obligation within a certain period of time, stating that a failure to do so will be regarded as a repudiatory breach giving rise to a right to terminate (thus making performance 'of the essence of the contract')? Two issues must be distinguished here. The first relates to the entitlement of the innocent party to serve such a notice; the second concerns the effect of the notice. In relation to the first issue, the innocent party is entitled to serve such a notice because the right to give notice is not confined to essential terms of the contract but can be exercised in relation to any term of the contract (*Behzadi* v. *Shaftesbury Hotels Ltd* [1992] Ch. 1). Notice can be served at the moment of breach: it is not necessary to wait for a reasonable time to elapse before serving it (see *Behzadi* (above)). The period of notice given must, however, be reasonable; an issue which depends upon all the facts and circumstances of the case. The vital issue is therefore the second one, namely the effect of such a notice. In *Re Olympia & York Canary Wharf Ltd (No. 2)* [1993] BCC 159, Morritt J rejected the argument that a failure to comply with a time of the essence notice was of itself sufficient to constitute a repudiation of the contract. It is suggested that this is correct because, if failure to comply did of itself amount to a repudiation it would, in effect, give to one party the power unilaterally to turn a non-essential term into an essential term. There is all the difference in the world between a term which both parties agree to classify as a condition and a term which both parties agree to classify as a warranty but one party purports unilaterally to elevate to the status of a condition. On this view the function of a 'time of the essence' notice is limited: a failure to comply in respect of a non-essential term will not constitute a repudiation of the contract but at most will provide evidence from which a court may be prepared to infer that a repudiatory breach has occurred.

10.4 The Need for Change?

It can be seen that the primary emphasis in these cases has been upon the importance of the *term* which has been broken rather than upon the importance of the consequences of the *breach* of that term. The result has been that, in cases such as *Arcos* v. *Ronaasen* (above), a term has been classified as a condition even though the consequences of breach were insignificant. The justification for this approach is, firstly, that the parties must be free to classify the relative importance of their own contractual terms (see *Lombard North Central* v. *Butterworth* (above)) and, secondly, the need for certainty in commercial transactions. Certainty can be most effectively achieved by deciding whether or not a term is a condition according to the nature of the term broken, not by requiring the parties to wait and examine the consequences of the breach before deciding whether or not they are sufficiently serious to justify the classification of the term as a condition. The cause of certainty is further advanced by the fact that, once a term is classified as a condition, the innocent party is, unless barred by estoppel or by his election to affirm the contract (on which see further 19.8), automatically entitled to terminate performance of the contract. But it is important not to over-state the certainty which is achieved by classifying a term as a condition. It is true that, once a term has been classified as a condition a significant measure of certainty is thereby achieved, but uncertainty can still arise in relation to the prior question of whether the term which has been broken is actually a condition. For example, in *The Naxos* [1990] 1 WLR 1337 a majority of the House of Lords held that the obligation of the seller to have the cargo ready for delivery at any time within the contract period was a condition, whereas a majority of the Court of Appeal and the first instance judge were of the opinion that it was not. This uncertainty is, however, largely confined to previously unclassified terms and, while it should not be ignored, it should not detract from the principal point which is that the classification of a term as a condition does give rise to a greater degree of certainty in commercial transactions.

But the cost of this emphasis on the need to promote certainty is an element of injustice, in cases such as *Arcos* v. *Ronaasen* (above), where the motive for terminating the contract was that the contract had turned out to be a bad bargain for the innocent party. Such injustice could be largely avoided if the critical factor in deciding whether a term was a condition (and hence whether the innocent party was entitled to terminate performance of the contract) was to become the consequences of the breach. Then the innocent party would only be entitled to terminate performance of the contract where the consequences to him of the breach were sufficiently serious (indeed there was authority for such a proposition in the early case of *Boone* v. *Eyre* (1777) 1 H Bl 273, before the emphasis switched to the importance of the term which had been broken in cases such as *Behn* v. *Burness* (1863) 3 B & S 751 and *Bettini* v. *Gye* (1876) 1 QBD 183). Yet the cost of such a shift in emphasis would be the sacrifice of a degree of certainty.

A further criticism which has been levelled against too great a willingness to classify a term as a condition is that it encourages termination of contracts rather than their performance. As Roskill LJ stated in *The Hansa Nord* [1976] QB 44, 'in principle, contracts are made to be performed and not to be avoided according to the whims of market fluctuation and where there is a free choice between two possible constructions I think the court should tend to prefer that construction which will ensure performance, and not encourage avoidance of contractual obligations'. The *Hansa Nord* was a case, like *Arcos* v. *Ronaasen*, where the buyer was searching for a way out of a bad bargain and it is true that, in this context, a refusal to classify a term as a condition is more likely to lead to contractual performance. But in other contexts this is not so. The classification of a term as a condition can give an incentive to a would-be contract-breaker to perform his obligations under the contract because breach will expose him to a claim for loss of bargain damages. The hirer in *Lombard North Central plc* v. *Butterworth* (above) will, presumably, take greater steps to perform his obligations under any future contract of hire he may conclude, knowing the draconian consequences which can follow from breach of a condition. In this sense, classification of a term as a condition could be said to act as an incentive to performance rather than termination. So this argument, ultimately, is not convincing and it is the apparent injustice of cases such as *Arcos* which is the real basis for arguments for reform.

So, in this context, what we have is, essentially, a conflict between the interests of 'certainty' and the interests of 'justice' or 'fairness'. 'Certainty' requires the focus to be upon the nature of the term broken and demands a high degree of remedial rigidity. 'Justice', on the other hand, requires the focus to be on the consequences of the breach and demands a high degree of remedial flexibility. The generally accepted view was that, in cases such as *Arcos* v. *Ronaasen*, the pendulum had swung too far in favour of the promotion of certainty and that it was time to redress the balance.

In seeking to redress the balance, two approaches have been adopted. The first is to seek to limit the number of terms which are classified as conditions. Thus, in *Reardon Smith Line Ltd* v. *Hansen Tangen* [1976] 1 WLR 989, Lord Wilberforce stated that some of the authorities which we have discussed were 'excessively technical and due for fresh examination' by the House of Lords. But these cases still await 'fresh examination' by the House of Lords and it is unlikely that this line of approach will be further developed. The second approach has been to focus more attention on the consequences of the breach and to give the courts greater remedial flexibility. This has been achieved through the recognition of the fact that the distinction between a condition and a warranty is not an exhaustive one.

10.5 Innominate Terms

A third classification has now been recognised in English law; the intermediate or the innominate term. The origin of this development can be found in the judgment of Diplock LJ in *Hong Kong Fir Shipping Co Ltd* v. *Kawasaki Kisen Kaisha Ltd* [1962] 2 QB 26, 70 when he said:

> 'There are many . . . contractual undertakings . . . which cannot be categorised as being "conditions" or "warranties". . . Of such undertakings all that can be predicated is that some breaches will and others will not give rise to an event which will deprive the party not in default of substantially the whole benefit which it was intended that he should obtain.'

An innominate term can be distinguished from a condition on the ground that breach of an innominate term does not automatically give rise to a right to terminate performance of the contract and it can be distinguished from a warranty on the ground that the innocent party is not confined to a remedy in damages. Thus the court is given a greater degree of remedial flexibility and it can focus attention on the consequences of the breach by allowing a party to terminate performance of the contract only where the breach of the innominate term has had serious consequences for him. Yet it is this remedial flexibility which is, itself, problematic because one can never be entirely sure whether one has the right to terminate when faced with a breach by the other party. In deciding whether or not the breach was of a sufficiently serious character the courts will have regard to all the relevant circumstances of the case. Carter (1991) has helpfully identified the following factors which are relied upon by the courts: (i) any detriment caused, or likely to be caused, by the breach; (ii) any delay caused, or likely to be caused, by the breach; (iii) the value of any performance received by or tendered to the party not in breach; (iv) the cost of making any performance given or tendered by the party in breach conform with the requirements of the contract; (v) any offer by the party in breach to remedy the breach; (vi) whether the party in breach has previously breached the contract or is likely to breach it in the future; and (vii) whether the party not in breach will be adequately compensated by an award of damages in respect of the breach. Not only is this list of factors extremely broad, but the weight which is accorded to each one must depend, to a large extent, on the facts of the case. The uncertainty thereby caused is important because, if a contracting party gets it wrong and purports to terminate when he was not in fact entitled to do so (because the breach was not repudiatory), he will be held to have repudiated his obligations under the contract and may be liable to pay substantial damages in consequence. Uncertainty can carry with it a real price.

The creation of this new category of innominate terms leaves us with the further difficulty of distinguishing between an innominate term, a condition and a warranty. In practice classification of a term as a warranty is rare, but such a classification is not entirely without significance. A party who is in breach of contract may wish to argue that the term which has been broken is a warranty rather than an innominate term so as to restrict the innocent party to a remedy in damages and to deprive him of the ability to terminate. Contracting parties are free to classify terms as warranties, just as they are free to classify terms as conditions, but if they wish to confine a term to the status of a warranty, they should 'make it plain from the contract as a whole' that that is their intention' (*Re Olympia & York Canary Wharf Ltd (No. 2)* [1993] BCC 159, 166). If the contract states that the term is a condition then, subject to *Schuler* v. *Wickman*, it will be treated as a condition. A term will also be regarded as a condition where it is classified as such by statute. Where the term has been previously classified by the judiciary as a condition then, cases such as *Arcos* v. *Ronaasen* apart, it is likely that the term will continue to be regarded as a condition. The principal difficulty is likely to arise in connection with previously unclassified terms.

At this point we return to the conflict which we have already noted between the interests of 'certainty' and 'justice'. If primary attention is given to considerations of fairness, this will favour classification of terms as innominate terms because the remedy can be tailored to the facts of the case. On the other hand, an approach which gives primary attention to considerations of certainty will favour classification as a condition because the remedial consequences will then be clear. Some indication of the likely resolution of this conflict can be gleaned from the case of *Bunge* v. *Tradax* (above). The House of Lords held that a term which related to the time of performance in a commercial contract was a condition and not an innominate term on the ground that time was generally of the essence in such contracts. However Lord Wilberforce said that 'the courts should not be too ready to interpret contractual clauses as conditions'. This suggests that, apart from terms which are commercially vital where the need for certainty is greatest, greater consideration will be given to the interests of 'justice' by classifying contract terms as innominate terms in order to give the courts flexibility in granting the appropriate relief. A good example of this is provided by *The Hansa Nord* [1976] QB 44, a case which bears some resemblance to *Arcos* v. *Ronaasen*. Buyers of citrus pulp purported to reject the cargo on the ground that shipment was not made in 'good condition'. The price of the cargo was £100 000. The sellers were compelled to sell the cargo and the buyers, acting through an agent, managed to repurchase it for £30 000 and they were able to use the citrus pulp for its original intended purpose. The Court of Appeal held that the term which had been broken was not a condition and, applying *Hong Kong Fir*, they concluded that that the term was an innominate one and that the consequences of the breach were not sufficiently serious to give rise to a right to terminate. The buyers were therefore confined to a claim in damages to reflect the loss in value of the cargo caused by its defective state. On this approach, the injustice of cases such as *Arcos* v. *Ronaasen* need no longer occur.

Summary

1 Contract terms can be classified either as conditions, warranties or innominate terms.

2 A condition is an essential term of the contract which goes to the root or the heart of the contract. This is a promissory condition which must be distinguished from a contingent condition, which is some event upon which the existence of the contract hinges. A contingent condition may be either a condition precedent or a condition subsequent.

3 A term may be classified as a promissory condition by statute, by judicial classification or by the classification of the parties. In the latter category the court must be satisfied that the parties intended to use the word condition in its technical sense.

4 Breach of a promissory condition entitles the innocent party either to terminate performance of the contract and claim damages or to affirm the contract and claim damages.

5 A warranty is a lesser, subsidiary term of the contract. Breach of a warranty only gives a remedy in damages.

6 The category of innominate terms was recognised by Diplock LJ in the *Hong Kong Fir* case.

7 An innominate term can be distinguished from a condition on the ground that breach of an innominate term does not automatically give rise to a right to terminate performance of the contract and it can be distinguished from a warranty on the ground that the innocent party's remedy is not confined to damages. Classification as an innominate term therefore gives the court an important degree of remedial flexibility.

Exercises

1 Distinguish between a promissory condition and a contingent condition.

2 When will a term be classified as a promissory condition?

3 What are the remedial consequences of classifying a term as

(a) a condition;

(b) a warranty; and

(c) an innominate term.

11 Exclusion Clauses

An exclusion clause may be defined as a 'clause in a contract or a term in a notice which appears to exclude or restrict a liability or a legal duty which would otherwise arise' (Yates, 1982, p. 1). Exclusion clauses are a common feature of contracts today and may take a number of different forms. The most frequently encountered types of exclusion clauses are those which seek to exclude liability for breach of contract or for negligence or which seek to limit liability to a specified sum. Another type of exclusion clause commonly encountered is an indemnity clause, under which one contracting party promises to indemnify the other for any liability incurred by him in the performance of the contract (for a description of other types of exclusion clauses see Yates, 1982, pp. 33-41).

11.1 Exclusion Clauses: Defence or Definition?

Despite the common occurrence of exclusion clauses in contracts, differing views remain as to their essential nature. Let us take an example to illustrate the point. John, who presently lives in Colchester, wishes to have his furniture transported to his new house in Preston and for this purpose he contracts with Peter. Peter, who is self-employed, offers a price which is substantially lower than any other removal firm because he offers no insurance cover for the goods while they are in transit; instead he relies on the owner of the goods either to use his existing insurance policy (if it is applicable) or to take out his own special insurance policy. In order to give effect to his pricing policy Peter inserts a clause into his contracts to the following effect: 'no liability is accepted for any damage, howsoever caused, to any goods during the course of transit'. Two views may be adopted as to the function of such a clause.

One view holds that this clause simply defines the obligations which the contracting parties have chosen to accept. Peter has only accepted a limited obligation to transmit the goods and has never accepted any liability for damage to the goods during the course of transit. On this view the function of the exclusion clause is to assist in *defining* the obligations of the parties. This view is not, however, the one which the courts have traditionally adopted. Courts have traditionally seen exclusion clauses as performing a defensive function. On this view a failure by Peter to deliver the goods safely to Preston constitutes a breach of contract and the role of the exclusion clause is to provide Peter with a *defence* to John's action for breach of contract.

Yet a closer examination of this traditional view reveals a serious difficulty. The difficulty is that Peter has not accepted an absolute obligation to deliver John's goods; such a conclusion could only be reached by ignoring the exclusion clause when defining Peter's obligations. But why should the exclusion clause be ignored in defining Peter's obligations, since it is via the exclusion clause that Peter has sought to define the extent of his obligations and it is only by this means that he can offer a service at a price lower than that of his competitors? There can surely be no justification for ignoring the exclusion clause in this manner. The clause is simply one means, albeit an important one, by which Peter has attempted to *define* his obligations. If this view of exclusion clauses is accepted, the justification for subjecting exclusion clauses to distinct regulation largely disappears because such clauses then become functionally indistinguishable from every other term of the contract which assists in defining the obligations which the parties have accepted towards each other (this theory was initially developed by Coote, 1964, and is also supported by Yates, 1982).

The argument that exclusion clauses define the obligations of the parties has recently been attacked by Adams and Brownsword (1988a) on the ground that it is 'elegantly formalistic' and that it ignores 'both the historical development of the problem, and the realities of the situation'. The 'historical development' is that the growth in the use of standard form contracts has been accompanied by a growth in the use of exclusion clauses and the 'realities' of the situation are that such terms are offered on a 'take it or leave it basis'. In short, these standard form contracts, which so often include sweeping exclusion clauses, are imposed on the weaker party to the transaction. They take away the rights of the weaker party and nullify his expectations rather than define the obligations of the parties. But it is only by looking outside the contract for the initial existence of these 'rights' or 'expectations' that exclusion clauses can be said to 'take away' the 'rights' of the weaker party or nullify his 'expectations'. There 'rights' and 'expectations' must exist outside the contract because the contract as a whole certainly did not confer them upon the weaker party. How then are we to ascertain the scope of these 'rights' or 'expectations'? Are they to be found in some conception of 'public policy'? Proponents of the 'defensive' view of exclusion clauses do not tell us. Surely the evil which we are seeking to eradicate is not the existence of exclusion clauses or even simply the existence of 'unreasonable exclusion clauses' but the existence of 'unfair' terms in a contract. If this is so, then the correct approach must be to deal with exclusion clauses as part of a general doctrine of duress, inequality of bargaining power or 'unconscionability' (see further Chapter 17) and not by the artificial and misleading process of subjecting exclusion clauses to distinct regulation on the basis that they are a defence to a breach of an obligation (see Yates, 1982, ch. 7). Notwithstanding the force of this criticism, the courts and Parliament have generally treated exclusion clauses as a defence to a breach of an obligation, although, as we shall see, this view has given rise to considerable difficulties.

11.2 The Functions of Exclusion Clauses

Before embarking upon an analysis of the detailed rules of law, we must identify the different functions of exclusion clauses. Exclusion clauses perform a number of useful functions. First, they help in the allocation of risks under the contract. In our example involving Peter and John the risk of damage to the goods is clearly allocated to John and there is no need for Peter to take out insurance cover; double insurance is thereby avoided. Secondly, exclusion clauses can help reduce litigation costs by making clear the division of responsibility between the parties. Thirdly, exclusion clauses are often used in standard form contracts which, by enabling people, such as Peter, to mass-produce their contracts, helps reduce the cost of negotiations and of making contracts.

On the other hand, exclusion clauses can perform a function which is socially harmful in that, as we have already seen, they can be used by the powerful in society to exclude liability towards the weaker party, thereby leaving the weak without a remedy. It is this socially undesirable function of exclusion clauses which has provided significant impetus for reform of this area of law and which explains the restrictive approach which the courts have adopted in their treatment of exclusion clauses.

11.3 An Outline of the Law

A contracting party who wishes to include an exclusion clause in a contract must overcome three hurdles before he can do so. First, it must be shown that the exclusion clause is properly incorporated into the contract (11.4). Secondly, it must be shown that, properly interpreted, the exclusion clause covers the loss which has arisen (11.5–11.7). Thirdly, there must be no other rule of law which would invalidate the exclusion clause (11.8–11.15).

Historically, it was the first two of these three stages which were important. The principal explanation for this is that, although at common law the court has power to strike down contract terms which are 'contrary to public policy' (see 15.6–15.16), it did not have the power to hold exclusion clauses invalid because they were unreasonable (despite arguments to the contrary by Lord Denning in cases such as *Levison* v. *Patent Steam Carpet Cleaning Co Ltd* [1978] QB 68). Deprived of the ability to strike down unreasonable exclusion clauses by such direct means, the courts sought to achieve such a goal by the indirect means of adopting a restrictive approach towards the incorporation (9.4 and 11.4) and the interpretation (11.5–11.7) of exclusion clauses. Lord Denning recognised this in *Gillespie Bros* v. *Roy Bowles Ltd* [1973] 1 QB 400, when he said that 'judges departed from the ordinary meaning, under the guise of construing the clause so as to reduce it to reasonable proportions'.

But now, since courts have been given statutory power under the Unfair Contract Terms Act 1977 (UCTA) to control exclusion clauses, there is less need for them to use the first two stages to control unreasonable exclusion clauses and hence it can be expected that the focus of attention will switch to the third stage (although constrast the restrictive approach which was adopted towards incorporation in the case of *Interfoto Picture Library Ltd* v. *Stiletto Visual Programmes Ltd* [1989] QB 433 (discussed at 9.4), which, although not an exclusion clause case, shows that the restrictive approach to incorporation is still very much alive).

11.4   Incorporation

At the first stage it must be shown that the exclusion clause was validly incorporated into the contract. Here the reader should refer to the discussion of incorporation at 9.4.

11.5   Construction of Exclusion Clauses

At the second stage it must be shown that the exclusion clause, properly interpreted or properly construed, covers the damage which was caused. Had the courts adopted a definitional approach to exclusion clauses then such clauses would have been subject to the same rules of interpretation as any other term of the contract. But one consequence of the courts' adoption of the defensive approach to exclusion clauses has been that exclusion clauses have not been interpreted in the same way as other terms of the contract; they have been interpreted more rigorously or restrictively.

The general approach which the courts have adopted to the interpretation of exclusion clauses is a restrictive one, under which the exclusion clause is interpreted strictly against the party seeking to rely on it. This rule is called the '*contra proferentem*' rule. The effect of the rule is that any ambiguity in the exclusion clause is resolved against the party seeking to rely on it. Although the *contra proferentem* rule is applicable to any ambiguous term in a contract, it has been applied particularly stringently to exclusion clauses. The 'proferens' is simply the person seeking to rely on the exclusion clause; it does not imply that the person seeking to rely on the exclusion clause has 'imposed' it on the other party (*Scottish Special Housing Association* v. *Wimpey Construction UK Ltd* 1986 SLT 173).

One consequence of the application of the *contra proferentem* rule has been a game of 'cat and mouse' between contract draftsmen and the courts, as draftsmen have sought to evade the restrictive interpretations adopted by the courts. This can be illustrated by reference to the following two cases. In *Wallis, Son and Wells* v. *Pratt and Haynes* [1911] AC 394, a contract for the sale of seeds contained a clause which stated that the sellers gave 'no warranty express or implied' as to the description of the seeds. The seeds did not correspond with the description so the buyers brought an action for damages against the sellers, who sought to rely on the exclusion clause. It was held that they could not do so because it only covered breach of a 'warranty' and, in failing to provide seeds which corresponded with the description, the sellers had broken a condition (the distinction between a condition and a warranty is discussed at 10.1). The impact of this ruling can be seen in *Andrews Bros (Bournemouth) Ltd* v. *Singer and Co Ltd* [1934] 1 KB 17. This time the exclusion clause stated that 'all conditions, warranties and liabilities *implied* by statute, common law or otherwise are excluded'. The plaintiffs contracted with the defendants to buy some 'new Singer cars'. One of the cars delivered by the defendants was a used car. The plaintiffs sued for damages and the defendants sought, unsuccessfully, to rely on the exclusion clause. Greer LJ said that the defendants were probably trying to escape the effect of *Wallis* but the only problem was that, although they had included the word condition, they had omitted the word 'express' and this was fatal because the court held that the defendants had broken an express term of the contract.

However, this strict approach may now be undergoing some reconsideration. In *Ailsa Craig Fishing Co Ltd* v. *Malvern Fishing Co Ltd* [1983] 1 WLR 964, the House of Lords held that, in the case of limitation clauses, the *contra proferentem* rule did not apply with the same rigour as it applied to exclusion clauses. Lord Fraser and Lord Wilberforce said that limitation clauses were not viewed with the same hostility as exclusion clauses because of their role in risk allocation and because it was more likely that the other party would agree to a limitation clause than an exclusion clause. This approach is open to the objection that it ignores the risk allocation function of exclusion clauses and it is by no means certain that the other party would be more willing to agree to a limitation clause, especially where the limit is derisory (see Palmer, 1982). Instead of differentiating between exclusion clauses and limitation clauses, one would have expected uniform rules of construction to be applied to all contract terms. Such an approach has not, however, commended itself to the House of Lords and they have since followed *Ailsa Craig* in *George Mitchell (Chesterhall) Ltd* v. *Finney Lock Seeds Ltd* [1983] 2 AC 803. On the other hand, the High Court of Australia in *Darlington Futures Ltd* v. *Delco Australia Pty Ltd* (1987) 61 ALJR 76, has refused to differentiate between exclusion clauses and limitation clauses in this manner. Instead the court held that

'the interpretation of an exclusion clause is to be determined by construing the clause according to its natural and ordinary meaning, read in the light of the contract as a whole, thereby giving due weight to the context in which the clause appears including the nature and the object of the contract and, where appropriate, construing the clause *contra proferentem* in case of ambiguity'.

This approach is to be welcomed in so far as it adopts a more natural interpretation of exclusion clauses. Some support for a more clement approach can also be found in some English cases. As we have already noted (9.4), in *Photo Production Ltd* v. *Securicor Transport Ltd* [1980] AC 827, Lord Diplock said that 'the reports are full of cases in which what would appear to be very strained constructions have been placed upon exclusion clauses'. He noted that many of these cases involved consumer contracts and continued, 'any need for this kind of judicial distortion of the English language has been banished by Parliament's having made these kinds of contract subject to the Unfair Contract Terms Act 1977'. It should be noted that in neither *Photo Production* nor *Darlington Futures* was the *contra proferentem* rule doubted; in both cases all that the court was saying was that it will operate only in cases of genuine ambiguity and that in future exclusion clauses should be given a more natural construction.

It is to be hoped that, in future cases, courts will continue to apply a more natural interpretation to exclusion clauses. However there remain at least two situations in which particular rules of construction are employed by the courts. These rules apply where one party seeks to exclude liability for his own negligence (11.6) or where he seeks to exclude liability for a 'fundamental breach' (11.7). We shall now discuss these two special rules of construction.

11.6   Negligence Liability

The first relates to the situation where a contracting party seeks to exclude liability for his own negligence (note that UCTA contains severe restrictions on the ability of a contracting party to exclude liability for his own negligence even where it is clear that the clause, on its proper construction, covers negligently inflicted damage, see 11.10). The courts regard it as inherently unlikely that one party will agree to allow the other contracting party to exclude liability for his own negligence. To give effect to this, the courts have evolved three specific rules of construction which find their origin in the speech of Lord Morton of Henryton in *Canada Steamship Lines Ltd* v. *The King* [1952] AC 192.

The first rule is that if a clause contains language which expressly exempts the party relying on the exclusion clause from the consequences of his own negligence then (subject to UCTA) effect must be given to the clause. This test may be fulfilled by using a word which is a synonym for negligence (*Smith* v. *UBM Chrysler (Scotland) Ltd* 1978 SC (HL) 1). The safest course, however, is to use the word negligence expressly.

If the first rule is not satisfied the court will then proceed to apply the second and the third limbs of Lord Morton's test. It is important to understand that, while the first rule stands alone, the second and the third rules constitute a double hurdle which must be overcome by a clause which fails to satisfy the first rule. The second rule is that the court must consider whether the words are wide enough, in their ordinary meaning, to cover negligence on the part of the party relying on the exclusion clause. If a doubt arises as to whether the words are wide enough, the doubt must be resolved against the party relying on the clause. Exclusion clauses which have been held wide enough to satisfy this test include clauses which exclude liability for 'any act or omission' or 'any damage whatsoever'.

Once the second rule has been satisfied the court must then apply the third rule and consider whether the exclusion clause may cover some kind of liability other than negligence. If there is such a liability, the clause will generally be confined in its application to that alternative source of liability and will be held not to extend to negligently inflicted loss. It was once thought that the mere existence of a possible alternative source of liability meant that the clause could not cover negligence, but the point has since been reconsidered by the Court of Appeal in *The Raphael* [1982] 2 Lloyd's Rep 42 (see Palmer, 1983). In the latter case it was held that the rules laid down in *Canada Steamship* were merely aids to be used by the courts in identifying the intention of the parties and it was emphasised that where the alternative source of liability was 'fanciful or remote' it would not prevent the exclusion clause covering liability in negligence. But what if the alternative source of liability was sufficiently realistic for the parties to intend the clause to apply to that other source of liability? Does such an alternative source of liability mean that the clause cannot apply to negligence? Stephenson LJ thought so. On the other hand Lord Donaldson and May LJ held that the point was ultimately one of construction but even they said that in such a case the clause would generally be interpreted as not excluding liability for negligence.

The combination of the second and the third rules can produce results which are unsatisfactory and contrary to the intention of the parties. Two particular problems can be identified. The first is that the two rules make contradictory demands of the draftsman. The second rule demands that the clause be drafted as widely as possible so that it will be held to encompass negligently inflicted damage. But the third rule demands that the clause be narrow in scope because the wider it is, the more likely it is that it will encompass some source of liability other than negligence and so be confined in its scope to that alternative source of liability. A number of clauses have been caught by this dilemma: they surmount the second rule, only to fall at the third because the clause is held to be confined to the alternative, non-negligent source of liability (see, for example, *Dorset County Council* v. *Southern Felt Roofing Co Ltd* (1989) 48 Build LR 96).

The second problem is that the parties may intend the same clause to apply both to negligently inflicted damage and to non-negligently inflicted damage. In our example involving Peter and John (see 11.1), Peter may wish the exclusion clause to cover not only negligence on his part, but also any liability which he may incur for late delivery of the furniture through no fault of his own (for example, his van may break down and John may incur expenses living in a hotel in Preston while waiting for the furniture to arrive). In such a case, the application of the *Canada Steamship* rules would be more likely to frustrate that intention than give effect to it, and rules which so frustrate the intention of the parties should be abandoned at the first opportunity. It is therefore suggested that the courts should no longer apply the *Canada Steamship* rules but should leave the issue as one of construction, with the courts simply having to decide, as a matter of construction, whether or not the exclusion clause covered negligently caused damage. Such a step was taken by the Supreme Court of Victoria in *Schenker & Co (Aust) Pty Ltd* v. *Malpas Equipment and Services Pty Ltd* [1990] VR 834, 846, where McGarvie J stated that the strained approach to construction adopted in *Canada Steamship* was inconsistent with the more natural and ordinary construction adopted by the High Court of Australia in *Darlington Futures* (above). He justified this departure from strained rules of construction on the following ground:

> 'To construe commercial contracts as they would be understood by business people serves primary aims of both the law and commerce. The law serves the community best if citizens understand it and are able to resolve their dispute themselves by reference to it, without resorting to lawyers or courts.'

It is suggested that there is much to be said for this view, but in *EE Caledonia Ltd* v. *Orbit Valve Co Europe* [1993] 4 All ER 165, 173, Hobhouse J took the opposite approach and chose to affirm and apply the *Canada Steamship* rules in emphatic terms. He stated:

> 'it has to be borne in mind that commercial contracts are drafted by parties with access to legal advice and in the context of established legal principles as reflected in the decisions of the courts. Principles of certainty, and indeed justice, require that contracts be construed in accordance with the established principles. The parties are always able by the choice of appropriate language to draft their contract so as to produce a different legal effect. The choice is theirs.'

While certainty is indeed an important commodity in the law of contract, the approach of Hobhouse J is open to criticism on a number of grounds. The first is that parties do not always have access to legal advice. The second is the fact that parties can contract out of the rule does not justify the rule itself. Finally, the continued existence of an unsatisfactory rule imposes costs on commerce because the parties must bear the cost of negotiating their way out of an inconvenient rule. The better approach, it is suggested, would be to rid the law of the arbitrary *Canada Steamship* rules, leaving the courts to apply the *contra proferentem* rule in the usual way.

11.7 Fundamental Breach

The second situation in which the courts have evolved specific rules of interpretation is where the breach of contract by the party relying on the exclusion clause is of a fundamental nature. Two distinct approaches have been adopted here and it is vital to understand the difference between the two. The first approach may be called the rule of law approach, under which it was not possible by a clause (however widely drafted) to exclude liability for certain breaches of contract which were deemed to be fundamental. This approach grew under the guiding hand of Lord Denning as a means of control over exclusion clauses which were thought to be unreasonable. The second approach may be called the rule of construction approach. According to this approach the question whether an exclusion clause covered a fundamental breach was a question of construction, under which the clause was interpreted against the party seeking to rely on it.

In *Suisse Atlantique Societe d'Armament Maritime SA* v. *NV Rotterdamsche Kolen Centrale* [1967] 1 AC 361, the House of Lords held that the latter approach was the correct one but, unfortunately, their Lordships' judgments were not a model of clarity and their ambiguities were seized upon in cases such as *Harbutt's Plasticine Ltd* v. *Wayne Tank Pump Co Ltd* [1970] 1 QB 477, to resurrect the rule of law approach. However, the rule of law approach was finally laid to rest by the House of Lords in *Photo Production Ltd* v. *Securicor Transport Ltd* [1980] AC 827. The plaintiffs, who were factory owners, entered into a contract with the defendants, under which the defendants contracted to provide periodic visits to the plaintiffs' factory during the night for the purpose of checking that the factory was secure. During one of these visits an employee of the defendants started a fire, apparently to keep himself warm, but which got out of control and burnt down the factory.

The plaintiffs sought to recover damages of £648 000 from the defendants, but the defendants relied on an exclusion clause which stated that 'under no circumstances' were they 'to be responsible for any injurious act or default by any employee . . . unless such act or default could have been foreseen and avoided by the exercise of due diligence on the part of [the defendants]'. The House of Lords held that it was a question of construction whether or not the exclusion clause covered a fundamental breach and that, on the facts, the defendants were not liable because the exclusion clause did, in fact, cover the damage which had arisen.

It is undoubtedly the case that much mystique surrounds the doctrine of fundamental breach. This is largely due to the difficulties and confusion created by the rule of law approach. Now that the rule of law approach has been laid to rest, the 'doctrine' simply exists as a rule of construction, according to which the more serious the breach, or the consequences of the breach, the less likely it is that the court will interpret the exclusion clause as applying to the breach. As Neill LJ stated in *Edmund Murray Ltd* v. *BSP International Foundations Ltd* (1993) 33 Con LR 1, 16, 'it is always necessary when considering an exemption clause to decide whether as a matter of construction it extends to exclude or restrict the liability in question, but, if it does, it is no longer permissible at common law to reject or circumvent the clause by treating it as inapplicable to "a fundamental breach"' (see also Unfair Contract Terms Act 1977, s.9).

Although the rule of law approach has gone, great care must still be taken when drafting a term which seeks to exempt one party from the consequences of a particularly serious breach. Therefore if a contracting party wishes to exclude liability for (i) breach of a fundamental term of the contract (that is a term which goes to the root of the contract or forms the essential character of the contract, see *Karsales (Harrow) Ltd* v. *Wallis* [1956] 1 WLR 936), (ii) a deliberate refusal to perform his obligations under the contract (*Sze Hai Tong Bank Ltd* v. *Rambler Cycle Co Ltd* [1959] AC 576) or (iii) a breach which will have particularly serious consequences for the other party, then he must use clear words to such an effect if he is to achieve his purpose. Yet even here, as we have already noted, the House of Lords in *Photo Production* stated that a strained construction should not be put upon words in an exclusion clause which are clearly and fairly susceptible of only one meaning.

11.8   Other Common Law Controls upon Exclusion Clauses

There are certain additional controls over exclusion clauses which exist at common law. The common law limitations are of much less significance since the intervention of Parliament (see 11.9). A party cannot rely on an exclusion clause, the effect of which he has misrepresented to the other party (*Curtis* v. *Chemical Cleaning and Dyeing Co Ltd* [1951] 1 KB 805). Similarly, an exclusion clause which is contained in a written document can be overridden by an express inconsistent undertaking given at or before the time of contracting (*Couchman* v. *Hill* [1947] KB 554). A defendant may also be prevented by the doctrine of privity from taking the benefit of an exclusion clause contained in a contract to which he was not a party (see 7.6). Finally, it must be remembered that the courts have no power at common law to strike down an exclusion clause simply because it is unreasonable (see 11.3).

11.9   The Unfair Contract Terms Act 1977

Parliament has now assumed the major role in regulating the use of exclusion clauses in contracts. The principal legislation which it has enacted in pursuance of this role is the Unfair Contract Terms Act 1977 (UCTA). The Act is a complex and technical piece of legislation. It is important to bear in mind that here we are dealing with an Act of Parliament and the *exact* words used by the Act must be studied and applied.

While the Act gives the courts considerable power to regulate exclusion clauses, it is vital to note that English law still does not recognise the existence of a general doctrine of unfairness or unconscionability (see

17.4). It is only particular types of clause, such as exclusion or limitation clauses, which are picked out for regulation. One consequence of this approach is that Parliament must define what constitutes an exclusion or a limitation clause and the courts must in turn interpret that definition. The focus is therefore upon the *form* of *the clause* which is the subject of the control rather than upon the *substance* of *the contract* taken as a whole. The result is that difficult threshold questions can arise in deciding whether or not the clause in the contract falls within the scope of the Act. If it does, it will be subjected to the reasonableness test (unless it is declared by the Act to be void), but if it falls outside the scope of the Act then there is no general doctrine of unfairness or unreasonableness to which the party seeking to set aside the term can appeal. This has given rise to various jurisdictional difficulties as contracting parties have sought to evade the clutches of the Act by arguing that the clause at issue does not fall within the scope of the Act. In the following sections of this chapter we shall look at the various clauses which fall within the scope of the Act and explore one or two of the 'jurisdictional' issues which have arisen.

11.10 Negligence Liability

The first issue which the Act deals with are attempts to exclude or restrict liability for negligently inflicted loss. Section 2 provides that:

'(1) A person cannot by reference to any contract term or to a notice given to persons generally or to particular persons exclude or restrict his liability for death or personal injury resulting from negligence.
(2) In the case of other loss or damage, a person cannot so exclude or restrict his liability for negligence except in so far as the term or notice satisfies the requirement of reasonableness.
(3) Where a contract term or notice purports to exclude or restrict liability for negligence a person's agreement to or awareness of it is not of itself to be taken as indicating his voluntary acceptance of any risk.'

A number of points should be noted about this section. The first is that it only applies to 'negligence', so that it does not apply to attempts to exclude or restrict liability which is strict. 'Negligence' is defined in s.1(1) as 'the *breach* –

(a) of any obligation, arising from the express or implied terms of a contract, to take reasonable care or exercise reasonable skill in the performance of the contract;
(b) of any common law duty to take reasonable care or exercise reasonable skill (but not any stricter duty);
(c) of the common duty of care imposed by the Occupiers' Liability Act 1957 or the Occupiers' Liability Act (Northern Ireland) 1957'.

An act is not prevented from being an act of negligence on the ground that the breach of duty was intentional rather than inadvertent, or because liability for it arose vicariously rather than directly (s.1(4)).

The second point to note about section 2 is that it applies only to attempts to exclude or restrict 'liability' and that liability for this purpose is confined to 'business liability'. Business liability is defined in s.1(3) as 'liability for breach of obligations or duties arising

(a) from things done or to be done by a person in the course of a business (whether his own business or another's) or
(b) from the occupation of premises used for business purposes of the occupier'.

'Business' is defined in s.14 as including a profession and the activities of any government department or local or public authority.

The third point to note is that the section is not confined in its application to contracts: it also extends to non-contractual notices which purport to exclude or restrict liability for negligence. Fourthly, it should be noted that section 2 adopts two methods of control. The first, contained in s.2(1), is that any contract term or notice which attempts to exclude or restrict liability for negligence causing death or personal injury is *void*. Personal injury is defined in s.14 as including 'any disease and any impairment of physical or mental condition'. The second method of control, contained in s.2(2), is that attempts to exclude or restrict liability for negligence causing loss or damage other than death or personal injury are valid only if they satisfy the requirement of *reasonableness* (the reasonableness test is discussed at 11.14).

Finally, we must turn to the 'jurisdictional' issues which have arisen, or may arise, under s.2. As has been noted, the section refers to a party attempting to 'exclude or restrict his liability' for negligence and negligence itself is defined in s.1 as the 'breach' of an obligation or a duty. Section 2 is therefore drafted in defensive terms, that is to say, it assumes that there has been a *breach* of duty and so does not appear to extend to clauses which define the obligations of the parties. So how would a court respond to the argument that the clause which was the subject-matter of the litigation simply defined the obligations of the parties and therefore fell outside the scope of section 2?

Such an argument was put to the Court of Appeal in *Phillips Products Ltd* v. *Hyland and Hamstead Plant Hire Co Ltd* [1987] 2 All ER 620. The defendants 'hired' a JCB excavator and driver to the plaintiffs. Condition 8 of the contract stated that the driver was to be regarded as the employee of the plaintiffs and that the plaintiffs alone should be responsible for all claims arising in connection with the driver's operation of the excavator. Due to the negligence of the driver, the JCB excavator crashed into the plaintiffs' factory wall. The plaintiffs sued for damages and the defendants sought to rely upon condition 8. The plaintiffs argued that condition 8 was caught by s.2(2) of UCTA and that it failed to satisfy the requirement of reasonableness. The defendants argued that condition 8 was not caught by s.2(2) on the ground that there was no negligence within the meaning of s.1(1)(b) because there had been no breach of their obligations as they had never accepted any liability for the acts of the driver. This argument was rejected by the Court of Appeal. Slade LJ asserted that, in considering whether there has been a breach of duty under s.1(1), the court must leave out of account the clause which is relied on by the defendants to defeat the plaintiffs' claim. But why should condition 8 be left out of account when it was via that clause that the defendants had sought to define their obligations? Slade LJ claimed to find further support for his analysis in s.13(1) of the Act which extends the scope of s.2 to encompass 'terms and notices which exclude or restrict the relevant obligation or duty'. It is clear that the function of this provision is to extend the scope of s.2 to certain duty-defining clauses. The aim of the provision is probably to prevent evasion of the Act by clever draftsmen employed by the more powerful party to the contract. But the difficulty which it causes lies in ascertaining the *extent* to which it applies to duty-defining clauses. Section 13(1) does not give us any criteria by reference to which we can decide which duty-defining clauses are caught by the Act and which are not.

The scope of s.13 was recently discussed by the House of Lords in *Smith* v. *Eric S Bush* [1990] 1 AC 831. Lord Templeman stated that the Act subjected to regulation 'all exclusion notices which would in common law provide a defence to an action for negligence'. Lord Griffiths interpreted s.13 as 'introducing a "but for" test in relation to the notice excluding liability'; that is to say, a court must decide whether a duty of care would exist 'but for' the exclusion clause. Lord Jauncey stated that the wording of s.13 was 'entirely appropriate to cover a disclaimer which prevents a duty coming into existence'. But surely the Act does not catch all duty-defining clauses? Ridiculous conclusions would be reached if it did (for some examples see Palmer and Yates, 1981, and Palmer, 1986). One example will suffice to illustrate the point: 'an overworked accountant says to a potential investor "this is all I can remember about Company X but I may be wrong so don't rely on me"' (Palmer, 1986). Is such a statement caught by the Act? The answer is not clear. But if it is, how can a person qualify his obligations without being caught by the Act? This lack of clarity is almost certain to result in confusion in the courts. Although the courts must share some responsibility for the creation of this confusion, the confusion lies, ultimately, at the heart of UCTA in its misconception of the function of exclusion clauses (see 11.1), and until that issue is resolved the courts will continue to experience considerable difficulty in identifying the clauses which fall within the scope of the Act.

Two further examples can be given of these difficulties. The first is provided by *Thompson* v. *T Lohan (Plant Hire) Ltd* [1987] 2 All ER 631, a case which can be usefully contrasted with *Phillips* v. *Hylands* (above). Once again the case concerned the hiring of an employee and a JCB excavator and a claim arising out of the negligence of the driver. The contract term which was the subject of the dispute was a new version of condition 8 (the variation is of no significance for present purposes). But this time it was held that condition 8 was not caught by section 2 of UCTA. In *Thompson* the driver's negligence led to the death of Mr Thompson. Mr Thompson's widow recovered damages from the general employers who then sought to recover an indemnity from the hiring employers under condition 8. The hiring employers argued that condition 8 was caught by s.2(1) of the Act and was therefore ineffective. However it was held that condition 8 was not caught by s.2(1) and so was effective to transfer liability to the hiring employer. The vital issue which divides these two cases is whether or not it is sought to *exclude* liability towards the *victim* of the negligent act. In *Thompson* condition 8 did not attempt to exclude liability towards the victim of the driver's negligence (Mr Thompson) because his widow had recovered from the general employers and the issue was whether that liability could be *transferred* from the general employers to the hiring employers. On the other hand, condition 8 in the *Phillips* case was relied upon in an effort to *exclude* liability towards the *victim* of the driver's negligence (the plaintiffs) and therefore was caught by s.2(2) (see further Adams and Brownsword, 1988b). This distinction between an *exclusion* and a *transfer* of liability can lead to haphazard results in practice. Suppose that the driver in *Phillips*, instead of damaging a wall belonging to the plaintiffs, had damaged a wall belonging to a third party, who sought and recovered damages from the general employer. In any action brought by the general employer against the hirers to recover the sum paid to the third party, s.2 would be irrelevant because there would be no attempt to exclude a liability towards the victim of the negligence (the third party). Such a conclusion makes it impossible for a lawyer to state in advance whether the clause will be caught by s.2 because it all depends upon whose wall is damaged and whether the person who is seeking to recover damages is the victim of the negligence. But should it not be the case that, whether the property which is damaged belongs to the plaintiffs or not, the result in each case should be the same? Either the risk has been fairly allocated or it has not. Distinctions of the type drawn in *Phillips* and *Thompson* are incoherent in policy terms and reflect the insecure foundations upon which UCTA is built.

The second example of these jurisdictional difficulties can be provided by reference to the decision of the House of Lords in *Scottish Special Housing Association* v. *Wimpey Construction UK Ltd* [1986] 1 WLR 995. Wimpey were employed by the SSHA to modernise some houses which were owned by SSHA. During the course of the work the houses were damaged by fire caused by the alleged negligence of Wimpey. Wimpey relied upon the terms of the contract as a defence to SSHA's claim for damages. Clause 18(2) of the contract stated that Wimpey were liable for any damage to the property caused by their negligence 'except for such loss or damage as is as the risk of the employer under clause 20(C)' of the contract. Clause 20(C) stated that 'the existing structures together with all contents thereof . . . shall be at the sole risk of the Employer as regards loss or damage by fire . . . and the Employer shall maintain adequate insurance against those risks'. The House of Lords held that the risk of damage to the property by fire (including fire caused by the negligence of Wimpey) had been allocated to SSHA and that therefore Wimpey were not liable for the damage caused. As Lord Keith observed, the essential question which clause 20(C) sought to answer was – who should insure against the contractor's negligence? The answer was that it was SSHA. Two puzzles emerge from this case. The first is that the House of Lords did not apply the *Canada Steamship* rules of construction to the clause (see 11.6), notwithstanding the fact that the *effect* of this clause was to enable Wimpey to exclude liability for the consequences of their own negligence. Thus the clause was held to exclude liability for negligence, even though the word negligence was not mentioned in the clause. Nor did the House of Lords consider whether there was any alternative source of liability to which the clause could apply - they simply sought to give the clause its natural interpretation. Welcome as this approach is (see 11.6), it does not explain why the rules were not invoked. The second puzzle relates to the applicability of UCTA. For procedural reasons, the Act was not in issue before the court. But would the clause have fallen with the scope of the Act? It can be argued that such clauses do not fall within its scope because they seek to allocate risk and the responsibility for insurance and do not seek to 'exclude or restrict a liability'. They are clauses which allocate responsibility or which define the obligations of the parties. But there are competing arguments. In the first place we have already noted that s.13(1) extends the scope of s.2 to certain duty-defining clauses. Secondly, the *effect* of the clause was to enable one party to exclude liability for the consequences of its own negligence. In deciding whether such clauses fall within the scope of the Act, much will depend upon whether the courts examine the form of the clause or its substance. If they examine its form it can be argued that this is an 'insurance clause' which regulates risk and the responsibility for taking out insurance and so falls outside the scope of the Act. But if they have regard to its substance, they are more likely to conclude that it falls within the scope of the Act.

This 'form or substance debate' is of great significance for the future of the Act. The courts have not made it clear which approach they will follow. In *Johnstone* v. *Bloomsbury Health Authority* [1992] QB 333, 346, Stuart-Smith LJ, relying in part upon the judgment of Slade LJ in *Phillips* v. *Hyland* (above), stated that 'when considering the operation of section 2 of the Act the court is concerned with the substance and not the form of the contractual provision'. On the other hand, it must be said that *Phillips* itself would appear to have fallen foul to reasoning of form rather than substance, as can be seen when *Phillips* is compared with *Thompson* v. *Lohan Plant Hire* (above). The issue therefore remains to be resolved by the courts, notwithstanding its importance for the future of the Act (see further 11.16).

11.11   Liability for Breach of Contract

The Act also regulates clauses which seek to exclude or restrict liability for
breach of contract. The principal section which performs this role is
section 3. However, by virtue of s.3(1), this section applies only to two
types of contract. The first is where one party 'deals as consumer', which is
defined in s.12 in the following terms:

'(1) A party to a contract 'deals as consumer' in relation to another
party if –
(a) he neither makes the contract in the course of a business nor holds
himself out as doing so; and
(b) the other party does make the contract in the course of a business;
and
(c) in the case of a contract governed by the law of sale of goods or
hire-purchase, or by section 7 of this Act, the goods passing under
or in pursuance of the contract are of a type ordinarily supplied for
private use or consumption.
(2) But on a sale by auction or by competitive tender the buyer is not
to be regarded as dealing as consumer.
(3) Subject to this, it is for those claiming that a party does not deal as
consumer to show that he does not'.

A contract is only made 'in the course of' a business where it forms part of
the regular course of dealing of that business (*R & B Customs Brokers Ltd
v. United Dominions Trust Ltd* [1988] 1 WLR 321).

The second type of contract to which s.3 applies is where one party
'deals . . . on the other's written standard terms of business'. No definition
is provided of this phrase. Does the requirement that the terms be 'written'
exclude a contract which is partly written and partly oral? How much of a
variation is needed before the terms applied cease to be 'standard'? The
latter issue was considered for the first time by Judge Stannard in *Chester
Grosvenor Hotel Co Ltd* v. *Alfred McAlpine Management Ltd* (1991) 56
Build LR 115, 131. He stated that the question was 'one of fact and
degree' and continued:

'what is required for terms to be standard is that they should be so
regarded by the party which advances them as its standard terms and
that it should habitually contract in those terms. If it contracts also in
other terms, it must be determined in any given case, and as a matter of
fact, whether this has occurred so frequently that the terms in question
cannot be regarded as standard, and if on any occasion a party has
substantially modified its prepared terms, it is a question of fact
whether those terms have been so altered that they must be regarded as
not having been employed on that occasion.'

This pragmatic approach has much to commend it and it will reduce the
ability of parties effectively to contract out of s.3 by regularly changing

their standard terms in minor respects. Aware that the effect of a narrow construction of s.3(1) will be to emasculate s.3, the courts are likely to continue to give the subsection a broad interpretation.

As against the party who deals as consumer or deals on the other's written standard terms of business, the other party cannot by reference to any contract term 'when himself in breach of contract, exclude or restrict any liability of his in respect of the breach except in so far as the contract term satisfies the requirement of reasonableness' (s.3(2)(a)). Note that liability once again means business liability and that the subsection is cast in defensive terms, that is to say it assumes the existence of a breach of contract. This time, however, s.13(1) is not available to apply to duty-defining clauses because it states that it only extends the scope of sections 2 and 5–7 of the Act.

Duty-defining terms may, however, be caught by s.3(2)(b) which states that the other party cannot by reference to any contract term claim to be entitled –

'(i) to render a contractual performance substantially different from that which was reasonably expected of him, or
(ii) in respect of the whole or any part of his contractual obligation, to render no performance at all,
except in so far as the contract term satisfies the requirement of reasonableness'.

This subsection must apply to situations other than a breach of contract because, if there was a breach of contract, it would be caught by s.3(2)(a). The type of situation the draftsman would appear to have in mind arises where a holiday company reserves the right to change the destination of the holiday or the hotel booked (without breaking the contract) and the alternative which it provides is less than the other contracting party reasonably expected. But how can a court identify the other party's 'reasonable expectations'? Presumably the exclusion clause will be ignored in identifying his reasonable expectations, but how many other terms will be disregarded in identifying his reasonable expectations? These questions remain to be answered by the courts.

The Act also regulates other terms which seek to exclude or restrict liability for breach of contract. In contracts for the sale or hire purchase of goods the implied terms as to title cannot be excluded or restricted by reference to any contract term (s.6(1)); and the sellers' implied undertakings as to the conformity of goods with the description or sample, or as to their quality or fitness for a particular purpose, cannot be excluded or restricted by reference to any contract term as against a person dealing as consumer, although as against a party dealing otherwise than as consumer the latter liabilities can be excluded or restricted by reference to a contract term only in so far as the term satisfies the requirement of reasonableness (s.6(2),(3)). Two additional points should be noted here. The first is that all attempts to exclude or restrict these implied terms are caught by UCTA, not simply those which seek to exclude or restrict a business liability under s.1(3) (s.6(4)). It should, however, be remembered that the implied terms relating to quality and fitness for purpose apply only where the seller sells the goods in the course of a business (see 9.8). The second is that the Act directs the courts to have regard to specific matters in considering whether such a term is reasonable (s.11(3) and Schedule 2).

In the case of a contract of hire or a contract of exchange, any term of the contract which purports to exclude or restrict liability for breach of an obligation arising by implication from the nature of the contract in respect of the goods' correspondence with their description or sample or their quality and fitness for any particular purpose is void as against a consumer (s.7(2)) and, as against anyone else, must satisfy the reasonableness test (s.7(3)). Liability for breach of the obligations contained in s.2 of the Supply of Goods and Services Act 1982 cannot be excluded or restricted by reference to any contract term (s.7(3A)), and liability in respect of the right to transfer ownership of the goods or give possession or the assurance of quiet possession to a person taking goods in pursuance of the contract cannot be excluded or restricted by reference to any such term except in so far as the term satisfies the requirement of reasonableness (s.7(4)).

11.12   Indemnity Clauses

An indemnity clause is a clause under which one contracting party promises to indemnify (that is to say, reimburse) the other for any liability incurred by him in the performance of the contract. Section 4 of the Act regulates indemnity clauses. Section 4(1) states that any person dealing as consumer cannot be required, as a term of the contract, to indemnify another in respect of liability that may be incurred by that other for negligence or breach of contract, except to the extent that the term satisfies the requirement of reasonableness. This section only applies where the party required to give the indemnity deals as consumer (see s.12 above). It has no application to commercial indemnity clauses. This point helps to explain some of the difficulties which arose in *Phillips* v. *Hyland* (above) and *Thompson* v. *Lohan Plant Hire* (above). Both of these cases essentially involved commercial indemnity clauses. But, because s.4 does not extend to such clauses, it was necessary to invoke s.2 in an effort to bring them within the scope of the Act.

11.13   Attempts at Evasion

The Act contains a number of controls upon attempts to evade the application of the Act. Two are worthy of note here. The first is s.13(1), the existence of which we have already had cause to note (11.10) The subsection states:

'To the extent that this Part of this Act prevents the exclusion or restriction of any liability it also prevents -

(a) making the liability or its enforcement subject to restrictive or onerous conditions;
(b) excluding or restricting any right or remedy in respect of the liability, or subjecting a person to any prejudice in consequence of his pursuing any such right or remedy;
(c) excluding or restricting rules of evidence or procedure;
    and (to that extent) sections 2 and 5 to 7 also prevent excluding or restricting liability by reference to terms and notices which exclude or restrict the relevant obligation or duty'.

The principal point which should be noted is that this subsection does not have independent effect: its function is to extend the scope of sections 2 and 5–7. It does not, of itself, render any contract term void, nor does it subject any contract term to the reasonableness test. That task is performed by sections 2 and 5–7 and a court ought always to refer back to whichever of these sections is applicable when applying the reasonableness test or declaring that the term is void. We have already noted that s.13(1) is open to criticism in that it fails to provide any guidance as to the extent to which it applies to duty-defining clauses (see 11.10). But, in other respects, the extensions which it makes are useful ones. For example, purporting to exclude a right of set-off falls within its scope (*Stewart Gill Ltd* v. *Horatio Myer & Co Ltd* [1992] QB 600) as would setting a short time-limit within which a claim must be made or excluding a particular remedy (such as termination) while leaving other remedies (such as damages) intact.

The second section which is worthy of note in this connection is section 10, which states that a term excluding or restricting liability, which is contained in a separate contract rather than in the contract giving rise to the liability, is ineffective in so far as it attempts to take away a right to enforce a liability which under the Act cannot be excluded or restricted. The mischief at which the section is aimed is the practice of seeking to evade the Act by the use of another contract, for example where a term in a contract between a manufacturer of a product and a purchaser purports to affect the rights of the purchaser against the vendor under the Sale of Goods Act 1979. The section therefore applies to attempts to evade the provisions of the Act by the introduction of an exclusion clause in a contract with a third party, but it does not apply to genuine compromises of existing claims (*Tudor Grange Holdings Ltd* v. *Citibank NA* [1992] Ch 53).

11.14 The Reasonableness Test

The reasonableness test is central to the operation of the Act and therefore requires separate discussion. Section 11(1) provides that 'in relation to a contract term, the requirement of reasonableness . . . is that the term shall have been a fair and reasonable one to be included having regard to the circumstances which were, or ought reasonably to have been known to or in the contemplation of the parties when the contract was made'.

It is important to note that reasonableness is to be assessed at the date of making the contract, not the date of breach. The onus lies on the party relying on the exclusion clause to show that it is reasonable (s.11(5)). The courts have taken into account a number of factors in deciding whether an exclusion clause is reasonable: the respective bargaining power of the parties, whether the exclusion clause was freely negotiated, the extent to which the parties were legally advised, the availability of insurance, the availability of an alternative source of supply to the innocent party and the extent to which the party seeking to rely on the exclusion clause sought to explain its effect to the other party (see also the factors listed in Schedule 2 of the Act which the court is specifically directed to take into account in the case of a contract which falls within the scope of sections 6 or 7 of the Act).

An example of the operation of the reasonableness test can be provided by reference to the case of *Phillips* v. *Hyland* (discussed above, 11.10). There it was held that condition 8 of the contract failed the reasonableness test because the plaintiffs did not generally hire JCB excavators and their drivers, the hire was for a very short period of time, there was little opportunity for the plaintiffs to arrange any insurance cover and the plaintiffs had no control over the choice of driver. The defendants were in the best position to take out insurance and to bear the loss. All these factors combined to suggest that condition 8 was not reasonable. But the question of the reasonableness of a particular clause is a highly discretionary one and the courts have not been wholly consistent in the exercise of their discretion. Some judges have been more interventionist than others (see Adams and Brownsword, 1988a). The consequence of this is an element of unpredictability and inconsistency in the case law. Appellate courts have largely abdicated their role as the guardians of predictability and consistency by holding that an appellate court must treat the trial judge's finding on the issue of reasonableness with the utmost respect and refrain from interference unless satisfied that the lower court proceeded on some 'erroneous principle or was plainly and obviously wrong' (*George Mitchell (Chesterhall) Ltd* v. *Finney Lock Seeds* [1983] 2 AC 803). Given this approach, it is likely that inconsistency will continue to be a feature of cases decided under the reasonableness test of UCTA and, to that extent, the interest in preserving commercial certainty has been sacrificed.

Although much depends upon the facts of the individual case, there are a number of propositions which can be advanced with a degree of certainty. The first is that the court will have regard to the clause as a whole in deciding whether or not it is reasonable: the court does not have regard only to that part of the clause which is being relied upon by the party seeking to exclude or restrict liability (see *Stewart Gill Ltd* v. *Horatio Myer & Co Ltd* [1992] QB 600). This proposition flows from the fact that s.11(1) states that the time for assessing the reasonableness of the clause is the time at which the contract was made (at which point it will not be known which part of it will be relied upon by the defendant) and not the time of the breach. The second point is that the court does not have the power to sever the unreasonable parts of an exclusion clause from the reasonable parts, leaving the latter in force (*Stewart Gill Ltd* v. *Horatio Myer & Co Ltd* (above)). This conclusion has important drafting consequences. It is now extremely unwise to rely upon a single all-embracing exclusion clause because, should it go too far at one particular point, it may fail in its entirety. It is much safer to separate out the different elements of the clause into sub-clauses so that a failure of one part will not necessarily invalidate the entire clause.

11.15 Excepted Contracts

Finally, it should be noted that the Act does not apply to certain contracts, such as contracts of insurance, contracts which concern the transfer of an interest in land and international supply contracts (see generally Schedule 1 and s.26)

11.16 Conclusion

The Unfair Contract Terms Act 1977 represents a major attempt to regulate the use of exclusion clauses in Britain. It cannot claim to be a wholly satisfactory piece of legislation. The main difficulty still lies in identifying the essential nature of an exclusion clause: does it define the nature and extent of the contractual obligation or is it a defence to a breach of an obligation? As we have noted, the courts have traditionally seen exclusion clauses in defensive terms and, although UCTA is cast primarily in defensive terms, s.13(1) and s.3(2)(b) do extend the Act to certain duty-defining clauses. But, once it is conceded that the Act does apply to duty-defining clauses, on what basis can it be decided which duty-defining terms are caught by the Act and which are not? This has become a question of some importance as contract draftsmen have sought to evade the clutches of the Act. Yet it is a question to which those who support the defensive view of exclusion clauses have provided no answer.

It is suggested that the only solution, however unpalatable it may be, lies in a reconsideration of the whole basis of the Act, in recognising that exclusion clauses perform duty-defining functions and treating them like any other term of the contract and only intervening to control them where they are shown to be 'unfair' or 'unconscionable'. An opportunity to reconsider the Act was presented by the EC Directive on Unfair Terms in Consumer Contracts (see 1.6 and 17.6). Clauses which seek to exclude or restrict liability fall within the scope of the Directive (see the Annex, paragraphs (a) and (b)) but so do many other contract terms which are unfair. It would appear that the Directive will be implemented into English law by means of a statutory instrument and that UCTA will not be amended in any way. Instead, consumers will be given rights under the Directive in addition to their existing rights under UCTA (the scope of the two rights is compared at 17.6). This is unfortunate. The Directive provided English law with an opportunity to reconsider the basis of UCTA and the piecemeal approach to regulation which it adopts. The jurisdictional problems which we have noted in this chapter would have been significantly reduced, if not eliminated, by the adoption of a more general test of unfairness. Sadly, English law has passed up the opportunity to reconsider the Act and the problems which we have noted will continue unabated.

Summary

1 Exclusion clauses may be seen either as defining the obligations of the parties or as a defence to a breach of an obligation. The latter is the view which the courts have primarily adopted.

2 Exclusion clauses must be validly incorporated into the contract. Incorporation may take place either by the party who is not relying on the exclusion clause signing the contract containing the exclusion clause, by giving reasonable notice of the exclusion clause or by a course of dealing.

3 The exclusion clause, properly interpreted, must cover the damage which has arisen. The general rule of construction is that the exclusion clause will be interpreted *contra proferentem* (that is, against the party seeking to rely on the exclusion clause).

4 In relation to an attempt by a contracting party to exclude liability for his own negligence three specific rules have been devised by Lord Morton in *Canada Steamship Lines Ltd* v. *The King*. However, these rules are only aids to be used by the court in identifying the intention of the parties.

5 The doctrine of 'fundamental breach' is a rule of construction, according to which the more serious the breach, or the consequences of the breach, the less likely it is that the court will interpret the exclusion clause as covering the breach.

6 The Unfair Contract Terms Act 1977 is now the major source of control of exclusion clauses.

7 Attempts by reference to a contract term or notice, to exclude or restrict liability for negligence causing death or personal injury are void. In relation to other loss or damage caused by negligence, such attempts are only valid if they are held to be reasonable.

8 Where one party deals as consumer or on the other's written standard terms of business, the other party cannot exclude or restrict liability for his own breach or claim to be entitled to render a contractual performance substantially different from that which was reasonably expected of him or render no performance at all, except in so far as the contract term satisfies the requirement of reasonableness.

9 Reasonableness is to be assessed as at the date of making the contract and the onus is upon the party relying on the exclusion clause to show that it is reasonable.

10 The court has a wide discretion in deciding whether or not an exclusion clause is reasonable and will consider a number of different factors in reaching its conclusion.

Exercises

Consider the example involving Peter and John set out at 11.1 on the assumption that it includes the following exclusion clause 'no liability is accepted for any damage, howsoever caused, to goods during the course of transit'.

1 What is the function of such a clause?

2 Peter wishes to know how he can incorporate such a clause into his contracts. How would you advise him?

3 Does the exclusion clause cover the damage done in the following cases

(i) Some of John's furniture is damaged as it is loaded into Peter's van;

(ii) John's furniture is damaged when Peter's van crashes because of Peter's negligent driving;

(iii) John's furniture is totally destroyed when Peter's van is destroyed by fire;

(iv) Peter sells John's furniture before he gets to Preston.

4 How does the Unfair Contracts Terms Act 1977 affect the exclusion clause in the situations described in question 3(i)–(iv)?

Part III

Policing the Contract

12 A Duty to Disclose Material Facts?

In this part of the book we shall consider various ways in which the law of contract regulates the agreement concluded by the parties and allocates the risk of unforeseen events between the parties. In Chapters 12 and 13 we shall discuss the obligations which are imposed upon contracting parties during the process of contractual negotiation. In Chapter 14 we shall analyse the methods by which the courts allocate the risk between contracting parties when they enter into a contract under a common fundamental mistake or an unforeseen event occurs after they have entered into the contract which destroys the basis on which they entered into the contract. In Chapters 15 and 16 we shall consider the limitations which are placed upon the enforceability of contracts by the doctrine of illegality and by the rules relating to capacity to enter the contracts. Finally, in Chapter 17 we shall discuss the recent EC Directive on Unfair Terms in consumer contracts, together with the doctrines of duress, undue influence and inequality of bargaining power and then conclude this part by discussing the extent to which the law of contract is concerned with the fairness of the bargain reached by the parties.

12.1 Introduction

In terms of disclosing information during the process of contractual negotiation, there are essentially two types of obligation which could be imposed by the courts upon contracting parties. The first is a duty to disclose all known material facts to the other contracting party. The second is a duty to refrain from making active misrepresentations: that is to say, a contracting party is not compelled to disclose information, but, once he does disclose, he must do so truthfully. English law has adopted the latter approach and does not recognise the existence of a general duty to disclose material facts known to one contracting party but not to the other (*Keates* v. *Cadogan* (1851) 10 CB 591).

A number of reasons can be identified for this refusal to countenance the existence of a general duty of disclosure. An instructive example provided by Professor Fried (1981, p. 79) will help us to appreciate these reasons:

'An oil company has made extensive geological surveys seeking to identify possible oil and gas reserves. These surveys are extremely expensive. Having identified one promising site, the oil company (acting through a broker) buys a large tract of land from its prosperous farmer owner, revealing nothing about its survey, its purposes or even its identity. The price paid is the going price for farmland of that quality in that region..

An English court would undoubtedly uphold the validity of such a contract and would not require the buyer to disclose his information to the seller prior to the making of the contract. A number of justifications can be provided for such a rule. The first is the simple proposition that the information acquired by the buyer has a financial value and to expect him to disclose it to the seller without compensation is to deprive him unfairly of his valuable information, to provide a disincentive to the acquisition of such information and to unjustly enrich the seller. The second is that contractual obligations are generally voluntarily assumed by parties who deal 'at arm's length', seeking to make the best bargain they can. In such a context contracting parties are not expected to share information with each other. The third justification is that, if such a duty were to be recognised, then questions would have to be resolved as to when it would arise and what would be its content. This justification may be called the floodgates argument. These are compelling justifications for the refusal of the law to recognise the existence of a *general* duty of disclosure.

But strong arguments can be adduced to support the recognition of a duty of disclosure in certain *particular* cases. For example, few would support a rule which enabled a car dealer to sell a car which he knew to be dangerous without revealing that fact to the purchaser. Thus we find that, in certain exceptional cases, a particular duty of disclosure is held to exist. We shall now consider these exceptions and conclude by considering whether they have any coherent rationale.

12.2   Snatching at a Bargain

The first example of a limited duty of disclosure arises from the rule, which we have already noted (see *Hartog* v. *Shields* [1939] 3 All ER 566, discussed at 2.2), that a plaintiff will be prevented from snatching at a bargain which he knew was not intended by the defendant. Thus, in *Smith* v. *Hughes* (1871) LR 6 QB 597, the principle was established that a seller who knows that the buyer has misunderstood the terms of his offer is under an obligation to inform the buyer of the true nature of his offer. In other words, he is under a duty to disclose the existence of the mistake. But, where the buyer makes a mistake and that mistake does not relate to the terms of the seller's offer, then the seller, even if he is aware of the buyer's mistake, is not under an obligation to disclose the mistake to the buyer. It is the responsibility of the buyer to discover his mistake and he cannot escape from his bad bargain by arguing that is was the responsibility of the seller to inform him of his mistake (see further, Kronman, 1978a and Brownsword, 1987).

12.3   Representation by Conduct

The second group of exceptions all concern liability for misrepresentation (12.3–12.5). A misrepresentation consists of a false statement of fact (see 13.3) but the courts have, in limited circumstances, been flexible in their identification of a 'statement' of fact so that, in effect, they have imposed a limited duty of disclosure by the back door. For example, a contracting party does not have to open his mouth to make a statement; he can make it by his conduct (see Gleeson and McKendrick, 1987). In *Walters* v. *Morgan* (1861) 3 D F & J 718, Campbell LC said that, while simple reticence does not amount to a legal fraud, ' a nod or a wink, or a shake of the head, or a smile from the purchaser intended to induce the vendor to believe the existence of a non-existing fact, which might influence the price of the subject to be sold' would be a sufficient ground for refusing to enforce a contract.

The refusal to draw a rigid distinction between statements and conduct seems eminently sensible in the examples given by Campbell LC in *Walters*. Conduct can be as misleading as words. An apparently straightforward example of the imposition of liability on the basis of the conduct of the defendant is provided by *Gordon* v. *Selico* (1986) 11 HLR 219. An independent contractor, employed by the defendants, was asked to bring a flat which was infected with dry rot up to a very good standard for the purpose of selling it. The independent contractor simply covered up the dry rot and made no attempt to eradicate it. The plaintiffs purchased the flat and later discovered the presence of the dry rot. It was held that, in concealing the dry rot, the independent contractor had knowingly made a false representation to the plaintiffs that the flat did not suffer from dry rot and that he and the vendors were therefore liable to the plaintiffs in damages.

But, once it is recognised that a representation may be made by conduct, difficulties arise in identifying the meaning to be ascribed to the conduct and in ascertaining the situations in which the defendant is under an obligation to correct the meaning conveyed by his conduct. For example, in a case such as *Gordon* v. *Selico*, what would have been the position if the independent contractor had papered the dining-room prior to selling the house, partly because it needed redecorating anyway and partly to hide the defective state of the plaster? What is the meaning to be attributed to such conduct and is such a vendor under a duty to disclose the reasons why he has papered the room? In the High Court in *Gordon* v. *Selico* (1985) 275 EG 899, 903, Goulding J said that

'the law must be careful not to run ahead of popular morality by stigmatising as fraudulent every trivial act designed to make buildings or goods more readily saleable even if a highly scrupulous person might consider it dishonest'.

The vagueness of such a principle highlights the fact that, in the absence of a general duty of disclosure, it is extremely difficult to mark out the limits of any particular duty of disclosure.

12.4 Representation Falsified by Later Events

A person may also be guilty of misrepresentation where he fails to correct a representation which, when made was true, but which subsequently, to his knowledge, has become false or which, at the time of making it he believed to be true, but which he has subsequently discovered to be false. In *With* v. *O'Flanagan* [1936] Ch 575, negotiations for the sale of a medical practice began at a time when the practice was valued at £2000. But when the contract of sale was concluded the practice had become worthless because of the ill-health of the vendor in the intervening period. It was held that the vendor was under an obligation to disclose the change of circumstances to the buyer. The justification for this rule appears to be that a representation, once made, is deemed to be a continuing representation so that, once it becomes false to the knowledge of the representor and he fails to correct it, it becomes a misrepresentation (*Shankland & Co* v. *Robinson and Co* 1920 SC (HL) 103, per Lord Dunedin). However, where the representation relates to a statement of intention and the contracting party changes his intention before the conclusion of the contract, then there is no obligation to communicate that change of intention (*Wales* v. *Wadham* [1977] 1 WLR 199).

12.5 Statement Literally True but Misleading

A further situation in which liability in misrepresentation may be incurred arises where the statement is literally true but is nevertheless misleading because the maker of the statement has failed to disclose all the relevant information. In *Notts Patent Brick and Tile Co* v. *Butler* (1866) 16 QBD 778, a purchaser of land asked the vendor's solicitors whether the land was subject to restrictive covenants. The solicitor replied that he was not aware of any, but he did not say that the reason for his ignorance was that he had not bothered to check. It was held that, although the solicitor's statement was literally true, it nevertheless amounted to a misrepresentation.

12.6 Contracts Uberrimae Fidei

There are a group of contracts which are known as contracts *'uberrimae fidei'* or contracts of the utmost good faith. Insurance contracts are contracts *'uberrimae fidei'*; in such contracts the insured is under a duty to disclose all facts which a reasonable or prudent insurer would regard as material. The insured is in the best position to know the relevant facts and therefore a duty of disclosure is placed upon him.

12.7 Fiduciary Relationships

There is also a limited class of fiduciary relationships in which the party in whom the trust is reposed is placed under an obligation to disclose information to the person who has placed his trust in him (a good example is provided by the cases in which the presumption of undue influence is held to arise, see 17.3). Where such a fiduciary relationship exists the parties do not bargain 'at arm's length' and the objection to the imposition of a duty of disclosure disappears.

12.8 A Duty of Disclosure in Tort?

Rather than seek a remedy in contract, a plaintiff may argue that the defendant committed the tort of negligence in failing to disclose the information to the plaintiff. But the law of tort does not impose a general duty of disclosure; indeed, Lord Keith has recently reaffirmed that a person who sees 'another about to walk over a cliff with his head in the air, and forbears to shout a warning' incurs no liability in the tort of negligence (*Yuen Kun-yeu* v. *Attorney General of Hong Kong* [1988] AC 175). On the other hand, a failure to speak may give rise to liability in the tort of negligence where the defendant has voluntarily assumed a responsibility to disclose information to the plaintiff and the plaintiff has relied upon that assumption of responsibility (*Banque Keyser Ullmann SA* v. *Skandia (UK) Insurance Co Ltd* [1990] 1 QB 665, 794). A duty of disclosure may also be imposed by the law of tort in certain other exceptional cases. Thus a doctor who fails to disclose to a patient the risks involved in a course of treatment may be liable in the tort of negligence if he fails to act in accordance with a standard accepted as proper by a responsible body of medical men (*Sidaway* v. *Bethlem Royal Hospital Governors* [1985] AC 871). There is some authority for the proposition that a bank may be liable in negligence if it fails to proffer 'some adequate explanation of the nature and effect of the document' which a customer is required to sign (*Cornish* v. *Midland Bank plc* [1985] 3 All ER 513, 523 per Kerr LJ), although in more recent cases the courts have refused to impose a duty of care in such circumstances (*Barclays Bank plc* v. *Khaira* [1992] 1 WLR 623 and *Barclays Bank plc* v. *O'Brien* [1993] QB 109). But these remain exceptions to the general rule and the law of tort has not taken, and is unlikely to take, the step of imposing a duty on contracting parties to bargain in good faith (but see *English* v. *Dedham Vale Properties* [1978] 1 WLR 93).

12.9 The Role of the Sale of Goods Act 1979

We have already noted (see 9.8) that the Sale of Goods Act 1979 implies certain terms into contracts for the sale of goods. Two of these terms are of particular significance here. First, where a seller sells goods in the course of a business, there is an implied condition that the goods supplied under the contact are of merchantable quality, except in relation to defects drawn to the buyer's attention before the contract was concluded or, in the case where the buyer examines the goods, as regards defects which that examination ought to reveal (s.14(2)). Secondly, where the seller sells goods in the course of a business and the buyer makes known to the seller any particular purpose for which the goods are being bought, there is an implied condition that the goods supplied under the contract are reasonably fit for that purpose (s.14(3)). In many ways the rights conferred by these provisions are greater than any protection afforded by any duty of disclosure because the seller may be liable even where he was unaware of the existence of the defect; it suffices that the goods were not of merchantable quality or were not reasonably fit for their purpose. The Supply of Goods and Services Act 1982 and, to a lesser extent, Part I of the Consumer Protection Act 1987 (which imposes strict liability for defective products) further extend the scope of such regulatory legislation and lessen the need for the creation of a general duty of disclosure because they protect the 'consumer' irrespective of whether the supplier of the goods, the provider of the services or the manufacturer of the product knew of the relevant defect.

12.10 Conclusion

In *Interfoto Picture Library Ltd* v. *Stiletto Visual Programmes Ltd* [1989] QB 433, 439, Bingham LJ noted that in many legal systems in the world 'the law of obligations recognises and enforces an overriding principle that in making and carrying out contracts parties should act in good faith'. A duty of good faith is, of course, wider in scope than a duty of disclosure because it is not confined to pre-contractual behaviour but can extend to the way in which the parties behave during performance of the contract and even to its termination. A case which might have been caught by a duty of good faith is *Arcos Ltd* v. *E. A. Ronaasen & Co* [1933] AC 470 (discussed in more detail at 10.3), where the buyers under a contract of sale rejected goods ostensibly on the ground that they did not conform with description but in reality because the market price for the goods had fallen. As Professor Brownsword has noted (1992), the real objection is that the buyers 'acted in bad faith'. But English law recognises no general principle that a party must exercise his contractual rights 'reasonably' or 'in good faith' and so there was no way in which an English court could challenge the buyers' actions on this ground. Nor is there any likelihood that the judiciary will introduce a doctrine of good faith into English law in the near future. In *Walford* v. *Miles* [1992] 2 AC 128 (discussed in more detail at 4.1), Lord Keith refused to imply a term that the parties would continue to negotiate in good faith on the ground that a 'concept of a duty to carry on negotiations in good faith is inherently repugnant to the adversarial position of the parties when involved in negotiations'. He maintained that each party 'is entitled to pursue his (or her) own interests, so long as he avoids making misrepresentations'. In this respect English law seems to be out of step with many other jurisdictions which recognise the existence of a doctrine of good faith. In America the Uniform Commercial Code states in s.1–203 that 'every contract or duty within this Act imposes an obligation of good faith in its performance or enforcement' and, for this purpose, s.1–201 defines good faith as 'honesty in fact in the conduct or transaction concerned' (see also the definition in s.2–103). Article 1.7 of the Draft Statement of Principles for Commercial Contracts prepared by Unidroit (see 1.7) states that 'each party must act in accordance with good faith and fair dealing in international trade' and further that 'the parties may not exclude or limit this duty'. The comment to the draft article states that 'good faith and fair dealing may be considered to be one of the fundamental ideas underlying the Principles'. The EC Directive on Unfair Terms in Consumer Contracts (see 1.6 and 17.6) also makes explicit reference to 'the requirement of good faith' and the statutory instrument which will give effect to the Directive will also contain a reference to good faith (notwithstanding the fact that there is no such doctrine in English law).

Why then does English law not recognise a doctrine of good faith or a general duty of disclosure? A number of reasons can be identified. The first is that English law starts from a premiss of rugged individualism, in which the parties are expected to look after their own interests and to bargain to obtain the best terms which they can for themselves. But, as we have noted, this is not the complete picture: the commitment to individualism is not an absolute one. The piecemeal exceptions which we have noted represent a limited attempt by the courts and Parliament to protect the expectations of consumers and to impose a limited duty of co-operation in an effort to avoid the unfairness and the excesses which would arise from an absolute refusal to recognise the existence of any duty of disclosure or a duty to bargain in good faith (for an alternative explanation of these exceptions in terms of a liberal theory of contract, see Fried, 1981, pp. 77–85). The second reason is that English law is reluctant to embrace broad general principles, such as a duty of good faith. It prefers to develop incrementally and by analogy to existing precedents rather than by reference to broad statements of general principle. As Bingham LJ noted in *Interfoto* while English law recognises no 'overriding principle' that parties must act in good faith, it has 'developed piecemeal solutions in response to demonstrated problems of unfairness'. It could be said that English law prefers to mark out on an incremental basis what constitutes 'bad faith' but that it refuses to lay down a broad principle that parties must act in good faith. The third reason, closely related to the second, is that a broad general principle would generate too much uncertainty. When would a duty of good faith arise and what would be its content? Is good faith a subjective standard or an objective one? Should it apply to all contracts, or only in a non-commercial context where the need for certainty is less pressing? These are difficult questions which the proponents of a doctrine of good faith must answer.

Finally, it should be stated that the fact that English law does not recognise the existence of a *doctrine* of good faith, does not mean that it is not *influenced or shaped* by notions of good faith. This point was recently made by Steyn LJ in *First Energy (UK) Ltd* v. *Hungarian International Bank Ltd* [1993] 2 Lloyd's Rep 194, 196, in the following terms:

> 'a theme that runs through our law of contract is that the reasonable expectations of honest men must be protected. It is not a rule or a principle of law. It is the objective which has been and still is the principal moulding force of our law of contract. It affords no licence to a Judge to depart from binding precedent. On the other hand, if the prima facie solution to a problem runs counter to the reasonable expectations of honest men, this criterion sometimes requires a rigorous re-examination of the problem to ascertain whether the law does indeed compel demonstrable unfairness'.

In this way, notions of good faith may be said to inform our law of contract. One of the aims of the law of contract is to produce fair and workable rules, which conform to the standards of fair and reasonable people. To the extent that a rule appears to encourage bad faith, it will be the subject of 'rigorous re-examination' by the courts. But those who advocate the introduction of a doctrine of good faith argue that this is not sufficient because, as Steyn LJ acknowledges, it does not enable judges to depart from 'binding precedent'. Thus good faith could not be used to overrule a case such as *Arcos* v. *Ronaasen* (above), nor to give effect to the agreement of the parties in *Walford* v. *Miles* (above). It can therefore be argued that the influence of good faith is at times rather muted and that judges require stronger weapons to combat bad faith, which can only be done by elevating good faith to the status of a legal doctrine or a principle of law. Yet, as we have noted, such a step would give rise to a number of problems, most notably the uncertainty which would thereby be caused and the difficulties involved in defining the scope of good faith. Further, it is not at all clear that English law presently countenances many examples of bad faith. It is therefore for those who advocate that English law would be improved by the recognition of a doctrine of good faith to make out their case.

Summary

1 English law does not recognise the existence of a general duty to disclose material facts known to one contracting party but not to the other.

2 A defendant who knows that the plaintiff has misunderstood the terms of his offer is under an obligation to inform the plaintiff of the true nature of his offer.

3 A representation may be made by conduct.

4. A person is under a duty to disclose material facts which come to his notice before the conclusion of a contract if they falsify a representation previously made by him.

5. A person may be guilty of misrepresentation if his statement is literally true but is in fact misleading.

6. A duty to disclose material facts is imposed in the case of contracts *uberrimae fidei* (of the utmost good faith) and in the case of certain fiduciary relations.

7. Exceptionally a duty of disclosure may be imposed by the law of tort.

8. The existence of the 'merchantable quality' and 'fitness for purpose' provisions in the Sale of Goods Act 1979 mitigate the hardships which would otherwise be caused by the refusal of English contract law to recognise the existence of a general duty of disclosure. Similar obligations are now contained in the Supply of Goods and Services Act 1982.

Exercises

1. Why does English law not recognise the existence of a general duty of disclosure? Do you think it should recognise the existence of such a duty?

2. List the exceptional situations in which English law does recognise the existence of a particular duty of disclosure. Do these exceptions have any coherent rationale?

3. In Professor Fried's illustration concerning the oil company and the farmer (see 12.1) should the oil company be required to disclose its information to the farmer? Give reasons for your answer. Can you distinguish this illustration from the case of *Gordon* v. *Selico*?

4. Joe papered his dining-room prior to selling the house, partly because it needed redecorating anyway and partly to hide the defective state of the plaster. Emma bought the house and later discovered that the defective state of the plaster was in fact caused by a serious structural fault in the dining-room wall. Has she a cause of action against Joe?

5. It is a noticeable feature of the duty of disclosure cases which have arisen this century that they concern contracts which fall outside the scope of regulatory legislation, such as the Sale of Goods Act 1979. Can we learn any lessons from this fact?

13 Misrepresentation

13.1 Introduction

Although English law does not recognise the existence of a general duty to disclose information during the process of contractual negotiation, the process of contractual negotiation is not left unregulated. Rather, a duty is imposed not to make any false statements of fact to the other contracting party and thereby to induce him to enter into the contract. As we shall see, the law relating to misrepresentation does have a crucial role to play in the policing of contractual negotiations (see 13.3).

At the outset a fundamental distinction must be drawn between a promise and a representation. A promise may be defined as a statement by which the maker of the statement accepts or appears to accept an obligation to do or not to do something. A representation, on the other hand, is a statement which simply asserts the truth of a given state of facts. The distinction can be illustrated by reference to the case of *Kleinwort Benson Ltd* v. *Malaysia Mining Corporation Berhad* [1989] 1 WLR 379. The plaintiffs agreed to make available to a subsidiary company of the defendants a £10 million credit facility. The defendants refused to act as guarantors but they gave to the plaintiffs a letter of comfort which stated that 'it is our policy to ensure that the business of [the subsidiary company] is at all times in a position to meet its liabilities to you under the above arrangements'. The subsidiary company ceased to trade after the collapse of the tin market at a time when its indebtedness to the plaintiffs was £10 million. The defendants refused to honour their undertaking in the letter of comfort and so the plaintiffs took proceedings against them, arguing that the defendants were in breach of contract in failing to pay. But the Court of Appeal held that the letter of comfort did not amount to a contractual promise by the defendants. Therefore they were not liable to the plaintiffs. It was held that the letter of comfort was simply a representation of fact as to the defendants' policy at the time when the statement was made. The defendants did not promise that they would not change their policy for the future; they did not state that 'it is *and will at all times continue to be* our policy to ensure that the subsidiary will at all times be in a position to meet its liabilities to you'.

Thus promises and representations are functionally different and have different legal consequences. A representation is a statement of fact which induces the other party to enter into a contract or otherwise act to his detriment. The representor does not promise anything; he simply asserts the truth of his statement and invites reliance upon that statement. If his statement of fact is false then it is a misrepresentation and the most appropriate remedy is to put the other party in the position which he would have been in had he not acted upon the misrepresentation to his detriment. Thus, on the facts of *Kleinwort Benson*, had the defendants' policy, at the time at which they made the statement, not been to ensure that the subsidiary would at all times be in a position to meet its liabilities, then their statement would have amounted to an actionable misrepresentation (see 13.3). A promise, on the other hand, creates an expectation that the promise will be fulfilled and the promisor accepts (or is deemed to accept) an obligation to carry out his promise. Having accepted such an obligation, the law will call upon the promisor to fulfil that obligation and will seek, by the remedy granted, to protect the expectation so created (see further 20.3). Although promises and representations are functionally different, it can be very difficult to tell whether a particular statement is a promise or a representation. For example, in *Kleinwort Benson* the trial judge, Hirst J, held that the letter of comfort was a contractual promise, whereas the Court of Appeal held that it was a representation of fact. But any difficulty experienced in drawing the line should not blind us to the fact that representations and promises are fundamentally different types of statement.

One final point must be made before we consider the substance of the law relating to misrepresentation. That point is that misrepresentation lies on the boundary of contract and tort. A party who was been induced to enter a contract by a misrepresentation may seek a remedy in contract or in tort. Therefore at various points in the chapter we shall have to consider liability in both contract and tort.

Our analysis will proceed in four stages. At the first stage we will define a misrepresentation; at the second stage we shall discuss the different types of misrepresentation; at the third stage we shall consider the remedies for misrepresentation and at the final stage we shall discuss the exclusion of liability for misrepresentation.

13.2   What is a Misrepresentation?

A misrepresentation may be defined as an unambiguous, false statement of fact which is addressed to the party misled and which materially induces the contract. This definition may be broken down into three distinct elements. The first is that the representation must be an unambiguous false statement of fact (13.3), the second is that it must be addressed to the party misled (13.4) and the third is that it must be a material inducement to entry into the contract (13.5).

13.3   A Statement of Existing Fact

The representation must be an unambiguous false statement of existing fact. The need for a statement underlines the point that a failure to disclose information will not generally constitute a representation, although, as we have noted, the courts have been flexible in their identification of a 'statement' so that, for example, a statement can be made by conduct as well as by words (see 12.3–12.5). The statement must also be one of *existing fact*. The following four categories of statement have been held *not* to constitute statements of existing fact and therefore cannot amount to actionable misrepresentations.

The first is a 'mere puff'. We have already noted (see 8.1) that a commendatory statement may be so vague as to be neither a promise which is incorporated into the contract as a term, nor a statement of fact. In *Dimmock* v. *Hallett* (1866) LR 2 Ch App 21, Turner LJ said that a representation that land was 'fertile and improveable' would not, except in an extreme case, be considered such a misrepresentation as to entitle the innocent party to rescind the contract. But there are limits to this principle. The more specific the statement, the less likely it is to be treated as a mere puff (*Carlill* v. *Carbolic Smoke Ball Co* [1893] 1 QB 256, discussed in more detail at 3.3).

Secondly, a statement of opinion or belief which proves to be unfounded is not a false statement of fact. In *Bisset* v. *Wilkinson* [1927] AC 177, a vendor of a farm in New Zealand, which had not been used for sheep farming before, represented to a prospective purchaser that, in his judgment, the land could carry 2000 sheep. In fact it could not carry 2000 sheep and the purchaser, when he discovered this, sought to set aside the contract on the ground of the vendor's misrepresentation. He was unable to do so because the vendor's statement was not a false statement of fact but a statement of opinion which he honestly held.

Bisset was distinguished, however, in the important case of *Esso Petroleum Ltd* v. *Mardon* [1976] QB 801. Esso represented to the defendant, a prospective tenant of a petrol filling station which was in the process of construction, that the throughput of petrol at the station was likely to reach 200 000 gallons per year. However the local authority refused planning permission for the petrol pumps to front on to the main street. Instead, the station had to be built back to front with the forecourt at the back of the station and the only access to the petrol pumps being from a side street. Esso, through their experienced officials, assured the defendant that this change would not affect the projected throughput of petrol. In fact, as a result of the change, the throughput only reached 78 000 gallons per year. The defendant incurred considerable losses in operating the station and he eventually reached the position where he could no longer pay Esso for his petrol. Esso consequently sought to repossess the station and to recover the money owed to them by the defendant. The defendant counterclaimed for damages for breach of contract and for negligent misrepresentation. Esso argued that their statement as to the throughput of petrol was a statement of opinion and hence was not actionable. But the Court of Appeal held that the statement was one of fact. Lord Denning distinguished *Bisset* on the ground that there 'the land had never been used as a sheep farm and both parties were equally able to form an opinion as to its carrying capacity'. Esso, on the other hand, had special knowledge and skill in the forecasting of the throughput of petrol and they were held to represent that they had made the forecast with 'reasonable care and skill'. On the facts it was held that they had not exercised reasonable care and skill and they were therefore liable to the defendant in damages. A similar approach to that adopted in *Esso* was espoused by Bowen LJ in *Smith* v. *Land and House Property Corp* (1884) 28 Ch D 7, when he said that where

> 'the facts are equally known to both parties, what one says to the other is frequently nothing but an expression of opinion . . . But if the facts are not equally well known to both sides, then a statement of opinion by one who knows the facts best involves very often a statement of material fact, for he impliedly states that he knows facts which justify his opinion'.

Combining the principles established in *Esso* and *Smith* we can deduce the following proposition: where the representor has greater knowledge than the representee the courts will imply that the representation must be made with reasonable care and skill (*Esso*) and that the representor knows facts which justify his opinion (*Smith*). In effect, these cases impose upon negotiating parties who have special skill a duty to take reasonable care in the preparation of forecasts and opinions.

Thirdly, a representation of law is not a statement of existing fact (although a *fraudulent* misrepresentation of law may give rise to liability in equity to restore any benefit obtained by virtue of the misrepresentation: *West London Commercial Bank Ltd* v. *Kitson* (1884) 13 QBD 360, 362–3). Finally, a statement of intention is not a statement of fact. Nor is a promise a statement of fact. A person who fails to carry out his stated intention does not thereby make a misrepresentation (*Wales* v. *Wadham* [1977] 1 WLR 199). But a person who misrepresents his present intention does make a false statement of fact because the state of his intention is a matter of fact. In *Edgington* v. *Fitzmaurice* (1885) 29 Ch D 459, directors of a company invited the public to subscribe for debentures on the basis that the money so raised would be used to expand the business. In fact, the real purpose in raising the money was to pay off company debts. It was held that the directors were guilty of misrepresentation because they had misrepresented their actual intention.

13.4 Addressed to the Party Misled

Secondly, it must be shown that the representation was addressed to the party misled. There are two ways in which a representation may be addressed to the party misled. The first and most obvious method is by the direct communication of the misrepresentation to the plaintiff by the representor. Alternatively, the misrepresentation may be addressed by the representor to a third party with the intention that it be passed on to the plaintiff. In *Commercial Banking Co of Sydney* v. *RH Brown and Co* [1972] 2 Lloyd's Rep 360, the defendant bank misrepresented to the plaintiffs' bank the financial standing of one of the plaintiffs' customers. The plaintiffs' bank communicated the information to the plaintiffs, who acted on it to their detriment. It was held that the defendants were liable to the plaintiffs because they knew that the plaintiffs' bank did not want the information for their own purposes and that it was to be passed on to a customer who was proposing to deal with a client of the defendant bank.

13.5   A Material Inducement

Finally the representation must be a material inducement to entry into the contract. Here there are two elements at work. The first is that the representation must be material, in the sense that it would affect the judgment of a reasonable man in deciding whether to enter into the contract on these terms (although a person who has been fraudulent cannot be heard to argue that the representation was immaterial). The second is that the representation must actually induce the contract, that is to say, it must induce the actual plaintiff to enter into the contract. In *Edgington* v. *Fitzmaurice* (above) it was held that the misrepresentation need not be the sole inducement; it is sufficient that it was *an* inducement which was actively present to the representee's mind. This requirement was not satisfied in the case of *JEB Fasteners* v. *Marks, Bloom and Co* [1983] 1 All ER 583. The defendants negligently prepared the accounts of a company which was taken over by the plaintiffs. The accounts had been made available to the plaintiffs, who had reservations about them, but they nevertheless decided to proceed with the take-over because they wished to acquire the services of two of the directors of that company. The take-over was not a commercial success and the plaintiffs brought an action against the defendants alleging that they had been negligent in the preparation of the accounts. The Court of Appeal dismissed the action on the ground that the defendants' representation did not play a 'real and substantial' part in inducing the plaintiffs to act. They had taken over the company, not in reliance upon the accounts, but because of their desire to acquire the services of the two directors.

There are at least three situations in which a plaintiff will be unable to show that the representation induced the contract. The first is where the plaintiff was unaware of the existence of the representation (*Horsfall* v. *Thomas* (1862) 1 H & C 90), the second is where the plaintiff knew that the representation was untrue and the third is where the plaintiff did not allow the representation to affect his judgment. A plaintiff does not allow a representation to affect his judgment where he regards the representation as being unimportant (*Smith* v. *Chadwick* (1884) 9 App Cas 187) or where he relies upon his own judgment. In *Atwood* v. *Small* (1838) 6 Cl & F 232, Atwood contracted to sell his mine to Small, but exaggerated its earning capacity. Small appointed agents to verify Atwood's representations and they reported that his statements were true. After the contract was concluded, Small discovered the exaggerations and sought to rescind the contract. He was unable to do so because he had relied upon his agents' report rather than upon Atwood's representation. It should be noted that this rule does not apply to the plaintiff who has the opportunity to discover the truth himself but does not take it. In such a case, the plaintiff remains entitled to relief against the misrepresentor (*Redgrave* v. *Hurd* (1881) 20 Ch D 1, although note that Professor Treitel (1991, p. 304) argues that, in the light of the decision of the House of Lords in *Smith* v. *Eric S Bush* [1990] 1 AC 831, *Redgrave* may no longer apply where it was reasonable to expect the representee to make use of the opportunity and he fails to do so).

13.6 The Types of Misrepresentation

There are four different types of misrepresentation. It is important to distinguish between the different types of misrepresentation because they may give rise to different remedial consequences. We shall see that all types of misrepresentation entitle the representee to rescind the contract but not all types of misrepresentation give rise to an action for damages.

The first type of misrepresentation is fraudulent misrepresentation. Fraudulent misrepresentation, in addition to being a ground on which a contract may be set aside, constitutes the tort of deceit. Although the word fraud bears a wide meaning in common parlance, its meaning in law is much narrower as a result of the decision of the House of Lords in *Derry* v. *Peek* (1889) 14 App Cas 337. In *Derry* Lord Herschell established the following three propositions. The first is that there must be proof of fraud and nothing short of that is sufficient. The second is that fraud is proved when it is shown that a false representation has been made (i) knowingly or (ii) without belief in its truth or (iii) recklessly, careless whether it be true or false. Unreasonableness of belief does not of itself constitute fraud; it simply provides evidence of dishonesty on the part of the maker of the statement (*Angus* v. *Clifford* [1891] 2 Ch 449). Thirdly, if fraud is proved the motive of the person guilty of it is immaterial. In *Polhill* v. *Walter* (1832) 3 B & Ad 114, the representor knew that his statement was false but his motive in making the statement was to benefit his principal and not to benefit himself, nor to injure anyone else. Notwithstanding his good motives, he was held liable in the tort of deceit. There are few cases brought in the tort of deceit today, largely because of the difficulty of proving that the representor was guilty of fraud.

The second type of misrepresentation is negligent misrepresentation at common law. In the period immediately after *Derry* v. *Peek*, it was thought that negligent misrepresentation was not actionable in tort because liability in tort arose only in cases of fraudulent misrepresentation (*Le Lievre* v. *Gould* [1893] 1 QB 491). However, this view was rejected by the House of Lords in *Nocton* v. *Lord Ashburton* [1914] AC 932. Although the House recognised that negligent misrepresentation could be actionable, they held that it was actionable only where there was a pre-existing contractual relationship between the parties or where the parties were in a 'fiduciary relationship'. This restrictive approach prevailed in England as late as 1951 (see *Candler* v. *Crane, Christmas and Co* [1951] 2 KB 164, but contrast the powerful dissenting judgment of Denning LJ).

However, in 1964 in *Hedley Byrne* v. *Heller* [1964] AC 465, the House of Lords finally expanded the ambit of liability for negligent misrepresentation. The plaintiffs were advertising agents who booked substantial advertising space on behalf of their clients, Easipower Ltd, on terms that they were personally liable if Easipower defaulted. The plaintiffs became concerned about the financial standing of Easipower and, through their bank, sought from the defendants, who were Easipower's bankers, a reference on the financial soundness of Easipower. The defendants replied that Easipower were 'considered good for its ordinary business transactions'. In reliance upon the reference, the plaintiffs placed orders which, because of the subsequent default of Easipower, resulted in a loss to them of £17 000. The plaintiffs alleged that the defendants were negligent in the preparation of the reference and were therefore liable to them in damages. Their claim failed because the defendants had provided the reference 'without responsibility'. However the importance of *Hedley Byrne* lies, not in the fact that the claim failed because of the disclaimer, but in the fact that the House of Lords significantly widened the scope of liability in tort for negligent misrepresentation. The important task which now remains for us is to ascertain the limits of *Hedley Byrne*.

The key to *Hedley Byrne* lies in the concept of a 'special relationship' between the plaintiff and the defendant. The content of this 'special relationship' is, however, a matter of controversy. For some time it appeared that its principal constituent elements were a voluntary assumption of responsibility by the defendant and foreseeable detrimental reliance by the plaintiff. But the courts have recently begun to distance themselves from the voluntary assumption of responsibility test (see, for example, *Caparo Industries plc* v. *Dickman* [1990] 2 AC 605, 637) and have chosen instead to rely upon a number of factors in deciding whether or not to impose liability (see, for example, the judgment of Neill LJ in *James McNaughten Papers Group plc* v. *Hicks Anderson & Co (a firm)* [1991] 2 QB 113, 125–8). Notwithstanding the adoption of this more flexible approach, it is possible to identify three principal factors which are invoked by the courts in defining the scope of *Hedley Byrne*.

The first is the knowledge of the representor. The greater the knowledge which the representor has of the representee and of the purposes for which the representee is likely to rely upon his statement, the more likely it is that the representor will be liable to the representee (contrast, in this respect, the decisions of the House of Lords in *Caparo* v. *Dickman* (above) and *Smith* v. *Eric S Bush* [1990] 1 AC 831). It is sometimes argued that the representor must also be possessed of a special skill. In *Mutual Life and Citizens Assurance Co* v. *Evatt* [1971] AC 793, the majority of the Privy Council interpreted this element as requiring that the representor be in the business of giving advice on the subject of his representation. On the facts, the defendant insurance company had given the plaintiff gratuitous advice on the wisdom of investing in the defendants' sister company. It was held that the defendants were not liable because they were an insurance company and not investment advisers. The status of *Evatt* is, however, unclear because the judgment of the minority, Lord Reid and Lord Morris, has commanded wider support in subsequent cases. The minority held that a duty of care is owed by anyone who takes it upon himself to make representations knowing that another will justifiably rely upon his representation. In *Esso Petroleum* v. *Mardon* [1976] QB 801 (see Gravells, 1976) Ormerod LJ supported the minority view in *Evatt*, as did Lord Denning and Shaw LJ in *Howard Marine and Dredging Co* v. *A Ogden and Sons* [1978] QB 574. On the basis of these dicta it is suggested that the majority view in *Evatt* will not be followed and that the minority view will be preferred.

The second factor is the purpose for which the statement was made. Where the representor makes the statement with the intention that the representee rely upon it, then liability is likely to be imposed (see *Smith* v. *Eric S Bush* (above)), but where the statement is put into general public circulation with no particular person in mind as the recipient, then it is unlikely that liability will be imposed (*Caparo* v. *Dickman* (above)). The third factor is that it must be reasonable for the representee to rely upon the representor's statement. Where, for example, the statement is made on a social occasion, the representee will generally find that it is difficult to persuade a court to conclude that it was reasonable to rely on the statement (cf *Chaudhry* v. *Prabhakar* [1989] 1 WLR 29). On the other hand, where the statement is made in a commercial context the courts will generally be much readier to infer that it was reasonable to rely upon the statement (see, for example, *Smith* v. *Eric S Bush* (above)).

Negligent misrepresentation at common law must be distinguished from the liability which may arise under section 2(1) of the Misrepresentation Act 1967. This is the third type of misrepresentation. Section 2(1) provides that

'Where a person has entered into a contract after a misrepresentation has been made to him by another party thereto and as a result thereof he has suffered loss then, if the person making the misrepresentation would be liable to damages in respect thereof had the misrepresentation been made fraudulently, that person shall be so liable notwithstanding that the misrepresentation was not made fraudulently, unless he proves that he had reasonable grounds to believe and did believe up to the time that the contract was made that the facts represented were true.'

Section 2(1) operates independently of the *Hedley Byrne* line of authority. The section is drafted in rather clumsy and unusual terms because it imposes liability by reference to liability for fraudulent misrepresentation, even though the misrepresentor has not been fraudulent (for a discussion of the possible consequences of the 'fiction of fraud' see Atiyah and Treitel, 1967, pp. 372–5). But, stripped of its convoluted drafting, the general effect of the section is clear; where a misrepresentation has been made by one contracting party to another, the party making the misrepresentation is liable to the other in damages unless he can prove that he had reasonable grounds to believe and did believe up to the time that the contract was made that his statement was true.

This statutory right has three advantages over a common law negligence claim. The first is that the Act does not require that there be a 'special relationship' between the parties, thus avoiding the difficulties inherent in establishing the existence of such a relationship. This was of crucial significance in *Gosling* v. *Anderson* [1972] EGD 709. The defendant, who was selling her flat, represented to the plaintiff, through her estate agents, that planning permission had been obtained for building a garage when, in fact, it had not been obtained. In the Court of Appeal Roskill LJ stated that, had the action been heard before 1967, the plaintiff's action would have failed unless she had been able to prove fraud, but that she was now able to rely on s.2(1) of the 1967 Act and was entitled to damages for the misrepresentation.

The second advantage of a claim under s.2(1) is that the representor is liable unless he proves that he had reasonable grounds to believe and did believe up to the time that the contract was made that the facts represented were true, whereas at common law it is for the representee to prove that the representor was negligent. It is no easy task for a representor to discharge the onus of proof under s.2(1), as can be seen from the case of *Howard Marine* v. *Ogden* (above). The defendants wished to hire barges from the plaintiffs and, during the course of the negotiations, the plaintiffs' manager represented that the deadweight capacity of each barge was 1600 tonnes when, in fact, it was only 1055 tonnes. The defendants used the barges for 6 troublesome months but, when they discovered the true deadweight capacity of the barges, they refused to continue to pay the hire. The plaintiffs sued for the hire charges and the defendants counterclaimed, *inter alia*, for damages under s.2(1) of the 1967 Act. The representation of the plaintiffs' manager as to the deadweight capacity of the barges was based upon his recollection of the figures in Lloyd's Register. His recollection was correct but, unusually, Lloyds were wrong. The Court of Appeal held, Lord Denning dissenting, that the plaintiffs had not discharged the burden of proof upon them of showing that they had reasonable grounds to believe that the statement was true. This was because the accurate figures were contained in the ships' documents and the plaintiffs had failed to show any 'objectively reasonable ground' for disregarding the figure in these documents and preferring the figure in Lloyd's Register. The burden upon the representor is therefore a heavy one and it is likely to enable a representee to recover where at common law he would have failed (for example, in *Howard Marine* itself, only Shaw LJ was of the opinion that a common law claim would have succeeded).

The third advantage is that the measure of damages recoverable under s.2(1) is the measure of damages for the tort of deceit. Authority for this proposition is derived from the recent controversial case of *Royscot Trust Ltd* v. *Rogerson* [1991] 2 QB 297. The plaintiff finance company was induced to enter into a hire purchase transaction with Mr Rogerson as a result of a misrepresentation by the defendant car dealers. As the defendants knew, it was the plaintiffs' policy not to enter into a hire purchase transaction unless 20 per cent of the purchase price of a car was paid to the dealer by the customer. Mr Rogerson agreed with the defendants to put down a deposit of £1200 on a car, the price of which was £7600. But that produced a deposit of only some 16 per cent of the purchase price. So the defendants falsely stated that the price of the car was £8000 and that Mr Rogerson had paid a deposit of £1600; thus producing the required 20 per cent deposit (it is vital to note here that there was no allegation that the defendants were guilty of fraud in making these changes: the case proceeded upon the assumption that the defendants had not been fraudulent). On this basis the plaintiffs agreed to enter into the transaction but Mr Rogerson subsequently, in breach of contract, sold the car and ceased to pay the hire purchase instalments. The Court of Appeal held that damages under s.2(1) were to be assessed as if the defendants had been fraudulent, so that the plaintiffs were entitled to recover their actual loss directly flowing from the misrepresentation, whether or not that loss was reasonably foreseeable. The remoteness rule applicable was that derived from the tort of deceit, not the tort of negligence (see further 13.9). The court held that the action of Mr Rogerson in dishonestly selling the car was a direct result of the defendants' misrepresentation, in the sense that there was no break in the chain of causation between the misrepresentation and the loss. The plaintiffs were therefore entitled to recover damages of £3625, namely the difference between the £6,400 they advanced to Mr Rogerson and the instalments of £2775 they received from him before his default. While there may remain some circumstances in which a representee will gain an advantage by bringing a claim in the tort of deceit rather than under s.2(1) (on which see Hooley, 1992), the effect of *Royscot* must surely be to reduce the practical significance of the tort of deceit. After all, why go to the trouble of proving that the representor was fraudulent when you can recover the same measure of damages under s.2(1) without even having to prove that the representor was negligent?

There is something distinctly odd about the result in *Royscot*. The defendants were not fraudulent, yet they were treated as if they had been. The point becomes even more apparent when applied to the facts of *Howard Marine* v. *Ogden* (above). What justification can there possibly be for treating the plaintiffs in *Howard Marine* as if they had been fraudulent, when it was not even proved that they had been guilty of negligence? These anomalies could have been avoided if the court in *Royscot* had accepted that the reference to fraud in s.2(1) was simply a 'fiction'. But Balcombe LJ rejected this argument on the ground that it was inconsistent with the authorities and contrary to the 'plain words of the subsection'. While the intention of Parliament in enacting s.2(1) may well have been to incorporate, by analogy, the rules for the tort of deceit (see Cartwright, 1987, pp. 429–33), it is almost certain that Parliament could not have foreseen the anomalies which would arise as a result of the analogy drawn. But *Royscot* makes the anomaly plain for all to see. There is no justification for treating an innocent party as if he had been fraudulent and legislation is required to remove this anomaly. The rules applicable to the assessment of damages should be derived from the tort of negligence, not deceit (see *Gran Gelato Ltd* v. *Richcliff (Group) Ltd* [1992] Ch 560, where an analogy was drawn with the tort of negligence, discussed further at 13.9).

Nothwithstanding the advantages which the statutory cause of action affords, there remain certain situations in which a plaintiff must have recourse to a common law claim. The first situation arises where, as in *Hedley Byrne*, the representation is made by a third party who is not party to the contract. Section 2(1) only applies where the representation has been made by the other party to the contract. The second situation in which it may be necessary to have recourse to the common law arises where the contract between the parties is void *ab initio* (for example, on the ground of *non est factum*). In such a case there is no contract to which s.2(1) can apply.

The final type of misrepresentation is innocent misrepresentation. An innocent misrepresentation is a misrepresentation which is neither fraudulent, nor negligent. This category is now of little practical significance.

13.7 Remedies

Once the existence of a misrepresentation has been established, consideration must be given to the remedies available for misrepresentation. There are two principal remedies. The first is the setting aside of the contract induced by the misrepresentation (this is called 'rescission' by lawyers). This is a classic contractual remedy. However a plaintiff may not be satisfied with rescission and may also want compensation for the financial loss which he has suffered. A claim for damages does not lie in contract when the contract has been rescinded but a claim for damages may lie in tort or under statute and so we must consider the relationship between these claims.

13.8 Rescission

Rescission is, in principle, available for all types of misrepresentation (subject to the discretion of the court to award damages in lieu of rescission under s.2(2) of the Misrepresentation Act 1967, see 13.9). It is, however, very important to be clear about the precise meaning of the word rescission. Atiyah and Treitel (1967) helpfully distinguish two types of rescission. The first type, entitled 'rescission for misrepresentation', arises where the contract is set aside for all purposes, that is to say, the contract is set aside both retrospectively and prospectively. Here the aim is to restore, as far as possible, the parties to the position which they were in before they entered into the contract. The second type of rescission, called 'rescission for breach', arises where one contracting party terminates performance of the contract because of the breach by the other party. In the latter case the effect of rescission is to release the parties from their obligations to perform in the future but the contract is not treated as if it had never existed. Therefore rescission for breach does NOT operate retrospectively (see further chapter 19). In this chapter we shall discuss only rescission for misrepresentation.

Rescission does not occur automatically when a misrepresentation is made. Misrepresentation renders a contract voidable. Therefore the representee can elect either to rescind or to affirm the contract. If he decides to rescind, the general rule is that he must bring his decision to rescind to the notice of the representor. This can be done in a number of ways: for example, by seeking a declaration that the contract is invalid, by restoring what he has obtained under the contract or by relying upon the misrepresentation as a defence to an action on the contract (*Redgrave* v. *Hurd* (above)). However, where the representor deliberately absconds and so makes it impossible for the representee to give him notice of his decision to rescind, then it is sufficient that the representee evidences his intention to rescind by some overt means, falling short of communication, which is reasonable in the circumstances. So, where a thief persuades an owner to part with his car by a fraudulent misrepresentation and the thief cannot subsequently be traced, the owner can validly rescind by notifying the police or the Automobile Association (*Car and Universal Finanace Co* v. *Caldwell* [1965] 1 QB 525, but contrast the Scottish case of *MacLeod* v. *Kerr* 1965 SC 253).

There are, however, certain limits to the right to rescind. The right to rescind may be lost by affirmation of the contract by the plaintiff after he discovered the truth, by the intervention of innocent third party rights or by lapse of time (*Leaf* v. *International Galleries* [1950] 2 KB 86, although lapse of time does not, of itself, bar rescission in cases of fraudulent misrepresentation). The principal ground on which the right to rescind may be lost arises where it is impossible to restore the parties to their pre-contractual position. The very object of rescission is to return the parties to the position which they were in before entering into the contract and where this is impossible it inevitably follows that rescission is unavailable. At common law the courts insisted upon precise restitution, but the harshness of this rule is mitigated by the intervention of equity. In equity a party who can make substantial, but not precise, restitution can rescind the contract if he returns the subject-matter of the contract in its altered form and gives an account of any profits made through his use of the product together with an allowance for any deterioration in the product (*Erlanger* v. *New Sombrero Phosphate Co* (1878) 3 App Cas 1218).

We have already noted that the effect of rescission is to set aside the contract for all purposes. A consequence of this is that *contractual* damages cannot be claimed because the contract has been set aside for all purposes and so there is no basis for any claim on the contract. But an indemnity may be claimed. An indemnity can only be claimed in respect of expenses incurred in the discharge of obligations created by the contract. The point can be illustrated by reference to the case of *Whittington* v. *Seale-Hayne* (1900) 82 LT 49. The plaintiffs took a lease of premises for the purpose of breeding prize poultry. They were induced to do so by representations of the defendant's agent that the premises were in good sanitary condition. Under the lease the plaintiffs covenanted to execute all such works as might be required by the local authority. The premises were not, however, in a sanitary condition and were in a state of disrepair. The water supply was poisoned and, as a result, the poultry died or became valueless and the manager of the farm became ill. The local authority declared the premises unfit for habitation and required the plaintiffs to renew the drains. It was held that the plaintiffs were entitled to an indemnity in respect of the rates which they had paid and the cost of carrying out the repairs ordered by the local authority because these were obligations which were actually created by the lease. On the other hand, the plaintiffs were not entitled to recover in respect of the value of the lost stock or their loss of profit because these were not obligations which were created by the lease. Such losses could be recovered in a damages action but, on the facts, a claim in damages was not available.

13.9 Damages

A contractual claim for damages does not lie for misrepresentation, unless the misrepresentation has been subsequently incorporated into the contract as a term, in which case damages can be claimed for breach of contract (see 8.1 and 8.6). But damages may be recoverable in *tort* where the misrepresentation was made fraudulently or negligently. Sections 2(1) and 2(2) of the Misrepresentation Act 1967 also make provision for the recovery of damages for misrepresentation. Provided there is no element of double recovery a plaintiff may rescind and claim damages (except under s.2(2) of the Misrepresentation Act 1967, see below). When considering the entitlement of a plaintiff to damages for misrepresentation it is vital to give separate treatment to each type of misrepresentation.

Where the misrepresentation is fraudulent then damages may be recovered in the tort of deceit. The aim of an award of damages in deceit is to put the plaintiff in the position which he would have been in had the tort not been committed; that is to say, it aims to protect his reliance interest. This was confirmed by the Court of Appeal in *Doyle* v. *Olby* [1969] 2 QB 158. The court also held that the defendant was liable for all the damage directly flowing from the fraudulent inducement which was not rendered too remote by the plaintiff's own conduct, whether or not the defendant could have foreseen such consequential loss. Exemplary (or punitive) damages cannot be recovered for fraudulent misrepresentation because there appears to be no case prior to *Rookes* v. *Barnard* [1964] AC 1129 in which such damages were awarded (*AB* v. *South West Water Services Ltd* [1993] QB 507). Aggravated damages may, however, be awarded (*Archer* v. *Brown* [1985] QB 401).

In the case of negligent misrepresentation at common law the misrepresentor has committed a tort and damages can therefore be claimed. Once again the award of damages seeks to put the plaintiff in the position which he would have been in had the tort not been committed. The representor will be liable for all losses which are a reasonably foreseeable consequence of the misrepresentation (*The Wagon Mound (No 1)* [1961] AC 388). Where the representee has also been at fault, the damages payable may be reduced on the ground of contributory negligence (Law Reform (Contributory Negligence) Act 1945, s.1; *Gran Gelato Ltd* v. *Richcliff (Group) Ltd* [1992] Ch. 560). Punitive damages are not recoverable (*AB* v. *South West Water Services Ltd* (above)).

In the case of a claim under s.2(1) of the Misrepresentation Act 1967, there was, until recently, some controversy relating to the measure of damages recoverable. Some argued that damages should seek to put the plaintiff in the position he would have been in had the representation not been made (thus protecting the reliance interest), while others argued that damages should put the plaintiff in the position he would have been in had the representation been true (thus protecting the expectation interest). In *Gosling* v. *Anderson* (above) and *Jarvis* v. *Swan's Tours* [1973] QB 233, Lord Denning appeared to suggest that the measure of recovery was the expectation measure and this view was followed by Graham J in *Watts* v. *Spence* [1976] Ch 165. But this view has since been rejected and it is now clear that the measure of recovery is the reliance measure (*Royscot Trust Ltd* v. *Rogerson* [1991] 2 QB 297; *Sharneyford Supplies Ltd* v. *Barrington Black and Co* [1987] Ch 305, 323). It is suggested that this is the correct approach because, as we have already noted (13.1), promises and representations are functionally different. A representor does not promise anything; he simply asserts the truth of his statement and invites *reliance* upon that statement. It is therefore appropriate that the measure of damages should be the reliance measure (see Taylor, 1982). Although damages are confined to the reliance measure, it must be remembered that damages are assessed as if the representor had been fraudulent (*Royscot Trust Ltd* v. *Rogerson* [1991] 2 QB 297), so that the remoteness rules applicable are those pertaining to the tort of deceit, not the tort of negligence. It has also been held that damages payable under s.2(1) may be reduced on the ground of the representee's contributory negligence (*Gran Gelato Ltd* v. *Richcliff (Group) Ltd* [1992] Ch. 560, although it should be noted that Sir Donald Nicholls V-C reached his conclusion by drawing an analogy with the tort of negligence. This reasoning does not appear to be consistent with the approach of the Court of Appeal in *Royscot* where it was held that the appropriate analogy was with the tort of deceit. The point is an important one because it appears that contributory negligence is not available as a defence to an action in deceit (see *Alliance and Leicester Building Society* v. *Edgestop Ltd* [1994] 2 All ER 38, and so, on the reasoning in *Royscot*, it should not have been in issue in *Gran Gelato* as a possible defence to the s.2(1) claim).

In cases of innocent misrepresentation, the traditional common law rule was that damages were not available. Innocent misrepresentation is not a tort and therefore the only remedy was rescission and an indemnity. In practice the courts tended to mitigate the rigours of this rule, either by finding that the representation was in fact not a representation at all but a contractual term (see further 8.1–8.4), or by finding that the representation was enforceable as a 'collateral contract'. The latter technique can be illustrated by reference to the case of *De Lassalle* v. *Guildford* [1901] 2 KB 215. The plaintiff was induced to enter into a lease by an oral statement made by the defendant that the drains were in good order. The drains were not in good order but the lease contained no reference to the drains. It was held that the defendant's representation was enforceable as a warranty which was collateral to the lease. Thus there were two contracts between the parties. The first one was the written lease and the second consisted of the oral statement that the drains were in good order, the consideration for which was the entry by the plaintiff into the lease. However, the courts were not able to find the existence of such a collateral contract in every case (see *Heilbut Symons and Co* v. *Buckleton* [1913] AC 30).

The need to seek out the existence of a collateral contract has been reduced by s.2(2) of the Misrepresentation Act 1967 which provides that

'where a person has entered into a contract after a misrepresentation has been made to him otherwise than fraudulently, and he would be entitled, by reason of the misrepresentation, to rescind the contract, then, if it is claimed in any proceedings arising out of the contract, that the contract ought to be or has been rescinded, the court or arbitrator may declare the contract subsisting and award damages in lieu of rescission, if of opinion that it would be equitable to do so, having regard to the nature of the misrepresentation and the loss that would be caused by it if the contract were upheld, as well as to the loss that rescission would cause to the other party.'

Thus the courts now have a discretion to award damages in lieu of rescission in the case of innocent misrepresentation. The following points should be noted about s.2(2). The first is that the power to award damages is discretionary. The representee has no right to damages. The second point is that damages are in lieu of rescission, so that if the plaintiff wishes to rescind he can only claim an indemnity. Thirdly, it is not entirely clear what is the appropriate measure of damages under s.2(2). The measure of damages is not necessarily the same as that recoverable under s.2(1), so that the deceit rules are not applicable to s.2(2). In *William Sindall plc* v. *Cambridgeshire County Council* (1993) *The Times* June 8, Evans LJ stated that the contract measure is 'the correct measure in circumstances where the plaintiff is entitled to an order for rescission, but rescission is refused under s.2(2)'. Hoffman LJ in turn stated that s.2(2) was designed to eliminate the anomaly by which 'a minor representation gave rise to a right of rescission whereas a warranty in the same terms would have grounded no more than a claim for modest damages'. The subsection was intended to eliminate the anomaly by enabling the court to uphold the contract and compensate the plaintiff for the loss he has suffered on account of the subject-matter of the contract not having been what it was represented to be. 'In other words, damages under s.2(2) should never exceed the sum which would have been awarded if the representation had been a warranty' (per Hoffman LJ). The final point relates to the situation where the plaintiff had the right to rescind but has lost it, for example because of lapse of time. Does such a plaintiff also lose the right to claim damages under s.2(2)? In *Alton House Garages (Bromley) Ltd* v. *Monk* (Hearing 31.7.81.) Cantley J held that the jurisdiction was one to grant damages *in lieu of* rescission and that the representee must therefore be entitled to rescind at the date of the court hearing. Therefore if the representee has lost his right to rescind the court cannot award him damages under s.2(2).

13.10   Excluding Liability for Misrepresentation

At common law a person could not exclude liability for his own fraudulent misrepresentation (*S Pearson & Son Ltd* v. *Dublin Corporation* [1907] AC 351), but he could exclude liability for negligent or innocent misrepresentation, although such exclusion clauses were subject to strict rules relating to incorporation and construction (see 9.4 and 11.4–11.7). However s.3 of the Misrepresentation Act 1967 (as amended by s.8 of the Unfair Contract Terms Act 1977) limits the freedom of the parties to exclude liability for the consequences of a misrepresentation. It provides that

'If a contract contains a term which would exclude or restrict –

(a) any liability to which a party to a contract may be subject by reason of any misrepresentation made by him before the contract was made; or

(b) any remedy available to another party to the contract by reason of such a misrepresentation

that term shall be of no effect except in so far as it satisfies the requirement of reasonableness as stated in section 11(1) of the Unfair Contract Terms Act 1977; and it is for those claiming that the term satisfies that requirement to show that it does'.

It should be noted that, once again, the Act is drafted in defensive terms (see 11.1) so that it attacks attempts to 'exclude or restrict' a 'liability' or a 'remedy'. This section applies both to business liability and to non-business liability. Clauses which seek to define the duty may therefore fall outside the scope of the Act, but it is unlikely that a representor will be able to evade the clutches of the Act merely by stating that the representee must satisfy himself as to the correctness of any statement made (*Cremdean Properties* v. *Nash* (1977) 244 EG 547; *South Western General Property Co Ltd* v. *Marton* (1982) 263 EG 1090 and *Walker* v. *Boyle* [1982] 1 All ER 634).

Summary

1 A misrepresentation may be defined as an unambiguous false statement of fact which is addressed to the party misled and which is a material inducement to entry into the contract.

2 Mere puffs, statements of opinion, statements of intention and representations of law are not statements of fact.

3 A representation does not induce the contract if the representation was unimportant, the representee was unaware of its existence or did not allow it to affect his judgment.

4 A fraudulent misrepresentation is made when it is proved that a false representation has been made (i) knowingly or (ii) without belief in its truth or (iii) recklessly, careless whether it be true or false.

5 Negligent misrepresentation is actionable at common law where there is a special relationship between the plaintiff and the defendant. The existence of a special relationship depends upon a number of factors, including the knowledge of the representor, the purpose for which the statement was made and the reasonableness of the reliance by the representee.

6 Section 2(1) of the Misrepresentation Act 1967 states that where a misrepresentation has been made by one contracting party to another, the party making the misrepresentation is liable to the other in damages unless he can prove that he had reasonable grounds to believe and did believe up to the time that the contract was made that his statement was true.

7 The principal remedies for misrepresentation are rescission and damages. Rescission is in principle available for all types of misrepresentation. The effect of rescission is to put the parties as far as possible into the position which they would have been in had the contract not been concluded.

8 Damages can be claimed for fraudulent and negligent misrepresentation and under s.2(1) of the 1967 Act. In all cases the measure of damages is the reliance measure. In the case of innocent misrepresentation the court has a discretion to award damages in lieu of rescission under s.2(2) of the 1967 Act.

9 The ability of a contracting party to exclude liability for misrepresentation is controlled by s.3 of the Misrepresentation Act 1967 which subjects any term which purports to exclude or restrict liability or a remedy for misrepresentation to the reasonableness test.

Exercises

1 What is a misrepresentation?

2 What is a statement of existing fact? Give examples to illustrate your answer.

3 Distinguish between fraudulent, negligent and innocent misrepresentation.

4 What are the advantages to a plaintiff in invoking s.2(1) of the Misrepresentation Act 1967 rather than the common law of negligent misrepresentation? Are there any disadvantages?
5 What are the principal remedies for misrepresentation? What is the difference between damages and an indemnity?
6 Can a defendant exclude liability for misrepresentation?

14 Common Mistake and Frustration

14.1 Introduction

Parties occasionally enter into a contract on the basis of a common assumption which they later discover was false. Alternatively, events occur after the formation of the contract which were not within the contemplation of the parties when they entered into the contract. In these circumstances, are the parties bound to carry out their contract according to its terms, even though the events which have occurred were not within their contemplation when they entered into the contract? The answer to this question is that the courts may, in certain circumstances, release the parties from their obligations to perform. But it is very important to understand the basis of the intervention of the courts in these cases. The basis is not that the parties failed to reach agreement. These cases are not like the mistake cases which we discussed at 4.6, where one party is claiming relief on the basis that he was mistaken and that mistake negatived his consent and so prevented a contract coming into existence.

Here the parties do actually reach agreement and a valid contract is initially concluded. But an event occurs which was unforeseen by the parties and which destroys the basis upon which they entered into the contract. In such a case the courts must decide who bears the risk of such an unforeseen event (see Swan, 1980). Where the courts intervene to grant relief they do so on the ground that it is no longer fair or just to hold the parties to their agreement in such radically changed and unforeseen circumstances.

Where the common misapprehension is present *at the date of entry* into the contract, the contract may be set aside on the ground of common (or, as it is sometimes called, 'mutual') mistake. On the other hand, where events have occurred *after* the making of the contract which render performance of the contract impossible, illegal or something radically different from that which was in the contemplation of the parties at the time at which they entered into the contract, then the contract may be discharged on the ground of 'frustration'.

Common mistake is often treated separately from frustration on the ground that the latter is concerned with the discharge of a contract, whereas mistake relates to the formation of a contract. It is true that mistake relates to events which exist or occur prior to the making of the contract, and frustration applies to events which occur after the making of the contract. But there is, in fact, a strong link between these two doctrines, as can be seen from a brief analysis of the following case.

In *Amalgamated Investment & Property Co Ltd* v. *John Walker & Sons Ltd* [1977] 1 WLR 164, the defendants sold property to the plaintiffs for £1 710 000. The property was advertised as being suitable for occupation or redevelopment and the defendants knew that the plaintiffs wished to redevelop the property. In their pre-contract enquiries the plaintiffs asked the defendants whether the property was designated as a building of special historic or architectural interest. The defendants replied that it was not but, unknown to both parties, officials at the Department of the Environment had, on 22 August 1973, unconditionally included the property in a list of buildings to be designated as buildings of special architectural or historical interest. The parties signed the contract of sale on 25 September 1973. On the following day the Secretary of State wrote to the defendants informing them that the building had been listed and that the listing would take effect the next day when signed by the Secretary of State. The effect of the listing was to cause the value of the property to drop by £1 500 000 to approximately £200 000.

In these circumstances, the plaintiffs sought to have the contract set aside. They argued that the contract should be set aside on the ground of mistake or, alternatively, that the contract was frustrated by the listing of the building. But into which category did the case fall? If the listing took effect before the contract was signed on 25 September 1973 the ground on which the plaintiffs sought relief was common mistake, but, if the listing took effect after the contract had been signed on the 25th, the ground upon which relief was sought was frustration. The Court of Appeal held that the building did not become a listed building until it was signed by the Secretary of State on 27 September. The ground on which relief was sought was therefore frustration. But the court held that the contract was not frustrated because the plaintiffs knew of the risk that the buildings could be listed, as was evidenced by their pre-contract enquiries and it was a risk which they had to bear. The listing of the building was not an unforeseen event which rendered the performance of the contract something radically different from that which had been contemplated by the parties (see 14.10).

This case demonstrates that there is a strong relationship between common mistake and frustration. The point at issue in the case was: who should bear the risk of the listing of the building? Whether the case is treated as one of common mistake or frustration the issue is exactly the same. In the remaining sections of this chapter we shall give separate treatment to the doctrines of common mistake and frustration and conclude by identifying the relationship between the two doctrines.

14.2 Common Mistake

Where the mistake is common to both parties, the parties have reached agreement, but that agreement is based upon a fundamental mistaken assumption. In such a case the court may nullify the consent of the parties and set aside the contract which they concluded. The leading case on common mistake is *Bell* v. *Lever Brothers Ltd* [1932] AC 161. The defendants, Bell and Snelling, entered into a contract with the plaintiffs under which they agreed to serve for five years as chairman and vice-chairman respectively of a subsidiary company of the plaintiffs. One of the terms of their service agreements was that they must not make any private profit for themselves, by doing business on their own account, while working for the subsidiary. But the defendants, unknown to the plaintiffs, did engage in business on their own account and did not disclose their profits to the plaintiffs. The plaintiffs later decided that they wished to terminate the defendants' contracts because of a re-organisation of their business. So they entered into compensation agreements with the defendants under which they agreed to pay Bell £30 000 and Snelling £20 000 in exchange for their consent to the termination of their service agreements. After the money had been paid, the plaintiffs discovered the breaches by the defendants of their service agreements. The significance of the breaches by the defendants was that they would have entitled the plaintiffs to terminate the service agreements without the payment of any compensation. In these circumstances the plaintiffs sought to recover the money which they had paid to the defendants. A crucial feature of the case was the finding of the jury that, when they entered into the compensation agreements, the defendants had forgotten about their breaches of duty. The parties therefore entered into the compensation agreements under a common mistake that the service agreements were valid when they were, in fact, voidable.

The House of Lords held, by a majority of three to two, that the plaintiffs could not recover the money. Lord Atkin and Lord Thankerton held that the mistake was not sufficiently fundamental to avoid the contract. Lord Blanesburgh held that the plaintiffs could not recover because they had not pleaded common mistake, but he also expressed his 'entire accord' with the judgments of Lord Atkin and Lord Thankerton. The test established by the majority was well expressed by Lord Thankerton when he said that the common mistake must 'relate to something which both [parties] must necessarily have accepted in their minds as an essential element of the subject matter'. Yet, even applying this test, why was the plaintiffs' mistake not fundamental? They had paid £50 000 to the defendants, which in 1929 must have been a colossal sum of money, when they could have dismissed them without paying any compensation. The answer to this question is not entirely clear. A partial answer is that the House of Lords did not want to lay down a principle which would enable parties to escape from what was merely a bad bargain. They wanted to hold men to their bargains and to emphasise the exceptional nature of the jurisdiction of the court to set aside a contract on the ground of mistake. But why did they not recognise that this was, in fact, such an exceptional case? After all, the plaintiffs had made a spectacular mistake. But a closer analysis of the facts suggests that the mistake may not have been as significant as it appears at first sight. It seems that the plaintiffs were very anxious to carry through the reorganisation and to secure the defendants' consent to the termination of their service agreements. This anxiety and urgency suggested to the majority of their Lordships that the plaintiffs *might* have entered into the same agreements, even if they had known of the defendants' breaches of duty. Since it was for the plaintiffs to establish that the mistake was a fundamental one, the existence of such a doubt was fatal to their claim (see the useful analysis of *Bell* adopted by Steyn J in *Associated Japanese Bank (International) Ltd* v. *Crédit du Nord* [1989] 1 WLR 255).

Nevertheless, it must be said that the test adopted by the majority is a relatively open-textured one and that it can admit of varying interpretations. This is demonstrated by the judgments in *Bell* itself because the minority, Lord Warrington and Lord Hailsham, held that the plaintiffs' mistake *was* sufficiently fundamental to avoid the contract. In the following sections (14.3–14.6), we shall seek to ascertain the circumstances in which the courts have held a common mistake to be sufficiently fundamental to avoid a contract.

14.3 Mistake as to the Existence of the Subject-matter of the Contract

A mistake may be sufficiently fundamental to avoid a contract where both parties are mistaken as to the existence of the subject-matter of the contract. For example, in *Galloway* v. *Galloway* (1914) 30 TLR 531, the defendant, assuming his wife to be dead, married the plaintiff. The defendant and the plaintiff later separated and entered into a deed of separation under which the defendant promised to pay a weekly allowance to the plaintiff. The defendant subsequently discovered that his first wife was still alive and fell into arrears. When the plaintiff sued to recover the arrears it was held that she could not do so because the separation agreement was void on the ground that it was entered into under the common mistake that the parties were, in fact, married.

Greater difficulties arise in the case of a contract for the sale of non-existent goods. Section 6 of the Sale of Goods Act 1979 provides that

'where there is a contract for the sale of specific goods, and the goods without the knowledge of the seller have perished at the time when the contract is made, the contract is void'.

This section was thought to give effect to the decision of the House of Lords in *Couturier* v. *Hastie* (1856) 5 HLC 673. The parties entered into a contract for the sale of a cargo of corn, which was believed to be in transit from Salonica to the United Kingdom. But, before the contract was made and unknown to both parties, the corn had deteriorated to such an extent that the master of the ship sold it. The seller argued that the buyer remained liable for the price of the corn because he had bought an 'interest in the adventure' or such rights as the seller had under the shipping documents. The House of Lords rejected the seller's argument, holding that the subject-matter of the contract was not the rights of the seller under the shipping documents but the corn and that, since the corn did not exist, there was a total failure of consideration and the buyer was not liable to pay the price. But the precise legal basis of the decision of the House of Lords in *Couturier* has been the subject of some debate and controversy among lawyers. We shall now consider the principal interpretations which have been placed upon *Couturier*.

The first interpretation is that a mistake as to the existence of the subject-matter of a contract inevitably renders a contract void. This appears to be the interpretation placed upon *Couturier* by the draftsman of section 6 of the Sale of Goods Act 1979. However the word 'mistake' was not used in any of the judgments in *Couturier*. The court was principally concerned with the construction of the contract and the question whether the consideration had totally failed. The court did not establish such an all-embracing proposition.

The second interpretation, adopted by Denning LJ in *Solle* v. *Butcher* [1950] 1 KB 671, 691, is that the contract in *Couturier* was void because there was an implied condition precedent that the contract was capable of performance. In *Couturier* the parties proceeded upon the assumption that the goods were capable of being sold when, in fact, they were not and the effect of the implied condition precedent was to render the contract void. The difficulty with this interpretation is that it does not tell us when, or on what basis, the courts will imply such a condition precedent.

The third interpretation is that the question whether or not a contract is void depends upon the construction of the contract. Such an interpretation was placed upon *Couturier* by the High Court of Australia in *McRae* v. *Commonwealth Disposals Commission* (1951) 84 CLR 377. In this rather bizarre case the defendants purported to sell to the plaintiffs the wreck of a tanker which was lying on the Jourmand Reef and was said to contain oil. The plaintiffs embarked upon an expedition in an attempt to salvage the vessel but no tanker was found and, indeed, no such tanker had ever existed. The plaintiffs succeeded in their action for damages for breach of contract. The defendants had argued that there could be no liability for breach of contract because the alleged contract was void owing to the non-existence of the subject-matter of the contract. This argument was rejected by the court on the ground that the defendants had promised that such a tanker was in existence and they were liable for breach of that promise. *Couturier* was distinguished on the ground that there the parties had entered into the contract under the shared assumption that the corn was still in existence and could be sold by the seller; that assumption proved to be unfounded and the contract was held to be void. But in *McRae* the defendants had actually promised that the tanker was in existence. They had assumed the risk of the non-existence of the tanker and for the breach of their promise they were held liable in damages.

But would an English court follow *McRae*? It seems clear that it is factually distinguishable from *Couturier* for the reasons already given. The result in *McRae* seems perfectly just because the defendants assumed the risk of the non-existence of the tanker and the effect of the decision was to place that risk upon the defendants. In policy terms there is little doubt that *McRae* should be followed. The difficulty lies in reconciling *McRae* with the wording of section 6 of the Sale of Goods Act 1979 (above). Section 6 does not provide an insuperable obstacle, however, because it can be argued that a case such as *McRae* is not caught by the actual wording of section 6 since the tanker never existed and therefore it could not have 'perished'. On this interpretation only contracts for the sale of goods which once existed but have since perished would be governed by section 6. Contracts for the sale of goods which never existed would not be caught by section 6 but would instead be governed by the more flexible approach adopted in *McRae*. But such a distinction has little to commend itself in policy terms.

Alternatively, it could be argued that section 6 is only a rule of construction which can, in a case such as *McRae*, be ousted by proof of contrary intention (see Atiyah, 1957). The difficulty with this argument is that many sections of the Sale of Goods Act 1979 explicitly state that they are subject to contrary agreement but there is no such provision in section 6. Finally, it could be argued that, although the main contract in a case such as *McRae* is void, the defendants could be liable to the plaintiffs under a collateral contract, the terms of which would be that the tanker was in existence. The consideration provided by the plaintiffs would be the entry into the void contract. It is doubtful whether entry into a void contract can constitute consideration (but see *Strongman (1945) Ltd* v. *Sincock* [1955] 2 QB 525) and see the more flexible approach to consideration adopted in *Williams* v. *Roffey Bros. & Nicholls (Contractors) Ltd* [1991] 1 QB 1, see 5.11). Even if the consideration hurdle could be overcome, such a solution would be inelegant and horribly artificial. The contortions which are required to evade section 6 and to achieve a satisfactory solution in a case such as *McRae* suggests that English contract law would be radically improved by the repeal of section 6 of the Sale of Goods Act 1979.

14.4 Mistake as to Identity of the Subject-matter

A mistake as to the identity of the subject-matter of the contract may be sufficiently fundamental to avoid a contract if both parties thought that they were dealing with one thing when in fact they were dealing with another. There is no English case on this point (but see the discussion in the Canadian case of *Diamond* v. *British Columbia Thoroughbred Breeders' Society* (1966) 52 DLR (2d) 146).

14.5   Mistake as to the Possibility of Performing the Contract

A mistake may be sufficiently fundamental to avoid a contract where both parties believe that the contract is capable of being performed when, in fact, it is not. Professor Treitel (1991) helpfully divides these cases into three categories.

The first category is physical impossibility. In *Sheikh Brothers Ltd* v. *Ochsner* [1957] AC 136, the appellants granted to the respondents a licence to enter and cut sisal growing on their land and in return the respondents agreed to deliver to the appellants 50 tons of cut sisal per month. Unknown to both parties, the land was incapable of producing an average of 50 tons of sisal per month throughout the term of the licence. The Privy Council held that the contract was void because the mistake of the parties related to a matter which was essential to the agreement and neither party had assumed the risk of the land being incapable of producing such a yield.

The second type of impossibility is legal impossibility, that is to say, the contract provides for something to be done which cannot, as a matter of law, be done. In *Cooper* v. *Phibbs* (1867) LR 2 HL 149, the appellant agreed to take a lease of a salmon fishery which both parties believed to be the property of the respondents. It was subsequently discovered that the appellant, as the tenant in tail, was the owner of the fishery. The contract was set aside on the ground that the contract was legally incapable of performance because the appellant was already the owner of the fishery.

The third type of impossibility is commercial impossibility. In *Griffith* v. *Brymer* (1903) 19 TLR 434, the parties entered into a contract for the hire of a room for the purpose of viewing the coronation procession of Edward VII. The procession was cancelled because of the illness of Edward VII. The parties had concluded their contract at 11 am but, unknown to both parties, the decision to operate on Edward VII was taken at 10 am. It was held that the contract was void because the mistake of the parties went to the root or the heart of their agreement. Although the contract was still physically and legally capable of performance, the cancellation of the procession had undermined the commercial object of the contract.

14.6   Mistake as to Quality

A mistake as to the quality of the subject-matter of the contract may be sufficiently fundamental to avoid a contract. But the courts are extremely reluctant to conclude that a mistake as to quality renders a contract void, as can be seen from *Bell* v. *Lever Brothers* itself (see 14.2). A further difficulty is created by the fact that the cases are not easy to reconcile. A brief account will be given of some of the leading cases and then an attempt will be made at some reconciliation.

In *Leaf* v. *International Galleries* [1950] 2 KB 86, the Court of Appeal stated that a contract for the sale of a picture would not be set aside on the ground of mistake if both parties entered into the contract erroneously believing the picture to be a Constable. In *Harrison and Jones* v. *Burton and Lancaster* [1953] 1 QB 646, the parties entered into a contract for the sale of a particular brand of kapok which was believed to be pure kapok whereas, in fact, it also contained some brush cotton which made it a commercially inferior product. It was held that the mistake was not sufficiently fundamental to avoid the contract. In *Oscar Chess Ltd* v. *Williams* [1957] 1 WLR 370 (see 8.4) both parties entered into a contract for the sale of a car under the belief that the car was a 1948 model when in fact it was a 1939 model. Once again the mistake was not sufficiently fundamental to avoid the contract. Finally, in *Solle* v. *Butcher* [1950] 1 KB 671, the defendant agreed to lease a flat to the plaintiff for seven years at an annual rental of £250. The parties entered into this agreement under the mistaken assumption that the flat was free from rent control. When the plaintiff discovered that the flat was subject to rent control and that the rent payable under the legislation was only £140, he sought to recover the rent which he had overpaid. The defendant counterclaimed for rescission of the lease on the ground of mistake. The Court of Appeal held that the contract could not be avoided at law (although the contract was set aside in equity, see further 14.7). In *Solle* Lord Denning clearly wished to restrict the scope of the doctrine of common mistake because a finding that the contract was void would have detrimental effects upon the rights of innocent third parties (see further 4.6).

On the basis of these cases it would appear to be extremely difficult, if not impossible, to establish that a common mistake as to quality renders a contract void. But there are cases in which a mistake as to quality has been held to be sufficiently fundamental to avoid the contract. One such case is *Scott* v. *Coulson* [1903] 2 Ch 249. A contract for the sale of a life assurance policy was held to be void when, unknown to both parties, the assured had died and the value of the policy had consequently increased from £460 to £777. Secondly, in *Nicholson and Venn* v. *Smith-Marriott* (1947) 177 LT 189, the defendants put up for auction table napkins 'with crest of Charles I and authentic property of that monarch'. In reliance upon this description, the plaintiff bought the napkins for £787. It was later discovered that the napkins were Georgian and were worth only £105. Hallet J held that the plaintiff was entitled to damages for breach of contract but he also held that the plaintiff could have avoided the contract on the ground of mistake. The authority of this case has been weakened, however, by doubts cast upon its correctness by Denning LJ in *Solle* v. *Butcher* (above).

How can these cases be reconciled? The general test can be identified reasonably easily. As Lord Thankerton stated in *Bell* v. *Lever Brothers* (above), the mistake of the parties must relate to an 'essential and integral element of the subject matter' of the contract. The difficulty lies in applying that test to the facts of any given case. Professor Treitel (1991,

p. 255) has put forward the following test: imagine that you can 'ask the parties, immediately after they made the contract, what its subject-matter was. If, in spite of the mistake, they would give the right answer the contract is valid at law'. Such a test works satisfactorily in most cases and helps explain the difference between cases such as *Oscar Chess* and *Nicolson and Venn*. But it does not appear to explain *Leaf*, where the parties would surely have said that they were purchasing a Constable and not simply a picture. Treitel concedes this point, but counters that the dicta in that case are not conclusive because 'the plaintiff did not claim that the contract was void'. It is also difficult to apply this test to *Scott* where it is arguable that the parties would have given the correct answer, namely an insurance policy. Although this test cannot reconcile all the cases, it does provide some useful guidance in considering whether a mistake as to quality relates to an 'essential and integral element of the subject matter of the contract'.

14.7   Mistake in Equity

As can be seen from our discussion of the case law (14.3–14.6), the decision of the House of Lords in *Bell* v. *Lever Brothers Ltd* has given birth to an extremely narrow doctrine of common mistake in English law. Such a restrictive approach can be justified on the ground that it promotes certainty and protects innocent third party rights. But the narrow approach adopted in *Bell* has since been 'supplemented by the more flexible doctrine of mistake in equity' (per Steyn J in *Associated Japanese Bank (International) Ltd* v. *Crédit du Nord* [1989] 1 WLR 255). A more flexible doctrine of mistake in equity has flourished since *Bell* because *Bell* has been interpreted as an authority on the scope of mistake at law and not on mistake in equity. But the relationship between mistake at law and mistake in equity is an uneasy one. Indeed, if the House of Lords in *Bell* had believed that there was a wider equitable jurisdiction to grant relief in cases of mistake, it is difficult to understand why no reference was made to such a jurisdiction. Although the leading cases on the scope of mistake in equity are now of respectable antiquity (for example, *Solle* v. *Butcher* was decided in 1949), the House of Lords has never had the opportunity to consider the relationship between the principles established in *Bell* and the equitable jurisdiction which has been developed since *Bell*. But the relationship has been considered by judges in the lower courts and the clearest rationalisation of the cases has been provided by Steyn J in *Associated Japanese Bank (International) Ltd* v. *Credit du Nord* (above). Steyn J stated that a court must first decide whether the contract is void at common law. If it is void, then no question of mistake in equity arises. But, if the contract is valid at law, then the court must consider whether the contract can be set aside in equity. The role of the equitable doctrine is therefore a supplementary one, designed to mitigate the hardships caused by the strict approach adopted at law.

Mistake in equity differs in three major respects from mistake at law. The first is that the scope of the doctrine is wider (see Cartwright, 1987). In *Solle* v. *Butcher* (above) Denning LJ stated that the mistake must be 'fundamental' and that the party seeking to set the contract aside must not himself be 'at fault'. But he also asserted that the court has power to set aside a contract which is valid at law 'whenever it is of the opinion that it is unconscientious for the other party to avail himself of the legal advantage which he has obtained'. Subsequent cases do not appear to support the proposition that 'unconscientiousness' is the basis of the court's jurisdiction to intervene; rather, they suggest that the mistake must be 'substantial', although it need not be so fundamental as to render the contract void at law. Two cases help illustrate the scope of the equitable doctrine.

The first is *Grist* v. *Bailey* [1967] Ch 532, in which the defendant contracted to sell property to the plaintiff for £850 'subject to the existing tenancy thereof'. At the time the agreement was concluded both parties believed that the property was in the occupation of a protected tenant. When the defendant discovered that the protected tenant had died he refused to complete and sought rescission of the contract. The property, with vacant possession, was worth £2250. Goff J set aside the contract in equity. The second case is *Magee* v. *Pennine Insurance Co* [1969] 2 QB 507. There the Court of Appeal set aside an insurance company's compromise of a claim which had been entered into by both parties in the belief that the policy was binding when, in fact, it was voidable on the ground of innocent misrepresentation.

These decisions are questionable on two grounds. The first is that they do not sit easily with *Bell* v. *Lever Brothers* (above). It is particularly difficult to distinguish between *Magee* and *Bell* v. *Lever Brothers* (and Winn LJ dissented in *Magee* on precisely this ground). In both cases the plaintiffs paid out in the belief that there was a valid contract between themselves and the defendants when the contract was, in fact, voidable: in *Magee* the plaintiffs recovered, in *Bell* they did not. If *Magee* is indeed correctly decided, it is hard to resist the inference that the plaintiffs in *Bell* would have recovered if they had pleaded mistake in equity. Yet if their Lordships in *Bell* had thought that the plaintiffs would have won had they brought their claim in equity, surely they would have said so? Here we see the potential of equity to undermine the common law rules and, indeed, the decision in *Bell* itself. This inconsistency must be faced up to directly. It is no longer sufficient simply to refer to the historical division between law and equity as if that is a justification in itself. It is not. Fusion of law and equity took place over 100 years ago and English law should now develop a uniform set of rules to define the circumstances in which a contract can be set aside on the ground of common mistake.

The second point on which *Grist* and *Magee* are open to criticism is that in both cases the court concluded that the mistake was substantial on rather flimsy evidence. It can be argued that the vendor in *Grist* and the insurance company in *Magee* entered into bad bargains on the basis of inadequate information and then invoked mistake in equity to relieve them from the consequences of their own imprudence. It is understandable that the courts, when exercising their equitable jurisdiction, should wish to avoid the perceived hardships created by the narrow doctrine of common mistake at law, but they must also be careful that their relaxed approach in equity does not give rise to hardship by enabling fools to escape the consequences of their own folly.

The second difference between mistake in equity and mistake at law is that mistake in equity renders a contract voidable and not void, so that when a contract is set aside on the ground of mistake in equity innocent third party rights are protected. The third difference is that in equity the courts have greater remedial flexibility because they can set aside the contract 'on terms'. Thus, in *Grist* v. *Bailey* (above) the contract was set aside on terms that the defendant should give to the plaintiff an opportunity to purchase the property for a 'proper vacant possession price' (see too the terms on which the lease was set aside in *Solle* v. *Butcher*). Despite its dubious legitimacy and the rather liberal way in which it has sometimes been applied, mistake in equity is generally regarded as a useful, flexible supplement to common law mistake (although its practical utility does not detract from the need to develop a uniform set of rules).

14.8 Frustration

A contract can only be set aside on the ground of common mistake where the parties were labouring under the mistake at the time at which they entered into the contract. Unforeseen events which occur after the contract has been concluded cannot form the basis of a claim for relief on the ground of mistake, but, in such a situation, a court may hold that the contract has been discharged by operation of the doctrine of frustration. A contract is frustrated where, *after* the contract was concluded, events occur which make performance of the contract impossible, illegal or something radically different from that which was in the contemplation of the parties at the time they entered into the contract. A contract which is discharged on the ground of frustration is brought to an end automatically by the operation of a rule of law, irrespective of the wishes of the parties (*Hirji Mulji* v. *Cheong Yue SS Co* [1926] AC 497).

It has been argued (14.1) that the principal difference between common mistake and frustration relates to the *time* at which the misapprehension or unforeseen event occurs. Yet it must be conceded that the time at which the misapprehension or unforeseen event occurs does have significant consequences; that is to say, it is easier to discover the true facts at the moment of entry into the contract than it is to foresee future events. Therefore it is to be expected that a court will be readier to discharge a contract on the ground of frustration than it will be to avoid a contract on the ground of mistake. But when one looks at the cases, that expectation is not clearly fulfilled because the doctrine of frustration presently operates within very narrow confines. What is it that explains the reluctance of the courts to invoke the doctrine of frustration?

14.9 Frustration, Force Majeure and Hardship

It is suggested that there are two principal reasons which help explain the reluctance of the courts to invoke the doctrine of frustration. The first is that the courts do not want to allow the doctrine to act as an escape route for a party for whom the contract has simply become a bad bargain. The attitude of the modern courts was well summed up by Lord Roskill when he said that the doctrine of frustration was 'not lightly to be invoked to relieve contracting parties of the normal consequences of imprudent bargains' (*The Nema* [1982] AC 724, 752). An example of this approach at work is provided by the case of *Davis Contractors Ltd* v. *Fareham UDC* [1956] AC 696. The plaintiff contractors agreed to build 78 houses for the defendants for £94 000. The work was scheduled to last for 8 months but, owing to shortages of skilled labour, the work took an extra 14 months to complete and cost £115 000. The plaintiffs, in an attempt to recover a sum of money in excess of the contract price, argued that the contract had been frustrated. Their argument was rejected by the House of Lords. Lord Radcliffe stated that it was not

'hardship or inconvenience or material loss itself which calls the principle of frustration into play. There must be as well such a change in the significance of the obligation that the thing undertaken would, if performed, be a different thing from that contracted for'.

Davis can be said to be the paradigm example of a bad bargain. The deal had undoubtedly turned out to be a poor one for the plaintiffs but the courts refused to rescue them. The decision may seem harsh but, had it gone the other way, it would have created a new principle of uncertain ambit which would have denied to the defendants the fruits of the good deal which they had negotiated. The hardship which *Davis* possibly creates is more than offset by the clear rule which it establishes and the signal which it gives to contracting parties that the courts will not lend their assistance to a party who is looking for a way out of a bad bargain. So frustration can be invoked only where the supervening event *radically* or *fundamentally* changes the nature of performance: it cannot be invoked simply because performance has become more onerous.

The second reason for the narrowness of the doctrine of frustration is that we all know that the future is uncertain; prices may suddenly increase, inflation may rise, labour disputes break out. Contracting parties are expected to foresee many such possibilities when entering into a contract and guard against them in the contract. Contracts today often make provision for the impact of unexpected events upon contractual performance. A clause which is frequently employed for this purpose is known as a 'force majeure' clause. In *Channel Island Ferries Ltd* v. *Sealink UK Ltd* [1988] 1 Lloyd's Rep 323, the contract between the parties contained the following force majeure clause:

> 'A party shall not be liable in the event of non-fulfilment of any obligation arising under this contract by reason of Act of God, disease, strikes, Lock-Outs, fire, and any accident or incident of any nature beyond the control of the relevant party.'

Another clause which is often found in commercial contracts is known as a 'hardship clause'. Such a clause will generally define what constitutes 'hardship' (usually of an economic variety) and will lay down a procedure to be adopted by the parties in the event of such hardship occurring. Generally the clause will impose an obligation on both parties to use best endeavours to renegotiate the contract in good faith in an attempt to alleviate the hardship which has arisen (although note in this context the difficulties which the decision of the House of Lords in *Walford* v. *Miles* [1992] 2 AC 128 (discussed at 4.1) might create for the enforceability of such an obligation to re-negotiate). A further type of clause which is often found in commercial contracts is an 'intervener clause'. Such a clause is similar to a 'hardship clause' except that it gives to a third party (the 'intervener') the authority to resolve the dispute which has arisen between the parties. Intervener clauses are regularly employed as a sanction to be invoked in the event of the parties themselves failing to negotiate their way out of a hardship event.

What advantages can be obtained by the use of such clauses? It is suggested that there are a number of advantages (see McKendrick, 1991a). The first is the provision of a degree of certainty. It is often difficult to know whether or not a contract has been frustrated. To an extent this uncertainty can be reduced by the parties agreeing a list of events which are to constitute force majeure or hardship events. The second is that frustration operates within very narrow limits (both in terms of the events which constitute frustrating events and the width of doctrines such as self-induced frustration which deny to a party the ability to argue that the contract was frustrated, see 14.16). On the other hand, force majeure and hardship clauses give to the parties the opportunity, should they want to avail themselves of it, to agree that a wider class of events shall constitute force majeure or hardship events. For example, an unexpected increase in prices does not constitute a frustrating event (see *Davis Contractors* v. *Fareham UDC* (above)) but it is not uncommon for a commercial contract to state that an 'abnormal increase in prices and wages' shall constitute a force majeure event.

The third advantage is that the parties can make provision for the consequences of the occurrence of a force majeure or hardship event. Frustration operates too drastically because it terminates the contract, irrespective of the wishes of the parties (see above). Very often the parties want to continue their relationship but to adapt the terms to meet the new situation. This cannot be done under the doctrine of frustration. But force majeure clauses often provide for a period of suspension of the contract (to allow more time for performance or to enable the parties to wait for the supervening event, such as bad weather or a strike, to subside) before resorting to the more drastic remedy of termination. Hardship and intervener clauses are particularly well suited to contracting parties who wish their relationship to continue through changing circumstances. The remedial rigidity of the doctrine of frustration contrasts unfavourably with the flexibility which can be obtained by drafting an appropriate force majeure or hardship clause.

It is suggested that the ability of contracting parties to make such provision in their contracts has had a significant impact upon the development of the doctrine of frustration. Indeed, at one point in its history, supervening or unforeseen events were not regarded as an excuse for non-performance because the parties could provide against such accidents in their contract. Once a party had assumed an obligation he was 'bound to make it good' (*Paradine* v. *Jane* (1647) Aleyn 26, 27). This absolutist approach was gradually relaxed during the latter half of the nineteenth century and, commencing with *Taylor* v. *Caldwell* (1863) 3 B & S 826 and culminating in cases such as *Jackson* v. *Union Marine Insurance Co Ltd* (1874) LR 10 CP 125 and *Krell* v. *Henry* [1903] 2 KB 740, the courts developed a wider role for the doctrine of frustration and it became significantly easier to invoke the doctrine. Today, the courts have reverted to a more restrictive approach and it is rare to find frustration being pleaded successfully. For this reason contracting parties frequently include force majeure and hardship clauses in their contracts so that they can allocate the risk of such unforeseen events (see further 14.16). It is often said that English law does not encourage the adjustment of bargains in the event of contractual performance becoming more onerous. This is not entirely accurate. The issue should not be seen as whether or not English law permits adjustment. The real issue is: who should do the adjusting? Is it the courts or is it the parties? The answer which English law gives is that it is for the parties to do the adjusting. While the courts will not adjust the bargain for the parties, they will not place significant obstacles in the way of attempts by the parties to adjust their bargain to meet changing circumstances.

14.10 Frustration: A Sterile Doctrine?

Although frustration is a difficult defence to invoke, it should not be thought that it has become a sterile doctrine which is incapable of development. The scope of the doctrine was, in fact, expanded by the decision of the House of Lords in *National Carriers* v. *Panalpina (Northern) Ltd* [1981] AC 675. For many years it was thought that the doctrine of frustration could not apply to a lease because a lease created an interest in land and that interest in land was unaffected by the alleged frustrating event. But in *Panalpina* it was held that, as a matter of principle, a lease could be frustrated, although, as a matter of practice, it would be rare for a court to conclude that a lease had been frustrated. Many leases run for a long period of time, such as 99 years, and it is difficult to conceive of such a lease being frustrated because the parties must anticipate that major changes will occur during the 99 year period and so, to a large extent, they will have assumed the risk of supervening events. The type of lease which might be frustrated is a lease of a holiday flat or some other lease of short duration. Although the practical significance of *Panalpina* may be minimal, the decision does display a willingness, in an appropriate case, to expand the horizons of the doctrine of frustration.

14.11   Impossibility

A contract which has become impossible of performance is frustrated. In *Taylor* v. *Caldwell* (1863) 3 B & S 826, the defendants granted to the plaintiffs a licence to use the 'Surrey Gardens and Music Hall' for a series of concerts at a fee of £100 per concert. After the contract had been concluded, but before the first concert was performed, the music hall was accidentally destroyed by fire so that it became impossible to stage the concerts. The plaintiffs argued that the defendants were in breach of contract in failing to supply the hall and sought to recover their wasted advertising expenditure. But the court held that the contract was frustrated because the destruction of the music hall rendered performance of the contract impossible. The frustrating event released both parties from their obligations under the contract and so the defendants were no longer under an obligation to supply the hall and were not in breach of contract. Partial destruction of the subject-matter may also frustrate a contract where it renders performance of the contract impossible. For example, in *Taylor* v. *Caldwell* the contract was for the hire of the music hall and the 'Surrey Gardens', but it was only the music hall which was destroyed. Nevertheless, because the destruction of the music hall rendered performance of the contract impossible the contract was frustrated.

Contracts for personal services, such as contracts of employment and contracts of apprenticeship, are frustrated by the death of either party to the contract. Similarly, a contract of employment may be frustrated if the ill-health of an employee renders him permanently unfit for work.

A contract may also be frustrated where the subject-matter of the contract is unavailable for the purpose of carrying out the contract. For example, a charterparty was held to be frustrated when the ship was requisitioned and so was unavailable to the charterer (*Bank Line Ltd* v. *Arthur Capel & Co Ltd* [1919] AC 435). Temporary unavailability of the subject-matter may also frustrate a contract. In *Jackson* v. *Union Marine Insurance Co* (1874) LR 10 CP 125, a ship was chartered in November 1871 and was required to proceed with all possible dispatch from

Liverpool to Newport, and there load a cargo for carriage to San Francisco. On her way to Newport in early January 1872, the ship ran aground and was not fully repaired until the end of August 1872. It was held that the contract was frustrated because the ship was not available for the voyage for which she was chartered. A voyage to San Francisco in late August 1872 was performance radically different from that originally contemplated.

Where the contract is one of fixed duration and the unavailability of the subject-matter is only temporary, the court must, in deciding whether the contract has been frustrated, consider the ratio of the likely interruption in contractual performance to the duration of the contract. The higher the ratio, the more likely it is that the contract will be frustrated. In *The Nema* (above) a charterparty was frustrated when a long strike closed the port at which the ship was due to load so that, of the six or seven voyages contracted to be made between April and December, no more than two could be completed (see also *Morgan* v. *Manser* [1948] 1 KB 184).

14.12 Frustration of Purpose

Where the common purpose for which the contract was entered into can no longer be carried out because of some supervening event the contract may be frustrated. Examples of frustration of purpose are, however, extremely rare. The reason for this is that the courts do not wish to provide an escape route for a party for whom the contract has simply become a bad bargain. A rare case in which a plea of frustration of purpose succeeded is *Krell* v. *Henry* [1903] 2 KB 740. The defendant hired a flat in Pall Mall from the plaintiff for two days. The object in entering into the contract was to view the coronation procession of Edward VII, although this was not actually expressed in the contract. After the contract had been concluded, the coronation of Edward VII was postponed because of the illness of the King. The Court of Appeal held that the contract was frustrated. *Krell* must, however, be contrasted with *Herne Bay Steam Boat Co* v. *Hutton* [1903] 2 KB 683, in which the defendant hired a ship from the plaintiff 'for the purpose of viewing the naval review and for a day's cruise around the fleet'. After the contract had been concluded, the naval review was cancelled because of the illness of Edward VII. Nevertheless, the court held that the contract was not frustrated. What is the difference between this case and *Krell*?

In answering this question, it is necessary to refer to an example considered by Vaughan Williams LJ in *Krell*. It was put to Vaughan Williams LJ that, if the contract was frustrated on the facts of *Krell*, then it 'would follow that if a cabman was engaged to take someone to Epsom on Derby Day at a suitably enhanced price for such a journey . . . both parties to the contract would be discharged in the contingency of the race at Epsom for some reason becoming impossible'. But Vaughan Williams LJ was of the opinion that such a contract would not be frustrated because he did not think that 'the happening of the race would be the foundation of the contract'. In *Krell*, on the other hand, the 'foundation of the contract' was the viewing of the coronation. However the contract in *Krell* was an extremely unusual one. The rooms were hired out by the day, excluding the night, and the only purpose which *both* parties had in entering into such an unusual contract was to hire the rooms for the purpose of viewing the coronation. So interpreted, the contract was frustrated. On the other hand, in *Herne Bay Steamboat Co* v. *Hutton* (above) the defendant could still see the fleet and, although the defendant's motive in entering into the contract might have been to see the naval review, it could not be said that that was the 'common foundation of the contract'. Similar reasoning explains the example of the cancellation of the Derby. Although the motive of the hirer might have been to see the Derby, that was not of itself sufficient to render the happening of the Derby the 'common foundation' of the contract. Thus interpreted, *Krell* becomes a very narrow decision indeed and it is not surprising that it has been distinguished in modern cases such as *Amalgamated Investment & Property Co Ltd* v. *John Walker & Sons Ltd* (above, 14.1).

14.13   Illegality

Supervening illegality can operate to frustrate a contract. In *Fibrosa Spolka Akcyjna* v. *Fairbairn Lawson Combe Barbour Ltd* [1943] AC 32, the respondents agreed to manufacture machines for the appellants and to deliver them to Gdynia in Poland. However before the respondents had completed the manufacture of the machines Gdynia was occupied by the German army. It was held that the contract was frustrated because in time of war it is against the law to trade with the enemy. The public interest in ensuring that no assistance was given to the enemy in time of war outweighed the fact that it remained physically possible to manufacture and deliver the machines. Where the illegality is only temporary or partial the contract will be frustrated only if the illegality affects the performance of the contract in a substantial or fundamental way (contrast *Denny, Mott & Dickinson* v. *James B Fraser & Co Ltd* [1944] AC 265 and *Cricklewood Property Investment Trust Ltd* v. *Leighton's Investment Trust Ltd* [1945] AC 221).

14.14   Express Provision

There are a number of limitations upon the scope of the doctrine of frustration. Three such limitations will be considered here (14.14–14.16). The first is that a contract is not frustrated where the parties have made express provision for the consequences of the alleged frustrating event in their contract. A frustrating event is a supervening, unforeseen event; it is not an event which has been anticipated in the contract itself. But where the contract is frustrated on the ground that further performance of the contract is against the law, because it involves trading with the enemy in time of war, the operation of the doctrine of frustration cannot be excluded by express provision in the contract. Overriding considerations of public policy deny effect to such a clause (*Ertel Bieber and Co* v. *Rio Tinto Co Ltd* [1918] AC 260).

The express provision rule has important consequences for force majeure clauses and hardship clauses. The effect of such clauses may be to exclude the operation of the doctrine of frustration because the contract, on its proper construction, will be held to have covered and made its own provision for the event which has occurred. But the courts have generally subjected to a narrow interpretation clauses which, it is alleged, make provision for what would otherwise be a frustrating event. In particular, the fact that the contract deals with events of the same general nature as the alleged frustrating event does not mean that the clause deals with every event in that class. A good example of this restrictive approach is provided by the decision of the House of Lords in *Metropolitan Water Board* v. *Dick Kerr and Co* [1918] AC 119. Here contractors agreed to construct a reservoir in six years. The contract provided that, in the event of delay 'whatsoever and howsoever occasioned', the contractors were to apply to the engineer for an extension of time. When the contractors were required by Government Order to stop the work and sell their plant it was held that the contract was frustrated because the delay clause was not intended to apply to such a fundamental change of circumstances. The clause was intended to cover only temporary difficulties and did not cover fundamental changes in the nature of the contract (see too *Jackson* v. *Union Marine Insurance Co Ltd* (above)).

So the courts insist that provision for the event be 'full and complete' before frustration is excluded, and the greater the magnitude of the event the less likely it is that it will be held to fall within the scope of the contract. One consequence of this approach is that it is extremely difficult, if not impossible, to draft a force majeure clause which will exclude the operation of the doctrine of frustration completely. As the *Metropolitan Water Board* case demonstrates, even the widest of clauses may be held not to encompass a particularly catastrophic event. Similarly, the fact that a force majeure clause makes provision for a temporary suspension of the contract on the occurrence of a force majeure event is likely to be interpreted by the court as an indication that the scope of the clause is confined to temporary interruptions in performance and that it does not apply to an event which renders further performance of the contract 'unthinkable' (*The Playa Larga* [1983] 2 Lloyd's Rep 171, 189).

14.15 Foreseen and Forseeable Events

Given that a frustrating event is a supervening, unforeseen event, the doctrine ought logically not to apply to an event which is within the contemplation of the parties. In *Walton Harvey Ltd* v. *Walker and Homfrays Ltd* [1931] 1 Ch 274, the defendant granted to the plaintiff the right to display an advertising sign for seven years on the defendant's hotel. Before the seven years had elapsed, the local authority compulsorily purchased the hotel and demolished it. The court held that the contract between the parties was not frustrated by the compulsory purchase and demolition of the hotel because it was within the contemplation of the defendant, at the time that the contract was concluded, that the property might be the subject of a compulsory purchase order. The proposition that a foreseeable event cannot frustrate a contract has been challenged, however, by Lord Denning in *The Eugenia* [1964] 2 QB 226 (see too *WJ Tatem Ltd* v. *Gamboa* [1939] 1 KB 132). The status of these dicta is uncertain. On the one hand they suggest that the general rule requires reconsideration, but, on the other hand, they can be reconciled with the orthodox analysis on the ground that the events in these cases were not sufficiently foreseeable to satisfy the very high test of foreseeability which is applicable here. An event is foreseeable and will prevent frustration of the contract only where it is one which 'any person of ordinary intelligence would regard as likely to occur' (see Treitel, 1991 p. 800, contrast Hall, 1984). Whatever the precise status of these dicta in *The Eugenia* and *Tatem* v. *Gamboa*, it is clear that the foresight of war is an irrelevant issue where the ground of frustration is trading with the enemy.

14.16   Self-Induced Frustration

A party cannot invoke the doctrine of frustration where the alleged frustrating event is brought about through his own conduct or the conduct of those for whom he is responsible. This inability to invoke frustration is generally referred to as 'self-induced frustration'. It is, however, important to be clear about the consequences of concluding that the 'frustration' was 'self-induced'. Frustration is generally invoked by a defendant who has not performed his contractual obligations as a defence to an action for breach of contract. But where the 'frustration' is held to be 'self-induced' the consequence is that the defendant is unable to rely on frustration and so, in the absence of any other defence, will be found to be in breach of contract.

Although the concept of self-induced frustration is clearly established in the cases, the courts have never established its limits with any degree of clarity. In *J Lauritzen AS* v. *Wijsmuller BV (The 'Super Servant Two')* [1989] 1 Lloyds Rep 148, Hobhouse J defined self-induced frustration as a 'label' which has been used by the courts to describe 'those situations where one party has been held by the courts not to be entitled to treat himself as discharged from his contractual obligations'. On his analysis frustration was self-induced where the alleged frustrating event was caused by a breach or an anticipatory breach of contract by the party claiming that the contract has been frustrated, where an act of the party claiming that the contract has been frustrated broke the chain of causation between the alleged frustrating event and the event which made performance of the contract impossible, and where the alleged frustrating event was not a supervening event, by which he meant 'something altogether outside the control of the parties'. Thus a negligent act by the defendant will generally amount to self-induced frustration because such an event is not 'altogether outside the control' of the defendant. On the contrary, it is within his control, notwithstanding the fact that his negligence is a result of his unreasonable failure to exercise that control (see *Joseph Constantine Steamship Ltd* v. *Imperial Smelting Corporation Ltd* [1942] AC 154).

Some insight into the scope of self-induced frustration can be gleaned from an analysis of the following two cases. The first case is *Maritime National Fish Ltd* v. *Ocean Trawlers Ltd* [1935] AC 524. The defendants chartered a ship from the plaintiffs but the vessel could only be used for its intended purpose if it was fitted with an otter trawl. An otter trawl could only be used under licence and, although the defendants applied for licences for the five vessels which they operated, they were allocated only three licences. They elected to apply the licences to the trawlers which they owned directly or indirectly rather than to the vessel chartered from the plaintiffs. The plaintiffs sued for the hire due under the terms of the contract but the defendants denied liability to pay on the ground that the contract had been frustrated by their failure to obtain a licence. The Privy Council held that the contract was not frustrated as a result of the defendants' failure to obtain a licence for the vessel; this was a case of self-induced frustration. But the ratio of the decision remained unclear. On the one hand, it could be argued that it was the fact that the defendants elected to allocate the licences to their own vessels which led the Privy Council to conclude that this was a case of self-induced frustration. On the other hand, it could be maintained that the mere fact that the defendants had a choice as to the distribution of the licences was sufficient to constitute self-induced frustration.

Our second case is *J Lauritzen AS* v. *Wijsmuller BV (The 'Super Servant Two')* [1990] 1 Lloyd's Rep 1 (see McKendrick, 1991a), where the Court of Appeal adopted the latter of our two possible interpretations of the *Maritime National Fish* case. The defendants agreed to transport the plaintiffs' oil rig using, at their option, either Super Servant One or Super Servant Two (both of which were self-propelling barges especially designed for the transportation of rigs). Prior to the time for performance of the contract the defendants made a decision, which they admitted was not irrevocable, to allocate Super Servant Two to the performance of the contract with the plaintiffs and to allocate Super Servant One to the performance of other concluded contracts. Unfortunately, after the contract had been concluded but before the time fixed for performance,

Super Servant Two sank while transporting another rig. The contract could not be performed by Super Servant One because of its allocation to the performance of other concluded contracts and so the contract was eventually performed by another, more expensive method of transportation. The plaintiffs brought an action for damages against the defendants, alleging that they were in breach of contract in failing to transport the rig in the agreed manner. The defendants denied liability on two grounds. The first was that they argued that the contract had been frustrated as a result of the sinking of Super Servant Two. This argument was rejected. The Court of Appeal held that the cause of the non-performance of the contract was not the sinking of Super Servant Two but the choice of the defendants to allocate Super Servant One to the performance of other contracts. The existence of such a choice was held to be sufficient to turn the case into one of self-induced frustration. The difficulty with this analysis is that the defendants had no *real* choice as to the allocation of Super Servant One. It was impossible to allocate it to the performance of all concluded contracts and so the sinking of Super Servant Two *compelled* them to make such a decision. The conclusion of the Court of Appeal appears to leave a seller or supplier of goods in an impossible position where his source of supply partially fails due to an unforeseen event.

But at this point it is important to turn to the defendants' second defence, which was that they were entitled to terminate performance of the contract without incurring any liability under the terms of a force majeure clause contained in the contract. One of the force majeure events listed in the contract was 'perils or dangers and accidents of the sea' and the Court of Appeal held that this phrase was apt to encompass the sinking of Super Servant Two *provided that* its sinking was not attributable to negligence on the part of the defendants or their employees. So, provided there was no negligence on the part of the defendants, the force majeure clause gave to the defendants an effective defence to the plaintiffs' claim for damages.

Super Servant Two is an interesting and important case because it provides us with an excellent example both of the narrow confines within which the doctrine of frustration currently operates and of the advantages which can be obtained by the incorporation of a suitably drafted force majeure clause in a contract. Indeed, the latter point was made abundantly clear by Hobhouse J at first instance when he said that if a promisor wished protection in the event of a partial failure of supplies 'he must bargain for the inclusion of a suitable force majeure clause in the contract'. The responsibility for adjusting and regulating the bargain is thus clearly allocated to the parties and not to the courts. Given the narrow confines within which frustration currently operates, *Super Servant Two* demonstrates that a contracting party who wishes to be released from his obligations to perform in a wider range of circumstances must bargain for the inclusion of a force majeure, hardship or intervener clause in the contract (see 14.9).

14.17 The Effects of Frustration

As we have already noted (14.8), a contract which is discharged on the ground of frustration is brought to an end automatically at the time of the frustrating event. For the purposes of ease of exposition we shall consider separately the effects of frustration upon a claim to recover money paid prior to the frustrating event and its effects upon a claim to recover the value of goods supplied or services provided prior to the frustrating event.

At common law it was held in *Fibrosa Spolka Ackcyjna* v. *Fairbairn, Lawson Combe Barbour Ltd* [1943] AC 32 (overruling *Chandler* v. *Webster* [1904] 1 KB 493 where it had been held, essentially, that the loss lay where it fell) that money paid prior to the frustration of the contract was recoverable upon a total failure of consideration. A total failure of consideration arises where the party seeking recovery has got no part of what he has bargained for. In *Fibrosa* (see 14.11) the appellants sought to recover the £1000 they had paid to the respondents on the signing of the contract. The House of Lords held that the consideration for the payment had wholly failed because the machines had not been delivered to the appellants and that they were entitled to the recovery of their prepayment. While it is true to say that *Fibrosa* represented an improvement upon the old common law rule established in *Chandler* v. *Webster* (above), it did not leave the law in an entirely satisfactory state. Two principal defects remained. The first was that the payer could only recover money paid upon a total failure of consideration; where the failure was only partial he could not recover (*Whincup* v. *Hughes* (1871) LR 6 CP 78, see further 21.2). The second defect was that the payee could not set off against the money to be repaid any expenditure which he had incurred in the performance of the contract. For example, on the facts of *Fibrosa*, the respondents had incurred expenditure in making the machines (although it was, admittedly, unclear whether that expenditure had been wasted), yet they were unable to retain any portion of the £1000 which represented their expenditure upon the machines.

This position has been rectified by the enactment of s.1(2) of the Law Reform (Frustrated Contracts) Act 1943. The effect of this subsection is threefold. The first is that moneys paid prior to the frustrating event are recoverable. The second is that sums payable prior to the time of discharge cease to be payable. The third is that the payee may be entitled to set off against the sums so paid expenses which he has incurred before the time of discharge in, or for the purpose of, the performance of the contract. Section 1(2) meets the two deficiencies of the common law in that the right to recover money is not confined to a total failure of consideration and the payee can set off against the sums repayable any reliance expenditure which he had incurred in the performance of the contract. But certain deficiencies remain (for fuller consideration see Goff and Jones, 1993 and McKendrick, 1991b). The first is that the section, however, does not make clear the basis upon which the court is to calculate the amount of expenditure which a payee is entitled to retain. Is it all of it, half of it, some other portion of it, or none of it? The subsection does not tell us (for a possible answer see *Lobb* v. *Vaisey Housing Auxiliary* [1963] VR 236, where it was held that the onus of proof was on the payee to show that it was just in all the circumstances of the case for him to retain any part of the prepayment, and for a legislative solution see s.5(3) of the British Columbia Frustrated Contracts Act 1974, which provides that the loss shall be apportioned equally between the parties). The second difficulty created by s.1(2) is that the payee cannot recover or retain more than the value of the prepayment, so that any reliance expenditure incurred which is in excess of the prepayment cannot be recovered under s.1(2), although it may be recoverable under s.1(3) where the expenditure results in a valuable benefit being obtained by the other party (see below).

We must now consider the effects of frustration upon a claim to recover the value of goods supplied or services provided prior to the frustrating event. At common law the leading case was *Appleby* v. *Myers* (1867) LR 2 CP 651. The plaintiffs contracted to make and erect machinery in the defendants' factory and to maintain the machinery for two years. Payment was to be upon completion of the work. After part of the machinery had been erected, an accidental fire destroyed the factory and machinery and frustrated the contract. It was held that the plaintiffs could not recover in respect of their work because they were only entitled to payment when performance was completed (called the 'entire obligations' or 'entire contracts' rule, see further 21.2) and, as the fire had prevented completion of the work, they were not entitled to payment. This rule caused obvious hardship to the provider of services under a frustrated contract and it has since been replaced by s.1(3) of the Law Reform (Frustrated Contracts) Act 1943. Section 1(3) states that

'where any party to the contract has, by reason of anything done by any other party thereto in, or for the purpose of, the performance of the contract, obtained a valuable benefit (other than a payment of money to which the last foregoing subsection applies) before the time of discharge, there shall be recoverable from him by the said other party such sum (if any), not exceeding the value of the said benefit to the party obtaining it, as the court considers just, having regard to all the circumstances of the case and, in particular –

(a) the amount of any expenses incurred before the time of discharge by the benefited party in, or for the purpose of, the performance of the contract, including any sums paid or payable by him to any other party in pursuance of the contract and retained or recoverable by that party under the last foregoing subsection, and

(b) the effect, in relation to the said benefit, of the circumstances giving rise to the frustration of the contract'.

This subsection is an unnecessarily complex provision (for details see Goff and Jones, 1993 and McKendrick, 1991b). Its basic effect is that, where one party to the contract has conferred upon the other party a 'valuable benefit' (other than a payment of money which is governed by s.1(2)) before the time of discharge, he shall be entitled to recover a 'just sum' which shall not exceed the value of the benefit which he has conferred upon the other party. In *BP* v. *Hunt* [1979] 1 WLR 783, Robert Goff J concluded that there were two steps involved in a section 1(3) claim. The first was the identification and valuation of the benefit. The subsection does not define what is to count as a benefit: it could be either the value of the services performed or it could be the end product of the services. In *BP* v. *Hunt* (above) Robert Goff J concluded that in 'an appropriate case' it was the end product which was to be regarded as the benefit. He appeared to envisage two circumstances in which a court could have regard to the value of the services in identifying the benefit; the first arising where the service by its very nature does not result in an end product (for example, the transportation of goods) and the second where the service results in an end product which has no objective value (for example, a plaintiff who commences 'the redecoration, to the defendant's execrable taste, of rooms which are in good decorative order'). But he held that, where the end product is destroyed by the frustrating event, the provider of the services has no claim under s.1(3) because the value of the benefit (namely, the end product) has been reduced to zero by the frustrating event. This interpretation of 'benefit' has unfortunate consequences. It means that the result in *Appleby* v. *Myers* (above) would be unaffected by the Act because the plaintiffs' work was destroyed by the fire and so did not result in any end product. Although this interpretation of 'benefit' has been heavily criticised (see Treitel, 1991, p. 813 and Haycroft and Waksman, 1984), such an interpretation has also been adopted in the Commonwealth (*Parsons Bros Ltd* v. *Shea* (1866) 53 DLR (2d) 86) and it appears to accord closely with the structure of s.1(3), which draws a distinction between the plaintiff's performance and the defendant's benefit and so it cannot be said that the defendant's benefit is the value of the plaintiff's performance.

The second step in a s.1(3) claim is the assessment of a 'just sum'. Here it must be remembered that the value of the benefit obtained acts as ceiling on the 'just sum'. Robert Goff J held that the contractual allocation of risk will always be a relevant factor in deciding what is a just sum. But it is very difficult to predict what a court will award as a just sum. Robert Goff J sought to provide a measure of certainty by stating that the aim of the court in assessing the just sum ought to be 'the prevention of the unjust enrichment of the defendant at the plaintiff's expense' and that the assessment should therefore be similar to that undertaken by a court in a *quantum meruit* claim. But this approach seems to have been rejected by the Court of Appeal when Lawton LJ stated that 'what is just is what the trial judge thinks is just' and that an appellate court is not entitled to interfere with the assessment of the just sum by the trial judge 'unless it is so plainly wrong that it cannot be just' (*BP* v. *Hunt* [1982] 1 All ER 925, 980). This leaves the issue virtually to the untrammelled discretion of the trial judge. It is regrettable that the Court of Appeal did not establish guidelines to assist trial judges in the exercise of their discretion to ensure a measure of consistency in decided cases and out of court settlements.

It must be concluded that s.1(3) is shoddily drafted and that it produces results which are, in principle, undesirable. A benefit should be identified as the value of the services and not as the end product of the services. The focus of the Act is upon the prevention of unjust enrichment (per Robert Goff J in *BP* v. *Hunt* [1979] 1 WLR 783, 799) and, consequently, it does not address itself to the recovery of reliance losses which do not result in a benefit to the other party, nor does it seek to apportion the losses between the parties. In failing to address itself to these issues, the 1943 Act is sadly deficient and it is no suprise to learn that its restricted approach has recently been rejected in the Commonwealth (see, generally, McKendrick, 1991b).

14.16   Conclusion

In this chapter we have sought to argue that in cases of common mistake and frustration the courts are dealing with the same issue; namely the allocation of risk of an unforeseen event. When the cases are put together in this way it can be seen that mistake in equity is very much the odd man out (note that no-one would appear to have argued that there is a corresponding doctrine of frustration in equity). Both mistake at common law and frustration operate within very narrow confines and emphasise the need to hold men to their bargains. Their concern is with the preservation of certainty and the desire to prevent the doctrine from being used as an escape route by those who are looking for a way out of a bad bargain. Mistake in equity, on the other hand, is a much broader doctrine. Its concern is not with the preservation of certainty but with doing justice between the parties and preventing unconscientious conduct. Seen in this light mistake in equity appears even more anomalous and, in fact, its survival as a part of English law may be attributable simply to the fact that there was no appeal from the decision of the Court of Appeal in *Solle* v. *Butcher* (above). To demonstrate this point, reference can be made to the fate of Lord Denning's judgment in *British Movietonews Ltd* v. *London and District Cinemas* [1951] 1 KB 190, 198. Six months after giving judgment in *Solle* v. *Butcher*, Lord Denning sought in *British Movietonews* to give the courts a broader power to qualify obligations in order to do what was just and reasonable after a subsequent uncontemplated turn of events. But, on appeal ([1952] AC 166) the House of Lords firmly rejected Lord Denning's innovation and held that the court had no such broad qualifying power. They held that the only doctrine which could be invoked to set aside a contract because of a subsequent uncontemplated turn of events was the traditional but narrow doctrine of frustration. There can be little doubt that a similarly constituted House of Lords would have given equally short shrift to Lord Denning's innovations in *Solle*. But the fact that there was no appeal prevented them from considering the issue. Thus the judgment of the Court of Appeal survived and, as has been noted (14.7), it has been applied by the Court of Appeal in subsequent cases. But it cannot be denied that its continued existence is an anomaly which is out of step with the conservative approach adopted in common law mistake and frustration cases. The future of mistake in equity therefore requires careful examination by the House of Lords.

Although it has been argued in this chapter that there is a very close relationship between common mistake and frustration, it is important to acknowledge that this analogy is not accepted by everyone. Thus, Professor Treitel (1991) has described the analogy between common mistake and frustration as an 'interesting and sometimes helpful' one but argues that it 'should not be pressed too far'. In particular, Treitel argues that mistake and frustration are 'different juristic concepts; the one relating to the formation and the other to the discharge of contracts'. Although it is true that one relates to formation and the other to discharge, they both relate to the same issue, as can be seen from the *Amalgamated Investments* case (14.1) and a comparison of *Griffiths* v. *Brymer* (14.5) and *Krell* v. *Henry* (14.10). Secondly, Treitel argues that events which frustrate a contract may not be sufficient to set aside a contract on the ground of mistake. This point I have already conceded, but the difference is a matter of degree, not kind. Finally, Treitel points out that the effects of frustration and mistake are different; frustration cases being subject to the Law Reform (Frustrated Contracts) Act 1943. This is true. But the 1943 Act was enacted as a response to the particular problems which had emerged in the law relating to the remedial consequences of frustration as a result of the decision of the Court of Appeal in *Chandler* v. *Webster* (above). The Act was not extended to mistake because it was based on a report prepared by the Law Revision Committee, whose terms of reference were confined to a reconsideration of *Chandler* v. *Webster* (see McKendrick, 1991b). The fact that Parliament did not or could not see fit to draw the analogy between common mistake and frustration in 1943 should not prevent us from drawing the analogy today. The same principles should be applicable to the remedial consequences of both common mistake and frustration. In both cases unjust enrichments should be reversed and, if this is thought to be insufficient to achieve a satisfactory result in all cases, consideration should be given to the principles upon which any loss caused by the mistake or the frustrating event should be apportioned between the parties. There is no need to provide a different remedial regime for the consequences of common mistake and frustration.

Summary

1 Where both parties enter into a contract under a common fundamental mistake which relates to an essential element of the subject-matter of the contract then the contract is void at law.

2   A mistake may be sufficiently fundamental to avoid a contract where both parties are mistaken as to the existence (or possibly the identity) of the subject-matter of the contract. Despite the enactment of s.6 of the Sale of Goods Act 1979, a mistake as to the existence of the subject-matter may not inevitably render a contract void; it may depend upon the construction of the contract (see *McRae* v. *Commonwealth Disposals Commission*).

3   A mistake may be sufficiently fundamental to avoid a contract where both parties believe that the contract is capable of being performed when, in fact, it is not. The impossibility may be physical, legal or commercial.

4   A mistake as to the quality of the subject-matter of the contract may be sufficiently fundamental to avoid a contract. But the courts are extremely reluctant to hold a contract void on such a ground. The mistake must relate to an essential and integral element of the subject matter' of the contract.

5   Mistake at law is supplemented by the more flexible doctrine of mistake in equity. A contract may be set aside in equity where the mistake is a substantial one. Such a mistake renders a contract voidable and the court may set aside the contract on terms.

6   A contract is frustrated where, after the contract was concluded, events occur which make performance of the contract impossible, illegal or something radically different from that which was in the contemplation of the parties at the time they entered into the contract.

7   A contract is not frustrated where the parties have made express provision for the consequences of the alleged frustrating event in their contract, where the alleged frustrating event was a foreseeable one and where the frustration was 'self-induced'. But express provision for, and foreseeablity of, the frustrating event are irrelevant in cases of trading with the enemy.

8   A contract which is discharged on the ground of frustration is brought to an end automatically by the operation of a rule of law, irrespective of the wishes of the parties.

9   Sums paid prior to the frustrating event are recoverable, sums payable prior to the time of discharge cease to be payable and the payee may be entitled to set off against the sums so paid expenses which he has incurred before the time of discharge in, or for the purpose of, the performance of the contract (s.1(2) of the 1943 Act).

10 Where one party to the contract has conferred upon the other party a 'valuable benefit' (other than a payment of money which is governed by s.1(2)) before the time of discharge, he shall be entitled to recover from that other party a 'just sum' which shall not exceed the value of the benefit which he has conferred upon the other party (s.1(3) of the 1943 Act).

Exercises

1   What is the scope of the doctrine of common mistake at law?
2   What is the proper interpretation to be placed upon the decision of the House of Lords in *Couturier* v. *Hastie*?
3   When will a mistake as to the quality of the subject-matter of the contract render a contract void?
4   What is the relationship between mistake at law and mistake in equity?
5   Compare and contrast *Bell* v. *Lever Brothers* and *Magee* v *Pennine Insurance Co.*
6   When will the courts hold that a contract has been frustrated? Illustrate your answer.
7   What is 'self-induced frustration'?
8   What are the effects of frustration upon a contract?
9   What is the relationship, if any, between common mistake and frustration?

15 Illegality

15.1 Introduction

In this chapter we turn to consider substantive limitations upon the enforceability of contracts. As a general rule the courts will not enforce a contract which is illegal or which is otherwise contrary to public policy. Nor, as a general rule, will they permit the recovery of benefits conferred under such a contract. It may seem perfectly sensible and just for the courts to refuse their assistance to a party to a transaction which is illegal or contrary to public policy. But the picture is more complex than would at first sight appear.

An example will help to illustrate the issues at stake here. In *Pearce* v. *Brooks* (1866) LR 1 Ex 213, the plaintiffs were coachbuilders who hired out an ornamental brougham (or carriage) to the defendant. The defendant was a prostitute and she planned to use the brougham to attract her customers. This fact was known to the plaintiffs. The defendant returned the brougham in a damaged condition, having paid only the second instalment on it. The plaintiffs' action for damages for breach of contract failed. The contract was illegal and could not be enforced.

A number of justifications can be adduced to support such a rule. The first is that the court cannot be called upon to aid a willing party to an illegal contract or to a contract which is contrary to public policy. The second is that justice would be tainted and the dignity of the court offended by intervention on behalf of the plaintiffs. The third is that a refusal to grant relief will make entry into illegal contracts a hazardous enterprise and will thus deter people from entering into such contracts.

But these arguments are not always persuasive. The first argument does not apply to the party who innocently enters into an illegal contract. Nor is the dignity of the court always offended by intervention on behalf a party to an illegal contract; there is a vast difference between a contract involving gross immorality or a contract to rob a bank and a contract which innocently infringes a piece of regulatory legislation. The third argument rests upon the rather dubious assumption that everyone knows the law and will take heed of its deterrent effect. Deterrence is also properly the function of the criminal law, not the civil law.

There are other competing policies which must be considered. The first is the argument from freedom of contract; that the parties should be as free as possible to regulate their own affairs. The second competing policy is the need to prevent unjust enrichment. For example, the defendant in *Pearce* v. *Brooks* obtained the use of the brougham without having to pay the hire. Now, on the facts of that case, the 'greater goal' of deterring entry into such contracts may have outweighed the need to prevent the unjust enrichment of the defendant. But in other cases we may not be prepared to countenance such unjust enrichment.

It is very important to understand that the legal regulation of illegal contracts and of contracts which are contrary to public policy is characterised by a tension between competing policies. The courts wish, on the one hand, to discourage entry into illegal contracts but, on the other hand, they also wish to uphold freedom of contract and prevent unjust enrichment. The result is tension and a degree of inconsistency in the case law.

15.2   Some Difficulties of Classification

Illegal contracts come in different shapes and sizes. Some involve gross immorality or a calculated attempt to break the law, while others involve innocent infringement of regulatory legislation. A contract to rob a bank has little in common with a contract which is performed by one of the parties in such a way that a statutory instrument is innocently infringed. Indeed, illegal contracts come in so many different shapes and sizes that it is difficult to find an appropriate classification for all the cases (see Furmston, 1965). Treitel (1991) distinguishes between contracts which involve the 'commission of a legal wrong', 'contracts contrary to public policy' and contracts which are declared by statute to be 'void' or 'unenforceable'. Cheshire, Fifoot and Furmston (1991) distinguish between contracts which are 'rendered void by statute', contracts which are 'illegal by statute or at common law' and 'contracts which are void at common law on grounds of public policy'. No two commentators appear to adopt the same classification. But these different classifications do not reflect radical disagreement as to the content of the relevant rules of law. Rather, the categorisation is undertaken largely for the purpose of ease of exposition.

The approach which will be adopted in the present chapter is, first, to discuss illegality in the performance of a contract, and then to distinguish between statutory illegality and common law illegality. The latter division should not be taken to suggest that it is easier to establish the existence of statutory illegality than common law illegality. The function of this division is to emphasise that the techniques employed by the courts in each case are rather different. In the case of statutory illegality, the courts are seeking to discern the intention of Parliament and the effect of the breach of the statute upon the contract. But in the case of common law illegality the courts have greater scope to identify their own conceptions of public policy. The limiting feature, however, is that the courts do not wish to be seen to be employing their own idiosyncratic conceptions of public policy and, at the same time, they are aware that Parliament now has the principal role to play in establishing the limits of public policy.

15.3 Illegality in Performance

Illegality may affect a contract in two principal ways. In the first place, the illegality may relate to the formation of the contract, so that the contract is illegal at the moment at which it is formed. Such a contract is void *ab initio* because it is infected with the illegality from the very outset. Secondly, the illegality may arise in the performance of an otherwise valid and enforceable contract. Here the contract is valid at the moment of formation and it is only infected with the illegality when it occurs during the performance of the contract. An example will illustrate the point. Two parties enter into a contract for the transportation of goods. At the moment of formation the contract is good and enforceable. But let us suppose that, while transporting the goods, the carrier commits a criminal offence by speeding. Does such an illegal act, committed in the course of the performance of the contract, invalidate the contract? In *St John Shipping Corporation* v. *Joseph Rank Ltd* [1957] 1 QB 267, 281, Devlin J rejected the argument that violation of the speed limit in the course of performance of the contract would, of itself, render the contract unenforceable by the party guilty of the offence. This must be right. The criminal courts will pass judgment on the offence committed; the civil courts should enforce the contract. But what are the limits of this rule? When will an illegal act committed in the course of performance of the contract invalidate the contract? This is not an easy question to answer. Separate consideration must be given to the position of the party who committed the criminal offence and the position of the other, 'innocent' party.

In deciding whether the party who committed the criminal offence can enforce the contract it is necessary to examine the judgment of Devlin J in *St John Shipping Corporation* v. *Joseph Rank Ltd* (above). A shipowner committed a statutory offence when he overloaded his ship in the performance of certain contracts for the carriage of goods. The shipowner was held to be entitled to sue to recover the freight, despite the illegality. Devlin J held that the purpose behind the statute was to penalise the conduct which led to the contravention of the statute and not to prohibit the contract itself. The contract therefore remained enforceable. Similarly, in *Shaw* v. *Groom* [1970] 2 QB 504, a landlord committed an offence by failing to give his tenant a rent-book. It was held that the landlord was nevertheless entitled to sue for the rent because the purpose behind the legislation was to punish his failure to issue a rent-book but not to invalidate the tenancy agreement (contrast the more restrictive approach adopted in the earlier case of *Anderson* v. *Daniel* [1924] 1 KB 138, where the 'guilty' party was held to be unable to enforce the contract). Although both of these cases concern statutory illegality, it is suggested that the question which should be asked in all cases is: was it the purpose of the statute (or the common law rule) that a breach committed in the course of the performance of a contract should invalidate the contract?

The claim by the innocent party to enforce the contract is a much stronger one, especially where he does not know of or consent to the illegality. This was recognised by the court in *Archbolds (Freightage) Ltd* v. *S Spangletts Ltd* [1961] 2 QB 374. A contract was made for the carriage of a consignment of whisky and, in performing the contract, the carrier committed a criminal offence because the vehicle which he used to transport the whisky was not licensed to carry goods belonging to a third party. It was held that the plaintiff could nevertheless sue for breach of the contract of carriage because he was unaware of the illegality and so was not tainted by it (see too *Marles* v. *Philip Trant & Sons Ltd* [1954] 1 QB 29). Devlin LJ stated that he thought that

> 'the purpose of this statute is sufficiently served by the penalties prescribed for the offender; the avoidance of the contract would cause grave inconvenience and injury to members of the public without furthering the object of the statute'.

But where the 'innocent' party has knowledge of the commission of the illegality, then it is more likely that he will be unable to enforce the contract. In *Ashmore, Benson, Pease & Co Ltd* v. *AV Dawson Ltd* [1973] 1 WLR 828, the parties entered into a contract for the transportation of tube banks. The defendants sent articulated lorries which could not lawfully be used to carry the load. The load was damaged in transit. The plaintiffs sued for damages. The action failed because there was evidence that the plaintiffs' transport manager knew of the illegal performance and that, by sanctioning the illegal performance of the contract, he had 'participated' in the illegality. The crucial role played by the knowledge of the innocent party appears, at first sight, to be inconsistent with the maxim that ignorance of the law is no excuse (*Nash* v. *Stevenson Transport Ltd* [1936] 2 KB 128). It is true that, where at the moment of formation, a contract is declared to be illegal, the knowledge of the parties is irrelevant. Where, on the other hand, the illegality occurs in the performance of a contract which is capable of lawful performance, the knowledge of the innocent party is a relevant consideration because his ignorance relates, not to the *law*, but to the *fact* that the other contracting party has performed the contract in an illegal manner. His knowledge of the illegality is therefore a relevant consideration.

15.4   Statutory Illegality

A contract is illegal if its formation is expressly or impliedly prohibited by statute. Where the making of the contract is expressly prohibited no difficulties arise; the contract is illegal. Greater difficulties arise where it is alleged that Parliament has impliedly prohibited the *making* of such a contract (see Buckley, 1975). The function of the court in such a case is to interpret the statute to discern whether, on its proper construction, the Act prohibits the making of such a contract. The difficulty is that

Parliament has often not addressed itself to this issue. So the process of 'finding' the 'intention' of Parliament is frequently an extremely artificial one.

In *Re Mahmoud and Ispahani* [1921] 2 KB 716, the Seeds, Oils and Fats Order 1919 stated that 'a person shall not . . . buy or sell or otherwise deal in' linseed oil without a licence. The defendant misrepresented to the plaintiff that he had a licence. The defendant later refused to accept delivery of the order. The plaintiff sued the defendant for damages. The defendant argued that the contract was illegal because he did not have a licence. The court held that the plaintiff could not maintain his action for damages because such an action would undermine the purpose behind the statute. Bankes LJ stated that the Order was 'a clear and unequivocal declaration by the Legislature in the public interest that this particular type of contract shall not be entered into'. Yet the consequences for the plaintiff were extremely harsh and it has been doubted whether the court correctly identified the intention of Parliament (see Greig and Davis, 1987, p. 1117). In an effort to avoid the possibility of a court misinterpreting the intention of Parliament, Acts of Parliament now frequently specify the consequences for a contract which has been entered into in breach of the Act (see Part I of the Resale Prices Act 1976). However, the courts are generally reluctant to conclude that a statute impliedly prohibits the making of a contract (see *Archbolds (Freightage) Ltd* v. *S Spanglett Ltd* (above) and *St John Shipping Corp* v. *Joseph Rank Ltd* [1957] 1 QB 267, 289).

15.5 Gaming and Wagering Contracts

Parliament will occasionally declare a particular type of contract to be 'void'. For example, s.18 of the Gaming Act 1845 states that 'all contracts or agreements, whether by parole or in writing, by way of gaming or wagering shall be null and void'. The section further provides that no action can be maintained in any court for the recovery of 'any money or valuable thing alleged to be won upon any wager'. Finally, the section provides that no action can be brought to recover any money or valuable thing which has been deposited in the hands of any stakeholder, although the interpretation placed upon the section is that a deposit can be recovered before it has been paid over to the winner (*Diggle* v. *Higgs* (1872) 2 Ex D 442).

15.6 Illegality at Common Law

A contract may be illegal at common law. The scope of the doctrine of illegality at common law is extremely wide. It is often summed up in the maxim that a court will not enforce a contract which is 'contrary to public policy'. 'Illegality' at common law therefore goes beyond contracts to commit a crime and extends, for example, to contracts which are contrary to good morals and contracts which are prejudicial to the institution of marriage. Some commentators seek to divide the cases into two distinct compartments (see Cheshire, Fifoot and Furmston, 1991), namely, contracts which are 'illegal' at common law on grounds of public policy and contracts which are 'void' at common law on grounds of public policy. But this division is a troublesome one because 'those who use the classification cannot always agree' on which contracts are 'illegal' and which are 'void' (see Treitel, 1991, p. 378). In this chapter we shall not attempt to divide the cases up in such a manner. Rather, we shall analyse the cases under the title of contracts which are 'illegal' at common law because they are 'contrary to public policy' (often referred to, for the sake of brevity, as 'illegal' contracts) and we shall seek to identify the scope of the doctrine of public policy at common law.

In deciding whether a particular contract is 'contrary to public policy', the courts cannot shelter behind the argument that they are simply giving effect to the intention of Parliament. They must evolve their own conceptions of public policy. Here the courts are open to the charge of usurping the function of Parliament and of giving effect to their own personal opinions on what is, and what is not, morally justifiable. Thus, we find that Burroughs J once described public policy as 'a very unruly horse, and when once you get astride it you never know where it will carry you' (*Richardson* v. *Mellish* (1824) 2 Bing 229, 252). On the other hand, Lord Denning has argued that: 'with a good man in the saddle, the unruly horse can be kept in control. It can jump over obstacles' (*Enderby Town Football Club Ltd* v. *The Football Association Ltd* [1971] Ch 591, 606).

The courts have, in fact, been extremely cautious and conservative in their formulation of public policy. We shall now survey the different grounds upon the courts have held a contract to be contrary to public policy and conclude with an examination of the scope of the doctrine of public policy at common law.

15.7 Contracts Contrary to Good Morals

A contract to promote sexual immorality is illegal on the ground that it is contrary to public policy. We have already noted that in *Pearce* v. *Brooks* (above) it was held that a contract to supply goods to a prostitute to be used by her in the furtherance of her profession was illegal. Similarly, a promise by a man to pay a woman if she will become his mistress is illegal (*Franco* v. *Bolton* (1797) 3 Ves 368). At one point in time contracts between cohabiting couples who were not married were contrary to public policy. But the attitude adopted by the courts towards extra-marital relationships has gradually changed to reflect the growing incidence of such relationships. Where the parties are living together in a 'stable' extra-marital relationship, it is highly unlikely that a court today would conclude that an agreement entered into by them in relation to the purchase of property is contrary to public policy (so, for example, in *Tinsley* v. *Milligan* [1993] 3 WLR 126, it was not argued that the parties' agreement to purchase property was unenforceable on the ground that they were lovers, see further 15.18).

15.8 Contracts Prejudicial to Family Life

Contract law is also protective of family relationships. Contracts which are prejudicial to the institution of marriage are contrary to public policy; thus a contract which restrains a party from marrying (*Lowe* v. *Peers* (1768) 2 Burr 2225) or a contract under which one person undertakes to procure the marriage of another in return for a fee is illegal (*Hermann* v. *Charlesworth* [1905] 2 KB 123, although it is questionable whether this case would be followed today as society's attitude to introduction agencies has changed considerably). But a promise to pay a sum of money to a person for as long as they remain single is valid (*Gibson* v. *Dickie* (1815) 3 M & S 463). In *Spiers* v. *Hunt* [1908] 1 KB 720, a promise by a man to marry the plaintiff after the death of his wife was held to be contrary to public policy because it encouraged sexual immorality and was likely to encourage the break-up of his marriage (although it should be noted that the action for breach of promise to marry has now been abolished by s.1 of the Law Reform (Miscellaneous Provisions) Act 1970). A separation agreement entered into by spouses who are living together is invalid (*Brodie* v. *Brodie* [1917] P 271), although such an agreement can validly be made once the parties have separated. Similarly, a parent cannot by contract transfer to another adult his rights and duties in relation to a child (although, in an appropriate case, an adoption order can be made by a court).

15.9 Contracts to Commit a Crime or a Civil Wrong

A contract to commit a crime is illegal on the ground that it is contrary to public policy. In *Bigos* v. *Bousted* [1951] 1 All ER 92, the parties entered into a contract which was contrary to the exchange control regulations. The contract was held to be unenforceable. Similarly, contracts to defraud the revenue are contrary to public policy (*Miller* v. *Karlinski* (1945) 62 TLR 85). In *Alexander* v. *Rayson* [1936] 1 KB 169, the parties entered into a contract to defraud the rating authority by showing the value of the property at less than its actual value. The contract was held to be illegal and unenforceable. A contract is also illegal where it makes provision for the payment of money to a person as a result of his commission of an unlawful act. In *Beresford* v. *Royal Exchange Assurance* [1938] AC 586, a person who had insured his life for £50 000 committed suicide. It was held that his estate was not entitled to enforce the policy even though it expressly covered death by suicide because, at that time, suicide was a criminal offence (the reasoning is now practically obsolete because suicide is no longer a crime). To permit a person, or his estate, to benefit from his own crime was held to be contrary to public policy.

A contract to commit a tort is illegal, for example a contract to publish a libel (*Clay* v. *Yates* (1856) 1 H & C 73). Where neither party knows that the performance of the contract involves the commission of a tort then the contract is not illegal.

A contract to indemnify a person against criminal liability is illegal where the criminal offence is committed with a guilty intent, but the position is unclear where the crime is committed with no guilty intent. A contract to indemnify a person against liability in tort is illegal if the tort is intentionally and knowingly committed.

15.10   Contracts Prejudicial to the Administration of Justice

Contracts which are prejudicial to the administration of justice are illegal. Thus a contract to stifle a prosecution may be illegal and a contract under which one party promises to give false evidence in criminal proceedings is illegal (*R* v. *Andrews* [1973] QB 422). Agreements to obstruct bankruptcy proceedings are illegal (*Elliott* v. *Richardson* (1870) LR 5 CP 744). Agreements which tend to abuse the legal process by encouraging litigation which is not bona fide are contrary to public policy.

Also contrary to public policy are contracts which seek to oust the jurisdiction of the courts by stipulating that a contracting party is not entitled to access to the courts in the event of a dispute between the parties. But contracting parties may validly provide that a dispute must be referred to arbitration before it can be brought to court (*Scott* v. *Avery* (1855) 5 HLC 811). The Arbitration Act 1979 has now reduced the scope of judicial control over arbitration proceedings (see s.1 of the Act and the guidelines laid down in *The Nema* [1982] AC 724) and the parties may now enter into a written 'exclusion agreement', which excludes the power of the court to intervene to control the arbitral proceedings, although in the case of a 'domestic arbitration agreement' such an agreement can only be made after the commencement of the arbitration.

15.11   Contracts Prejudicial to Public Relations

Contracts which are prejudicial to foreign friendly countries are contrary to public policy and unenforceable. Thus a contract to facilitate the forcible overthrow of the government of a friendly country is unenforceable (*De Wutz* v. *Hendricks* (1824) 2 Bing 314). A similar rule applies to contracts which are prejudicial to the interests of the State; trading with the enemy is declared to be illegal under the Trading with the Enemy Act 1939.

Contracts which seek to further or promote corruption in public life are illegal. Thus a contract to sell a public office or a public honour is illegal. In *Parkinson* v. *College of Ambulance Ltd* [1925] 2 KB 1, the parties entered into a contract under which one party promised to procure a knighthood for the other. The contract was held to be contrary to public policy.

15.12 Contracts in Restraint of Trade

A contract or a covenant in restraint of trade is an undertaking whereby one party agrees to restrict his freedom to trade or his freedom to conduct his profession or business in a particular locality for a specified period of time. A contract which is in restraint of trade is void and unenforceable unless it can be shown to be reasonable. The doctrine of restraint of trade is based upon considerations of public policy. But every contract contains an element of restraint of trade. Let us suppose that I enter into a contract to give a course of fifty lectures over a two year period. The contract restricts my freedom to trade during the hours in which I have agreed to give the lectures. But such a contract is not caught by the restraint of trade doctrine.

What types of contract are caught by the doctrine? There are two principal contracts to which the doctrine applies. The first is a covenant by an employee not to compete with his employer either during or after his employment and the second is a covenant by the seller of a business and its goodwill not to carry on a business which will compete with the business bought by the purchaser. The doctrine can also apply to other contracts but it is extremely difficult to define its limits. In *Esso Petroleum Co Ltd* v. *Harper's Garage (Stourport) Ltd* [1968] AC 269, the doctrine was applied to a contract under which a garage agreed to accept all of its petrol from one supplier for a considerable period of time. Lord Reid stated that he 'would not attempt to define the dividing line between contracts which are and contracts which are not in restraint of trade' and that the better approach was 'to ascertain what were the legitimate interests of the [suppliers] which they were entitled to protect and then to see whether these restraints were more than adequate for that purpose'.

Once it is decided that the contract is subject to the doctrine then it is for the party who is seeking to rely on the clause to show that it is reasonable in two respects. The first is that it must be reasonable as between the parties and the second is that it must be reasonable in the public interest. In analysing the reasonableness requirements we shall discuss separately covenants in contracts of employment, covenants in contracts for the sale of a business and, finally, other contracts to which the doctrine applies.

15.13 Contracts of Employment

A contract of employment may contain a covenant which purports to restrict the freedom of the employee to work either during or after the termination of his employment. Such covenants are scrutinised with great care by the courts. In deciding whether the restraint clause is reasonable as between the parties two factors are particularly relevant. The first is that the covenant must seek to protect some legitimate interest of the employer. Lord Parker stated in *Herbert Morris Ltd* v. *Saxelby* [1916] 1 AC 688, that an employer must establish that he has: 'some proprietary right, whether in the nature of a trade connection or in the nature of trade secrets, for the protection of which such a restraint is . . . reasonably necessary'. Thus, an employer can legitimately restrain an employee who has come into contact with customers of the employer in such a way as to acquire influence over them (*Fitch* v. *Dewes* [1921] 2 AC 158) or who has acquired trade secrets or confidential information belonging to the employer (*Forster and Sons* v. *Suggett* (1918) 35 TLR 87). But an employer is not entitled to protect himself against the use of the 'personal skill and knowledge' acquired by the employee in the course of the employer's business. Such skills belong to the employee and he is free to exploit them in the market-place.

The second factor is that the restraint must be reasonable in terms of subject-matter, locality and time. An employer is not generally entitled to restrain an employee from carrying on a business which is different from that in which he was employed. Similarly, the restraint must not be wider in area than is necessary to protect the employer's interest (see *Mason* v. *Provident Clothing and Supply Co* [1913] AC 724, in which a clause restraining an employee from working in a similar business within 25 miles of London was held to be unreasonable). The restraint must also be reasonable in terms of time, although it is possible for the restraint clause to be unlimited in time and still be reasonable (*Fitch* v. *Dewes* (above)).

Once it is demonstrated that the restraint is reasonable as between the parties, it must also be demonstrated that it is reasonable in the interests of the public. However, the courts are extremely reluctant to conclude that an agreement, which is reasonable as between the parties, is unenforceable because it is contrary to the interests of the public, especially in the case of a restraint clause in a contract of employment (but see *Wyatt* v. *Kreglinger and Fernau* [1933] 1 KB 793).

15.14   Contracts for the Sale of a Business

A contract for the sale of a business frequently contains a clause under which the vendor of the business agrees not to set up a similar business in the immediate vicinity for a period of time. The purchaser has bought the goodwill in the business and he is entitled to protect his purchase by an appropriately drawn restraint clause. Such a clause is not viewed with the hostility of a restraint clause in a contract of employment.

The restraint clause must be reasonable as between the parties and two factors are of particular relevance here. The first is that the buyer must establish a proprietary interest which the clause is seeking to protect. That is to say, when a buyer purchases a business and pays for the goodwill of the business, he is entitled to take reasonable steps to protect that interest. The second factor is that the clause must be reasonable in the light of all the circumstances of the case. It will be unreasonable if it goes further than reasonably necessary for the protection of his interest in point of space, time or subject-matter. The reasonableness of a clause depends upon all the facts of each case (see *Nordenfelt* v. *Maxim Nordenfelt* [1894] AC 535, in which a worldwide restraint was upheld because of the limited number of manufacturers in the particular industry).

Once the clause is shown to be reasonable as between the parties, it must be shown to be reasonable in the public interest. The courts have, once again, been reluctant to conclude that an agreement which is reasonable as between the parties is unenforceable because it is contrary to the public interest.

15.15 Restrictive Trading and Analogous Agreements

We have already noted that it is extremely difficult to define the limits of the doctrine of restraint of trade. For example, it was once thought that exclusive dealing agreements were not within the scope of the doctrine or, if they were, they were valid because they were not contrary to the public interest. But that view received a fatal blow as a result of the decision of the House of Lords in *Esso Petroleum Ltd* v. *Harper's Garage (Stourport) Ltd* (above). A garage company, which owned two garages, entered into a solus agreement with Esso under which it agreed to buy all its petrol from Esso, to keep the garage open at all reasonable hours and not to sell the garage without ensuring that the purchaser entered into a similar agreement with Esso. One agreement was to last for 5 years and the other for 21 years. In effect, the garage owners were tied to Esso for 21 years. It was held that the agreements were governed by the restraint of trade doctrine, that the 5 year agreement with Esso was valid but that the 21 year agreement was invalid. Although the courts have been prepared to extend the scope of the doctrine of restraint of trade to such contracts, they have not subjected such contracts to stringent scrutiny (but contrast the more interventionist approach adopted by the House of Lords in *Schroeder Music Publishing Co Ltd* v. *Macaulay* [1974] 1 WLR 1308, where there was a considerable disparity in bargaining power between the parties). The courts are willing to find the existence of a legitimate interest which such exclusive dealing agreements seek to protect, such as maintaining retail outlets or protecting a competitive position in the market-place, and they have adopted a *laissez faire* approach to the reasonableness requirements (see *Alec Lobb (Garages) Ltd* v. *Total Oil (Great Britain) Ltd* [1985] 1 WLR 173). The consequence of this *laissez faire* approach has been that the courts have played a secondary role in the regulation of anti-competitive practices and the primary role is now played by Parliament (see the Fair Trading Act 1973, the Resale Prices Act 1976, the Restrictive Practices Act 1976 and the Competition Act

1980) and by European Community law (see Article 85 of the Treaty of Rome). There is no doubt that Parliament is better equipped than the common law to engage in the regulation of such allegedly anti-competitive practices (see Trebilcock, 1976, where he subjects the decision of the House of Lords in *Schroeder* v. *Macauley* (above) to substantial criticism).

15.16   The Scope of Public Policy

The doctrine of public policy at common law is an extremely conservative one and operates within relatively rigid confines. Indeed, Lord Halsbury once stated that the courts cannot 'invent a new head of public policy' (*Janson* v. *Driefontein Consolidated Mines Ltd* [1902] AC 484). Such a restrictive approach is no longer generally accepted. The courts are prepared gradually to adapt the existing categories to reflect changing social and moral values (see, for example, the discussion of contracts between cohabiting couples at 15.7), although they remain extremely reluctant to extend the doctrine to a contract of a type to which the doctrine has never been applied before. Such a rigidly controlled doctrine has the merit of limiting the ability of individual judges to develop their own idiosyncratic conceptions of public policy. The task of placing limits upon freedom of contract in the name of public policy is therefore left largely to Parliament. A judge in a modern case would not conclude that a contract which was supported by 'inadequate consideration' was void because it was 'contrary to public policy'. But he might be able to say that the contract was voidable because it had been procured by undue influence or as a result of 'inequality of bargaining power' (see 17.3–17.4). Doctrines such as undue influence, the rules relating to contractual capacity (Chapter 16), the legal regulation of exclusion clauses (Chapter 11) and the penalty clause rule (21.7) can all be regarded as 'disguised extensions or applications of the doctrine of public policy' (Treitel, 1991, p. 427). While the courts remain reluctant to expand the doctrine of 'public policy' beyond the contracts to which it has traditionally been applied, the influence of 'public policy' in English law is more likely to be found in cases of alleged undue influence or 'inequality of bargaining power' than in the cases which we have discussed in this chapter.

15.17   The Effects of Illegality

We have already noted the general rule that an illegal contract will not be enforced by the courts. Although the courts will not enforce the contract, they may be prepared to give to the 'innocent party' a remedy on some alternative basis. In *Strongman (1945) Ltd* v. *Sincock* [1955] 2 QB 525, the defendant stated that he would obtain the necessary licences to enable the plaintiff builders lawfully to modernise his house. The defendant failed to obtain all the licences and he refused to pay for some of the work which the plaintiffs had done, arguing that the contract was illegal. The plaintiffs were unable to sue on the building contract because of the failure to obtain all the licences, but they were able to recover the value of the work which they had done on the ground that the defendant had breached a *collateral warranty* that he would obtain the necessary licences. In *Shelley* v. *Paddock* [1980] QB 348, it was also recognised that an innocent party to an illegal contract could recover damages for fraudulent misrepresentation. By searching out the existence of remedies other than on the contract itself, the court can take steps to protect an innocent party who has relied to his detriment upon a contract which he has subsequently discovered to be illegal.

15.18 The Recovery of Money or Property

A further question which must be asked is: do the courts permit a party to an illegal contract to recover any benefits which he has conferred upon the other party to the contract? The general rule is that the courts will not permit the recovery of benefits transferred under an illegal contract (*Holman* v. *Johnson* (1775) 1 Cowp 341). Once again the courts are seeking to reconcile two competing policies, namely the prevention of unjust enrichment and the need to deter entry into illegal contracts. The general rule reflects the latter policy. But there are a number of exceptions to the general rule and these exceptions reflect the former policy.

Before analysing the general rule and the exceptions a further question must be asked. That question is: on what ground can a party who has conferred a benefit on the other party to the contract seek recovery? The illegality does not, of itself, confer a cause of action. In many cases the illegality is employed as a *defence* to an action for the recovery of the benefit. It could be argued that the general rule denying recovery is based upon considerations of public policy but that, where the parties are not *in pari delicto* (equally guilty), the policy objection to recovery simply disappears. Alternatively, it can be argued that the grounds on which recovery is sought are the normal grounds of restitution, such as mistake or duress, and that the illegality is used simply as a *defence* to a restitutionary action which would otherwise have succeeded (see Birks, 1985).

Although the precise basis of the claim may not be clear, there are three exceptional cases in which a party can recover benefits conferred under an illegal contract. The first exception arises where the parties are not *in pari delicto*. There are two groups of cases here. The first is where the plaintiff was under a mistake of fact which rendered him unaware of the illegal nature of the contract (*Oom* v. *Bruce* (1810) 12 East 225). The second arises where the plaintiff was induced to enter into the illegal transaction by the fraudulent representation of the defendant which had the effect of concealing the illegal nature of the transaction from the plaintiff (*Hughes* v. *Liverpool Victoria Legal Friendly Society* [1916] 2 KB 482) or where the plaintiff was induced to enter into the contract under some form of compulsion amounting to oppression (*Smith* v. *Cuff* (1817) 6 M & S 160).

Another aspect of the *in pari delicto* rule is that recovery is permitted where a transaction is rendered illegal under a statute which was enacted in an effort to protect parties in the position of the plaintiff (*Kasumu* v. *Baba-Egbe* [1956] AC 539 and *Kiriri Cotton* v. *Dewani* [1960] AC 192).

Secondly, a plaintiff is entitled to recover a benefit conferred under an illegal contract if he repudiates the illegal purpose in time. The payer has a *locus poenitentiae* and may withdraw from the illegal contract and recover his payment (see *Taylor* v. *Bowers* (1876) 1 QBD 291 and *Kearley* v. *Thomson* (1890) 24 QBD 742, usefully discussed by Beatson, 1975). The justification for this exception is that the parties to an illegal contract should be provided with an incentive to refrain from performing an illegal contract.

Thirdly, a plaintiff may be able to recover money paid or property transferred under an illegal contract if he can establish his right to the money or the property without relying upon the illegal nature of the contract. The source of this exception lies in the difficult case of *Bowmakers Ltd* v. *Barnet Instruments Ltd* [1945] KB 65 (see also *Belvoir Finance* v. *Stapleton* [1971] 1 QB 210 and the discussion by Hamson (1949) and Higgins (1962)). In *Bowmakers* the plaintiffs bought machine tools in contravention of the Defence Regulations and they delivered the tools to the defendants under three illegal hire-purchase agreements. The defendants, in breach of the agreements, sold some of the tools and refused to return the remainder. The plaintiffs sued successfully for damages in the tort of conversion. The defendants' right to possess the goods terminated on their breach of the hire-purchase agreements and so the plaintiffs were able to establish their title to the machine tools without placing any reliance upon the illegal transactions.

Bowmakers was a case in which the plaintiffs were able to establish their title to the goods at law: but the same principle has since been held to be applicable to a party who can establish the existence of an *equitable* proprietary interest in the goods. This was the conclusion reached by the House of Lords in *Tinsley* v. *Milligan* [1993] 3 WLR 126. Miss Tinsley (the plaintiff) and Miss Milligan (the defendant) were lovers. They jointly purchased a house which was registered in the sole name of the plaintiff in order to enable the defendant, with the knowledge of the plaintiff, to make false benefit claims from the Department of Social Security. The defendant later repented of her fraud and informed the DSS of what she had done. The parties subsequently quarrelled and the plaintiff moved out. She then brought an action seeking possession of the house, asserting that she was the sole owner. The defendant could not argue that she had an interest in the property at law (because it was registered in the sole name of the plaintiff) but she asserted that she had an equitable interest in it by virtue of her contributions to the purchase price. The plaintiff argued that the defendant was not entitled to assert any such equitable interest because of her participation in the fraud: she could not invoke the assistance of a court of equity because she had not come to equity 'with clean hands'. While this argument was accepted by Lord Goff and Lord

Keith, it was rejected by the majority. The majority refused to draw a distinction between the rule at law and the rule in equity. Thus Lord Browne-Wilkinson stated that 'if the law is that a party is entitled to enforce a property right acquired under an illegal transaction, in my judgment the same rule ought to apply to any property right so acquired, whether such right is legal or equitable'. Applying this proposition to the facts of the case the majority held that the defendant was entitled to succeed because she did not have to rely on the illegality to establish her equitable interest. Her equitable interest arose on ordinary principles of the law of trusts. This is because English law presumes that where two parties provide the purchase money to buy a property which is conveyed into the name of only one of them, the latter is presumed to hold the property on a resulting trust for both parties in shares proportionate to their contributions to the purchase price (known as the 'presumption of resulting trust'). The defendant was therefore able to establish her equitable interest by virtue of the common intention of the parties and her contribution to the purchase price. She did not need to rely on the illegality. On the contrary, it was the *plaintiff* who was forced to rely on the illegality to rebut the presumption of resulting trust and this she could not do. The defendant's counterclaim therefore succeeded.

In different ways both *Bowmakers* and *Tinsley* illustrate the inadequacy of the present remedial regime concerning illegal contracts. Although *Tinsley* may be said to have produced a degree of coherence by its refusal to draw a distinction between law and equity, in another respect the decision is arbitrary. A simple example will illustrate the point. Suppose the parties in *Tinsley* had been husband and wife. If the husband had been in the position of the defendant in *Tinsley* his claim would have failed because English law presumes that when a husband advances money to his wife, he does so as a gift (known as the 'presumption of advancement'). Although the presumption is rebuttable, the husband could only have done so by relying on the illegality, which the courts say cannot be done. Yet, why should it matter whether the parties are husband and wife or lovers? Surely the answer ought to be the same in both cases? It could be argued that the source of this problem lies in the law of trusts; that the presumption of advancement and the presumption of resulting trust are outmoded presumptions which no longer reflect modern life. Although there is a degree of truth in this argument, it should be noted that it does not deny that the law is presently in an unsatisfactory state.

Nor is the decision in *Bowmakers* entirely free from difficulty. The principal problem is that, by awarding damages assessed by reference to the value of the machine tools, the result was *de facto* enforcement of the contract. On the other hand, to refuse a remedy would have been to confer a *de facto* gift upon the defendants. As Coote has pointed out (1972), 'the real difficulty lies in the arbitrary, all-or-nothing character of the common law governing illegal contracts'.

The common law is, in fact, a poor instrument for the regulation of illegal contracts because of the lack of remedial flexibility. For some time it appeared that English law was moving in the direction of a more flexible, discretionary test under the guise of the so-called 'public conscience' test which was adopted by the Court of Appeal on a number of occasions (see, for example, *Euro-Diam Ltd* v. *Bathurst* [1990] 1 QB 1). According to this test the court should consider the public conscience in deciding whether or not to afford the plaintiff a remedy and should refuse to grant relief only where 'it would be an affront to public conscience . . . because the court would thereby appear to assist or encourage the plaintiff in his illegal conduct or to encourage others in similar acts'. In *Tinsley* Lord Goff rejected such a test, stating that it was 'little different, if at all, from stating that the court has a discretion whether to grant or refuse relief'. He held that such a test could not be accepted because it was inconsistent with a long line of authority going back to *Holman* v. *Johnson* in 1775 where it was clearly established that the courts will not lend their aid to someone who founds their cause of action upon an illegal act.

Yet it is important to note that Lord Goff did not rule out reform completely. Indeed, he acknowledged that the present rules are 'indiscriminate in their effect, and are capable therefore of producing injustice' but he concluded that the introduction of major reform was the province of Parliament, not the courts. There is a precedent for reform. New Zealand has enacted the Illegal Contracts Act 1970, which gives to the court wide discretionary powers to grant such relief as the court 'in its discretion thinks just' (see Furmston, 1972). Lord Goff referred to this Act in his judgment in *Tinsley* and continued:

> 'your Lordships have no means of ascertaining how successful the Act has proved to be in practice. . . In truth, everything points to the conclusion that, if there is to be a reform aimed at substituting a system of discretionary relief for the present rules, the reform is one which should only be instituted by the legislature, after a full inquiry into the matter by the Law Commission, such inquiry to embrace not only the perceived advantages and disadvantages of the present law, but also the likely advantages and disadvantages of a system of discretionary relief, no doubt with particular reference to the New Zealand experience.'

The 'New Zealand experience' would appear to have been rather mixed. Professor Coote has recently written (1992) that the 'choice of relief and the criteria for its application have in practice turned out to be significantly different from what the reformers appear to have expected or intended' and that the courts like to have 'broadly expressed discretions and to apply them broadly'. He concludes by saying that widely drafted legislation, such as the 1970 Act, 'quickly assumes a life of its own and that implied constraints which would once have appeared obvious can as quickly be ignored or forgotten'. This underlines the need for clearly articulated principles to guide the courts if they are to be entrusted with discretionary powers. Such principles can be found in a fully-developed law of restitution (see Burrows, 1993c, pp. 461–72). But it may be that not all cases can be resolved by reference to the law of restitution. It may be necessary to address the problem of losses incurred as well as benefits conferred in the performance of illegal contracts. The courts may therefore require a discretionary power to award compensation for losses incurred in the performance of an illegal contract and also a residual power to vary an illegal contract in order to make it comply with the law. Reform along such lines might strike a better balance between the need to deter entry into illegal contracts and the desire to prevent unjust enrichment.

15.19 Severance

Finally, it may be possible to 'sever' the illegal part of the contract and enforce the remainder. If the illegal part of the contract can be separated from the rest of the contract, without rendering the remainder of the contract radically different from the contract which the parties originally concluded, then the court may be prepared to sever the illegal part, provided that severance is not contrary to the public policy which rendered the contract illegal (see further Treitel, 1991, pp. 446–53).

Summary

1 As a general rule the courts will not enforce a contract which is illegal or which is otherwise contrary to public policy.
2 Where the illegality arises in the performance of a contract which was valid at the moment of formation, the contract can be enforced by the guilty party only when it was not the purpose of the statute broken or the common law rule violated that the contract should be invalidated. In the case of the innocent party, the contract can generally be enforced by him where he had no knowledge of the illegality.
3 A contract is illegal if its formation is expressly or impliedly prohibited by statute. The function of the court is to interpret the statute to discern whether, on its proper construction, the Act prohibits the making of such a contract.
4 A contract may be illegal at common law on the ground that it is contrary to public policy. Contracts which are contrary to public policy include contracts which are contrary to good morals, contracts which are prejudicial to family life, contracts to commit a crime or a civil wrong, contracts which are prejudicial to the administration of justice, contracts prejudicial to public relations and contracts in unreasonable restraint of trade.
5 A contract which is in restraint of trade is void and unenforceable unless it can be shown to be reasonable. The doctrine applies principally to a covenant by an employee not to compete with his employer either during or after his employment and to a covenant by the seller of a business and its goodwill not to carry on a business which will compete with the business bought by the purchaser. A clause which is caught by the doctrine is void unless it is reasonable as between the parties and reasonable in the public interest.
6 Although the courts are prepared gradually to adapt the doctrine of public policy to reflect changing social and moral values they remain extremely reluctant to extend the doctrine to a contract of a type to which the doctrine has never been applied before.

7   The general rule is that the courts will not permit the recovery of benefits conferred under an illegal contract. But recovery will be allowed where the parties were not *in pari delicto*, where the plaintiff has effectively repudiated the illegal purpose or where the plaintiff can establish his right to the money or the property without relying upon the illegal nature of the contract.

Exercises

1   Will the courts ever enforce an illegal contract? Should the courts ever enforce an illegal contract?
2   Compare and contrast the decisions in *Re Mahmoud and Ispahani* and *Archbolds (Freightage) Ltd* v. *S Spanglett Ltd*.
3   What impact does illegality in performance have on the enforceability of a contract?
4   When will a contract be held to be contrary to public policy? Does the doctrine of public policy reflect any values other than the idiosyncratic values of the judiciary?
5   A 35 year-old employee agrees with his employer that he will not work for the rest of his life if the employer pays him a lump sum of £1 million. The employer pays the money but the employee has now decided that he wishes to return to work. Discuss. (see *Wyatt* v. *Kreglinger and Fernau* [1933] 1 KB 793)
6   Joe employs six travelling salesmen. They sell insurance policies. Joe wishes to insert a restraint of trade clause in their contracts of employment. Advise him and draft a clause which will be suitable to his needs.
7   Can benefits conferred under an illegal contract be recovered?

16 Capacity

16.1 Introduction

Adults of sound mind have full contractual capacity. On the other hand, minors, the mentally incapacitated and companies have limited contractual capacity. In the case of minors and the mentally incapacitated, contract law seeks to protect such persons from the consequences of their own inexperience or inability. The limitations placed upon the contractual capacity of companies raise rather different issues, to which we shall return at 16.4.

Although contract law seeks to play a role in protecting minors and the mentally incapacitated, a competing policy is that the law does not wish to expose to hardship those who deal fairly and in all good faith with such persons. We shall see that the rules of law reflect an uneasy compromise between these competing policies. We shall begin our analysis by a consideration of the contractual capacity of minors (16.2), then we shall discuss the contractual capacity of the mentally incapacitated (16.3) and, finally, we shall analyse the contractual capacity of companies (16.4).

16.2 Minors

A minor is a person under the age of 18. The law adopts a particularly protective attitude towards minors, often at the expense of those who deal with them in all good faith. The general rule is that a minor is not bound by a contract which he enters into during his minority. But this general rule is subject to three principal exceptions.

The first is that a contract to supply a minor with 'necessaries' is binding upon the minor where the contract as a whole is for the benefit of the minor; where its terms are harsh or onerous it is not binding upon the minor. The definition of 'necessaries' is a wide one. In the case of a contract for the sale of goods, necessaries have been defined in s.3(3) of the Sale of Goods Act 1979 as 'goods suitable to the condition in life of the minor . . . and to his actual requirements at the time of the sale and delivery'. At common law a wide definition of necessaries has also been adopted. Regard must be had to the station in life of the minor; the higher the status, the greater the range of necessaries. So in *Peters* v. *Fleming* (1840) 6 M & W 42, rings, pins and a watch chain were held to be necessaries for an undergraduate who had a rich father. But there is a trap for the trader here because, in deciding whether a particular article is a necessary, a court will have regard to the status of the minor and his actual needs at the time of entry into the contract. Thus, in *Nash* v. *Inman*

[1908] 2 KB 1, a tailor sold 11 fancy waistcoats to a minor, who was a Cambridge undergraduate. The minor refused to pay for them. The tailor's action for payment failed because he could not establish that the defendant was not already amply supplied with clothing; the waistcoats were not therefore necessaries. Although a minor is bound by an executed contract for necessaries, it remains unclear whether a minor is bound by an executory contract for necessaries (contrast *Nash* v. *Inman* (above) and *Roberts* v. *Gray* [1913] 1 KB 520).

Secondly, a minor is bound by a contract of employment if that contract is generally for his benefit (contrast *Clements* v. *L & NW Rly* [1894] 2 QB 482 and *De Francesco* v. *Barnum* (1889) 43 Ch D 430). This principle, however, is confined to contracts of employment and analogous contracts (such as a contract to give publishers the exclusive rights to publish the minor's memoirs, see *Chaplin* v. *Leslie Frewin (Publishers) Ltd* [1966] Ch 71). But there is no general principle of law that a contract with a minor is binding simply because it is for his benefit.

Thirdly, certain contracts with minors are not void but are only voidable; that is to say, the contract is valid and binding upon the minor unless he repudiates liability before majority or within a reasonable time thereafter. Only the minor can repudiate; the adult is bound by the contract. For example, a contract under which a minor acquires an interest in land or shares in a company is voidable, as is a partnership agreement to which a minor is a party. The effect of the repudiation is to release the minor from his obligations to perform in the future. But the minor can only recover back money paid under such a contract where there has been a total failure of consideration (*Steinberg* v. *Scala (Leeds) Ltd* [1923] 2 Ch 452). A total failure of consideration arises where the basis upon which the minor paid the money has wholly failed, that is to say, he has received no part of the performance which he has bargained for.

Outside these three categories, the general rule is that, as we have noted, minors are not bound by the contracts into which they enter. However, a minor may incur liability to an adult in a number of other ways. In the first place, the minor will be liable on the contract if he ratifies it after he has reached majority. Secondly, where a contract is unenforceable against the minor or he has repudiated it, the court may 'if it is just and equitable to do so', require the minor to transfer to the other party any 'property acquired' by the minor under the contract, or any 'property representing it' (s.3(1) of the Minors' Contracts Act 1987: it should be noted in this context that the Act contains no definition of 'property'; in particular, it is unclear whether 'property' includes money). The aim of this section is to prevent the unjust enrichment of the minor in cases such as *Nash* v. *Inman* (above), by enabling the court to order the minor to restore to the vendor the fancy waistcoats. But the court cannot order the minor to return the property where he has disposed of it and obtained nothing in return for it. This limitation has been criticised on the ground that it should be irrelevant that the benefits conferred are no longer identifiable in the minor's hands. Nevertheless, this provision is to be welcomed in so far as it reduces the possibility of the unjust enrichment of the minor. But it should be noted that the Act did not abolish the existing common law rules (see *Stocks* v. *Wilson* [1913] 2 KB 235 and *Bristow* v. *Eastman* (1794) 1 Esp 172), so that the adult may still have resort to these rules where, for some reason, a remedy is not available to him under the 1987 Act. However, it is unlikely that an adult will wish, in future, to have resort to the pre-1987 common law because s.3(1) of the Act generally improves the position of the adult vis-a-vis the minor.

Thirdly, a minor who has actually performed his side of the contract may be unable to recover the benefits which he has conferred upon the other party. At first sight this seems rather anomalous. The foolish minor enters into improvident bargains; the very foolish minor actually carries through his side of the bargain. The courts have, however, approached this issue from a different perspective. Their approach has been to allow minority to act as a *defence* to a claim brought against the minor by an adult (as in *Nash* v. *Inman* (above)), but they have refused to allow that same minority to be used as the foundation of an *active* claim by the minor: that is to say, they have refused to recognise that minority can act as a factor rendering the conferral of a benefit unjust so as to trigger an unjust enrichment claim. On the contrary, a minor who seeks to recover the value of a benefit which he has conferred upon an adult must satisfy the same requirements as an adult making a restitutionary claim (except that, where the claim is based on a total failure of consideration, the minor can make out a restitutionary claim even though the adult was ready and willing to perform his side of the bargain). It is for this reason that we find in the cases that minors have relied upon traditional grounds of restitution, such as total failure of consideration (see, for example, *Steinberg* v. *Scala (Leeds) Ltd* (above)). The failure to recognise minority as a ground of restitution presents an odd contrast with the case of mental incapacity (see 16.3) where it is clear that it is the incapacity (together with the knowledge of the other party) which constitutes the unjust factor. There is much to be said for the view that minority should also constitute a ground of restitution subject to the requirement that the minor make counter-restitution to the adult (that is to say, the minor must restore to the adult any benefit which he has obtained at the expense of the adult). Indeed, this may have been the view that English law originally adopted in *Valentini* v. *Canali* (1889) 24 QBD 166, before the case was (wrongly) interpreted as an authority for the proposition that the minor must establish the existence of a total failure of consideration.

Fourthly, a contract with a minor is effective to pass property to the minor (s.3(1) of the Minors' Contracts Act 1987); similarly it is effective to pass property from the minor to the adult. Finally, a minor may incur liability in tort, but, where the effect of the tort action would be to undermine the protection afforded by the law of contract, then the tort action will also be barred. In *R Leslie Ltd* v. *Sheill* [1914] 3 KB 607, a minor obtained a loan of £400 by fraudulently misrepresenting his age. It was held that the minor could not be sued in the tort of deceit because the effect of granting damages in the tort action would be indirectly to enforce the contract and thus undermine the protection afforded by the law of contract.

Despite the enactment of the Minors' Contracts Act 1987, the law relating to the contractual capacity of minors remains in a confused state. The rules relating to necessaries can act as a trap for persons who deal in all good faith with minors. On the other hand, given that in the vast majority of cases a minor can avoid liability without the need to repudiate, it is difficult to understand why certain contracts are treated as voidable so that the minor can only avoid liability by a timely repudiation. The rules of law remain in need of further rationalisation in an effort to provide a better balance between, on the one hand, the protection of minors and, on the other hand, the interests of those who deal in all good faith with them.

16.3   Mental Incapacity and Drunkenness

A contract entered into by a person whose property is subject to the control of the court under Part VII of the Mental Health Act 1983 is voidable at the instance of such a party, although the contract does bind the other party (*Re Walker* [1905] 1 Ch 60). The justification for this rule would appear to be that, where the patient's property is subject to the control of the court, an attempted disposition of the property does not bind him, since it would interfere with the court's control over the property.

Where the property is not subject to the control of the court under the 1983 Act, then mental incapacity is not a ground for the setting aside of a contract or for the return of benefits conferred under a contract, unless the incapacity is known to the other party to the contract (*Imperial Loan Co* v. *Stone* [1892] 1 QB 599). Where the incapacity is not known to the other party, the contract cannot be set aside, unless the contract is of such a nature as to attract the equitable jurisdiction to relieve against unconscionable bargains between two persons of sound mind (*Hart* v. *O'Connor* [1985] AC 1000, see further 17.4). This requirement that the other party be aware of the incapacity should be contrasted with the case of minors, where there is no requirement that the other party be aware of the minority and, indeed, the minor may be relieved even when he has misrepresented his age. In Scotland the rule is that knowledge of the insanity is not a relevant consideration (*John Loudon & Co* v. *Elder's CB* 1923 SLT 226). It is therefore no surprise to learn that the requirement that the other party be aware of the incapacity has been subjected to severe criticism (see Hudson, 1986), although its harshness may be mitigated in practice by the existence of the equitable jurisdiction to set aside an improvident bargain made with a poor and ignorant person (*Creswell* v. *Potter* [1978] 1 WLR 255, see further 17.4)).

Drunkenness is treated in the same way as mental incapacity, so that the contract may only be set aside by the drunken party where the drunkenness prevented him from understanding the transaction and the other party to the contract knew of his incapacity (*Gore* v. *Gibson* (1843) 13 M & W 623). Finally, it should be noted that in the case of a contract for the sale of goods, 'where necessaries are sold and delivered to a person who by reason of mental incapacity or drunkenness is incompetent to contract, he must pay a reasonable price for them' (s.3(2) of the Sale of Goods Act 1979).

16.4 Companies

A company is a legal person which is separate and distinct from its shareholders. But the capacity of the company is limited by the objects for which the company is set up and which are contained in the company's memorandum of association. If the company acts beyond its objects then it has acted *ultra vires*, that is to say, it has acted beyond its capacity. In *Ashbury Railway Carriage and Iron Co* v. *Riche* (1875) LR 7 HL 653, it was held that a contract which was *ultra vires* the company was void. One of the principal justifications for the *ultra vires* rule is that it gives protection for shareholders who can learn from the objects clause 'the purposes to which their money can be applied' (*Sinclair* v. *Brougham* [1918] AC 514). In theory, it also provides protection for those who lend money to the company because they can infer from the objects clause the extent of the company's powers. But, in practice, a strict application of the rule caused hardship to innocent third parties who entered into a contract with a company, unaware of the *ultra vires* nature of the contract.

So it is not surprising to learn that the courts have created a number of exceptions to the rule in an effort to provide some protection for innocent third parties who deal in all good faith with the company (see Farrar, 1991, pp. 102–11). The most significant protection is now provided by statute in s.35(1) of the Companies Act 1985 (as amended by the Companies Act 1989) which states that:

'The validity of an act done by a company shall not be called into question on the ground of lack of capacity by reason of the fact that it is beyond the objects of the company stated in the memorandum of association'.

The intention behind this section is to abolish the *ultra vires* rule as regards innocent third parties who deal in all good faith with the company (see further s.35A and s.35B), while retaining it for internal purposes concerning the relationship between the shareholders and the company (s.35(2) and (3)). Therefore, in effect, this section has abolished the *ultra vires* rule in relation to third parties who deal in all good faith with the company, so that the contract remains valid and enforceable.

Summary

1 The general rule is that a minor is not bound by a contract which he enters into during his minority.

2 But a minor is bound by a contract to supply him with 'necessaries' where the contract as a whole is for the benefit of the minor and he is also bound by a beneficial contract of employment. Certain contracts involving minors are voidable and the minor can escape liability only by a timely repudiation.

3 However a minor may incur liability in a number of other ways. He may incur liability on the contract if he ratifies it after attaining majority, he may incur liability in tort, he may be ordered to restore any property he has acquired under the contract or any property representing it (s.3(1) of the Minors' Contracts Act 1987) and it is more difficult for a minor to obtain a remedy where the contract has been performed.

4 A person whose property is subject to the control of the court under Part VII of the Mental Health Act 1983 appears to be incapable of entering into a contract. In all other cases mental incapacity is not a ground for the setting aside of a contract, unless the incapacity is known to the other party to the contract.

5 The rule established in *Ashbury Railway Carriage and Iron Co* v. *Riche* was that a contract which is ultra vires a company is void. The effect of s.35 of the Companies Act 1985 (as amended) is virtually to abolish the doctrine of *ultra vires* in relation to third parties who deal in all good faith with the company.

Exercises

1 John, who is aged seventeen, agrees to buy a motor bike from Trike Ltd for £2500. He takes delivery of the bike but refuses to pay for it. Advise Trike Ltd.

2 In what circumstances may a minor incur liability to an adult as a result of entering into a contract?

3 John, who suffers from senile dementia, agrees to sell a portrait to Brian for £5000. Brian does not know that John is suffering from senile dementia. It is later discovered that the portrait is, in fact, an original nineteenth century painting, which is worth £125 000. Advise John whether he has any rights against Brian.

4 What does *ultra vires* mean? What effect does it have on a contract with a party who is unaware of the *ultra vires* nature of the transaction?

17 Duress, Undue Influence, and Inequality of Bargaining Power

17.1 Introduction

The law of contract has always placed limits upon the exercise of economic power by contracting parties (see Reiter, 1981). This role has traditionally been played by the doctrines of duress and undue influence, although recent years have also witnessed a (largely abortive) attempt to introduce into the common law a doctrine of inequality of bargaining power. While the English courts appear to have abandoned the attempt to create a doctrine of inequality of bargaining power, the recent EC Directive on Unfair Terms in Consumer Contracts (see 1.6 and 17.6) will bring about considerable change in this area and compel Parliament to bring forward regulations which will give to the courts significant powers to regulate unfair terms in consumer contracts. In this chapter we shall give separate consideration to each of these issues and conclude by discussing the extent to which the law of contract is concerned with the fairness of the bargain reached by the parties.

17.2 Common Law Duress

The doctrine of duress has been a relatively late developer in English contract law. Although the courts have had little difficulty in setting aside a contract on the ground of duress to the person, they have had more difficulty in recognising the existence of more subtle forms of duress, such as duress to goods and economic duress (see below). Historically, some of the work was done by the doctrine of consideration (see 5.3, 5.6 and 5.11). For example, if X puts a gun to Y's head and extracts from Y a promise to pay him £10 000, then Y's promise is unenforceable because of the absence of any consideration provided by X. But the doctrine of consideration was never well equipped to deal with duress and this is largely because of the rule that consideration must be sufficient but need not be adequate (see 5.6). So if X agrees to give Y his pen worth £1 in return for the promise to pay £10 000, the consideration hurdle is overcome.

  The role of consideration in regulating duress-type situations is likely to diminish still further as a result of the decision of the Court of Appeal in *Williams* v. *Roffey Bros & Nicholls (Contractors) Ltd* [1991] 1 QB 1 (discussed in more detail at 5.11–5.14). The approach of the Court of Appeal strongly suggests that the modern courts will be more willing to find the presence of consideration in the renegotiation of a contract and leave it to duress to regulate the fairness of the renegotiation. Indeed, one of the factors which was relied upon in adopting a more liberal approach to consideration was the fact that the court could always set aside the contract on the ground of duress where the ingredients of duress were established. Thus, a case such as *Stilk* v. *Myrick* (1809) 2 Camp 317 and 6 Esp 129 (see 5.11 and 5.13) was reclassified as a duress case rather than a consideration case. So, post-*Williams* v. *Roffey Bros*, it is clear that the doctrine of duress assumes greater significance. The difficulty is that duress has been bedevilled by conceptual confusion with the result that it is not easy to identify its limits and it is not obvious that it is ready to play the role which has been allocated to it. Having set duress in its context, we must now turn to consider the scope of the doctrine of duress at common law.

A contract which has been entered into under duress is voidable. There are three types of duress at common law. The first, and least controversial, is duress to the person. This may consist of actual violence to the plaintiff or to members of his family or threats of such violence. In *Barton* v. *Armstrong* [1976] AC 104, the Privy Council held that the threats need not be the sole reason for entry into the contract; it was sufficient that the threats were *a* factor influencing the victim to enter into the contract.

The second type of duress is duress to goods, that is a threat of damage to the victim's goods rather than to his person. Here the development of the law has been hindered by the old case of *Skeate* v. *Beale* (1840) 11 Ad & E 983, in which it was held that the unlawful detention of another's goods does not constitute duress. On the other hand, there was authority for the proposition that money paid to release goods which had been unlawfully detained could be recovered back in an action for money had and received (*Astley* v. *Reynolds* (1731) 2 Str 915). The decision in *Skeate* v. *Beale* has come under heavy academic criticism (see Beatson, 1974) and in *The Siboen and The Sibotre* [1976] 1 Lloyd's Rep 293, Kerr J refused to follow it. Given the development of the doctrine of economic duress (see below), it can be predicted with some confidence that *Skeate* will not be followed today and in *The Evia Luck* [1992] 2 AC 152, Lord Goff stated that the limitation in *Skeate* that only duress to the person would entitle a party to avoid a contract had been 'discarded'. So it now clear that duress to goods can, in an appropriate case, form the basis of a claim for relief.

The third type of duress, and the most difficult to stabilise, is economic duress. This type of duress arises where one party uses his superior economic power in an 'illegitimate' way so as to coerce the other contracting party to agree to a particular set of terms. The existence of this doctrine was first recognised in England by Kerr J in *The Siboen and The Sibotre* (above) and it has since been recognised in a number of cases, most importantly by the House of Lords in *Universe Tankships of Monrovia* v. *International Transport Workers Federation ('The Universe Sentinel')* [1983] 1 AC 366. In the latter case the defendant trade union 'blacked' the plaintiffs' ship in port and refused to release it until certain monies were paid, including a payment to the union's welfare fund. The House of Lords held that the latter payment was recoverable because the will of the shipowners had been coerced into making the payment and the pressure applied by the defendant union had been 'illegitimate'.

One question which must be asked here is: on what basis do the courts intervene to set aside a contract on the ground of duress? The traditional answer is that the courts will intervene where the victim's will has been 'coerced', such as 'to vitiate his consent'. This emphasis upon the need to establish a 'coercion of the will' can be seen in *The Siboen and the Sibotre* and, albeit to a lesser extent, in *The Universe Sentinel*. However the difficulties inherent in the 'coercion of the will' theory have been convincingly exposed by Professor Atiyah (1982). The principal difficulty is that duress does not deprive a person of all choice, but merely presents him with a choice between evils. For example, if a man forces me at gun point to enter into a contract, I do in fact consent to entering into the contract. Indeed, the more real the pressure, the more real is my willingness to enter into the contract, even if it is only to extricate myself from my predicament. What is wrong with the contract is not the absence of consent, but the wrongful nature of the threats which have been used to bring about the consent.

The role of consent should simply be to provide the necessary element of causation, namely that the threats used were a cause of the victim acting as he did (*Barton* v. *Armstrong* (above)). Consent also has a role to play in distinguishing between duress and a settlement of an honest claim (*Pau On* v. *Lau Yiu Long* [1980] AC 614) and in barring a claim, which would otherwise have succeeded, where a party has subsequently affirmed the contract (*North Ocean Shipping Co Ltd* v. *Hyundai Construction Co Ltd* [1979] QB 705). Any attempt to create a wider role for consent will deflect the court's attention from the real issues towards irrelevant inquiries into the psychological processes of the victim. It is therefore not surprising that the courts have begun to distance themselves from the coercion of the will test and in *The Evia Luck* (above) Lord Goff, giving the principal judgment of the House of Lords, noted the criticisms which have been levelled against the theory and doubted whether 'it is helpful to speak of the plaintiff's will having been coerced'. Hopefully, the courts will soon abandon the test completely and have regard to the consent of the victim only for the purpose of ensuring that there is a sufficient causal link between the pressure and the entry into the contract.

This suggests that greater emphasis should be placed in future cases upon the nature of the pressure applied by the more powerful party. So the principal task which remains for the courts is to ascertain what constitutes 'illegitimate' pressure. It is clear that it encompasses unlawful threats, such as a threat to commit a crime, a tort or a breach of contract (see *Pao On* v. *Lau Yiu Long* (above)). Lord Scarman stated in *The Universe Sentinel* that it should extend to threats which, though lawful in themselves, are used to attain a goal which is unlawful, such as blackmail. On the other hand, a threat to refuse to contract should not constitute duress because, in the absence of an obligation to enter into a contract, no wrongful threat is made in refusing to contract (*Smith* v. *William Charlick Ltd* (1924) 124 CLR 38). Equally, a refusal to waive existing contractual obligations should not amount to duress because of the absence of a wrongful threat (*Alec Lobb (Garages) Ltd* v. *Total Oil Great Britain Ltd* [1983] 1 WLR 87, 94). Although a refusal to contract or to waive existing contractual obligations may have serious consequences for the victim and may 'coerce his will', such threats should not constitute duress because no wrongful threat has been made by the more powerful party. This suggests that, in future cases, the primary focus of the court's inquiry should be upon the nature of the pressure applied by the more powerful party rather than the state of mind of the victim.

While the focus of attention upon the nature of the pressure applied will, ultimately, bring greater coherence to the law, it will not eliminate all the difficult questions. The courts are likely to experience considerable difficulties where the duress is alleged to take the form of a threatened breach of contract. The emphasis on the need for an illegitimate threat has led us to the conclusion that a threat to break a contract can constitute duress, whereas a refusal to waive an existing contractual obligation cannot. While this sounds very neat in theory, it can be difficult to apply in practice because, in many cases, one of the most difficult and contentious issues is whether or not the party who has exerted the pressure was threatening to break the contract, or whether he was entitled to make the demand which he was making. This has led some commentators to suggest that not all breaches of contract should count as the application of illegitimate pressure: some additional element should be required. Thus Burrows (1993c) has argued that bad faith should play a critical role in deciding whether or not a threatened breach of contract is illegitimate. One problem with this test lies in identifying what constitutes bad faith. Burrows defines it in the following terms: 'a threatened breach of contract should be regarded as illegitimate if concerned to exploit the plaintiff's weakness rather than solving financial or other problems of the defendant'. Another problem with the emphasis on bad faith is that English law does not generally invoke notions of bad faith in the context of breach of contract: either one is in breach of contract, or one is not. A threatened breach of contract is a threat which, under the terms of the contract, one is not entitled to make, irrespective of one's good faith.

A case which may illustrate the difficulties here is *Williams* v. *Roffey Bros* (the facts of which are set out at 5.11). It is a little difficult to apply the duress analysis with any confidence to this case because duress was, for some reason, not pleaded. But it is not very easy to ascertain why duress was not in issue in the case: there was a potential breach of contract by the sub-contractors and the probability of that breach was a cause of the main contractors offering to pay more for the performance of the agreed work. Yet most people seem to feel content with the conclusion that there was no duress on the facts of the case. One reason for this is that it was the main contractors who called the meeting and who made the offer to pay more. But the fact that they made the suggestion cannot, of itself, be decisive because the reason for them making the offer of extra payment may well have been the pressure which they were under as a result of the lack of progress being made and the possible inability of the plaintiff to complete the work. The second point which tends to suggest that there was no duress is the fact that the plaintiff was obviously incompetent: not only was he unable to supervise his workforce but he could not cost the job properly. But how would we feel about the sub-contractor who deliberately priced the job very low so that he was awarded the contract and who then, without making any explicit threats, made it clear to the main contractor that he was unlikely to complete on time unless offered more money? The latter example seems more akin to duress. Yet how can the courts distinguish between the incompetent sub-contractor (as in *Williams* v. *Roffey*) and the contractor who deliberately underprices the job? Do these examples suggest that there might be a role for an additional factor, such as bad faith, to distinguish those breaches of contract which are illegitimate, from those which are legitimate? Or should we conclude that all breaches of contract are illegitimate and that a vital error was made in *Williams* in failing to bring the duress issue before the court? The fact that these fundamental questions remain to be answered suggests that the law relating to duress remains rather undeveloped in English law and that it is not yet ready to play the role given to it by the Court of Appeal in *Williams* v. *Roffey Bros.*

17.3 Undue Influence

Undue influence, being a creation of equity, has emerged separately from common law duress. Although undue influence is a well-worn phrase, its meaning has not been subjected to precise analysis by the courts. What does 'undue' mean? Does it mean 'illegitimate' (and, if so, does it have the same meaning as in common law duress?) or does it mean 'too much'? And what about 'influence'? Does it mean 'pressure' or is it a more subtle, continuing form of domination? The courts have not provided any clear answer to these questions.

The traditional approach is to divide undue influence into two distinct categories: presumed and actual undue influence. But an important preliminary point was considered by the House of Lords in *National Westminster Bank plc* v. *Morgan* [1985] AC 686. There it was held that, before a transaction could be set aside on the ground of presumed undue influence, it had to be shown that the transaction was wrongful, in the sense that it constituted a *manifest and unfair disadvantage* to the person seeking to have the contract set aside. In *Bank of Credit and Commerce International SA* v. *Aboody* [1990] 1 QB 923, the Court of Appeal held 'that a disadvantage would be a manifest disadvantage if it would have been obvious as such to any independent and reasonable persons who considered the transaction at the time with knowledge of all the relevant facts'. A disadvantage will not be manifest if it emerges only 'after a fine and close evaluation of [the transaction's] various beneficial and detrimental features' (although contrast the rather more generous approach to manifest disadvantage adopted by the Court of Appeal in *Cheese* v. *Thomas* [1994] 1 All ER 35).

In *Aboody* the Court of Appeal held that the manifest disadvantage requirement was also applicable to cases of actual undue influence but this argument was rejected by the House of Lords in *C.I.B.C. Mortgages plc* v. *Pitt* [1994] AC 200. Lord Browne-Wilkinson stated that actual undue influence was a 'species of fraud' and that, once a plaintiff had proved actual wrongdoing, there was no need for him to assume the additional obligation of proving manifest disadvantage. This must be right. If I subject you to illegitimate pressure or to undue influence so that you enter into a contract into which you would not otherwise have entered, the fairness of the bargain is irrelevant: the fact that my wrongdoing caused you to enter into the transaction is enough to give you a ground for relief. So why do the courts insist on manifest disadvantage in the context of presumed undue influence? The answer which Lord Browne-Wilkinson gave is that its function is 'to raise a presumption of undue influence'. An example will illustrate the point. Suppose that a solicitor purchases an antique from his client at a fair market value. There is nothing suspicious about this transaction and so the solicitor is not called upon to prove that he did not subject the client to undue influence. But let us suppose that the antique was sold for half the market value. Here the manifestly disadvantageous nature of the transaction causes us to suspect that something has gone wrong in the bargaining process: in other words, the presumption of undue influence has been raised. This seems to make sense. But two caveats must be entered. The first is that Lord Browne-Wilkinson pointed out that the manifest disadvantage requirement does not apply to an obscure line of cases sometimes referred to as the 'abuse of confidence cases'. In an abuse of confidence case it is for the fiduciary (the one in whom the confidence is reposed) to show that the transaction was a fair one (in contrast to the presumed undue influence cases where the burden is upon the weaker party to show manifest disadvantage). It is possible to argue that these abuse of confidence cases are all examples of actual undue influence (by focusing upon the word 'abuse') and if this is right no problem arises because we know that manifest disadvantage does not apply to actual undue influence. But if these cases cannot be so confined, then plaintiffs will obviously plead abuse of confidence rather than presumed undue influence in order to escape the manifest disadvantage requirement. The second caveat is that the fact that manifest disadvantage applies to presumed but not to actual undue influence assumes that a clear line can be drawn between the two categories. But this is not so and plaintiffs will now be tempted to plead actual undue influence rather than presumed in order to avoid the manifest disadvantage requirement. On the other hand, the courts may well be reluctant to make a finding of actual undue influence in the absence of clear evidence because once they reach such a conclusion there are very few control devices which they can then employ to deny a claim to relief.

As has already been stated, undue influence cases are traditionally divided into two categories. The first group of cases are cases of 'presumed undue influence'. In this group of cases the relationship between the parties plus manifest disadvantage gives rise to a presumption of undue influence and the onus of proof switches to the recipient to show that he did not exercise undue influence. In *Bank of Credit and Commerce International SA* v. *Aboody* (above) the Court of Appeal held that cases of presumed undue influence can themselves be divided into two categories. The first group of cases concern the 'well established categories of relationship', such as solicitor and client, doctor and patient and religious adviser and disciple, where 'the relationship as such will give rise to the presumption'. The second category consists of relationships which do not fall within the first class but which 'may be shown to have become such as to justify the court in applying the same presumption'. In the latter category is *Re Craig* [1971] Ch 95, in which an elderly widower employed a young woman as his secretary and companion. He employed her only 2 months after the death of his wife and over the next 6 years gave her gifts worth £28 000. It was held that there was a relationship of confidence between the two, such as to give rise to a presumption of undue influence, and that the young woman had failed to rebut the presumption that she had obtained the gifts by the use of undue influence.

Once the presumption of undue influence has arisen it may be rebutted by showing that the donor acted independently of any influence of the recipient and with full appreciation of what he was doing. The most usual, although not the only way of rebutting the presumption, is to show that the donor had competent and independent advice before acting. But the presumption may also be rebutted by showing that the act of the donor in making the gift had been a 'spontaneous and independent act' (*Re Brocklehurst* [1978] Ch 14).

The second group of undue influence cases are cases of 'actual undue influence'. They arise, not from the relationship between the parties, but because there has been some unfair and improper conduct on the part of the party alleged to have exercised the undue influence. Here the undue influence must be proved by the party seeking to establish its existence; there is no presumption of undue influence. Cases within this category tend to be a rather rare species because they are either argued as cases of common law duress or it is sought to establish that there is a relationship between the parties such as to give rise to a presumption of undue influence. A case such as *Re Craig* (above) can be decided either as a case of presumed undue influence (in the second category) or as a case of actual undue influence. As the Court of Appeal acknowledged in *Aboody*, the border between the second category of presumed undue influence and actual undue influence may be a 'slender' one. But now that we know that manifest disadvantage does not apply to actual undue influence a plaintiff in a case such as *Re Craig* is more likely to opt for actual undue influence rather than presumed. A rare case of actual undue influence is *Williams* v. *Bayley* (1866) LR 1 HL 200. A father sought to rescind a mortgage which he had executed in favour of a banker. He proved that he had executed the mortgage because he was frightened by the banker's warning that he had it in his power to prosecute his son for forgery. It was held that he was entitled to rescind the mortgage on the ground of undue influence.

17.4 Inequality of Bargaining Power

The issue whether a doctrine of inequality of bargaining power exists in English law has been one of some controversy in recent years. The primary source of this controversy lies in the seminal judgment of Lord Denning in *Lloyds Bank* v. *Bundy* [1975] QB 326. The facts of the case were, in many ways, unremarkable. Mr Bundy, an elderly man not well versed in business affairs, gave his bank a guarantee regarding his son's business debts and mortgaged his house to the bank as security for the guarantee. In entering into this transaction Mr Bundy relied implicitly on his bank manager as his adviser, but the bank manager was also acting on behalf of the son, thereby creating a conflict of interest. When the bank sought to enforce the guarantee against old Mr Bundy and obtain possession of the house, Mr Bundy defended the action on the ground that the mortgage had been improperly obtained. The majority of the court decided the case on orthodox grounds, holding that the bank had failed to rebut the presumption of undue influence because they could not show that Mr Bundy had been independently advised. All this, however, was not for Lord Denning. He set out the following general principle:

> 'English law gives relief to one who without independent advice enters into a contract upon terms which are very unfair or transfers property for a consideration which is grossly inadequate, when his bargaining power is grievously impaired by reason of his own needs and desires, or by his own ignorance or infirmity, coupled with undue influence or pressures brought to bear on him by or for the benefit of the other.'

Lord Denning envisaged that this new general principle would unify hitherto discrete areas of law and provide a basis for a solution to a wide range of problems. But it has since received a rather frosty reception in the appellate courts. In *Pao On* v. *Lau Yiu Long* (above) Lord Scarman, giving the judgment of the Privy Council, said that agreements were not voidable simply because they had been 'procured by an unfair use of a dominant bargaining position'. A much more severe rebuff was handed out by Lord Scarman, giving the judgment of the House of Lords in *National Westminster Bank plc* v. *Morgan* (above). He specifically disapproved of Lord Denning's principle of inequality of bargaining power and questioned whether there was any need for such a doctrine, given that Parliament, in statutes such as the Consumer Credit Act 1974, has undertaken the task of placing 'such restrictions upon freedom of contract as are necessary' to protect the most likely victims of inequality of bargaining power.

However, although Lord Denning's principle of inequality of bargaining power has been rejected, it should not be assumed that courts will stand by and allow the strong 'to push the weak to the wall' (*Alec Lobb (Garages) Ltd* v. *Total Oil (Great Britain) Ltd* [1985] 1 WLR 173, 183). Even in *National Westminster Bank* v. *Morgan*, Lord Scarman recognised the existence of an equitable jurisdiction to grant relief against an unconscionable (or unfair) bargain. He refused to confine the jurisdiction of equity within rigid limits, saying that the 'court in the exercise of this equitable jurisdiction is a court of conscience'. Thus we find that equity intervenes to relieve against unconscionable bargains (*Earl of Chesterfield* v. *Janssen* (1751) 2 Ves Sen 125), to set aside an agreement made with an expectant heir (*Earl of Aylesford* v. *Morris* (1873) LR 8 Ch App 484), to set aside an improvident bargain made with a poor and ignorant person (*Creswell* v. *Potter* [1978] 1 WLR 255) and to grant relief where there has been an abuse of a relationship of confidence (*Demarara Bauxite Co Ltd* v. *Hubbard* [1923] AC 673). There are two objections here. The first is that the failure of the courts to define the basis of their jurisdiction leads to uncertainty and inconsistency. Is the basis of these doctrines the inequality between the parties, the unfair nature of the terms, the knowing taking advantage of the weakness of another or some combination of these factors? The answer is unclear. The second objection is that, although there is no general principle of inequality of bargaining power, it remains to be seen how far these residual equitable doctrines will be resurrected to play the role which Lord Denning envisaged would be played by his doctrine of inequality of bargaining power. In this way the courts may achieve covertly what they refuse to do overtly and such subterfuge should not be encouraged in the law.

17.5 The Role of Parliament

Parliament has also had a role to play in regulating contracts in an effort to protect the most likely victims of inequality of bargaining power. For example, section 137(1) of the Consumer Credit Act 1974 states that

'If the court finds a credit bargain extortionate it may reopen the credit agreement so as to do justice between the parties.'

An extortionate credit bargain is one which requires the debtor or a relative of his to make payments which are 'grossly exorbitant' or which 'otherwise grossly contravenes ordinary principles of fair dealing' (s.138(1)). In deciding whether these requirements have been satisfied, the court must engage in a wide-ranging inquiry but must, in particular, have regard to the interest rates prevailing at the time that the agreement was made, the relevant characteristics of the borrower (such as age, experience, health and the presence or absence of financial pressure upon him), the risks accepted by the creditor and the creditor's relationship to the debtor. The court is also given considerable discretion to remake the agreement according to its conception of what justice requires on the facts of the case.

Other examples of statutes enacted in an attempt to protect the most likely victims of inequality of bargaining power include the Unfair Contract Terms Act 1977 and the Supply of Goods and Services Act 1982. Parliament has also intervened to regulate the employment relationship and the relationship between landlords and tenants in an effort to provide greater protection for employees and tenants (see 1.2). But, as we have already noted, Lord Scarman in *Morgan* used the existence of such legislation as a justification for refusing to create a doctrine of inequality of bargaining power. But the better approach would surely have been to create such a doctrine and follow the policy being pursued by Parliament. Instead, the common law has been left pursuing an individualistic policy which is diametrically opposed to the policies being pursued by Parliament in statutes such as the Consumer Credit Act 1974 and the Unfair Contract Terms Act 1977.

17.6   The EC Directive on Unfair Terms in Consumer Contracts

Further legislative intervention is on the horizon, this time as a result of our membership of the European Community. A Directive on Unfair Terms in Consumer Contracts has recently been agreed (93/13 EEC, see Dean, 1993) and it will be implemented into UK law by regulations made under s.2(2) of the European Communities Act 1972. It is not planned to make any amendments to the Unfair Contract Terms Act 1977 (UCTA) (on which see 11.9–11.16) and so this new right of action will be in addition to the consumer's existing rights of action under the 1977 Act. This will inevitably give rise to some confusion as the scope of the two rights differ in significant respects. The most important one for present purposes is that the 1977 Act is confined in its application to particular types of clauses (principally exclusion clauses, see 11.16), while the Directive is not confined to any particular type of term. Thus the jurisdictional problems which we noted under the 1977 Act (see, for example, 11.10) should not arise under the Directive. We shall not discuss the Directive in great detail here, largely because the regulations which will implement them are still in draft form. All that will be done is to set out the basic structure of the Directive.

The aim of the Directive is to regulate 'unfair terms in contracts concluded between a seller or supplier and a consumer' (Article 1). A consumer is defined in Article 2 as any natural person who is acting for purposes which are outside his trade or business. It should be noted that this definition is narrower than the corresponding provision in s.12 of

UCTA which does not necessarily exclude a company from the definition of a consumer (see 11.11). A seller or supplier is defined in Article 2 as any natural or legal person who is acting for purposes relating to his trade, business or profession, whether publicly owned or privately owned. This is similar, if not identical to the definition of business in UCTA.

The vital question, however, is: when is a contract term to be regarded as unfair? Article 3 is the central provision in the Directive. It states:

'A contractual term which has not been individually negotiated shall be regarded as unfair if, contrary to the requirement of good faith, it causes a significant imbalance in the parties' rights and obligations arising under the contract, to the detriment of the consumer.'

There are a number of requirements here. The first is that the contractual term must not have been individually negotiated. A term has not been individually negotiated 'where it has been drafted in advance and the consumer has therefore not been able to influence the substance of the term, particularly in the context of a pre-formulated standard contract' (Article 3(2)). The burden of proof is upon the supplier to show that the term has been individually negotiated.

The second point relates to the definition of an unfair term. The Directive does give some guidance as to its possible scope by including in an Annex 'an indicative and non-exhaustive list of the terms which may be regarded as unfair'. It should be noted that inclusion on the list does not mean that the term *is* unfair. It only means that it *may be* unfair: in this sense it is a 'grey list' rather than a black list. Thus exclusion clauses which purport to exclude or restrict liability for death or personal injury are included in the grey list, whereas under UCTA such clauses are void, at least where the death or injury has been caused by negligence (see UCTA, s.2, discussed at 11.10). But the grey list goes beyond exclusion clauses and encompasses, for example, terms which purport to make excessive sums payable by the consumer in the event of breach, clauses which enable the seller or supplier to alter the terms of the contract unilaterally without a valid reason which is specified in the contract, and even clauses which have the effect of irrevocably binding the consumer to terms with which he had no real opportunity of becoming acquainted before the conclusion of the contract. The Directive therefore has a broad reach.

But the Directive gives very little guidance as to the meaning of 'unfair' beyond the terms listed in the Annex. Some further guidance is provided by the preamble which states that 'in making an assessment of good faith, particular regard shall be had to the strength of the bargaining positions of the parties, whether the consumer had an inducement to agree to the term and whether the goods or services were sold or supplied to the special order of the consumer'. Article 4 further provides that:

'the unfairness of a contractual term shall be assessed, taking into account the nature of the goods or services for which the contract was concluded and by referring, at the time of conclusion of the contract, to all the circumstances attending the conclusion of the contract and to all the other terms of the contract or of another contract on which it is dependent.

Assessment of the unfair nature of the terms shall relate, neither to the definition of the main subject matter of the contract nor to the adequacy of the price and remuneration, on the one hand, as against the services or goods supplied in exchange, on the other, in so far as these terms are in plain intelligible language.'

These factors are similar to those which are taken into account by the courts in assessing the reasonableness of an exclusion clause under UCTA and the government has argued that the inquiry to be undertaken by the courts under the Directive is similar to that which they already undertake in their interpretation of UCTA (although it should be said that the government's interpretation is hotly contested).

The third point is that there are two phrases in the definition of an unfair term which are worthy of further comment. The first is 'good faith' and the second is 'significant imbalance'. As we have already noted (see 12.8), good faith is not a standard which is generally employed in English contract law, although it is more familiar to our civilian counterparts. But it is not clear what good faith adds to the definition in Article 3: does it simply mean that, where there is a significant imbalance, there is a lack of good faith, or can there be a lack of good faith even where there is no significant imbalance? Earlier drafts of the Directive distinguished clearly between significant imbalance and incompatibility with the requirements of good faith: they were alternative rather than cumulative grounds of unfairness. Thus a draft of the Directive stated that a contract term was unfair if:

'– it causes to the detriment of the consumer a significant imbalance in the parties' rights and obligations arising under the contract, or
– it causes the performance of the contract to be unduly detrimental to the consumer, or
– it causes the performance of the contract to be significantly different from what the consumer could legitimately expect, or
– it is incompatible with the requirements of good faith'.

But in the final version of the Directive the test appears to be cumulative so that the primary focus is upon whether there is a significant imbalance and not on good faith. It is unfortunate that the drafting lacks clarity on this particular point.

The second point relates to the meaning of 'significant imbalance'. The use of this phrase suggests that the Directive is directed towards substantive unfairness (that is, unfairness in the terms or the substance of the contract) rather than procedural unfairness (that is, unfairness in the procedure by which the contract was concluded). But if the focus of the Directive is upon substantive unfairness, why does Article 4 (above) state that an assessment of the unfair nature of the terms shall not relate to the adequacy of the price, provided that the price is stated in intelligible language? Surely the adequacy of the price is central to any notion of substantive unfairness? While those responsible for the drafting of the Directive may have wanted to avoid the conclusion that a term was unfair simply because the subject-matter of the contract was overpriced, is it not taking matters too far to say that the supplier is not subject to review under the Directive provided that he ensures that the price is in 'plain intelligible language'?

The final point relates to the effect of a court concluding that a term is unfair. Article 6 states that an unfair term 'shall not be binding on the consumer' and 'that the contract shall continue to bind the parties upon those terms if it is capable of continuing in existence without the unfair terms'. Basically, the term is voidable at the instance of the consumer. Article 7 of the Directive also contains more elaborate enforcement mechanisms, which deal with collective means of enforcement, but it would appear that the regulations which will give effect to the Directive will contain no reference to such collective means of enforcement.

Despite one or two drafting difficulties, the EC Directive should be welcomed on the basis that it strengthens the rights of consumers in this country and will help bring about greater uniformity within the European Community. And the fact that the Directive is confined in its scope to consumer contracts means that it is kept out of the commercial sphere where the need for certainty is greatest. So the uncertainty which the Directive will initially create is not the grave cause for concern which it would be if it applied to international contracts for the sale of goods.

17.7 A General Doctrine of Unconscionability?

Despite the efforts of Parliament and the European Community, any discussion of the desirability of a general doctrine of unconscionability may seem rather academic, given the rejection of Lord Denning's doctrine of inequality of bargaining power. At first sight English contract law seems unconcerned with the fairness of the contract concluded by the parties. The courts have rejected a doctrine of inequality of bargaining power and, as we have already noted (5.6), the general rule is that consideration must be sufficient but need not be adequate. Freedom of contract reigns and the adequacy of the consideration is irrelevant.

But, despite initial appearances to the contrary, the rules which make up English contract law are concerned with the fairness of the bargain reached by the parties. We have seen the hostility which the courts have displayed towards exclusion clauses, both in terms of the interpretative devices adopted (11.5) and their reluctance to incorporate exclusion clauses and other onerous clauses into a contract (9.4). Innominate terms (10.5) were created to give the courts greater remedial flexibility, so that the injustice of cases such as *Arcos* v. *Ronaasen* [1933] AC 470 need no longer occur. We have also noted the protective attitude which the courts have adopted towards minors (see 16.2). Later in this book we shall see that the courts are reluctant to order specific performance of a contract which is unfair (21.9), they have an equitable jurisdiction to grant relief against forfeiture (21.7) and they have developed a penalty clause jurisdiction, under which a court will not enforce a term of a contract which seeks to punish a contracting party who is in breach of contract (21.6). Surely conceptions of fairness must underpin, to a greater or lesser extent, these rules and doctrines (see Waddams, 1976). If these conceptions of fairness permeate the law of contract, would it not be better to acknowledge these considerations openly by the creation of a general doctrine of unconscionability?

Three principal objections can be raised against the creation of such a doctrine. The first is that the courts are unable to identify contracts which are unfair because of their inability to understand the operation of financial markets (see Trebilcock, 1976). The second is that such a general doctrine would create an unacceptable degree of uncertainty. The third is that it is not the function of contract law to engage in the redistribution of wealth (Fried, 1981, contrast Kronman, 1980 who defends 'the view that the rules of contract law should be used to implement distributional goals whenever alternative ways of doing so are likely to be more costly or intrusive').

These are powerful objections to the creation of such a general doctrine. But they are not necessarily conclusive. We have already noted (1.3) the conflicting ideologies which run through the law of contract and it is here that market-individualism and consumer-welfarism are in direct conflict (although contrast Tiplady, 1983). Given that these conceptions of fairness run throughout the law of contract, they cannot be dismissed as an insignificant aspect of contract law. Although Parliament must continue to play the principal role in regulating the economy and placing restrictions upon freedom of contract, a residual role can nevertheless be played by the courts and that role can best be recognised by the creation of a general doctrine of unconscionability. Uncertainty can be reduced by the recognition of the fact that unfairness can take different forms. Broadly speaking, two types of unfairness can be recognised. The first may be called procedural unfairness and the second substantive unfairness (although it should be noted that the distinction between the two has been doubted by Atiyah (1986d), who maintains that the two 'feed upon each other'). The first is concerned with the process by which the contract is negotiated. The second is concerned with the fairness of the terms or the substance of the contract. It is easier to identify the procedural tactics which are unacceptable as part of the process of contractual negotiation than it is to define substantive unfairness (see Thal, 1988). Unacceptable tactics might include threats to commit a crime, a tort or a breach of contract and the courts might recognise that there are certain bargaining weaknesses, such as infirmity and necessity, which should not be exploited. More difficulty is experienced in defining substantive unfairness; all that can be said is that it should only be a ground of relief in the very rare case where the consideration is manifestly and totally inadequate and that the courts must be left to work out the principles on a case-by-case basis. Such a narrowly drawn doctrine of unconscionability would not create an unacceptable level of uncertainty, but it would prevent injustice arising in the few cases in which it was needed.

Summary

1 A contract may be set aside on the ground of duress. The duress may be to the person, to his goods or economic duress.
2 Duress can be shown to exist where the consent of the victim has been obtained by illegitimate pressure.
3 Undue influence is an equitable doctrine. Before a contract can be set aside on the ground of presumed undue influence it must be demonstrated that the contract was manifestly disadvantageous to the person seeking to set it aside.
4 In cases of presumed undue influence, the relationship between the parties gives rise to a presumption of undue influence and the onus of proof switches to the recipient to show that he did not exercise undue influence. In cases of actual undue influence, there must be some unfair and improper conduct on the part of the party alleged to have exercised the undue influence. Actual undue influence must be proved by the party seeking to establish its existence.
5 English law does not recognise the existence of a general doctrine of inequality of bargaining power. But equity may intervene to set aside unconscionable bargains, agreements made with expectant heirs, improvident bargains made with poor and ignorant persons and contracts procured by an abuse of a relationship of confidence.
6 Parliament has also intervened, in statutes such as the Consumer Credit Act 1974 and the Unfair Contract Terms Act 1977, in an effort to protect the most likely victims of inequality of bargaining power.

Exercises

1 A threatens B that he (A) will shoot the next person he sees unless B pays him £10. B pays the £10. Can he recover it? Would your answer be the same if A had threatened to burn one of B's old family heirlooms unless he paid the £10?
2 What is the relationship between the doctrine of consideration and duress? (see *Stilk* v. *Myrick* (5.11) and *D & C Builders* v. *Rees* [1966] 2 QB 617)
3 What is economic duress? What are its limits?
4 What is undue influence? How does it differ from duress?
5 Does English law recognise the existence of a doctrine of inequality of bargaining power? Should it?
6 Do you think that the courts are concerned with the fairness of the bargain reached by the parties?
7 An old lady is 'induced by her solicitor under strong pressure to sell him a large and inconvenient family home at full market value'. Can the transaction be set aside by the old lady? If so, on what grounds?
8 Assess the likely significance of the EC Directive on Unfair Terms in Consumer Contracts.

Part IV

Performance, Discharge and Remedies for Breach of Contract

18 Performance and Discharge of the Contract

18.1 Performance

Contracts are made to be performed. When parties enter into a contract, they generally do so in the expectation that it will be performed according to its terms. Indeed, a contract consists of a number of terms which determine the scope of the performance obligations which the parties have accepted. A failure to perform in accordance with these terms is a breach of contract, which will entitle the other party to the contract to an appropriate remedy (*Photo Production Ltd* v. *Securicor Transport Ltd* [1980] AC 827, see further, 19.3).

However, in many cases the formation of the contract and the performance of the contract are practically simultaneous. For example, I purchase a newspaper at a nearby shop. Here my offer to buy the paper and the shopkeeper's acceptance of my offer occur at virtually the same time as the performance of the contract in the handing over, and the payment for, the newspaper. Atiyah asks (1986b): 'Is it really sensible to characterise these transactions as agreements or exchanges of promises?' He argues that obligations are really created by what we do, not what we promise or what we intend: in other words, it is the payment of the money and the handing over of the newspaper which form the basis of the obligations created, not the *promise* to pay or the *promise* to hand over the newspaper.

It must be conceded that in many cases formation and performance are practically simultaneous. This fact is often obscured by contract textbooks because formation appears at the beginning of the book and performance towards the end. But in the real world the two often occur at virtually the same time. On the other hand, there may be a considerable time lapse between formation and performance. For example, I may order a special anniversary issue of a newspaper which is not due for publication for another three weeks. In such a case I want to know at the moment that I reach agreement with the shopkeeper that he will order and deliver to me a copy of the newspaper. Here there appears to be no doubt that the agreement is the basis of our obligations, not any action in reliance upon the agreement. It is submitted that the same is true when formation and performance are virtually simultaneous. In my example of the purchase of a newspaper, the source of the obligations created remains my promise to buy the paper and the promise of the shopkeeper to sell the newspaper; our actions are simply evidence of the fact that we have reached agreement (see 1.4).

18.2 Discharge of the Contract

Contracts may be discharged or brought to an end in four principal ways. We shall deal with three forms of discharge in this chapter. They are discharge by performance (18.3), by agreement (18.4) and by operation of law (18.5). Contracts can also be discharged by breach, but breach is a sufficiently important topic to deserve a chapter in its own right (see Chapter 19).

18.3 Discharge by Performance

A contract is discharged by performance where the performance by both parties complies fully with the terms of the contract. The vast majority of contracts are discharged by performance. We do not read about such contracts in textbooks because, when the contract is discharged by performance, no legal problems arise. Indeed, the discussion of 'performance' in most contract textbooks is, in fact, a discussion of breach of contract because the point which is being made is that performance which fails to comply fully with the terms of the contract is a breach of contract. We shall deal with such issues in the chapter on breach of contract (see Chapter 19).

It is, however, extremely important to realise that, in the real world, most contracts are discharged by performance. Students who read contract textbooks tend to get a distorted view of reality because they believe that all contracts go wrong for one reason or another. In fact, most contracts are performed according to their terms and the role of the lawyer is confined to giving advice on the formation or the drafting of the contract. It is only in the minority of cases that contracts go wrong and a dispute breaks out between the parties and, even when such a dispute does occur, empirical studies show us that the rules of contract law are often but one factor among many to be taken into account in the resolution of the dispute (see 1.5).

18.4 Discharge by Agreement

The parties can agree to abandon or to discharge the contract. The limiting factor here is that an agreement to discharge a contract must be supported by consideration (5.20). Where performance has not been completed by either party to the contract, there is generally no difficulty in finding consideration because, in giving up their rights to compel each other to perform, each party is giving something to the bargain and so consideration is given. But where the contract is wholly executed on one side, an agreement to abandon the contract (unless the agreement to abandon the contract is itself supported by fresh consideration) will not be supported by consideration and will be unenforceable unless the agreement is in the form of a deed, the party who has fully performed his obligations under the contract is estopped from going back upon his representation that he will not enforce the original contract or he is held to have waived his rights under that contract (see 5.24–5.25).

Finally, a contract may be discharged by the operation of a condition subsequent which has been incorporated into the contract. A condition subsequent states that a previously binding contract shall come to an end on the occurrence of a stipulated event (see 10.2). The effect of the occurrence of the stipulated event is to discharge the contract, without either party being in breach of contract.

18.5 Discharge by Operation of Law

A contract may be discharged by operation of law. The principal example of a contract which is brought to an end by the operation of a rule of law is a contract which is frustrated. Frustration, it will be remembered, automatically brings a contract to an end by the operation of a rule of law, irrespective of the wishes of the parties (14.8). Other examples of the discharge of a contract by operation of law are discussed by Anson (1984, pp. 485–88).

Summary

1 Contracts are made to be performed. The vast majority of contracts are discharged by performance.
2 Contracts may be discharged by performance, agreement, operation of law or breach.
3 A contract is discharged by performance where the performance by both parties has complied fully with the terms of the contract.
4 An agreement to discharge a contract must be supported by consideration, unless one party is held to have waived his rights under the contract or is estopped from asserting them.
5 A contract may be discharged by operation of law, for example, by the occurrence of a frustrating event.

Exercises

1 List the different ways in which a contract can be discharged.
2 When will performance be sufficient to discharge the contract?
3 Jenny agrees to buy Sarah's car for £2500. Sarah gives Jenny the car but Jenny does not pay the £2500. Jenny and Sarah then agree to abandon the contract and Sarah tells Jenny that she 'does not need the money anyway'. Jenny then uses the £2500 to pay for the installation of double glazing in her house. Sarah has now decided that she wants her car back and she alleges that the agreement to discharge the contract is not an enforceable agreement. Advise Jenny.

19 Breach of Contract

19.1 Introduction: Breach Defined

Professor Treitel (1991) has defined a breach of contract in the following terms:

> 'a breach of contract is committed when a party without lawful excuse fails or refuses to perform what is due from him under the contract, performs defectively or incapacitates himself from performing'.

It should be noted that in all cases the failure to provide the promised performance must be 'without lawful excuse'. Thus where the contract has been frustrated there is no liability for breach of contract because both parties have been provided with a 'lawful excuse' for their non-performance. Similarly, where one party has breached the contract and the breach has given to the other party the right to terminate performance of the contract, that party is not in breach of contract in refusing to continue with performance because he is given a 'lawful excuse' for his non-performance.

Although the breach can take the form of words (such as an express refusal to perform the terms of the contract), it need not do so and can be evidenced by the conduct of one party in disabling himself from performing his obligations under the contract or by performing defectively. Where it is alleged that one party has incapacitated himself from performing his obligations under the contract, his inability to perform must be established on a balance of probabilities. This is relatively easy to do where the party alleged to be in breach has sold the subject-matter of the contract to a third party, but greater difficulty arises where he enters into alternative obligations which it is alleged are inconsistent with his existing contractual obligations. The fact that a party has entered into inconsistent obligations 'does not in itself necessarily establish [an inability to perform], unless these obligations are of such a nature or have such an effect that it can truly be said that the party in question has put it out of his power to perform his obligations' (*Alfred C Toepfer International Gmbh* v. *Itex Hagrani Export SA* [1993] 1 Lloyd's Rep 360, 362).

19.2 When Does Breach Occur?

The question whether or not a particular contract has been breached depends upon the precise construction of the terms of the contract. No universal legal principle can be established which displaces the need for a careful analysis of the terms of each individual contract. It is for the party alleging the existence of the breach of contract to prove that a breach has occurred. It is not generally necessary to prove that a party has been at fault before breach can be established. Many obligations created by a contract are strict; that is to say, liability does not depend upon proof of fault. A good example of a strict contractual obligation is provided by s.14(2) of the Sale of Goods Act 1979 which states that, where a seller sells goods in the course of a business, there is an implied condition that the goods supplied under the contract are of merchantable quality, except in relation to defects drawn to the buyer's attention before the contract was concluded or, in the case where the buyer examines the goods, as regards defects which that examination ought to have revealed. The purchaser is not required to prove that the seller was at fault in selling goods which were not of merchantable quality; the seller may have taken all reasonable steps to ensure that the goods were of merchantable quality but he will still be in breach of contract if they are not of such quality.

On the other hand, a contractual term may impose a duty to take reasonable care, in which case a breach can only be established where it is proved that the party alleged to be in breach has failed to exercise reasonable care. An example in this category is provided by s.13 of the Supply of Goods and Services Act 1982 which provides that a person who supplies a service in the course of a business impliedly undertakes to 'carry out the service with reasonable care and skill'.

19.3 The Consequences of Breach

A breach of contract does not automatically bring a contract to an end (*Decro-Wall International SA* v. *Practitioners in Marketing Ltd* [1971] 1 WLR 361). Rather, a breach of contract gives various options to the party who is not in breach ('the innocent party'). The extent of these options depends upon the seriousness of the breach. Even the most serious breach, such as a fundamental breach (see 11.7), does not, of itself, terminate or discharge the contract (*Photo Production Ltd* v. *Securicor Transport Ltd* [1980] AC 827).

The consequences of a breach of contract depend upon the facts of each individual case, but three principal consequences of a breach of contract can be identified. The first is that the innocent party is entitled to recover damages in respect of the loss which he has suffered as a result of the breach. The second is that the party in breach may be unable to sue to enforce the innocent party's obligations under the contract. The third consequence is that the breach may entitle the innocent party to terminate the performance of the contract. We shall now deal with these consequences individually.

19.4 Damages

Every breach of a valid and enforceable contract gives to the innocent party a right to recover damages in respect of the loss suffered as a result of the breach, unless the liability for breach has been effectively excluded by an appropriately drafted exclusion clause. An action for damages lies whether the term which is broken is a condition, a warranty or an innominate term (see further Chapter 10). The basis upon which the courts assess the damages payable will be discussed in Chapter 20.

19.5   Enforcement by the Party in Breach

The second consequence of a breach of contract is that the party who is in breach may be unable to enforce the contract against the innocent party. Where the obligations of the parties are independent, that is to say, the obligation of one party to perform is not dependent upon performance by the other party, then breach by one party does not entitle the innocent party to abandon performance of his obligations under the contract. For example, a landlord's covenant to repair the premises and a tenant's covenant to pay rent are independent obligations so that a landlord is not entitled to refuse to repair the premises because the tenant has failed to pay his rent (*Taylor* v. *Webb* [1937] 2 KB 370). But, where the obligations of the parties are dependent, then a contracting party must generally be ready and willing to perform his obligations under the contract before he can maintain an action against the other party for breach of contract. Obligations created by a contract are generally interpreted as dependent obligations (see, for example, s.28 of the Sale of Goods Act 1979) so that breach will generally preclude the party in breach from bringing an action to enforce the contract.

19.6   The Right to Terminate Performance of the Contract

A breach of contract may entitle the innocent party to take the further step of terminating performance of the contract. Here it is necessary to recount a little of the material which we discussed in Chapter 10. It will be remembered that contractual terms can be classified as conditions, warranties or innominate terms. Breach of a warranty does not give the innocent party a right to terminate performance of the contract; it only enables him to claim damages. But breach of a condition and breach of an innominate term, where the consequences of the breach are sufficiently serious (see 10.5), do give the innocent party the additional right to terminate performance of the contract. It should be noted that I have used the rather clumsy expression 'right to terminate performance of the contract'. Contract scholars and judges have disagreed as to the correct 'title' to be given to this right of the innocent party. Professor Treitel (1991) calls this right a 'right to rescind'. This terminology is acceptable, if dangerous. The danger lies in the fact that it tends to create confusion between 'rescission for breach' and 'rescission for misrepresentation'. Where a contract is rescinded for misrepresentation, it is set aside for all purposes. The contract is set aside both retrospectively and prospectively and the aim is to restore the parties, as far as possible, to the position which they were in before they entered into the contract (see 13.8). But a contract which is 'rescinded' for breach is set aside prospectively, but not retrospectively (*Johnson* v. *Agnew* [1980] AC 367 and *Photo Production Ltd* v. *Securicor Transport Ltd* [1980] AC 827). Provided this fundamental distinction is grasped, no objection can be raised to the use of the term 'right to rescind for breach'. We must now turn to give further consideration to the consequences of the rule that breach operates prospectively but not retrospectively.

19.7   The Prospective Nature of Breach

The point that breach operates prospectively but not retrospectively is an important one. It is for this reason that I have termed the right of the innocent party a right to 'terminate performance of the contract' and not a right to terminate the contract. It is the obligations of the parties to perform their future primary contractual duties which are terminated (see Carter, 1991, p. 66). The contract is not set aside *ab initio* and so a contract term which is intended to regulate the consequences of breach or the termination must be taken into consideration by the court (*Heyman* v. *Darwins Ltd* [1942] AC 356). The prospective nature of a breach of contract becomes clearer if we adopt the language of primary and secondary obligations.

The modern source of this distinction between primary and secondary obligations is the judgment of Lord Diplock in *Photo Production Ltd* v. *Securicor Transport Ltd* (above). Lord Diplock stated that 'breaches of primary obligations give rise to substituted secondary obligations'. There are two principal types of secondary obligation. The first is a 'general secondary obligation'. In such a case the primary obligations of both parties, in so far as they have not yet been fully performed, remain unchanged, but the breach gives rise to a secondary obligation, imposed upon the party in breach, 'to pay monetary compensation to the [innocent] party for the loss sustained by him in consequence of the breach'. Such a general secondary obligation arises on the breach of a warranty; the primary obligations of the parties in so far as they have not been fully performed remain unchanged and a secondary obligation to pay damages for the loss suffered as a result of the breach is created.

But, where the breach of a primary obligation entitles the innocent party to elect to terminate performance of the contract, and he does so elect, all primary obligations of both parties remaining unperformed are put to an end and

> 'there is substituted by implication of law for the primary obligations of the party in default which remain unperformed a secondary obligation to pay monetary compensation to the other party for the loss sustained by him in consequence of their non-performance'.

This obligation Lord Diplock called an 'anticipatory secondary obligation'. The crucial feature of an 'anticipatory' secondary obligation is that it enables damages to be assessed by reference to those obligations which would have fallen due for performance at some time in the future (see further 21.3). Although the judgment of Lord Diplock is not entirely clear on this point, it is suggested that he intended that an anticipatory secondary obligation should arise in every case of termination following upon a breach of a condition (an interpretation which is supported by the approach of the Court of Appeal in *Lombard North Central plc* v. *Butterworth* [1987] QB 527, discussed at 10.3 and 21.3). English law does not generally distinguish between a condition which is created by the general law and a condition which has been expressly agreed by the parties (that is to say, it would not otherwise have constituted a condition). The reason why parties choose to elevate a term to the status of a condition is to emphasise the importance of the term and to give to the innocent party, not only the right to terminate performance in the event of breach, but also the right to claim loss of bargain damages (see Opeskin, 1990).

The distinction between primary and secondary obligations is therefore a useful one in that it helps us to see why there is no inconsistency between electing to terminate performance of the contract and, at the same time, claiming damages for the breach which gave rise to the right to terminate performance. Rather, the exercise of the right to terminate performance of the contract simply discharges the primary obligations of both parties *for the future* and imposes on the party in breach, by way of substitution, an anticipatory secondary obligation to pay damages to the innocent party.

19.8   The Right of Election

An innocent party is not obliged to exercise his right to terminate performance of the contract. As we have already noted, a breach which gives to the innocent party a right to terminate performance of the contract (often termed a 'repudiatory breach') in fact gives him an option. He can either terminate performance of the contract and claim damages ('accept the repudiation') or he can affirm the contract and claim damages. Although this right of election between termination and affirmation is notionally free, in practice it may be restricted by the rule that the innocent party must take reasonable steps to mitigate his loss (see further 20.5). For example, a seller, faced with a buyer who has breached a contract in such a way as to give to the seller a right to terminate performance of the contract, may elect not to affirm the contract but to sell the goods elsewhere, thereby disabling himself from performing his obligations under the contract. A seller may take such a course of action because, if he fails to take reasonable steps to sell the goods elsewhere, a court may conclude that he has failed to mitigate his loss and he will be unable to recover the loss caused by his failure to mitigate.

Where the innocent party wishes to accept the breach and terminate performance of the contract he must generally communicate his decision to the party in breach, although a sufficiently overt act which is inconsistent with the continuation of the contract, such as selling the subject-matter of the contract to a third party, may suffice even though there is no concurrent communication with the party in breach (*State Trading Corporation of India Ltd* v. *M. Golodetz Ltd* [1989] 2 Lloyd's Rep. 277, 286). Acceptance of a repudiation must be clear and unequivocal and mere inactivity will generally not be sufficiently unequivocal to constitute an acceptance for this purpose (*State Trading Corporation of India Ltd* v. *M. Golodetz Ltd* [1989] 2 Lloyd's Rep. 277, 286; cf. *The Santa Clara* [1993] 2 Lloyd's Rep. 301, 304). As we noted in Chapter 10, the party electing to terminate need not put forward the 'real reason' for his decision; as long as the terms of the contract entitle him to terminate he is justified in doing so, irrespective of his motive (*Arcos Ltd* v. *EA Ronaasen & Son* [1933] AC 470, see further 10.3). Indeed, the law goes so far as to allow the innocent party to put forward no reason or even an invalid reason for deciding to terminate but, provided that the innocent party can subsequently point to a good reason which, unknown to him, existed at the moment of breach, he will still be entitled to terminate (*The Mihalis Angelos* [1971] 1 QB 164, 200, 204).

If, on the other hand, the innocent party elects to affirm the contract, the contract remains in force, so that both parties remain bound to continue with the performance of their respective contractual obligations. An innocent party who accepts further performance of the contract after the breach may be held thereby to have affirmed the contract (*Davenport* v. *R* (1877) 3 App Cas 115). Affirmation does not prevent the innocent party from claiming damages for any loss which he has suffered as a result of the breach, unless the innocent party waives not only the right to terminate performance of the contract but also the right to claim damages for the breach (sometimes known as 'total waiver', see below).

Once the innocent party has exercised his right of election and chosen either to terminate or to affirm, that decision cannot be revoked. Thus, an innocent party who has exercised his right to terminate performance of the contract cannot subsequently affirm the contract because the effect of the termination of performance is to release *both* parties from their obligations to perform in the future and, once released from these obligations, they cannot subsequently be resurrected (*Johnson* v. *Agnew* (above)).

Confusion is sometimes caused by referring to this right of election as a species of 'waiver'. This terminology is confusing but is now probably too well established to be abandoned. 'Waiver', in the sense of election, must be distinguished from 'waiver by estoppel'. These two types of waiver were clearly distinguished by Lord Goff in his judgment in *The Kanchenjunga* [1990] 1 Lloyd's Rep 391, 397–9. A contracting party who is faced by a repudiatory breach has a choice: he can either terminate or he can affirm, but he cannot do both. When the innocent party makes his choice ('makes an election'), for example by choosing to affirm, he thereby *abandons* his inconsistent right, in this case to terminate. The exercise of this right of election may be called 'waiver by election', although it is suggested that less confusion would arise if this right was simply known as 'election' and the word 'waiver' was dropped from the title. But there is another sense in which the word 'waiver' may be used. In this sense waiver does not mean the abandonment of a right but rather it refers to the forbearance from exercising a right. This species of waiver is closely linked to, if not identical with the line of authority exemplified by *Hughes* v. *Metropolitan Railway Co* (1877) 2 App Cas 439 (discussed in more detail at 5.25). This type of waiver may be called 'waiver by estoppel' and it arises when the innocent party represents clearly and unequivocally to the party in default that he will not exercise his right to treat the contract as terminated or so conducts himself as to lead the party in default to believe that he will not exercise that right.

Both waiver by estoppel and waiver by election share some common elements. The principal similarity is that both appear to require that the party seeking to rely on it (that is, the party in default) must show a clear and unequivocal representation, by words or conduct, by the other party that he will not exercise his strict legal right to treat the contract as repudiated. But there are also important differences between the two types of waiver (see generally *The Kanchenjunga* (above) at p. 399). In the case of waiver by election the party who has to make the choice must either know or have obvious means of knowledge of the facts giving rise to the right, and possibly of the existence of the right. But in the case of waiver by estoppel neither knowledge of the circumstances nor of the right is required on the part of the person estopped; the other party is entitled to rely on the apparent election conveyed by the representation. Waiver by election is final and so has permanent effect, whereas the effect of estoppel may be suspensory only (although in the context of waiver of breach, the waiver may have permanent effect because, where the party in breach has relied to his detriment on the waiver – for example, by not attempting to remedy the situation when there was time to do so – the innocent party may, as a result of the waiver, lose for ever the right to terminate on account of that particular breach). Finally, waiver by estoppel requires that the party to whom the representation is made rely on that representation so as to make it inequitable for the representor to go back upon his representation. There is, however, no such requirement in the case of waiver by election; once the election has been made it is final whether or not the party has acted in reliance upon the election having been made.

One final distinction must be drawn. It is between the case in which a party waives his right to treat the contract as repudiated but does not abandon his right to claim damages for the loss suffered as a result of the breach, and the case where the innocent party waives not only his right to terminate performance of the contract but also his right to claim damages. The former is an example of waiver by election and so is governed by the rules relating to election, while the latter appears to be an example of estoppel (because the innocent party is purporting to abandon all of his rights under the contract, without any consideration being provided for that abandonment) and so should be subject to the rules relating to waiver by estoppel.

19.9 Anticipatory Breach

One contracting party may inform the other party, before the time fixed for performance under the contract, that he will not perform his obligations under the contract. This is called an anticipatory breach of contract, which entitles the innocent party to terminate performance of the contract immediately. The novel feature of anticipatory breach is that acceptance of the breach entitles the innocent party to claim damages at the date of the acceptance of the breach. He does not have to wait until the date fixed for performance, even though this has the effect of accelerating the obligations of the party in breach. It does seem somewhat illogical to say that a party can be in breach of contract *before* the time fixed for performance under the contract. The doctrine of anticipatory breach can best be rationalised as a breach of an implied term of the contract that neither party will, without just cause, repudiate his obligations under the contract before the time fixed for performance.

The operation of the doctrine of anticipatory breach can be illustrated by reference to the case of *Hochster* v. *De La Tour* (1853) 2 E & B 678. In April of 1852 the defendant agreed to employ the plaintiff to act as his courier for 3 months from 1 June. But on 11 May the defendant wrote to the plaintiff informing him that his services would no longer be required. The plaintiff commenced his action on 22 May and it was held that he was entitled to commence his action for damages at that date; he did not have to wait until 1 June when performance was due.

Once again the innocent party is not obliged to exercise his right to terminate performance of the contract; he can elect to affirm the contract and demand performance from the other party at the time stipulated in the contract. But where the innocent party does decide to terminate performance of the contract he must give notice to the party in breach that he is accepting the anticipatory breach (or otherwise overtly evidence his acceptance of the breach) and he must not act inconsistently with his decision to accept the breach.

Where the innocent party does decide to affirm the contract and demand performance at the stipulated time, a number of consequences flow from this decision. The first is that affirmation does not prevent the innocent party accepting the breach if, at the date fixed for performance, the other party still refuses to perform. The second is that the innocent party, in addition to affirming the contract, may continue with the performance of his obligations under the contract, even though he knows that the performance is not wanted by that other party. This is what happened in the controversial case of *White and Carter (Councils) Ltd* v. *McGregor* [1962] AC 413. The defendants entered into a contract with the plaintiffs under which the plaintiffs agreed to display advertisements of the defendants' garage for a period of three years on plates attached to litter bins. Later the same day, the defendants wrote to the plaintiffs stating that they no longer wished to continue with performance of the contract. The plaintiffs refused to accept the cancellation and proceeded to display the advertisements for the three year period and then brought an action to recover the contract price. The House of Lords held, by a majority of three to two, that the plaintiffs were entitled to recover the contract price. The minority held that the plaintiffs were not entitled to succeed because they had failed to mitigate their loss. But the majority held, quoting from the judgment of Asquith LJ in *Howard* v. *Pickford Tool Co Ltd* [1951] 1 KB 417, 421, that 'an unaccepted repudiation is a thing writ in water and of no value to anybody'. The plaintiffs were not under an obligation to accept the defendants' breach, even though it was 'unfortunate' that the plaintiffs had 'saddled themselves with an unwanted contract causing an apparent waste of time and money'.

The principle laid down in *White and Carter* is, in fact, the subject of a number of qualifications. The first is that the innocent party cannot compel the party in breach to co-operate with him so that, where the innocent party cannot continue with performance without the co-operation of the party in breach, he will be compelled to accept the breach (*Hounslow LBC* v. *Twickenham Garden Developments Ltd* [1971] Ch 233). The second qualification is derived from the judgment of Lord Reid in *White and Carter* when he said that

'it may well be that, if it can be shown that a person has no legitimate interest, financial or otherwise, in performing the contract rather than claiming damages, he ought not to be allowed to saddle the other party with an additional burden with no benefit to himself'.

Lord Reid's view on this point did not appear to be shared by the other members of the House of Lords, but it has subsequently been regarded as part of the ratio of the case (see *Hounslow LBC* v. *Twickenham Garden Developments Ltd* (above)) and it has been developed in subsequent cases as a means of limiting the principle established in *White and Carter*. In *Clea Shipping Corp* v. *Bulk Oil International Ltd (The Alaskan Trader)* [1984] 1 All ER 129, after an extensive review of the authorities, Lloyd J concluded that:

'there comes a point at which the court will cease, on general equitable principles, to allow the innocent party to enforce his contract according to its strict legal terms'.

This 'equitable principle' cannot be invoked simply because the innocent party has behaved 'unreasonably'. The plaintiffs in *White and Carter* behaved unreasonably in continuing with performance of the contract, but they were nevertheless entitled to recover the contract price. But, where the innocent party acts 'wholly unreasonably' (*The Odenfield* [1978] 2 Lloyds Rep 357, 373), then the court may refuse to allow the innocent party to continue with performance and claim the contract price. Such was the case in *The Alaskan Trader* (above). The plaintiffs chartered a ship to the defendants for 24 months. After one year the ship required extensive repairs. The defendants stated that they had no further use for the ship but the plaintiffs nevertheless spent £800 000 in repairing the ship and, when it was repaired, they kept the ship and its crew ready to receive instructions from the defendants. The arbitrator held that the plaintiffs had acted wholly unreasonably in failing to accept the breach and this finding was upheld on appeal to Lloyd J.

On the other hand, a decision to affirm the contract may work to the disadvantage of the innocent party. The first disadvantage is that an innocent party who affirms the contract may lose his right to sue for damages completely if the contract is frustrated between the date of the unaccepted anticipatory breach and the date fixed for performance (*Avery* v. *Bowden* (1856) 6 E & B 953). Secondly, an innocent party who affirms the contract but subsequently breaches the contract himself cannot argue that the unaccepted anticipatory breach excused him from his obligation to perform under the contract. Where the breach is not accepted the parties remain subject to their obligations under the contract, so that the 'innocent party' may find himself liable to pay damages for breach of contract if he fails to accept the breach and subsequently breaches the contract himself (*The Simona* [1989] AC 788).

Summary

1 A breach of contract is committed when a party without lawful excuse fails or refuses to perform what is due from him under the contract, performs defectively or incapacitates himself from performing.

2 The question whether or not a particular contract has been breached depends upon the precise construction of the terms of the contract. Many contractual duties are strict.

3 A breach of contract does not automatically bring a contract to an end. A breach of contract gives to the innocent party a right to claim damages and it may give him the additional right to terminate performance of the contract.

4 When the performance of a contract is terminated because of breach, the obligation to perform is only terminated for the future. The contract is not set aside *ab initio*.

5 An innocent party is not obliged to exercise his right to terminate performance of the contract; he can elect to terminate or to affirm, although the effect of the doctrine of mitigation is to reduce the scope for affirmation.

6 A party who is in breach of contract may be unable to enforce the contract against the innocent party. But where the breach is of an independent, rather than a dependent obligation, breach will not entitle the innocent party to abandon performance of his obligations under the contract.

7 One contracting party may inform the other party, before the time fixed for performance under the contract, that he will not perform his obligations under the contract. This is called an anticipatory breach of contract, which entitles the innocent party to terminate performance of the contract immediately.

8 An innocent party who affirms the contract after an anticipatory breach may continue with the performance of his obligations under the contract, even though he knows that the performance is not wanted by that other party, provided that contractual performance does not require the co-operation of the other party to the contract and he has a 'legitimate interest' in the performance of the contract.

Exercises

1 What is a breach of contract and what are its consequences?
2 Distinguish between 'rescission for breach' and 'rescission for misrepresentation'.
3 Distinguish between a primary obligation and a secondary obligation.
4 What is an anticipatory breach?
5 What 'legitimate interest' did the plaintiffs in *White and Carter (Councils) Ltd* v. *McGregor* have in the performance of the contract?
6 Did the plaintiffs in *The Alaskan Trader* (above) act 'wholly unreasonably'? (see further Burrows, 1987 pp. 278–282).
7 Adam Ltd employ Steve to go to Japan and prepare an elaborate report for the company on the state of the Japanese market. Two days before Steve's departure, Adam Ltd inform Steve that they no longer require the report because they have decided not to commence trading in Japan. Steve nevertheless goes to Japan and prepares the report at a cost of £25 000. Adam Ltd are now refusing to pay for the report. Advise Steve.

20 Damages for Breach of Contract

20.1 Introduction

We have already noted that a breach of contract gives rise to an action for damages, whether the term broken is a condition, a warranty or an innominate term. In this chapter we shall discuss the principles which are applied by the courts when assessing the damages payable on a breach of contract. The principles applied by the courts are of great significance to the debate about the basis of the law of contract, to which we referred in Chapter 1. The claim that contract law can be separated from the law of tort and the law of restitution rests, to a large extent, on the proposition that the law of contract seeks to fulfil the expectations engendered by a binding promise (see 1.4). In this chapter we shall put that claim to the test by asking ourselves the fundamental question: does the law of contract really fulfil the expectations engendered by a binding promise? But before we seek to answer that question we must define the 'expectation interest' with greater precision and we must also examine the question whether the law of contract protects either the 'reliance interest' or the 'restitution interest'.

20.2 Compensation and the Different 'Interests'

The starting point must be that the aim of an award of damages is to compensate the plaintiff for the loss which he has suffered as a result of the defendant's breach of contract. The aim is not to punish the defendant. A breach of contract is a civil wrong; it is not a criminal offence. Although punitive damages can, in certain narrowly defined circumstances, be awarded in a tort action, they cannot be awarded in a purely contractual action, even where the defendant has calculated that he will make a profit from his breach of contract (*Cassell & Co* v. *Broome* [1972] AC 1027). The defendant may be said to have behaved 'badly', but he will not be punished by an award of punitive damages (the Law Commission has recently issued a Consultation Paper (1993a) on the subject but its provisional recommendation (p. 139) is that there should be no reform of this area of the law).

The proposition that damages are compensatory gives rise to a further question. That question is: for what is it that the plaintiff is entitled to be compensated? Theoretically, a plaintiff could claim compensation on one of a number of different grounds (see Fuller and Perdue, 1936 and the discussion by the High Court of Australia in *Commonwealth of Australia* v. *Amann Aviation Pty Ltd* (1991) 66 ALJR 123, noted by Treitel, 1992). In the first place, a plaintiff could claim the protection of his 'expectation interest'. The basis of such a claim is that the plaintiff's expectations, engendered by the promise of the defendant that he will perform his contractual obligations, have not been fulfilled and that damages should compensate him for his disappointed expectations by putting him 'in as good a position as he would have occupied had the defendant performed his promise'. Secondly, a plaintiff may claim the protection of his 'reliance interest', that is to say that, as a result of the defendant's promise to perform his contractual obligations, the plaintiff has acted to his detriment in entering into the contract and the award of damages should compensate him to the extent that he has relied to his detriment upon the promise of the defendant. The aim here is 'to put the plaintiff in as good a position as he was in before the [defendant's] promise was made'. Finally, a plaintiff may assert that his 'restitution interest' should be protected. A plaintiff who claims the protection of his restitution interest does not wish to be compensated for the loss which he has suffered; rather, he wishes to deprive the defendant of a gain which he has made at the plaintiff's expense. Which of these 'measures' can be claimed by a plaintiff in an action for damages for breach of contract? More importantly, what factors would persuade a plaintiff to elect to seek the recovery of one measure rather than another?

The most important factor is obviously the amount of damages which a plaintiff can recover by way of compensation. Which is more advantageous to the plaintiff; the expectation measure, the reliance measure or the restitution measure? A very simple example will help us to answer this question. Let us suppose that I enter into a contract to purchase a word processor for £2000. Let us make the further assumption that the market value of such a word processor is, in fact, £2000. In breach of contract the seller provides me with a defective word processor which is worth only £1000. I fulfil my side of the bargain and pay £2000.

An award of damages which protected my expectation interest would aim to put me in the position which I would have been in had the contract been performed according to its terms. Had the contract been performed according to its terms, I would have obtained a word processor worth £2000, whereas I have obtained a word processor which is worth only £1000. Therefore the expectation measure is calculated by deducting the value of what I have actually received (£1000) from the value of what I expected to receive (£2000). Damages would therefore be assessed at £1000.

An award of damages which sought to protect my reliance interest would seek to put me in the position which I would have been in had I not entered into the contract. Had I not entered into the contract, I would not have parted with my £2000 and I would not have received a word processor worth £1000. So the reliance measure is calculated by deducting the value of what I have received (£1000) from the amount which I have paid out (£2000). Damages would, once again, be assessed at £1000 so that, on the facts of this case, the expectation measure and the reliance measure would be exactly the same.

An award which sought to protect my restitution interest would restore to me the benefit which I had conferred upon the seller. So I would be entitled to the return of the £2000 and the seller would be entitled to the return of the word processor.

Although we have noted that the reliance measure and the expectation measure can be exactly the same, in other cases they can be radically different. The reason for the coincidence in my example was that the contract price and the market value of a word processor which complied with the contractual specifications were exactly the same. Had these figures been different, then the measures would have been different. Let us suppose that I had promised to pay £2000 but that the word processor was, in fact, worth only £1500. This time the expectation measure would be £1500 (the value of what I expected to receive) less £1000 (the value of what I actually received), which equals £500. But the reliance measure would be £2000 (what I paid out) minus £1000 (the value of what I received), which equals £1000. So a plaintiff will wish to resort to the reliance measure where he has made a bad bargain, in an effort to escape from the consequences of his own bargain. On the other hand, if I had made a good bargain so that the market value of the word processor was £2500, the expectation measure would be £2500 less £1000, which equals £1500, whereas the reliance measure would remain at £2000 less £1000, which equals £1000. Therefore it is only where the plaintiff has made a bad bargain that he will want to claim the reliance measure; in other cases the expectation measure will be more advantageous to a plaintiff.

20.3 The Expectation Interest

The general rule is that an award of damages for breach of contract seeks to protect the plaintiff's expectation interest. The classic statement of this general principle can be found in the judgment of Parke B in *Robinson* v. *Harman* (1848) 1 Ex 850, 855:

'the rule of the common law is, that where a party sustains loss by reason of a breach of contract, he is, so far as money can do it, to be placed in the same situation, with respect to damages, as if the contract had been performed'.

The justification for the award of the expectation measure is that a binding promise creates in the promisee an expectation of performance and the remedy granted for the breach of such a binding promise seeks to fulfil or to protect that expectation. But there is an element of ambiguity in the proposition that damages seek to put the plaintiff in the position he would have been in had the contract been performed.

Two possible measures could put the plaintiff in the position which he would have been in had the contract been performed according to its terms. The first is the difference in value between what the plaintiff has received and what he expected to receive and the second is the cost of putting the plaintiff into the position which he would have been in had the contract been fully performed. In many cases the two measures will produce the same result. For example, if, in breach of contract, a seller fails to deliver the promised goods, and the buyer goes out into the market place and purchases substitute goods, the diminution in value and the cost of cure will be exactly the same. But in some cases the two measures can produce very different results. The case of *Tito* v. *Waddell (No 2)* [1977] Ch 106, 328–338 neatly illustrates such a divergence. The defendants were granted licences to mine phosphate on Ocean Island, a small island in the Pacific Ocean. They covenanted with the plaintiffs, who were the owners of the island, to restore the land to its original condition when they had finished mining by replanting trees on the island. In breach of contract the defendants failed to carry out the replanting. The plaintiff islanders claimed damages for breach of contract. They claimed the cost of cure measure which they calculated at $A73 140 per acre. The defendants argued that the plaintiffs' damages should be nominal, being measured by the diminution in value of the island caused by their breach of contract. Megarry VC held that the cost of replanting did not represent the true loss to the plaintiffs, essentially because he did not think that the plaintiffs had any intention of carrying out the replanting (by the time of trial they were well established on another island some 1500 miles away). But he held that, in 'normal circumstances', a plaintiff would be entitled to the cost of cure measure if he had carried out the work necessary to bring about the cure or if he satisfied the court that he intended to carry out that work. Having rejected the cost of cure measure, Megarry VC also rejected the argument that damages should be nominal. Applying the diminution in value measure he held that, while there was no market for 'worked-out plots of land in Ocean Island', damages should be assessed at $A75 per acre. While it was better than nominal damages, the sum appears insignificant when it is realised that it is fractionally over 0.1 per cent of the sum claimed by the plaintiffs as the cost of replanting the island.

The cost of cure measure was successfully recovered by the plaintiff in *Radford* v. *De Froberville* [1977] 1 WLR 1262. The plaintiff sold a portion of his land to the defendant and part of the agreement was that the defendant would build a boundary wall which would divide the plot which the defendant had bought from the plot which the plaintiff had retained. The defendant failed to build the wall. The plaintiff brought an action for damages for breach of contract. The defendant argued that the plaintiff was entitled to damages based on the diminution in value of the land as a result of his breach of contract. However, the difference in value was nominal so the plaintiff claimed the cost of cure, which was £1200 at the date of breach but, by the time of the trial of the action, had risen to £3400. Oliver J held that the plaintiff was entitled to the cost of cure measure because that measure was the most likely to achieve the aim of putting the plaintiff in the position which he would have been in had the contract been performed according to its terms and he was satisfied that the plaintiff genuinely wanted the work carried out. What would have been the position if the plaintiff in *Radford* had intended to sell the property? It is suggested that, in such a case, the proper measure should be the diminution in value because the plaintiff's interest in the property would then be a purely financial one, namely to realise a profit on its sale, and the diminution in value would adequately protect his interest in that profit.

The approach in *Tito* and *Radford* has been criticised by Professor Birks (1987) on the ground that 'the condition for securing a substantial award in respect of that part of the consideration unperformed is evidence of an intent on the part of the plaintiff as to the future, which intent can be abandoned once the damages are safely in his pocket'. There are now some signs that this criticism has been accepted by the judiciary. Indeed, the Court of Appeal in *Ruxley Electronics & Construction Ltd* v. *Forsyth* [1994] 1 WLR 650, held, by a majority, that a plaintiff was not required to give an undertaking to the court that he would carry out the work of repair before he could obtain cost of cure damages.

Instead the court emphasised that a party who wishes to recover the cost of cure measure must show that it is reasonable for him to carry out the work of repair. But the critical point to note is that the court concluded that this reasonableness requirement is no more than a matter of mitigation of loss. Thus Staughton LJ stated that the difference in value measure was 'often appropriate' when 'the building or chattel which has been damaged . . . is of a kind that is commonly available'. This is because the 'cheapest way to make good the loss will often be to sell the building or chattel in question, and buy another which . . . is not damaged or does answer to the specification in the contract'. But the difference in value may be inadequate when the innocent party's building or chattel has some unique quality and so cannot be replaced. In such a case it may be entirely reasonable for the innocent party to claim the cost of cure measure, even 'if the cost of repair or reinstatement . . . is very expensive'.

20.4 The Restitution Interest

Can a plaintiff seek the protection of his restitution interest rather than his expectation interest? The answer is that a plaintiff does not have a free choice between the two measures. A plaintiff can obtain a restitutionary remedy only when he can establish that the defendant was enriched, that the enrichment was at the plaintiff's expense and that it is unjust that the defendant retain the benefit without recompensing the plaintiff. The classic example of a restitutionary claim is a claim to recover money paid under a mistake of fact (see, for example, *Barclays Bank Ltd* v. *WJ Simms Ltd* [1980] 1 QB 677). But, where the ground on which restitution is sought is that the defendant has broken his contract with the plaintiff, then a restitutionary remedy is available only within very narrow confines. There are essentially two grounds (20.5–20.6) on which a plaintiff may seek to protect his restitution interest consequent upon a breach of contract by the defendant.

20.5   Failure of Consideration and Enrichment by Subtraction

The first ground on which a plaintiff may seek a restitutionary remedy is that the *basis* upon which he has conferred the benefit upon the defendant has failed because of the defendant's breach of contract. The argument of the plaintiff is that he has conferred a benefit upon the defendant only for the purpose of the performance of the contract and, now that performance has been abandoned because of the defendant's breach of contract, the benefit ought to be restored to him.

But money paid to a defendant is only recoverable upon such a ground where there has been a total failure of consideration, that is to say, the plaintiff has received no part of what he has bargained for. A simple example is a buyer who pays a seller in advance and the seller, in breach of contract, subsequently refuses to deliver the goods. The buyer can recover the prepayment on the ground that there has been a total failure of consideration. Such a claim may prove to be very useful to a plaintiff who has entered into a bad bargain, because his restitution interest will exceed his expectation interest. Let us suppose that I agree to buy a desk for £200, which is in fact worth only £150. If, for some reason, the seller refused to deliver the desk, I would be able to recover the £200 because the consideration for the payment has wholly failed. I received no part of the promised performance and there is nothing to prevent me from recovering my £200 and purchasing a desk elsewhere for £150. Since there has been no performance of the contract, such a claim does not involve the court in placing a different value upon contractual performance than that agreed by the parties and so no objection can be raised to such a restitutionary claim. But, where the failure of consideration is only partial, that is to say, the plaintiff has received some part, no matter how small, of the promised performance then the restitutionary claim is barred (*Whincup* v. *Hughes* (1871) LR 6 CP 78). The reason for this would appear to be that, once contractual performance has begun, there is a real risk that a restitutionary claim would result in the court placing a different value upon contractual performance than that agreed by the parties because it cannot be assumed that the contract price is earned incrementally (contrast Burrows, 1984a).

Where the claim is not for the return of money but for the value of goods supplied or services rendered under the contract then more difficult questions arise. It is clear that, where the contract is terminated on the ground of the defendant's breach of contract, the plaintiff has a right to elect either to proceed in contract or in restitution (*Planché* v. *Colburn* (1831) 8 Bing 14), but it is not clear whether in a restitutionary action the contract price acts as a ceiling on the sum recoverable. Dicta can be found to support the proposition that the contract price does not act as a ceiling (*Lodder* v. *Slowey* [1904] AC 442, *Rover International Ltd* v. *Cannon Film Sales Ltd (No. 3)* [1989] 1 WLR 912) and such a rule was adopted in the American case of *Boomer* v. *Muir* 24 P 2d 570 (1933). But it is suggested that, given that breach operates prospectively (19.7), and the goods are supplied and services rendered under what was, at the time, a valid subsisting contract, it is difficult to see why the courts should ignore the contract in assessing the value of the goods supplied or services performed.

20.6 Enrichment by Wrongdoing

Secondly, a plaintiff may seek a restitutionary remedy on the ground that the defendant has, as a result of his breach of contract, obtained an unjust benefit, in the form of a profit which he would not otherwise have made. This claim differs from the first type of restitutionary claim because here the defendant's enrichment is not by subtraction from the plaintiff (see Birks, 1985). In the 'failure of consideration' claim the defendant was enriched by the receipt of a benefit which passed from the plaintiff to the defendant. But in this type of case the defendant has been enriched by his wrongdoing, namely his breach of contract, and, in such a case, there is no requirement that the enrichment be by subtraction from the plaintiff.

The nature of such a claim can be illustrated by the fact situation of *Teacher* v. *Calder* (1899) 1 F (HL) 39. The plaintiff agreed to invest £15 000 in the defendant's timber business. In return the defendant promised that he would keep at least £15 000 of his own money in the business. In breach of contract the defendant withdrew much of his capital from the business and invested the money in a distillery, where he earned large profits. The plaintiff sought to recover, by way of damages, the profits which the defendant had made as a result of his investment in the distillery. But it was held that the damages should be assessed by reference to the loss which the timber business had suffered as a result of the failure of the defendant to keep the promised sum of money invested in it.

This approach is consistent with the traditional expectation measure of recovery; that is to say, the aim of the award of damages was to put the plaintiff in the position which he would have been in had the defendant carried out his obligations under the contract. The aim of the award of damages was to compensate the plaintiff, not to require the defendant to disgorge the gain which he had obtained from his breach. But is it ever possible for a plaintiff to recover the gains which the defendant has made from his breach of contract? Should such a claim have succeeded on the facts of *Teacher*?

The answer to the first question is that gain-based damages are not generally recoverable for a breach of contract. The issue was recently considered by the Court of Appeal in *Surrey County Council* v. *Bredero Homes Ltd* [1993] 1 WLR 1361. The plaintiffs entered into a contract with the defendant development company, under which the plaintiffs agreed to sell to the defendants a portion of land which they no longer required. The defendants covenanted to develop the land in accordance with the planning permission given and to pursue diligently the development of the land to its completion, complying with the planning permission and the scheme approved for the development of the land. The defendants subsequently obtained fresh planning premission which had the effect of rendering the development more profitable for them by increasing the number of dwellings from 72 to 77. They did not, however, apply to the plaintiffs for a variation of their covenant to build in accordance with the initial grant of planning permission. The plaintiffs sought to recover damages assessed by reference to the profits which the defendants had made from their breach of covenant. The Court of Appeal rejected their claim and held that the plaintiffs were only entitled to recover nominal damages because they had suffered no loss as a result of the breach. This seems unsatisfactory. Here we have a flagrant breach of contract for which there was no effective remedy.

The plaintiffs put forward a number of arguments to support their claim to gain-based (or restitutionary) damages. All were rejected. The first was that the defendants' breach of contract was deliberate or cynical. The court refused to regard this is as the vital factor. Steyn LJ stated that to focus on the motive of the party in breach was contrary to the general approach of contract law. It is also a test which is difficult to apply in parctice. One reason why a party breaks a contract is that he has found a better deal elsewhere. Such a breach is deliberate but English law does not allow gain-based damages to be recovered solely on this ground. As Steyn LJ remarked, a rule which compelled a contract-breaker to disgorge gains on such a ground might have a tendency to discourage economic activity.

Secondly, the plaintiffs argued that a court should be prepared to award gain-based damages where the party in breach could have been restrained by an injunction from committing the breach or been compelled by specific performance to perform the contract. It is an observable phenomenon that jurisdictions which are more willing to grant specific performance are also more willing to award gain-based damages. But the Court of Appeal rejected the argument on the ground that the availability of gain-based damages should not depend upon the availability of the wholly different remedy of specific performance.

Despite the general hostility of the Court of Appeal to the award of gain-based damages, cases can be found in the books in which damages appear to have been assessed, not by reference to the plaintiff's loss, but by reference to the gain which the defendant has made as a result of the breach. One such case is *Penarth Dock Engineering* v. *Pound* [1963] 1 Lloyd's Rep 359 (another is *Wrotham Park Estate Co Ltd* v. *Parkside Homes Ltd* [1974] 1 WLR 798, which was extensively discussed by the Court of Appeal in *Bredero*). In *Penarth* the defendants bought a floating dock and, in breach of contract, they failed to remove it from its berth. The plaintiff sellers sued for damages for breach of contract. The defendants argued that damages should be nominal because the sellers would not have made any other use of the berth as the docks were to be shut down. This argument was rejected by Lord Denning on the ground that the measure of damages was not what the plaintiffs had lost, but the benefit which the defendants had obtained as a result of the breach and so damages were awarded on the basis of a fair market rental of the berth. Although this case appears to be a clear example of the award of gain-based damages, there are two difficulties which surround it. The first is that the plaintiff also brought a claim in the tort of trespass, where it is clear that gain-based damages can be recovered and so the case could be explained away as a tort case (on the other hand, Lord Denning did not place any emphasis on the fact that it was also a tort claim). The second is that it is possible to bring the case within the fold of compensatory damages by arguing that the plaintiff had suffered a real loss, namely the loss of the right to sell to the defendant the right to use his property (see Sharpe and Waddams, 1982). Although it can be squeezed within the compensatory framework, the more natural interpretation is that it is a case in which the aim of the award of damages was to strip the defendant of the gain which he had made as a result of his breach of contract (and see the rejection of the loss of opportunity to bargain analysis by Steyn LJ in *Surrey County Council* v. *Bredero* (above)).

So it cannot be said that gain-based damages are *never* available for a breach of contract, although it has to be recognised that they are only available within very narrow (and uncertain) limits. It has been argued that the aim of the law would be better served if there were to be available to the innocent party a 'restitutionary claim for an accounting of the profit which a promisor has gained from his breach of contract' (Jones, 1983) and the issue is presently under consideration by the Law Commission (1993a). Thus, Professor Jones argues that it is difficult to accept the 'justice' of a case such as *Tito* v. *Waddell (No 2)* (above), where the defendants saved themselves considerable expense by refusing to carry out the replanting and yet the plaintiffs' damages were 'trivial' because they had suffered no 'loss'. This does seem harsh. But, once it is recognised that a claim for the profits of the breach can be made, it is very difficult to define the limits of the claim and there is no consensus among commentators as to the circumstances in which such a claim should lie (see Burrows, 1993b). Professor Jones maintains that gain-based damages should always be available subject to the discretion of the court 'to refuse an accounting if it thinks proper to do so'. The Law Commission has suggested (1993a) that gain-based damages should be available if a two-stage test is satisfied. First, there must be 'either interference with a proprietary right or an analogous right (such as confidentiality and the rights enjoyed by the beneficiary of a fiduciary relationship) or deliberate wrongdoing which could have been restrained by injunction'. Second, 'the gains made by the defendant must be attributable to the interest infringed'. Such an approach could be applied to the facts of *Penarth Dock* where the defendants did interfere with a proprietary right of the plaintiff. The difficulty with this approach relates to the definition of 'proprietary'. It can be argued that a contractual right is a form of property. In *Bredero* Steyn LJ argued that 'property' must be interpreted in a wide sense, yet he could not have intended it to encompass a right of action for breach of contract because he would then have had to award restitutionary damages on the facts of *Bredero*. The exact meaning of 'property' therefore remains to be ascertained.

An alternative analysis is that a plaintiff should only be entitled to claim restitutionary damages where compensatory damages are 'demonstrably an inadequate remedy, having regard to the objectives which the victim of the breach had hoped to achieve through full performance of the contract' (Birks, 1987). The injustice of a case such as *Tito* v. *Waddell* stems from the fact that compensatory damages appear to be manifestly inadequate (the same analysis can be applied to *Penarth Dock*). The difficulty with this analysis is that it suggests that it is the assessment of compensatory damages which is defective and that the response should be to reform the rules relating to the assessment of compensatory damages and not to award gain-based damages. On the other hand, it may help to explain a case such as *Teacher* v. *Calder* (above), where compensatory damages were adequate. The plaintiff was made whole and his expectations fulfilled by the award of compensatory damages and he had no claim on the profits made by the defendant as a result of the breach.

There is no one theory which has yet been able to explain the circumstances when gain-based damages are available or should be available for a breach of contract. As Burrows has recently stated (1993b), 'consolidation of the present range of restitutionary damages is more important than problematic and controversial expansion'.

20.7 Reliance Interest

The plaintiff may wish to claim the protection of his reliance interest so that he is put in the position which he would have been in had he not entered into a contract with the defendant. It should be noted, however, that, where damages are awarded to fulfil the plaintiff's expectation interest, then the sum awarded will often include both gains prevented and losses caused because, had the contract been performed according to its terms, the plaintiff would have been reimbursed for his expenditure incurred as well as being rewarded by the receipt of his profit. A plaintiff is really only interested in attempting to recover his reliance interest alone where that interest exceeds his expectation interest.

The general rule, affirmed in *CCC Films (London) Ltd* v. *Impact Quadrant Films Ltd* [1985] QB 16, is that a plaintiff has an unfettered right to elect whether to claim for loss of bargain damages or for wasted expenditure (contrast the view taken by some members of the High Court of Australia in *Commonwealth of Australia* v. *Amann Aviation Pty Ltd*

(1991) 66 ALJR 123, 153, 164 where it was argued that there was no right of election and that a claim for reliance loss was only available where the plaintiff had not suffered or could not prove a loss of profit and that the reliance loss was therefore simply a way of putting the plaintiff into the position which he would have been in had the contract been performed). The general right of election is subject to an exception where the plaintiff seeks to recover his reliance loss in an attempt to escape the consequences of his bad bargain. In *C and P Haulage Co Ltd* v. *Middleton* [1983] 3 All ER 94, the plaintiff was given a licence to occupy premises on a renewable six monthly basis. He spent some money on improving the property, even though it was expressly provided in the contract that the fixtures were not to be removed at the end of the licence. The defendants ejected the plaintiff from the premises in breach of contract and the plaintiff sought to recover as damages the cost of the improvements which he had carried out to the property. His action failed on the ground that the breach had not caused him any loss because he would have been in the same position had the contract been terminated lawfully. The Court of Appeal held that the plaintiff's loss did not flow from the breach but from the fact that he had entered into a contract under which he had agreed that he would not be able to remove the fixtures at the end of the lease. It was held that a plaintiff could not recover his reliance losses where that would enable him to escape from his bad bargain or would reverse the contractual allocation of risk. It is for the defendant to show that the bargain was a bad one for the plaintiff. The only situation in which an innocent party can escape the consequences of his bad bargain is where there has been a total failure of consideration (see 20.5). In such a situation there has been no performance under the contract and so there is no objection to the reversal of the contractual allocation of risk.

A plaintiff may, however, wish to recover his reliance loss where he has incurred reliance expenditure before the conclusion of the contract. In *Anglia Television Ltd* v. *Reed* [1972] 1 QB 60, the plaintiffs engaged the defendant to star in a film which they were making. At the last moment the defendant repudiated the contract and the plaintiffs had to abandon the film because they were unable to find a replacement actor. Lord Denning said that, where the plaintiffs claimed their loss of expenditure, they were not limited to expenditure incurred after the contract was concluded but that they could also claim for expenditure incurred before the contract was concluded provided that it was within the reasonable contemplation of the parties that it would be likely to be wasted as a result of the defendant's breach. Such pre-contract expenditure could not be regarded as part of the expectation interest because there was no evidence that the plaintiffs would have made a net profit from the film and so would have recovered their pre-contract expenditure.

On the other hand, a plaintiff may be confined to the recovery of his reliance losses where he cannot prove what his expectation losses would have been. Such was the case in *McRae* v. *Commonwealth Disposals Commission* (1951) 84 CLR 377 (see 14.6), where the speculative nature of the enterprise made it impossible for the plaintiffs to quantify their expectations with any degree of precision. The High Court of Australia confined the plaintiffs to the recovery of their expenses incurred in mounting the salvage expedition and to the return of their prepayment. But *McRae* is an extreme case and the courts are extremely reluctant to conclude that the plaintiff's expectations are so speculative that they cannot be valued. In *Chaplin* v. *Hicks* [1911] 2 KB 786, the defendant, by his breach of contract, denied the plaintiff the opportunity to participate in a beauty contest. The court could not assess the likelihood of the plaintiff winning the contest but they awarded her damages of £100 to represent her loss of a chance to win the contest.

20.8 The Date of Assessment

One very important point relates to the date on which damages fall to be assessed. It was established in *Johnson* v. *Agnew* [1980] AC 367, that damages are to be assessed as at the date of breach. But, where the plaintiff is unaware of the breach, damages will generally be assessed as at the date on which the plaintiff could, with reasonable diligence, have discovered the breach. Similarly, where it is not reasonable to expect the plaintiff to take immediate steps to mitigate his loss, the date of assessment will be postponed until such time as it is reasonable to expect the plaintiff to mitigate his loss (*Radford* v. *De Froberville* (above)).

20.9 The Commitment to the Protection of the Expectation Interest

Although the stated purpose of the law of contract is to put the innocent party in the position which he would have been in had the contract been performed, there are a number of doctrines and rules which weaken the commitment of the law of contract to the protection of the expectation interest. In the following sections (20.10–20.14) we shall consider some of these doctrines.

20.10 Mitigation

A plaintiff is under a 'duty' to mitigate his loss. It is, however, technically incorrect to state that the plaintiff is under a 'duty' to mitigate his loss because he does not incur any liability if he fails to mitigate his loss. The plaintiff is entirely free to act as he thinks fit but, if he fails to mitigate his loss, he will be unable to recover that portion of his loss which is attributable to his failure to mitigate. The aim of the doctrine of mitigation is to prevent the avoidable waste of resources. There are two aspects to the mitigation doctrine.

The first is that the injured party must take all reasonable steps to minimise his loss. The plaintiff is not required to 'take any step which a reasonable and prudent man would not ordinarily take in the course of his business' (*British Westinghouse Co* v. *Underground Electric Ry Co* [1912] AC 673); he is only obliged to take *reasonable* steps to minimise his loss. Thus, where a seller fails to deliver the goods, the buyer must generally go out into the market place and purchase substitute goods. But a plaintiff need not take steps which would embroil him in complicated litigation (*Pilkington* v. *Wood* [1953] Ch 770), nor is he required to put his commercial reputation at risk (*James Finlay & Co Ltd* v. *Kwik Hoo Tong* [1929] 1 KB 400). The second aspect of the mitigation doctrine is that the plaintiff must not unreasonably incur expense subsequent to the breach of contract (*Banco de Portugal* v. *Waterlow & Sons Ltd* [1932] AC 452).

As Professor Atiyah has pointed out (1986b), the doctrine of mitigation 'does in practice make an enormous dent in the theory that the promisee is entitled to full protection for his expectations'. In Chapter 1 we discussed the following example. I enter into a contract to sell you 10 apples for £2. I refuse to perform my side of the bargain and am in breach of contract. But you must mitigate your loss. So you buy 10 apples for £2 at a nearby market. If you sue me for damages, what is your loss? You have not suffered any and you cannot enforce my promise. As Professor Atiyah has stated (1979):

'the reality is that the bindingness of executory contracts protects not the expectation of performance, but the expectation of profit; and even that is only protected so long as the promisee cannot secure it elsewhere'.

This point is an extremely good one. Professor Fried (1981) has argued that the 'duty' to mitigate is 'a kind of altruistic duty, towards one's contractual partner, the more altruistic that it is directed to a partner in the wrong. But it is a duty without cost, since the victim of the breach is never worse off for having mitigated'. But, as Professor Atiyah has pointed out (1986g), altruism finds little favour within a liberal theory of contract and it is surprising to find it being invoked here in favour of a contract breaker. He has also challenged the view that the 'duty' to mitigate is a duty without cost on the ground that, in practice, it 'often places the innocent party in a dilemma. If he fails to mitigate, his damages will be cut, and if he does mitigate, he may find that his only recoverable damages are trivial reliance costs not worth pursuing'. It is probably true to say that there is no one factor which explains the present role of mitigation within the law of contract (see Bridge, 1989), but that it is attributable to such factors as the need to avoid waste, the remoteness of the loss and the responsibility of the plaintiff to seek to minimise the loss. It underlines the fact that the law of contract is not wholeheartedly committed to the protection of the expectation interest but that, in the words of Burrows (1983), the doctrine of mitigation simply adds:

'a supplementary policy to those policies justifying protection of the expectation interest; and this supplementary policy is that the promisee should not leave it simply to the courts to ensure fulfilment of his expectations, but should rather take it upon himself to adopt other reasonable means to ensure the fulfilment of his expectations'.

20.11 Remoteness

A plaintiff's expectation interest will not be fully protected where some of the loss which he has suffered is too 'remote' a consequence of the defendant's breach of contract. The doctrine of remoteness limits the right of the innocent party to recover damages to which he would otherwise be entitled. The principal justification for the existence of this doctrine is that it would be unfair to impose liability upon a defendant for all losses, no matter how extreme or unforeseeable, which flow from his breach of contract. The general test is that the plaintiff can only recover in respect of losses which were within the reasonable contemplation of the parties at the time of entry into the contract. But the courts have experienced great difficulty in deciding when a loss is, or is not, within the reasonable contemplation of the parties.

The foundation of the law can be traced back to the case of *Hadley* v. *Baxendale* (1854) 9 Exch 341. A shaft in the plaintiffs' mill broke. The defendant carriers agreed to carry the shaft to Greenwich so that it could be used as a pattern in the manufacture of a new shaft. The shaft was delayed in transit because of the negligence of the defendants and, in consequence, production was halted at the plaintiffs' mill. The plaintiffs sought to recover their loss of profits as damages for breach of contract. Alderson B held that:

'where two parties have made a contract which one of them has broken, the damages which the other party ought to receive in respect of such breach of contract should be such as may fairly and reasonably be considered either arising naturally, that is, according to the usual course of things, from such breach of contract itself, or such as may reasonably be supposed to have been in the contemplation of both parties, at the time they made the contract, as the probable result of the breach of it'.

There are two distinct limbs to the test established by Alderson B. The first is that the defendant is liable for such losses as occur 'naturally' or as a result of the 'usual course of things' after such a breach of contract. To qualify as a loss which has occurred 'naturally' there must have been a 'serious possibility' or a 'real danger' or a 'very substantial' probability that the loss would occur (*Koufos* v. *C Czarnikow Ltd (The Heron II)* [1969] 1 AC 350). A defendant who agrees to supply or repair a chattel which is obviously being used for profit-making purposes is liable for the ordinary loss of profits suffered as a result of his failure to supply or repair the chattel timeously (*Fletcher* v. *Tayleur* (1855) 17 CB 21). Why could the plaintiffs not recover their loss of profits in *Hadley* when it must have been obvious to the carrier that the mill was being used for profit-making purposes? The answer is that the stoppage of the mill was not a 'natural' consequence of the carrier's delay because the plaintiffs might have had a spare shaft which could have kept the mill in production while the new shaft was being made.

Under the second limb a defendant may be liable for losses which did not arise 'naturally' but were within the reasonable contemplation of both parties at the time they made the contract. This test was not satisfied on the facts of *Hadley* because, although the plaintiffs were aware of the consequences of delay, they had not informed the defendants that delay would result in the halting of production and so the loss could not be said to have been in the reasonable contemplation of *both* parties. The defendant must at least know of the special circumstances (*Simpson* v. *London and North Western Railway Co* (1876) 1 QBD 274, *Seven Seas Properties Ltd* v. *Al-Essa (No. 2)* [1993] 1 WLR 1083), and there is some suggestion in the case law that the plaintiff must go further and establish that the defendant agreed to assume liability for the exceptional loss (*Horne* v. *Midland Railway* (1873) LR 6 CP 131).

The distinction between losses which arise 'naturally' and 'special' losses is illustrated by the case of *Victoria Laundry (Windsor) Ltd* v. *Newman Industries Ltd* [1949] 2 KB 528. The defendants contracted to sell and deliver a boiler to the plaintiffs. The defendants knew that the plaintiffs wished to put the boiler into immediate use in their laundry business. The boiler was delivered some five months late. The plaintiffs sued to recover the loss of profits which they had suffered as a result of the late delivery. The Court of Appeal held that the defendants were liable for the loss of profits which naturally flowed from their breach of contract. But the defendants were not liable for the loss of profits on some exceptionally lucrative contracts which the plaintiffs had entered into with the Ministry of Supply. The defendants did not know of the existence of these contracts and so the loss of profit on these contracts was not within the reasonable contemplation of both parties.

The effect of the second limb of the test established by Alderson B is to encourage contracting parties to disclose exceptional losses which may be suffered as a result of the breach. Where, as in the *Victoria Laundry* case, the plaintiff suffers an unusually large loss, he will be unable to recover that loss unless he draws it to the attention of the defendant at the time of contracting. The rule therefore encourages risk sharing, it enables the parties to assess the scope of their likely liability and to take out insurance cover accordingly.

One difficult question which remains to be discussed is whether the test for remoteness of damage in contract differs from the test for remoteness of damage in tort. In a negligence action damage is too remote a consequence of the defendant's breach of duty where the kind of damage which the plaintiff has suffered was not reasonably foreseeable by the defendant (*Overseas Tankship (UK) Ltd* v. *Morts Dock and Engineering Co Ltd (The Wagon Mound) (No 1)* [1961] AC 388). Despite suggestions that reasonable foresight of loss is also the determining factor in a contractual action (see Asquith LJ in *Victoria Laundry (Windsor) Ltd* v. *Newman Industries Ltd* (above)), it was established by the House of Lords in *The Heron II* (above) that the remoteness test in contract is narrower than the the remoteness test in tort because in a contractual action the loss must be within the reasonable contemplation of the parties at the time of entry into the contract. However, this view was, however, challenged by Lord Denning in *H Parsons (Livestock) Ltd* v. *Uttley Ingham & Co Ltd* [1978] QB 791, when he argued that, at least in relation to physical damage cases, the remoteness test was the same in contract and in tort. Although Lord Denning was in the minority in *Parsons*, it must be noted that Scarman LJ did state that it would be absurd if the amount of damages recoverable were to depend upon whether the plaintiff's cause of action was in contract or in tort. This issue awaits clarification by the House of Lords. It may be that, where the plaintiff has a cause of action in contract or in tort, the remoteness test applicable will be the reasonable foresight test (being more favourable to the plaintiff) but that, where the action is a purely contractual one, the test applicable will be the narrower reasonable contemplation test.

20.12 Causation

A plaintiff will be unable to recover damages in respect of the loss which he has suffered if he cannot establish a causal link between his loss and the defendant's breach of contract. The defendant's breach need not be the sole cause of the loss to the plaintiff, but it must be a cause of the loss.

For example, the independent act of a third party may break the chain of causation between the defendant's breach and the plaintiff's loss, unless the defendant has actually promised to guard against the very thing which has actually happened (*London Joint Stock Bank* v. *Macmillan* [1918] AC 777). Natural events may also break the chain of causation, as was argued in the case of *Monarch Steamship Co* v. *Karlshamns Oljefabrieker* [1949] AC 196. The defendants entered into a contract in April 1939 to carry goods from Manchuria to Sweden. In breach of contract, the defendants failed to provide a ship which was seaworthy. This resulted in a delay in the voyage so that the ship failed to get to Sweden before the outbreak of war in September 1939. As a result of the outbreak of war, the ship was ordered to a Scottish port where the goods had to be transferred to neutral vessels before being shipped to Sweden. The plaintiffs had to pay the cost of the transport in the neutral vessels and they sought to recover the sums paid as damages for breach of contract. The defendants argued that the outbreak of war broke the chain of causation between their breach of contract and the cost incurred by the plaintiffs in shipping the goods to Sweden in neutral vessels. This argument was rejected by the House of Lords on the ground that the outbreak of war was a likely event at the time that the contract was concluded in April 1939 and so it could not be held to amount to a break in the chain of causation.

An act of the plaintiff may be so unreasonable that it breaks the chain of causation between the defendant's breach and the plaintiff's loss. In *Lambert* v. *Lewis* [1982] AC 225, a farmer continued to use a trailer coupling after it was broken. The farmer was held to be liable in damages to persons who were injured in an accident caused by the coupling giving way. The farmer sought to recover an indemnity from the supplier of the coupling. It was held that the farmer could not recover because his continued use of the coupling, in the knowledge that it was damaged, broke the chain of causation between the supplier's breach of contract and the 'loss' suffered by the farmer in having to pay damages to the accident victims.

Where the plaintiff has been negligent and that negligence has contributed to the damage which he has suffered, but it is not sufficient to break the chain of causation, the question then arises whether the damages payable to the plaintiff can be reduced under the Law Reform (Contributory Negligence) Act 1945. This is a vexed issue. The answer depends upon the nature of the obligation which the defendant has broken. Damages may be reduced where the defendant has broken a contractual duty of care where the breach also constitutes a tort. Where the defendant has broken a contractual obligation which is expressed in terms of taking reasonable care but which does not correspond to a common law duty to take care, it remains unclear whether or not the Act is applicable. But where the defendant is sued for the breach of a strict contractual duty, then the 1945 Act is inapplicable and damages cannot be reduced on the ground of contributory negligence (see *Forsikringsaktie-selskapet Vesta* v. *Butcher* [1989] AC 852). The latter case can result in the *overcompensation* of the plaintiff as no reduction is made to reflect the plaintiff's contribution to the loss which has arisen (see Burrows, 1993a). The Law Commission has recently proposed (1993b) that contributory negligence be available as a defence to claims for breach of a contractual duty to take reasonable care or exercise reasonable skill.

20.13 Damages for Pain and Suffering and the 'Consumer Surplus'

Damages are generally assessed by reference to the market value of the promised contractual performance; that is to say, the plaintiff's loss is objectively assessed. Such an objective approach may lead to the undercompensation of a plaintiff because it does not take account of the plaintiff's subjective valuation of the contractual performance, which may be considerably more than the market value (called the 'consumer surplus', see Harris, Ogus and Phillips, 1979). Occasionally, the courts will protect the 'consumer surplus'; for example, by granting a specific performance order when the subject-matter of the contract is 'unique' or by awarding damages assessed on a cost of cure basis (see *Radford* v. *De Froberville* (above)).

But the courts are generally unwilling to compensate a plaintiff for his purely 'subjective' losses. Yet consumers frequently suffer such 'subjective' losses. For example, the value of family wedding photographs will generally exceed their market value because of their sentimental value to members of the family. But the courts have traditionally refused to award damages to compensate a plaintiff for any mental distress which he has suffered as a result of the defendant's breach of contract. In *Addis* v. *Gramophone Co Ltd* [1909] AC 488, the plaintiff sought to recover damages for the indignity which he had suffered in being sacked from his job in a 'humiliating' manner. The House of Lords held that the plaintiff was not entitled to be compensated for the injury to his feelings.

However there is no longer an absolute rule that damages cannot be recovered for mental distress. The courts have recognised that damages for mental distress can be awarded where the predominant object of the contract was to obtain some mental satisfaction (such as a holiday, *Jarvis* v. *Swan's Tours Ltd* [1973] QB 233), or to relieve a source of distress (*Heywood* v. *Wellers* [1976] 1 QB 446). It is not enough for this purpose that the plaintiff hoped to obtain peace of mind as a result of the defendant's contractual performance; the defendant must have promised, expressly or impliedly, that he would provide the plaintiff with peace of mind or freedom from distress. In *Watts* v. *Morrow* [1991] 1 WLR 1421, the plaintiff house purchasers no doubt hoped to enjoy peace of mind and freedom from distress as a result of a survey carried out by the defendant surveyor on a house which they were planning to buy. But the defendant did not promise that he would provide the plaintiffs with such peace of mind or freedom from distress and so he was not liable for the mental distress which the plaintiffs suffered as a result of his failure to discover significant defects in the property (although he was liable for mental distress caused by the physical discomfort or inconvenience resulting from his breach of contract).

In the immediate aftermath of cases such as *Jarvis* v. *Swan's Tours Ltd* (above), it seemed that damages for mental distress would be available in a wider range of circumstances than had previously been the case (see *Cox* v. *Phillips Industries Ltd* [1976] 3 All ER 161). But such an expansive approach was subsequently rejected by the Court of Appeal in *Bliss* v. *South East Thames RHA* [1987] ICR 700. Indeed, in *Hayes* v. *Dodds* [1990] 2 All ER 815, Staughton LJ stated that, while damages for mental distress are recoverable where the object of the contract is the provision of comfort or pleasure or the relief of discomfort, damages are not recoverable for mental distress where the object of the contract is 'simply carrying on a commercial activity with a view to profit'. He stated that he did not 'view with enthusiasm the prospect that every shipowner in the Commercial Court, having successfully claimed for unpaid freight or demurrage, would be able to add a claim for mental distress suffered while he was waiting for his money'.

The courts therefore remain reluctant to award damages to compensate a plaintiff for his 'subjective' losses or to protect his 'consumer surplus' and, to that extent, damages may undercompensate a plaintiff.

20.14 Conclusion

It can be seen that there are a number of doctrines which limit the commitment of the law of contract to the protection of the plaintiff's expectation interest. The existence of these rules and doctrines throws into doubt the validity of the claim that the law of contract protects the expectation interest. However, before reaching a conclusion on this fundamental issue, it is necessary to consider the steps which can be taken by contracting parties to ensure that an adequate remedy is obtained and that the expectation interest is fully protected. These issues are the subject-matter of our final chapter.

Summary

1 The aim of an award of damages is to compensate the plaintiff for the loss which he has suffered as a result of the defendant's breach of contract. The aim is not to punish the defendant.
2 The aim of an award of damages is to put the plaintiff in the position which he would have been in had the contract been performed according to its terms. This is generally calculated by the diminution in value measure, not the cost of cure measure.
3 A plaintiff can recover a benefit which he has conferred on the party in breach where there has been a total failure of consideration. A defendant is not generally required to disgorge the benefits which he has obtained as a result of his breach of contract.
4 A plaintiff may elect to recover his reliance rather than his expectation loss, unless he is seeking to escape the consequences of a bad bargain.
5 A plaintiff must take reasonable steps to mitigate his loss. The existence of a 'duty' to mitigate demonstrates that contract law is not wholeheartedly committed to the protection of the expectation interest.
6 Damages cannot be recovered where the loss which the plaintiff has suffered is too remote a consequence of the defendant's breach of contract. The general rule is that a loss is not too remote if it was within the reasonable contemplation of both parties at the time of entry into the contract.
7 The plaintiff must establish that his loss was caused by the defendant's breach of contract.
8 The general rule is that damages cannot be recovered for mental distress suffered as a result of the defendant's breach of contract, unless the predominant object of the contract was to obtain some mental satisfaction or to relieve a source of distress.

Exercises

1   Define and distinguish between the expectation interest, the reliance interest and the restitution interest.
2   Is the law of contract committed to the protection of the expectation interest?
3   Is a court ever justified in awarding damages by reference to the gain which the defendant has made as a result of the breach rather than by reference to the loss which the plaintiff has suffered?
4   Fire Prevention Ltd entered into a contract with Borchester Town Council, under which they agreed to provide a fire-fighting service of 15 fire engines and 40 firemen. In breach of contract Fire Prevention only supplied 12 fire engines and 35 men and thereby saved themselves £40 000. Borchester cannot show that they have suffered any loss as a result of Fire Prevention's breach because they cannot prove that Fire Prevention failed to extinguish any fire. Can Borchester recover damages from Fire Prevention? If so, on what basis would a court assess damages? (see *City of New Orleans* v. *Fireman's Charitable Association* 9 So 486 (1891)).
5   John, who had recently left his wife, booked a holiday with Harry's Tour Company Ltd. The holiday did not live up to expectations. John now suffers from severe depression. He has been advised by his doctors to give up his job. The depression has been caused partly by the break up of his marriage and partly by the aggravation of his disappointing holiday. Advise John.

21 Obtaining an Adequate Remedy

21.1 Introduction

In Chapter 20 the point was made that the law of contract is not wholeheartedly committed to the protection of the plaintiff's expectation interest and that a damages award may therefore undercompensate the plaintiff. We also noted that such undercompensation throws into doubt the claim that contract law protects the expectation interest. In this chapter we shall consider the extent to which the law of contract provides alternative remedies or enables contracting parties to incorporate into their contracts clauses which will ensure that the 'innocent party' (that is, the party who is not in breach) can obtain an adequate remedy in the event of a breach of contract.

At the beginning of this book (1.5) we noted that the role of the lawyer and of the law of contract is greater at the planning stage of a contract than after a breach has occurred. It is at the remedial stage that the role of the lawyer and of contract law is at its most important. On the one hand, one contracting party will probably wish to exclude or restrict his liability for breach of contract by an appropriately drafted exclusion or limitation clause, while the other party will wish to ensure that an effective and adequate remedy is available to him in the event of a breach of contract.

In seeking to ensure that a contracting party obtains an adequate remedy in the event of a breach of contract, we must extend our discussion beyond the remedy of damages. There are many methods which can be used in an effort to ensure that an effective remedy is obtained. In the first place the contract can be structured in such a way as to entitle one party to withhold the performance of his obligations (21.2) or to entitle one party to terminate performance and claim loss of bargain damages (21.3) or to make a claim in debt for the contract price (21.4). Such remedies may provide a powerful incentive to the other party to refrain from breaking the contract and to perform his obligations under the contract. Alternatively, the parties may make provision in their contract for a sum of money to be payable by way of damages in the event of breach (21.5–21.8). Finally, an adequate remedy can be obtained by seeking an order of specific performance (21.9) or an injunction restraining a threatened breach of contract (21.10). We shall now consider these remedies in greater detail and conclude with a very brief assessment of the significance of the remedial consequences of a breach of contract for the basis, or the theory, of contract law.

21.2   The Entire Obligations (or 'Contracts') Rule

The ability of one contracting party to withhold performance of his obligations under the contract gives to the other party an extremely powerful incentive to perform his contractual obligations. An example will illustrate the point. A house-owner and a builder enter into a contract under which the builder agrees to build a garage for £8000. The contract states that payment shall be made upon satisfactory completion of the work by the builder. The house-owner's obligation to pay the promised sum is therefore dependent upon satisfactory completion by the builder. Should the builder, in breach of contract, fail to complete the work he will, as a general rule, be unable to sue for payment. His claim will be barred by the entire obligations rule or, as it is sometimes known, the 'entire contracts' rule.

It is suggested that 'entire obligations' is the more accurate title for this rule. In some cases there may be little practical difference between an entire contract and an entire obligation. In our example involving the construction of a garage, the builder can only recover payment when he has completed contractual performance, so, from his perspective, there is no difference between an entire contract and an entire obligation: his obligation is to perform the contract in its entirety. But in other cases the difference between an entire contract and an entire obligation is clear. Where a construction contract makes provision for payment upon the completion of distinct stages of the project, the completion of each stage being a condition precedent to the right to claim payment, the obligation to complete each stage may be said to be entire, even though the contract as a whole is not entire.

The origin of the entire obligation rule can be traced back to the old case of *Cutter* v. *Powell* (1795) 6 TR 320. Cutter agreed with Powell to 'proceed, continue and do his duty as second mate' on a ship sailing from Jamaica to England. Cutter died on the journey to England and his widow sued to recover the wages which she alleged were payable in respect of the period of time in which Cutter had satisfactorily performed his duties before his death. Her action failed because Cutter was not entitled to payment unless he completed the voyage. The rule was no completion, no pay. This rule gives a powerful incentive to a contracting party to ensure, as far as is possible, that the contract is carried out according to its terms. But it can lead to the apparent unjust enrichment of the 'innocent party'. In *Cutter* v. *Powell*, Powell obtained the services of Cutter for some seven weeks but was not required to pay for any 'benefit' which he had obtained.

In practice, the hardships to which this rule can give rise are mitigated by its many exceptions. The principal exception is that the rule is alleged not to apply where the party in breach has substantially performed his obligations under the contract (*Hoenig* v. *Isaacs* [1952] 2 All ER 176; *Williams* v. *Roffey Bros & Nicholls (Contractors) Ltd* [1991] 1 QB 1). In such a case the innocent party must perform his obligations under the contract (usually pay the price) and content himself with an action for damages for any loss suffered as a result of the breach. But the doctrine of substantial performance has been heavily criticised by Professor Treitel (1991, at pp. 688–9) on the ground that 'it is based on the error that *contracts*, as opposed to particular *obligations*, can be entire'. He asserts that to 'say that an obligation is entire *means* that it must be completely performed before payment becomes due' and that in 'relation to "entire" obligations, there is no scope for any doctrine of "substantial performance"'. On this view a court is required to identify with some care the obligation which is alleged to be entire. Thus, he argues, the obligation to complete the work is generally entire but the obligation to do so in a workmanlike manner generally is not. So, in *Hoenig* v. *Isaacs* (above), where the builder had completed the work, albeit defectively, there was no need to resort to any doctrine of substantial performance. The obligation which was entire, namely the obligation to complete the work, had been performed and so the employer was required to pay the price, subject to a claim for damages in respect of the breach of the non-entire obligation to do the work in a workmanlike manner. Although there is much to be said for this view, it has not yet been expressly adopted by the courts, who still tend to insist that, upon substantial performance, the party in breach is entitled to claim the price, subject to a counterclaim for damages (see *Hoenig* v. *Isaacs* (above), *Bolton* v. *Mahadeva* [1972] 1 WLR 1009 and *Williams* v. *Roffey Bros & Nicholls (Contractors) Ltd* (above)).

The second exception is that an innocent party may be required to recompense the party in breach if he accepts the latter's part performance. This is usually difficult to establish because the acceptance of the innocent party occurs in the context of complete contractual performance and is generally not pro-ratable. Part performance was not what was requested. It was full performance or nothing. In our example, a garage is a benefit to the house-owner, but a partly built garage is not; indeed, it may be more of a nuisance (*Sumpter* v. *Hedges* [1898] 1 QB 673). Finally, the court may interpret the contract as consisting of a number of obligations so that, once each obligation has been completely performed, the party in breach may claim the sum promised in relation to the performance of that obligation. Many contracts are so divided; for example, a building contract will often provide for payment at intervals, usually against an architect's or engineer's certificate.

The ability of contracting parties to take steps to minimise the impact of the entire obligations rule has probably preserved the rule as part of English law. Although the Law Commission originally recommended (1983) that the party in breach be given a restitutionary remedy for the value of his part performance, their recommendation did not gain much support and legislation to abrogate the rule is no longer forthcoming (see Burrows, 1984a).

21.3   The Creation of Conditions

Another effective remedy is to threaten to terminate performance of the contract in the event of a repudiatory breach of contract and claim loss of bargain damages. The effectiveness of such a step can be seen from the case of *Lombard North Central plc* v. *Butterworth* [1987] QB 527 (see 10.3). By providing in clause 2 of the agreement that the obligation to pay each instalment punctually was of the essence of the contract, the owners were able to terminate performance of the contract and claim loss of bargain damages when the hirer failed to pay an instalment timeously. Clause 2 was not subject to the penalty clause rule (see 21.5–21.6) because the Court of Appeal held that the parties were free to classify as a condition a clause which would not otherwise be regarded as a condition. Therefore, by careful draftsmanship which ensures that any term likely to be broken is elevated to the status of a 'condition' which is of the 'essence of the contract', the innocent party can be given the ability to threaten termination of performance of the contract and to claim loss of bargain damages. This will give the other party a powerful incentive to perform his obligations under the contract and ensure that, if the contract is broken, an effective remedy is obtained.

21.4   A Claim in Debt

A debt is a definite sum of money which the defendant, under the terms of the contract, is due to pay to the plaintiff. It is therefore distinct from a claim in damages. The principal issue in a debt action is whether the money is *due* to the plaintiff. The plaintiff does not have to show that he has mitigated his loss, nor are the remoteness rules applicable. His action is simply to recover the sum due; no more, no less. The classic example of a claim in debt is an action to recover the contract price where goods have been delivered and the buyer has not paid for them. The advantage of a claim in debt can be seen from an examination of *White and Carter (Councils) Ltd* v. *McGregor* [1962] AC 413 (see 19.9), where the plaintiffs were able to recover the contract price and were not obliged to take steps to mitigate their loss. Such an action also enjoys certain procedural advantages (see Rules of the Supreme Court, Order 14). There are therefore distinct advantages in drafting a contract in such a way as to create a debtor-creditor relationship between the parties so as to provide the creditor with an effective remedy should the 'debtor' default in making payment.

21.5   Liquidated Damages

An alternative method of avoiding undercompensation is to insert into the contract a clause which states the amount of money which shall be payable in the event of a breach of contract. Such a clause also helps to eliminate uncertainty because it enables the parties to know in advance the extent of their potential liability and to take out insurance cover accordingly. However, the courts have retained a jurisdiction to control the content of such clauses. The basic rules which the courts have established may be stated in the following terms. If the clause represents a genuine pre-estimate of the loss which is likely to be occasioned by the breach, then it is a 'liquidated damages clause' and is enforceable. In quantifying the 'loss' which is likely to be occasioned by the breach, it is the *actual* loss which is the relevant sum, so that it is no objection that part of that loss would have been irrecoverable on the ground that it was too remote (*Robophone Facilities Ltd* v. *Blank* [1966] 1 WLR 1428, 1447). The sum stipulated in the liquidated damages clause is the sum recoverable, even though that sum is greater or smaller than the loss which has actually been suffered.

But if the sum stated in the clause is not a genuine pre-estimate of loss, it is a 'penalty clause' and is unenforceable. The aim of such a clause is to punish the party in breach and the courts have held that such an aim is impermissible. A clause which is held to be a penalty clause is not struck out of the contract, but it will not be enforced by the court beyond the actual loss of the party seeking to rely on the clause (*Jobson* v. *Johnson* [1989] 1 All ER 621). The court is not required to consider whether the party in breach is entitled to relief; the court automatically relegates the party seeking to rely on the penalty clause to a claim in damages.

The distinction between a liquidated damages clause and a penalty clause rests ultimately on the intention of the parties at the time of entry into the contract: that is to say, was the clause a genuine attempt to assess the loss likely to be occasioned by the breach or was it designed to punish the party in breach? The fact that the parties have described the clause as a 'liquidated damages clause' or a 'penalty clause' is a relevant factor but it is not conclusive (*Elphinstone* v. *Monkland Iron and Coal Co* (1886) 11 App Cas 332). The difference between a liquidated damages clause and a penalty clause is in fact a question of construction and the courts have established a number of rules of construction which they apply in deciding whether a particular clause is a penalty clause or a liquidated damages clause.

The source of these rules of construction can be found in the judgment of Lord Dunedin in *Dunlop Pneumatic Tyre Co Ltd* v. *New Garage & Motor Co Ltd* [1915] AC 79. Lord Dunedin stated, firstly, that a clause will be held to be a penalty clause

'if the sum stipulated for is extravagant and unconscionable in amount in comparison with the greatest loss that could conceivably be proved to have followed from the breach'.

The second rule is that a clause is a penalty clause

'if the breach consists only in not paying a sum of money, and the sum stipulated is a sum greater than the sum which ought to have been paid'.

The third rule is that

> 'there is a presumption (but no more) that it is a penalty when "a single lump sum is made payable by way of compensation, on the occurrence of one or more or all of several events, some of which may occasion serious and others but trifling damage"'.

This presumption can act as a trap for the unwary. Contract draftsmen must seek to distinguish between serious and trifling breaches of contract because a failure to distinguish between the two may result in the clause being held to be a penalty clause. The fourth rule of construction is that

> 'it is no obstacle to the sum stipulated being a genuine pre-estimate of damage, that the consequences of the breach are such as to make precise pre-estimation almost an impossibility. On the contrary, that is just the situation when it is probable that pre-estimated damage was the true bargain between the parties'.

When applying these presumptions to the facts of a particular case it must be remembered that the penalty clause jurisdiction is an exceptional one and that the courts will generally be slow to conclude that a formula is oppressive or penal, especially when it has been agreed by commercial parties who are capable of protecting their own interests in the bargaining process. That this is so can be demonstrated by reference to the recent decision of the Privy Council in *Philips Hong Kong Ltd* v. *Attorney-General of Hong Kong* (1993) 61 Build LR 41. Lord Woolf, giving the judgment of the Privy Council, expressly recognised the value of liquidated damages clauses in enabling the parties to 'know with a reasonable degree of certainty the extent of their liability and the risks which they run as a result of entering into the contract' and he refused to adopt an approach to their construction which would undermine these purposes. He therefore emphasised the exceptional nature of the penalty clause jurisdiction: 'the principle was always recognised as being subject to fairly narrow constraints and the courts have always avoided claiming that they have any general jurisdiction to rewrite the contracts that the parties have made'. He adopted the following passage from the judgment of Mason and Wilson JJ in the High Court of Australia in *AMEV UDC Finance Ltd* v. *Austin* (1986) 162 CLR 170:

> '[t]he courts should not . . . be too ready to find the requisite degree of disproportion lest they impinge on the parties' freedom to settle for themselves the rights and liabilities following a breach of contract'.

The particular argument which was put to the Privy Council in *Philips* was that, although the sum claimed was not exorbitant in the light of what had actually happened, the clause was nevertheless a penalty clause on the ground that there were various hypothetical situations (none of which had actually occurred on the facts) in which the application of the clause could have resulted in a sum larger than the actual loss being recovered by the injured party. The Privy Council, adopting a robust approach, rejected the argument in the following terms:

'Except possibly in the case of situations where one of the parties to the contract is able to dominate the other as to the choice of the terms of a contract, it will normally be insufficient to establish that a provision is objectionably penal to identify situations where the application of the provision could result in a larger sum being recovered by the injured party than his actual loss. Even in such situations so long as the sum payable in the event of non-compliance with the contract is not extravagant, having regard to the range of losses that it could reasonably be anticipated it would have to cover at the time the contract was made, it can still be a genuine pre-estimate of the loss that would be suffered and so a perfectly valid liquidated damage provision. The use in argument of unlikely illustrations should therefore not assist a party to defeat a provision as to liquidated damages.'

Of course, it must be remembered that the question whether a particular clause is a liquidated damage clause or a penalty clause must be asked at the date of the formation of the contract, not the date of breach. Therefore what has actually happened cannot be conclusive evidence of the status of the clause because the court must have regard to the wider range of events which were in the contemplation of the parties at the time of entry into the contract. But equally, as Lord Woolf stated, this does not mean that what happens after the formation of the contract is irrelevant. What actually happened can 'provide valuable evidence as to what could reasonably be expected to be the loss at the time the contract was made'. The approach and tenor of the judgment of Lord Woolf suggests that, in future, the courts will not be receptive to technical arguments which seek to set aside a clause which has operated in a fair and reasonable manner and further that, in the absence of compelling evidence, they will be reluctant to set aside an agreed pre-estimation of loss by parties of equal bargaining power. The penalty clause jurisdiction is the anomaly, not the rule.

We have already noted that a penalty clause is invalid and unenforceable. This leads to a potential anomaly where the loss which the innocent party has suffered is greater than the sum stipulated in the contract. In such a case, can the innocent party argue that the clause is a penalty clause so that it can be ignored and he can recover his actual loss? In *Wall* v. *Rederiaktiebogalet Luggude* [1915] 3 KB 66, it was held that the innocent party could do this and recover his actual loss, although the issue has been the subject of vigorous debate among academic lawyers (see Hudson, 1974, Gordon, 1974, Hudson, 1975 and Barton, 1976). It should also be noted that a liquidated damages clause may validly provide for the payment of a sum of money which is less than the estimated loss (*Cellulose Acetate Silk Co* v. *Widnes Foundry (1925) Ltd* [1933] AC 20, although where the clause is held to 'exclude or restrict' liability for breach of contract it may be caught by s.3 of the Unfair Contract Terms Act 1977, see 11.11).

21.6   Evading the Penalty Clause Rule

Although the approach of the Privy Council in *Philips Hong Kong* (above) appears to suggest that contracting parties will, in future, have greater latitude in making provision for agreed damages in the contract itself, parties may wish to avoid any uncertainty by evading the clutches of the penalty clause rule entirely by clever draftsmanship. Three principal devices can be used to avoid the rule. The first is that the penalty clause rule does not apply to a clause which simply accelerates an existing liability. An example will illustrate the point. Suppose that two parties enter into a contract of hire under which the entire rental is stated to be payable at the date of entry into the contract. The contract further provides that the hirer shall be entitled to pay the rental by instalments provided that certain conditions are met but that, in the event of default in payment of any instalment, the whole balance shall immediately become payable. Such an acceleration of liability is not caught by the penalty clause rule (*Protector Loan Co* v. *Grice* (1880) 5 QBD 592). The same principle applies where a creditor agrees to accept part payment of a debt in full discharge of the debt, provided that certain conditions are met, but stipulates that, if the conditions are not met, he will be entitled to recover the original debt in full (*The Angelic Star* [1988] 1 Lloyd's Rep 122). The crucial ingredient in these cases is that there must be 'a present debt, which by reason of an indulgence given by the creditor is payable either in the future, or in a lesser amount, provided that certain conditions are met' (*O'Dea* v. *Allstates Leasing System (WA) Pty Ltd* (1983) 57 ALJR 172, 174). So by clever draftsmanship a 'present debt' can be created and the subsequent 'acceleration' of that liability to pay is outside the scope of the penalty clause rule.

The second device is to stipulate that the sum shall be payable on an event which is not a breach of contract. The penalty clause rule applies *only* to sums of money which are payable on a breach of contract. A good example of the potential for evasion is provided by the case of *Alder* v. *Moore* [1961] 2 QB 57. The defendant, who was a professional footballer, suffered serious injury and he was certified as being disabled to such an extent that he was unable to play professional football. The plaintiff insurers paid him £500 under an insurance policy which had been taken out to cover the defendant in the event of him suffering permanent total disablement. The defendant covenanted with the plaintiffs that:

'In consideration of the above payment I hereby declare and agree that I will take no part as a playing member of any form of professional football and that in the event of infringement of this condition I will be subject to a penalty of [£500]'.

The defendant later resumed his playing career and the insurers sought to recover the £500 which they had paid to him. The defendant argued that the clause was unenforceable because it was a penalty clause. But the majority of the Court of Appeal held that the penalty clause rule was not applicable. The defendant had not promised that he would not play football again. Therefore the £500 was not payable upon a breach of contract and the penalty clause rule was irrelevant. This rule can lead to anomalous results. For example, a hirer who breaks a contract of hire-purchase by failing to pay the instalments can invoke the penalty clause rule if the owners seek to recover an 'excessive' sum of money from him as a result of his breach of contract. But, where the hirer honestly admits that he can no longer pay the instalments, and exercises his right under the contract to return the goods, such a hirer will have no defence to an action by the owners for an 'excessive' sum of money because the sum is not payable on a breach of contract (see *Bridge* v. *Campbell Discount Co Ltd* [1962] AC 600). Lord Denning pointed out the absurdity of this rule. He stated that equity has committed itself to the 'absurd paradox' that 'it will grant relief to a man who breaks his contract but will penalise the man who keeps it'. The response of the courts has been that the penalty clause rule only regulates the sums payable upon a breach of contract; any unfairness which lies in other parts of the contract cannot be dealt with by the penalty clause rule (see *Export Credits Guarantee Department* v. *Universal Oil Products Co* [1983] 1 WLR 399). The 'absurdity' which Lord Denning has pointed out stems from the fact that English law has refused to recognise the existence of a general doctrine of unconscionability (see 17.4). Instead, it has sought to deal with problems of contractual unfairness in a piecemeal manner. The price of such an approach is that, where the weaker contracting party is unable to bring his case within one of the existing identifiable categories, his claim for relief is likely to fail.

The third device which can be used to evade the penalty clause rule is to avoid the use of a clause which states that a specified sum of money shall be payable in the event of a breach of contract because there is always a risk that such a clause will be held to be a penalty clause. But, if the parties simply provide that the term is a condition which is of the essence of the contract, breach of that term will entitle the innocent party to terminate performance and claim loss of bargain damages. The elevation of a particular term into a condition is not caught by the penalty clause rule (see *Lombard North Central plc* v. *Butterworth* (above), noting in particular that clause 6, which did seek to quantify the sum payable on breach, was held to be a penalty clause and was therefore unenforceable. Contrast the decision of the Court of Appeal in *Financings Ltd* v. *Baldock* [1963] 2 QB 104).

21.7   Deposits and Part Payments

A clause in a contract which states that a certain sum of money shall be payable on a breach of contract inevitably runs the risk that it will be held to be a penalty clause. It also has the disadvantage that the innocent party has to take the initiative to obtain the money. A preferable alternative might therefore be to obtain payment of a sum of money in advance and then refuse to return it in the event of the other party breaking the contract.

In such a case, can the party in breach recover the prepayment? The answer to that question depends upon whether the money was paid as a deposit or as a part payment of the price. A deposit is paid by way of security and is generally irrecoverable, whereas a part payment is paid towards the contract price and is generally recoverable. The difference between the two is a matter of construction. Where the contract is neutral then a payment will generally be interpreted as a part payment (*Dies* v. *British and International Mining and Finance Co* [1939] 1 KB 715).

Where the payment is held to be a deposit, the rule established in *Howe* v. *Smith* (1884) 27 Ch D 89, is that a deposit is irrecoverable. A deposit which was due before the date of discharge but which has not been paid is forfeitable (*Hinton* v. *Sparkes* (1868) LR 3 CP 161). The general rule that a deposit is irrecoverable is capable of causing great hardship to the party in breach because the deposit may have been much larger than the loss occasioned by the breach of contract. However a critical limit upon the ability of parties to stipulate for excessive deposits was firmly established by the Privy Council in *Workers Trust and Merchant Bank Ltd* v. *Dojap Investments Ltd* [1993] AC 573 (see Beale, 1993). Vendors of property sought to forfeit a deposit of 25 per cent of the purchase price when the purchaser failed to pay the balance of the purchase price within the 14 days stipulated in the contract, time being of the essence of the contract. The purchasers did tender the balance of the purchase price with interest a week later but the vendors returned the cheque and purported to forfeit the deposit of almost three million Jamaican dollars. The Privy Council held that the vendors were not entitled to retain the deposit and ordered that it be repaid to the purchasers after subtracting from it any loss which the vendors could prove they had suffered as a result of the purchasers' breach.

Lord Browne-Wilkinson, giving the judgment of the Privy Council, stated that it was 'not possible for the parties to attach the incidents of a deposit to the payment of a sum of money unless such sum is reasonable as earnest money'. There is, however, some difficulty in establishing what is a 'reasonable deposit' given that even a reasonable deposit need not represent a genuine pre-estimate of the loss likely to be occasioned by the breach. On the facts, the Privy Council concluded that the customary deposit in the case of the sale of land has been 10 per cent and that 'a vendor who seeks to obtain a larger amount must show special circumstances which justify such a deposit'. This the vendors could not do. The

Privy Council admitted that this reliance upon the practice of asking for a 10 per cent deposit was 'without logic' but they were nevertheless content to use it as a benchmark. It is not at all clear how the courts will decide what constitutes a 'reasonable deposit' where there is no such objective benchmark.

The most difficult aspect of the case was whether the court had jurisdiction to relieve against the forfeiture of the deposit when the party claiming relief was not ready and willing to perform his obligations under the contract. In *Stockloser* v. *Johnson* [1954] 1 QB 476, Romer LJ stated that the jurisdiction of the court was confined to allowing late completion by the defaulting party and did not extend to ordering the repayment of a sum which had been paid in accordance with the contract and which, on breach, was stated to be forfeit. On the other hand, both Denning and Somervell LJJ in *Stockloser* stated that a deposit may be recoverable in equity if the forfeiture clause was of a penal nature and if it was unconscionable for the innocent party to retain the money. Lord Browne-Wilkinson found it unnecessary to resolve this conflict. He distinguished *Stockloser* on the ground that it was a case in which the purchaser seeking relief against the forfeiture of instalments had been let into possession of the subject-matter of the contract (although it is not entirely clear what basis in principle there is for so distinguishing the case). Whatever the answer to the problem in *Stockloser*, Lord Browne-Wilkinson stated that a stipulation for the forfeiture of a 25 per cent deposit was a 'plain penalty' and, on the authority of *Commissioner of Public Works* v. *Hills* [1906] AC 368, he held that the court was entitled to order repayment of the sum paid, less any damage actually proved to have been suffered as a result of the default. One further point of note which arises out of *Dojap* is that, in the event of a deposit being held to be unreasonable, the court will not re-write the contract by inserting into it a 'reasonable' deposit. The vendors were therefore not entitled to retain 10 per cent of the sum paid because they had not contracted for a 10 per cent deposit. This refusal to re-write the terms of the contract will give an incentive to contracting parties to err on the side of caution when setting the level of any deposit payable. *Dojap* is therefore to be welcomed in so far as it places limits upon the ability of contracting parties to provide for excessive deposits.

Where the sum paid is held to be a part payment, the general rule is that the sum is recoverable by the party in breach. This rule can be traced back to the case of *Dies* v. *British and International Mining and Finance Co* (above). The plaintiff contracted to purchase ammunition and made a prepayment of £100 000. In breach of contract the plaintiff refused to accept delivery. The defendants terminated the contract and the plaintiffs sued to recover the £100 000. Stable J held that the plaintiff was entitled to recover the money paid, subject to the right of the defendants to recover damages for the breach. The initial payment was a conditional one; it was conditional upon subsequent performance of the contract and, when that condition failed because of the termination of the contract consequent upon the plaintiff's breach of contract, the defendants' right to retain the money simultaneously failed (see Beatson, 1981). However, the rule in *Dies* did not emerge unscathed from a re-examination by the House of Lords in *Hyundai Shipbuilding and Heavy Industries Co Ltd* v. *Papadopoulos* [1980] 1 WLR 1129. Shipbuilders sought to recover an instalment which they alleged was due to them by the defendant guarantors. It was held that the shipbuilders were entitled to recover the instalment. Lord Fraser distinguished *Dies* on the ground that the latter case was not one in which the vendors were required to incur any expenditure or perform any work in the performance of their obligations under the contract. It was a simple contract of sale. *Hyundai*, on the other hand, involved a contract for work and materials, under which the shipbuilders incurred expense in the building of the ship. The conclusion that can be derived from *Hyundai* is that, where it is clear from the contract that the payee will have to incur reliance expenditure before completing his performance of the contract, then, in the absence of a stipulation in the contract to the contrary, the part payment will be irrecoverable. A part payment is therefore recoverable only where it is clear from the contract that the payee will not have to incur reliance expenditure before completing his performance of the contract.

21.8   Liquidated Damages, Penalty Clauses and Forfeitures: An Assessment

Two groups of questions must be considered here. The first is: why should we differentiate between penalty clauses and deposits? Why not have a uniform set of rules? The answer may be that, after *Workers Trust and Merchant Bank Ltd* v. *Dojap Investments Ltd* (above), we no longer distinguish between the two: the penalty clause rule is simply applied to deposits. While it is true to say that, after *Dojap*, the difference between the two sets of rules is not as great as it once was, it is not yet possible to say that the rules have been completely assimilated. As we have noted, the distinction between a penalty clause and a liquidated damages clause rests on whether or not the clause is a 'genuine pre-estimate of the loss' (21.5). But, in the case of a deposit, the vital question is whether or not the deposit is 'reasonable' and, crucially in this context, Lord Browne-Wilkinson stated that, at least in the case of a contract for the sale of land, a deposit may be 'reasonable' notwithstanding the fact that it is not a genuine pre-estimate of the loss. So it cannot yet be said that the 'genuine pre-estimate of loss' test is applicable to deposits. On the other hand, it is vital to note that Lord Browne-Wilkinson's observation was confined to contracts for the sale of land and it may be that, in other contexts, the courts will have regard to whether or not the deposit was a genuine pre-estimate of the loss in deciding whether or not it was 'reasonable'. There is, in fact, much to be said for the assimilation of the rules. The only difference between an agreed damages clause and a deposit is that the latter is payable in advance and so belongs to the recipient before the breach, while the former only becomes payable upon breach. Although this distinction may have important practical consequences, in the sense that the recipient of a deposit is less likely than the intended recipient of a sum payable by way of agreed damages to have to engage in litigation to obtain the sum stipulated, it does not demand the existence of two sets of controls upon the freedom of the contracting parties to make provision for the consequences of breach. A single set of rules should suffice.

The second group of questions which must be asked is: can the existence of these jurisdictions to grant relief to defaulting contracting parties be justified? Should freedom of contract not prevail so that the parties can be left free to stipulate the amount of damages payable in the event of a breach? What is the point of these rules if they can be evaded by the clever draftsmanship of the more powerful party? These are all difficult questions to answer.

Given the tendency which we have noted for damages to under-compensate, a number of arguments can be adduced in favour of leaving the parties free to make their own assessment of the damages payable upon a breach. The first is the argument from freedom of contract, that the parties should be free to stipulate the sums payable on breach. The second is that it would avoid the artificiality of the present rules, many of which can be evaded by careful draftsmanship. The third is that it would reduce the uncertainty caused by the present possibility of judicial review.

On the other hand, a number of arguments can be adduced against the abolition of these equitable jurisdictions. It can be argued that it is for the courts to decide the compensation which is payable upon a breach of contract and that it is not for the parties to set compensation at a level higher than that permitted by the courts. The principal objection, however, is that the courts would have to create a doctrine of unconscionability to play the role once played by these equitable jurisdictions. Thus far, the English courts have refused to recognise the existence of a general doctrine of unconscionability (*National Westminster Bank* v. *Morgan* [1985] AC 686, see further 17.4). On the other hand, the case for incorporating these traditional equitable jurisdictions within a wider doctrine of unconscionability or unfairness appears to have been strengthened by the recent EC Directive on Unfair Terms in Consumer Contracts (see further 1.6 and 17.6). It includes within the list of terms which may be regarded as unfair a term which has the object or effect of 'permitting the seller or supplier to retain sums paid by the consumer where the latter decides not to conclude or perform the contract, without providing for the consumer to receive compensation of an equivalent amount from the seller or supplier where the latter is the party cancelling the contract' and a term which has the object or effect of 'requiring any consumer who fails to fulfil his obligation to pay a disproportionately high sum in compensation'. This more general jurisdiction is unlikely to be conducive to the interests of certainty (at least in the short to medium term) but it does have the merit of avoiding the artificiality inherent within the present rules and it also reduces the scope for the evasion of the rules by clever draftsman employed by the more powerful party to the contract (see further on these issues Goetz and Scott, 1977, Kaplan, 1977, Muir, 1985 and Milner, 1979).

21.9 Specific Performance

A plaintiff who wishes to secure an adequate remedy may, finally, seek an order of specific performance. An order of specific performance is an order of the court which requires the party in breach to perform his primary obligations under the contract. This is, of course, one of the most effective methods of protecting the expectation of performance because it orders that performance take place, albeit at a later point in time than originally agreed. We have already noted that damages are available as of right upon a breach of contract, but specific performance is an equitable remedy which is only available in the discretion of the court. Historically, English law has conceived of specific performance as a supplementary remedy, only to be granted when damages were inadequate. But the scope of the remedy has gradually expanded in recent years. The crucial case in the development of the law is *Beswick* v. *Beswick* [1968] AC 58 (see 7.2). In granting an order of specific performance to the plaintiff, it is clear that the House of Lords envisaged a wider role for specific performance, based upon the appropriateness of the remedy in the circumstances of the case, rather than as a supplementary remedy in a hierarchical system of remedies. Lord Reid awarded specific performance to achieve a 'just result' and Lord Pearce granted the order because it was 'the more appropriate remedy'.

The extent to which this more expansive view has been implemented in subsequent cases remains unclear. One commentator has gone so far as to cite *Beswick* for the proposition that there is now 'a right to specific performance of all contracts where there is no adequate reason for the courts to refuse it' (Lawson, 1980). Other commentators, while recognising the possibilities inherent in *Beswick*, have been more hesitant, as subsequent cases have not always followed the lead given in *Beswick* (see Burrows, 1984). Cases can be found, however, which have adopted a more liberal approach (see *Evans Marshall and Co Ltd* v. *Bertola SA* [1973] 1 WLR 349 and *Sudbrook Estates Ltd* v. *Eggleton* [1983] 1 AC 444) and it is suggested that Professor Treitel is correct to conclude (1991) that the 'availability of specific performance depends on the *appropriateness* of that remedy in the circumstances of each case'.

Nevertheless there remain a number of situations in which an order of specific performance is not normally available. The remedy is generally unavailable where it would cause severe hardship to the defendant (*Patel* v. *Ali* [1984] Ch 283), where the contract is unfair to the defendant, even though the unfairness is not such as to amount to a ground on which the contract can be set aside (*Walters* v. *Morgan* (1861) 3 D F & J 718), where the conduct of the plaintiff demonstrates that he does not deserve the remedy (*Shell UK Ltd* v. *Lostock Garages Ltd* [1976] 1 WLR 1187), where the plaintiff has sought to take advantage of a mistake by the defendant (*Webster* v. *Cecil* (1861) 30 Beav 62), where performance is impossible (*Watts* v. *Spence* [1976] Ch 165), where the contract is one of personal service (s.236 of the Trade Union and Labour Relations (Consolidation) Act 1992), where the contract is one which requires constant supervision (*Ryan* v. *Mutual Tontine Association* [1893] 1 Ch 116), where the contract is too vague (*Tito* v. *Waddell (No 2)* [1977] Ch 106, 322) and finally, the court 'will not compel a defendant to perform his obligations specifically if it cannot at the same time ensure that any unperformed obligations of the plaintiff will be specifically performed, unless perhaps damages would be an adequate remedy for any default on the plaintiff's part' (*Price* v. *Strange* [1978] Ch 337).

However, the law is in an uncertain state here because many of the cases which form the foundation of these rules where decided before *Beswick* and their status must be regarded as uncertain in the light of that decision. For example, in *Hill* v. *CA Parsons Ltd* [1972] Ch 305 and *Irani* v. *Southampton AHA* [1985] ICR 590 the courts were prepared to specifically enforce a contract of employment, even though it was a contract of personal service. Admittedly, the facts of each case were rather exceptional but both cases display a growing willingness to grant orders of specific performance. Similarly, *Ryan* v. *Mutual Tontine Association* (above) was restrictively interpreted by Mervyn Davies J in *Posner* v. *Scott-Lewis* [1987] Ch 25, when he held that an order of specific performance could be made, despite alleged difficulties of supervision, provided that the contract stated with sufficient precision the performance intended by the parties.

Can the parties contract for an order of specific performance? In *Quadrant Visual Communications Ltd* v. *Hutchison Telephone UK Ltd* [1993] BCLC 442, Stocker LJ stated that 'once the court is asked for the equitable remedy of specific performance, its discretion cannot be fettered' by the stipulation of the parties. The parties could not, by the terms of their contract, confine the role of the court to that of a 'rubber stamp'. It should be noted, however, that this was a case in which the plaintiffs had been guilty of 'trickery' in failing to disclose to the defendants an agreement which the court held that they should have disclosed to the defendants: the plaintiffs had not come to court with 'clean hands'. In such a case, it is easy to understand why the court paid little or no attention to any agreed stipulation for specific performance. But in other contexts, where there is no 'wrongdoing' on the part of the plaintiff, it is arguable that, while the parties should not be able to exercise the discretion for the court, their stipulation should be *a* factor which is taken into account by the court in the exercise of its discretion (see *Warner Bros Pictures Inc.* v. *Nelson* [1937] 1 KB 209, 220–1). So it is possible that some limited advantage can be obtained by contracting for specific performance.

Given the gradual willingness of the courts to expand the scope of the remedy, should the courts take the further step of holding that specific performance is generally available on a breach of contract? It can be argued that damages undercompensate in more cases than is commonly supposed and the fact that a plaintiff asks for specific performance is good evidence that damages are inadequate. Indeed, in many cases plaintiffs have an incentive not to ask for an order of specific performance. They will want to go out into the market place and purchase alternative goods and sue for damages for the difference in value rather than wait for a court to make an order of specific performance. A further consideration which must be borne in mind is that the performance obtainable from an unwilling contracting party may well be inferior to that obtainable from another, willing performer. So it can be argued that, where the plaintiff asks for specific performance, the remedy should be generally available because the mere fact that he has asked for the remedy demonstrates that damages are an inadequate remedy.

But a number of arguments can be adduced against such a proposition. The first is that some limitations must be placed upon the availability of the remedy in the case of contracts involving personal or intimate relations and in cases where it would be impossible for the court to supervise the order because of the vagueness inherent in the contract. It should not be assumed, however, that an order of specific performance will necessarily result in the performance of the contract. An order of specific performance gives to the plaintiff a choice. He can either insist upon performance of the contract or he can sell his right, at a price of his own choice, to the defendant (see Calabresi and Melamed, 1972). A defendant who wished to be released from his contract with the plaintiff, in order to enter into a more lucrative contract with a third party, would then have to negotiate his way out of the contract with the plaintiff. It is suggested that, because of the fact that damages do tend to undercompensate, specific performance should be generally available and that the courts should be willing to grant the remedy unless the defendant can satisfy the court that there is a good reason to refuse the remedy, or that an order of specific performance would violate, or be inconsistent with, established rules and doctrines of contract law (see Kronman, 1978b, Schwartz, 1979b; Bishop, 1985 and McKendrick, 1986).

21.10   Injunctions

A breach of a negative contract or a negative stipulation in a contract may, in an appropriate case, be restrained by means of an injunction. An injunction is also an equitable remedy which is available within the discretion of the court. An injunction will not be granted where its effect would be directly or indirectly to compel the defendant to perform acts which he could not have been required to do by an order of specific performance. An injunction is commonly sought in restraint of trade cases to restrain the employee or vendor acting in breach of his covenant (see further Treitel, 1991, pp. 919–24).

21.11 Damages in Lieu of Specific Performance

Finally, the High Court has a discretion to award a plaintiff damages in lieu of an injunction or specific performance (s.50 of the Supreme Court Act 1981). Where the court decides to exercise its discretion to award damages, damages are assessed on the same basis as common law damages for breach of contract (*Johnson* v. *Agnew* [1980] AC 367, 400; cf. *Surrey County Council* v. *Bredero Homes Ltd* [1993] 1 WLR 1361, 1366–7, discussed in more detail at 20.6).

21.12 Conclusion

What is the significance of the remedial consequences of a breach of contract for the basis of contract law? It is suggested that there are three principal lessons which we can glean from our brief survey of the remedies available on a breach of contract. The first is the scope which is given to the parties to make provision for their own remedies on a breach of contract. In this chapter we have seen that a number of options are open to the parties and, although the courts do place limitations upon the remedies available, in many cases these restrictions can be evaded by careful draftsmanship. It is not true to say that the law of contract resembles the law of tort in that it simply imposes remedies upon the parties. In many cases the remedies are dependent upon the agreement of the parties. The second point relates to the 'interests' which the law of contract seeks to protect. We have seen that the law of contract seeks to protect the expectation interest, rather than the reliance interest or the restitution interest, thus separating contract law from the law of tort and the law of restitution. A promise engenders in the promisee an expectation that the promise will be performed and, as a general rule, the courts will order the party in default to fulfil the expectations which he has so created.

Thirdly, and finally, our study of remedies has demonstrated that the law of contract is not wholeheartedly committed to the protection of the expectation interest. Supplementary policies, such as the doctrines of mitigation and remoteness and the reluctance of the courts to grant an order of specific performance in certain situations, weaken the commitment of the law to the protection of the expectation interest. This illustrates a point which was made in the opening chapter of this book (1.4). Contract law is committed to the protection of individual autonomy and the protection of the expectation interest but that commitment is tempered in its application by considerations of fairness, consumerism and altruism. These conflicting ideologies are present within the rules relating to remedies; sometimes the courts are committed to 'market-individualism' (see, for example, *White and Carter (Councils) Ltd* v. *McGregor* (above, 21.4)), but on other occasions the courts are committed to 'consumer-welfarism' (see, for example, *Patel* v. *Ali* (above, 21.9) and the cases on the penalty clause rule). Contract law is a complex subject in which competing ideologies battle for predominance. The struggle to resolve this endemic conflict will continue to be a feature of contract law in the years to come.

Summary

1 A party who, in breach of contract, fails to perform an obligation which is entire cannot generally make any claim for payment from the innocent party. But the rule is subject to exceptions where the party in breach has substantially performed his obligations under the contract (although this exception is the subject of some controversy), where the innocent party has accepted the part performance and where the court holds that the obligation is not entire but divisible.

2 Where the term which is broken is a 'condition' which is of the 'essence of the contract', the innocent party can terminate performance of the contract and claim loss of bargain damages.

3 A claim in debt is a claim for a definite sum of money which the defendant is, under the terms of the contract, due to pay to the plaintiff. The plaintiff is not under a duty to mitigate his loss and the remoteness rules are inapplicable.

4 A liquidated damages clause is a genuine pre-estimate of the loss which is likely to be occasioned by the breach. Such a clause is enforceable and the sum recoverable is the sum stated in the clause, not the actual loss. A clause which seeks to punish the party in breach is a penalty clause. A penalty clause is unenforceable and is ignored for all purposes.

5 The penalty clause rule can be evaded by merely accelerating an existing liability, by making the sum payable on an event other than a breach of contract or by simply elevating the status of the term broken to a condition which is of the essence of the agreement.

6 A deposit is paid by way of security and is generally irrecoverable, provided that the sum payable by way of deposit is reasonable.

7 A part payment is a payment towards the contract price. Such a payment is recoverable where it is clear from the contract that the payee will not have to incur reliance expenditure before completing his performance of the contract.

8 Specific performance is an equitable remedy which is available within the discretion of the court. The availability of specific performance depends upon the appropriateness of the remedy on the facts of the case. There are a number of contexts in which specific performance is not normally available.

9 An injunction is an equitable remedy which may be used in an effort to prevent a threatened breach of contract. A court will not grant an injunction where to do so would be directly or indirectly to compel the defendant to do an act which he could not have been ordered to do by a decree of specific performance.

10 The court has a discretion in equity to grant damages in lieu of an injunction or specific performance.

Exercises

1 John agreed to build two houses on Brian's land. The contract price was agreed at £130000 and the price was payable upon completion of the work. After completing work to the value of £65000 John abandoned the contract. He is now seeking payment from Brian. Advise him. Would your answer differ if Brian had employed Julian to complete the work and had paid him £75000 to complete the two houses?

2 What is a claim in debt?

3 Distinguish between a liquidated damages clause and a penalty clause.

4 A contractor enters into a contract with an employer to erect some buildings at a cost of £900000. The contract states that, if the contractor fails to complete the work by the completion date, then the contractor has either to 'pay to or allow to the Employer the whole or such part as may be specified in writing by the Employer of a sum calculated at the rate stated in the Appendix as liquidated and ascertained damages'. The Appendix stated under the heading 'liquidated and ascertained damages' that the figure payable was '£ nil'. The contractor has failed to complete the work on time and the employer is now seeking damages from the contractor in accordance with the clause set out above. What advice would you give to the employer?

5 Distinguish between a deposit and a part payment. When are such payments recoverable by the party in breach?

6 Should specific performance be the normal remedy for breach of contract?

7 Outline the circumstances in which the courts will normally refuse to grant an order of specific performance.

Bibliography

Adams and Brownsword (1987) 'The Ideologies of Contract Law', 7 *Legal Studies*, 205.

Adams and Brownsword (1988a) 'The Unfair Contract Terms Act: A Decade of Discretion', 104 *Law Quarterly Review*, 94.

Adams and Brownsword (1988b) 'Double Indemnity - Contractual Indemnity Clauses Revisited', *Journal of Business Law*, 146.

Anson (1879) Law of Contract (1st edn), Oxford UP.

Anson (1984) Law of Contract (26th edn), Oxford UP.

Atiyah (1957) 'Couturier v. Hastie and the Sale of Non-Existent Goods', 78 *Law Quarterly Review*, 340.

Atiyah (1979), *The Rise and Fall of Freedom of Contract*, Oxford UP.

Atiyah (1982) 'Economic Duress and the Overborne Will', 98 *Law Quarterly Review*, 197.

Atiyah (1986a) 'The Modern Role of Contract Law', in Atiyah, *Essays on Contract*, Oxford UP.

Atiyah (1986b) 'Contracts, Promises and the Law of Obligations', in Atiyah, *Essays on Contract*, Oxford UP.

Atiyah (1986c) 'Consideration: A Restatement', in Atiyah, *Essays on Contract*.

Atiyah (1986d) 'Contract and Fair Exchange', in Atiyah, *Essays on Contract*.

Atiyah (1986e) *Pragmatism and Theory in English Law*, Stevens.

Atiyah (1986f) 'The Hannah Blumenthal and Classical Contract Law', 102 *Law Quarterly Review*, 363.

Atiyah (1986g) 'The Liberal Theory of Contract', in Atiyah, *Essays on Contract*.

Atiyah (1989) *An Introduction to the Law of Contract* (4th edn) Oxford UP.

Atiyah and Treitel (1967) 'Misrepresentation Act 1967', 30 *Modern Law Review*, 369.

Ball (1983) 'Work Carried Out in Pursuance of Letters of Intent – Contract or Restitution?', 99 *Law Quarterly Review*, 572.

Barton (1976) 'Penalties and Damages', 92 *Law Quarterly Review*, 20.

Beale (1993) 'Unreasonable Deposits', 109 *Law Quarterly Review*, 524.

Beale and Dugdale (1975) 'Contracts between Businessmen: Planning and the Use of Contractual Remedies', 2 *British Journal of Law and Society*, 45.

Beale, Bishop and Furmston (1990) *Contract: Cases and Materials* (2nd edn) Butterworth.

Beatson (1974) 'Duress as a Vitiating Factor in Contract', 33 *Cambridge Law Journal*, 97.

Beatson (1975) 'Repudiation of Illegal Purpose as a Ground for Restitution' 91 *Law Quarterly Review*, 313.

Beatson (1981) 'Discharge for Breach: The Position of Instalments, Deposits and Other Payments due before Completion', 97 *Law Quarterly Review*, 389.

Beatson (1992) 'Reforming the Law of Contracts for the Benefit of Third Parties: A Second Bite at the Cherry', *Current Legal Problems*.

Birks (1985) *An Introduction to the Law of Restitution*, Oxford UP.

Birks (1987) 'Restitutionary Damages for Breach of Contract: Snepp and the Fusion of Law and Equity', *Lloyd's Maritime and Commercial Law Quarterly*, 421.

Bishop (1985) 'The Choice of Remedy for Breach of Contract', 14 *Journal of Legal Studies*, 299.

Bojczuk (1987) 'When is a Condition not a Condition?', *Journal of Business Law*, 353.

Bridge (1989) 'Mitigation of Damages in Contract and the Meaning of Avoidable Loss', Quarterly *Law Review*, 398.

Brownsword (1987) 'New Notes on the Old Oats' 131 *Solicitors Journal*, 384.

Brownsword (1992) 'Retrieving Reasons, Retrieving Rationality? A New Look at the Right to Withdraw for Breach of Contract', *Journal of Contract Law*, 83.

Buckley (1975) 'Implied Statutory Prohibition of Contracts', 38 *Modern Law Review*, 535.

Burrows (1983) 'Contract, Tort and Restitution – a Satisfactory Division or Not?', 99 *Law Quarterly Review*, 217.

Burrows (1984a) 'Law Commission Report on Pecuniary Restitution on Breach of Contract', 47 *Modern Law Review*, 76.

Burrows (1984b) 'Specific Performance at the Crossroads', 4 *Legal Studies*, 102.

Burrows (1987) *Remedies for Torts and Breach of Contract*, Butterworth.

Burrows (1993a) 'Contributory Negligence in Contract: Ammunition for the Law Commission', *Law Quarterly Review*, 175.

Burrows (1993b) 'No Restitutionary Damages for Breach of Contract', *Lloyd's Maritime and Commercial Law Quarterly*, 453.

Burrows (1993c) *The Law of Restitution*, Butterworth.

Calabresi and Melamed (1972) 'Property Rules, Liability Rules and Inalienability – One View of the Cathedral', 85 *Harvard Law Review*, 1089.

Carter (1991) *Breach of Contract*, (2nd edn) Law Book Co.

Cartwright (1987) 'Damages for Misrepresentation', *The Conveyancer and Property Lawyer*, 423.

Cartwright (1987) 'Solle v. Butcher'and the Doctrine of Mistake in Contract', 103 *Law Quarterly Review*, 594.

Cheshire, Fifoot and Furmston (1991) *Law of Contract* (11th edn), Butterworth.

Coote (1964) *Exception Clauses*.

Coote (1972) 'Another Look at Bowmakers v. Barnet Instruments', *Modern Law Review*, 38.

Coote (1992) 'Validation under the Illegal Contracts Act', 15 *New Zealand Universities Law Review*, 80.

Corbin (1930) 'Contracts for the Benefit of Third Parties', 46 *Law Quarterly Review*, 12.

Corbin (1963) *on Contracts* (rev. edn, New York).

Dean (1993) 'Unfair Contract Terms: The European Approach', 56 *Modern Law Review*, 581.

Denning (1952) 'Recent Developments in the Doctrine of Consideration', 15 *Modern Law Review*, 1.

Dugdale and Yates (1976) 'Variation, Waiver and Estoppel' – a Reappraisal', 38 *Modern Law Review*, 680.

Ellinghaus (1971) 'Agreements Which Defer "Essential" Terms', 45 *Australian Law Journal*, 4 and 72.

Farrar (1991) *Company Law* (3rd edn), Butterworth.

Flannigan (1987) 'Privity – The End of an Era (Error)', 103 *Law Quarterly Review*, 564.

Fridman (1962) 'Construing, without Constructing, a Contract', 76 *Law Quarterly Review*, 521.

Fridman (1986) *The Law of Contract in Canada* (2nd edn), Carswell.

Fried (1981) *Contract as Promise*, Harvard UP.

Fuller (1941) 'Consideration and Form', 41 *Columbia Law Review*, 799.

Fuller and Perdue (1936) 'The Reliance Interest in Contract Damages', 46 *Yale Law Journal*, 52.

Furmston (1960) 'Return to Dunlop v. Selfridge?', 23 *Modern Law Review*, 373.

Furmston (1965) 'The Analysis of Illegal Contracts', *University of Toronto Law Journal*, 267.

Furmston (1972) 'The Illegal Contracts Act 1970 – An English View', 5 *New Zealand Universities Law Review*, 151.

Gardner (1982) 'The Proprietary Effect of Contractual Obligations under Tulk v. Moxhay and De Mattos v. Gibson' 98 *Law Quarterly Review*, 279.

Gardner (1992) 'Trashing with Trollope: A Deconstruction of the Postal Rules in Contract', 12 *Oxford Journal of Legal Studies*, 170.

Gilmore (1974) *The Death of Contract*, Columbus.

Gleeson and McKendrick (1987) 'The Rotting Away of Caveat Emptor', *The Conveyancer and Property Lawyer*, 121.

Goetz and Scott (1977) 'Liquidated Damages, Penalties and the Just Compensation Principle', 77 *Columbia Law Review*, 554.

Goff and Jones (1993) *The Law of Restitution* (4th edn), Sweet & Maxwell).

Goodhart (1941) 'Mistake as to Identity in the Law of Contract', 57 *Law Quarterly Review*, 228.

Goodhart (1951) 'Unilateral Contracts', 67 *Law Quarterly Review*, 456.

Goodhart (1953) 'A Short Replication', 69 *Law Quarterly Review*, 106.

Gordon (1974) 'Penalties Limiting Damages', 90 *Law Quarterly Review*, 296.

Gower (1952) 'Auction Sales of Goods Without Reserve', 68 *Law Quarterly Review*, 457.

Gravells (1976) 'Negligent Misrepresentation – A Wasted Opportunity for Clarification', 39 *Modern Law Review*, 462.

Greig and Davis (1987) *The Law of Contract*, Law Book Co.

Hall (1984) 'Frustration and the Question of Foresight' 4 *Legal Studies*, 300.

Halson (1990) 'Sailors, Sub-Contractors and Consideration', 106 *Law Quarterly Review*, 183.

Halson, (1991) 'Opportunism, Economic Duress and Contractual Modifications', 107, *Law Quarterly Review*, 649.

Hamson (1949) 'Illegal Contracts and Limited Interests', *Cambridge Law Journal*, 249.

Harris, Ogus and Phillips (1979) 'Contract Remedies and the Consumer Surplus', 95 *Law Quarterly Review*, 581.

Haycroft and Waksman (1984) 'Frustration and Restitution', *Journal of Business Law*, 207.

Hedley (1985) 'Keeping Contract in its Place: Balfour v. Balfour and the Enforceability of Informal Agreements', 5 *Oxford Journal of Legal Studies*, 391.

Higgins (1962) 'The Transfer of Property under Illegal Transactions', *Modern Law Review*, 149.

Hobhouse (1990) 'International Conventions and Commerical Law: The Pursuit of Uniformity', 106 *Law Quarterly Review*, 530.

Hooley (1992) 'Remedies for Misrepresentation', 142 New *Law Journal*, 60.

Howarth (1984) 'The Meaning of Objectivity in Contract', 100 *Law Quarterly Review*, 265.

Hudson (1968) 'Gibbons v. Proctor Revisited', 84 *Law Quarterly Review*, 503.

Hudson (1974) 'Penalties Limiting Damages', 90 *Law Quarterly Review*, 31.

Hudson (1975) 'Penalties Limiting Damages', 91 *Law Quarterly Review*, 25.

Hudson (1986) 'Mental Incapacity Revisited', *The Conveyancer and Property Lawyer*, 178.

Jackson (1982) 'How Many Kinds of Estoppel?', *The Conveyancer and Property Lawyer*, 450.

Jaffey (1985) 'Contract in Tort's Clothing', 5 *Legal Studies*, 77.

Jones (1983) 'The Recovery of Benefits Gained from a Breach of Contract', 99 *Law Quarterly Review*, 443.

Kaplan (1977) 'A Critique of the Penalty Limitation on Liquidated Damages', 55 *Southern California Law Review*, 1055.

Kennedy (1976) 'Form and Substance in Private Law Adjudication', 89 *Harvard Law Review*, 1685.

Kronman (1978a) 'Mistake, Disclosure, Information and the Law of Contracts', 7 *Journal of Legal Studies*, 1.

Kronman (1978b) 'Specific Performance' 45 *University of Chicago Law Review*, 351.

Kronman (1980) 'Contract Law and Distributive Justice', 89 *Yale Law Journal*, 472.

Lando (1992) 'Principles of European Contract Law: An Alternative to or a Precursor of European Legislation', 40 *American Journal of Comparative Law*, 573.

Law Commission (1976) Working Paper No. 70 *The Parol Evidence Rule*.

Law Commission (1983) Report No. 21 Law of Contract: *Pecuniary Restitution on Breach of Contract*.

Law Commission (1986) *Law Commission Report on the Parol Evidence Rule* (Law Com No. 154).

Law Commission (1991) Consultation Paper No. 121 *Privity of Contract: Contracts for the Benefit of Third Parties*.

Law Commission (1993a) Consultation Paper No. 132 *Aggravated, Exemplary and Restitutionary Damages.*

Law Commision (1993b) *Report No. 219 Contributory Negligence as a Defence in Contract.*

Lawson (1980) *Remedies of English Law* (2nd edn, Butterworth).

Lewis (1982) 'Contracts between Businessmen: Reform of the Law of Firm Offers and an Empirical Study of Tendering Practices in the Building Industry', 9 *Journal of Law and Society,* 153.

Macdonald (1988a) 'The Duty to give Notice of Unusual Contract Terms', *Journal of Business Law,* 375.

Macdonald (1988b) 'Incorporation of Contract Terms by a 'Consistent Course of Dealing', 8 *Legal Studies,* 48.

McBryde (1987) *The Law of Contract,* W. Green & Sons Ltd.

McKendrick (1986) 'Specific Implement and Specific Performance – A Comparison', *Scots Law Times,* 249.

McKendrick (1988) 'The Battle of the Forms and the Law of Restitution', 8 *Oxford Journal of Legal Studies,* 197.

McKendrick (1991a) 'Frustration and Force Majeure – Their Relationship and a Comparative Assessment', in McKendrick (ed.) *Force Majeure and Frustration of Contract.*

McKendrick (1991b) 'Frustration, Restitution and Loss Appointment', in Burrows (ed.), *Essays on the Law of Restitution.*

Miller (1972) 'Felthouse v. Bindley Revisited', 34 *Modern Law Review,* 489.

Milner (1979) 'Liquidated Damages: An Empirical Study in the Travel Industry', 42 *Modern Law Review,* 508.

Montrose (1954) 'The Contract of Sale in Self-Service Stores', *American Journal of Comparative Law,* 235.

Moriarty (1984) 'Licenses and Land Law: Legal Principles and Public Policies' 100 *Law Quarterly Review,* 376.

Muir (1985) 'Stipulations for the Payment of Agreed Sums', *Sydney Law Review,* 503.

Opeskin (1990) 'Damages for Breach of Contract Terminated under Express Terms', 106 *Law Quarterly Review,* 293.

Palmer (1982) 'Limiting Liability for Negligence' 45 *Modern Law Review,* 322.

Palmer (1983) 'Negligence and Exclusion Clauses Again', *Lloyd's Maritime and Commercial Law Quarterly,* 557.

Palmer (1986) 'Clarifying the Unfair Contract Terms Act 1977', *Business Law Review,* 57.

Palmer and Yates (1981) 'The Future of the Unfair Contract Terms Act 1977', *Cambridge Law Journal,* 108.

Patterson (1958) 'An Apology for Consideration', 58 *Columbia Law Review,* 929.

Phang (1990) 'Whither Economic Duress? Reflections on Two Recent Cases', 53 *Modern Law Beview,* 107.

Phang (1993) 'Implied Terms in English Law – Some Recent Developments', *Journal of Business Law,* 242.

Pollock (1875) *Law of Contract,* London.

Reiter (1981) 'The Control of Contract Power', 1 *Oxford Journal of Legal Studies,* 347.

Reynolds (1989) 'Privity of Contract, the Boundaries of Categories and the Limits of the Judicial Function', 105 *Law Quarterly Review*, 1.

Samek (1970) 'The Requirement of Certainty of Terms in the Formation of Contract – A Quantitative Approach'. *Canadian Bar Review*, 203.

Schwartz (1979) 'The Case for Specific Performance' 89 *Yale Law Journal*, 271.

Scottish Law Commission (1977) *Memorandum No. 36: Constitution and Proof of Voluntary Obligations: Formation of Contract*.

Sharpe and Waddams (1982) 'Damages for Lost Opportunity to Bargain', 2 *Oxford Journal of Legal Studies*, 290.

Simpson (1976) 'Innovation in Nineteenth Century Contract Law', 91 *Law Quarterly Review*, 247.

Slade (1952) 'Auction Sales of Goods Without Reserve', 68 *Law Quarterly Review*, 238.

Slade (1953) 'Auction of Sales of Goods Without Reserve', 69 *Law Quarterly Review*, 21.

Spencer (1974) 'Signature, Consent, and the Rule in L'Estrange v. Graucob', 32 *Cambridge Law Journal*, 104.

Swan (1980) 'The Contractual Allocation of Risk in Mistake and Frustration' in Reiter and Swan (eds), *Studies in Contract Law*.

Taylor (1982) 'Expectation, Reliance and Misrepresentation' 45 *Modern Law Review*, 139.

Tettenborn (1982) 'Contracts, Privity of Contract, and the Purchaser of Personal Property', *Cambridge Law Journal*, 58.

Thal (1988) 'The Inequality of Bargaining Power Doctrine: The Problem of Defining Contractual Unfairness', 8 *Oxford Journal of Legal Studies*, 17.

Thompson (1983) 'From Representation to Expectation: Estoppel as a Cause of Action', 42 *Cambridge Law Journal*, 257.

Tiplady (1983) 'The Judicial Control of Contractual Unfairness', 46 *Modern Law Review*, 601.

Trebilcock (1976) 'The Doctrine of Inequality of Bargaining Power: Post-Benthamite Economics in the House of Lords', 126 *University of Toronto Law Journal*, 359.

Treitel (1976) 'Consideration: A Critical Analysis of Professor Atiyah's Fundamental Restatement', 50 *Australian Law Journal*, 439.

Treitel (1991) *The Law of Contract* (8th edn, Stevens).

Treitel (1992) 'Damages for Breach of Contract in the High Court of Australia', 108 *Law Quarterly Review*, 226.

Vergne (1985) 'The "Battle of the Forms" Under the 1980 United Nations Convention on Contracts for the International Sale of Goods', 33 *American Journal of Comparative Law*, 233.

Vorster (1987) 'A Comment on the Meaning of Objectivity in Contract', 103 *Law Quarterly Review*, 274.

Waddams (1976) 'Unconscionability in Contracts', 39 *Modern Law Review*, 369.

Wedderburn (1959) 'Collateral Contracts', *Cambridge Law Journal*, 58.

Wightman (1989) 'Reviving Contract', 52 *Modern Law Review*, 116.

Winfield (1939) 'Some Aspects of Offer and Acceptance' 55 *Law Quarterly Review*, 499.

Yates (1982) *Exclusion Clauses in Contracts* (2nd edn, Sweet & Maxwell).

Index